The science of education in its sociological and historical aspects

Otto Willmann

THE SCIENCE OF EDUCATION

IN ITS

SOCIOLOGICAL AND HISTORICAL ASPECTS

BY

OTTO WILLMANN, Ph.D.

Authorized Translation from the Fourth German Edition

BY

FELIX M. KIRSCH, O.M.Cap.

m. g. oliver.
St. michael's college.
Nov. 3. 1921.

IN TWO VOLUMES

VOLUME I

ARCHABBEY PRESS, BEATTY, PENNSYLVANIA
1921

IMPRIMI PERMITTITUR.

Fr. Thomas Petrie, O. M Cap., Min. Prov.

Pittsburgi, Pa., die 20a Jul , 1921.

———— — - - - ···

IMPRIMATUR   ,

✠ Hugo Carolus,

Episcopus Pittsburgensis

To

The Right Reverend Archabbot

Aurelius Stehle, O.S.B.,

The Present Volume

Is

Respectfully and Gratefully

Dedicated

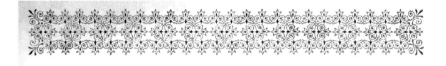

PREFACE.

IN his latest Report the President of Columbia University, Dr. Nicholas Murray Butler, makes the following confession: "For a quarter century past, American educational practice has been steadily losing its hold upon guiding principle and has, therefore, increasingly come to float upon the tide of mere opinion, without standards, without purpose and without insight." Any one familiar with recent educational history will bear out the truth of this statement.

Hence the writer ventures to think that *The Science of Education* by the late Dr. Otto Willmann, now made accessible to English readers, has a mission for our day and our country, since it offers those guiding principles of which American education stands in sore need. Dr. Willmann acts on the principle that the history of education must be our guide in educational matters. Whatever has stood the test of the ages, bids fair to prove of value in the future also. The present volume undertakes to ascertain from the history of education, what is the basis of our culture and civilization and what must, consequently, ever remain the essence of our courses of study. This volume is probably the best defence extant of what may be called the "ars educandi perennis."

But Dr. Willmann is not a blind worshipper of past glory. He is fully alive to the achievements of modern educationists, especially of Herbart; but while adopting all that is of practical value in his pedagogy, he is at pains to correct Herbart's mistakes in metaphysics and psychology. This phase of the work will appear in detail in the second volume which is now in the press

What gives a particular value to the present work is the broad vision of the author Dr. Willmann does not minimize the importance of education, yet with his philosophical mind he realizes that the school is but one of the forces that are engaged in the momentous task of social reconstruction. Hence he treats the subject of education in its sociological aspects and traces the interdependence between the school and other social factors This broad view of the field is needed most urgently to-day to prevent our educational leaders from drawing conclusions that are based on narrow professional grounds

The Science of Education is considered a pedagogical classic in Europe It has even been called the greatest achievement of modern pedagogy, and competent authorities do not hesitate to declare that the author is the greatest educationist of our time. The present work has given rise to a school of educational writers, and its principles are consistently developed and illustrated in Professor Roloff's "Lexikon der Padagogik" (five vols., Herder, 1913-1917) The Society of Christian Pedagogy has undertaken to spread the teachings of Dr Willmann among all classes of teachers Several educational periodicals serve the same purpose. Catholics and Protestants are one in paying tribute to Dr Willmann's genius, and thus it is not surprising that his *Science of Education* has exerted a profound influence on the development of educational thought in Europe The work has been translated into Dutch, and a Spanish version is in course of preparation. May we not, then, hope that the book in its English dress will not only assist our educators to solve the problems now confronting them on all sides, but that it will also prove to them an inspiration and a guide in their work?

The translator owes a debt of gratitude to the late Rev. Dr. Thomas E. Shields, of the Catholic University of America, for reading the entire manuscript and for suggesting a wide variety of changes. He is likewise indebted to Mr. Arthur Preuss, Editor of the "Fortnightly Review," for his scholarly revision of the Introduction. Valuable assistance was also received from the Rev. Dr. Patrick J. McCormick, Editor of the "Catholic Educational Review," the Rev. Clarence Tschippert, O. M. Cap., and other confrères. To all these friends the translator begs herewith to express his grateful appreciation of their many kindnesses.

HERMAN, PA., Sept. 1, 1921.

F. M. K.

CONTENTS.

INTRODUCTION.

I.

II.

III.

IV.

~~~~~~~~~

PART I.

THE HISTORICAL TYPES OF EDUCATION

I

EDUCATION IN ITS RELATION TO CULTURE, CIVILIZATION, AND MORAL REFINEMENT

Chapter I

Chapter II

Chapter III

II.

ORIENTAL EDUCATION.

Chapter IV.

1. The *Vedas*. 2. Vedic studies: grammar and the art of language. 3. Mathematics. 4. Teaching methods. Elementary instruction. 5. Appreciation of education.

Chapter V.

1. The Hermetic Books. 2. The art of writing. 3. Mathematics. Music and physical culture. 4. The temple schools. Character of the educational system of ancient Egypt.

Chapter VI.

1. Education among the Semitic peoples. Chaldean education. 2. Persian education.

Chapter VII.

1. Unique position of the Hebrews. High regard for learning. 2. Early beginnings of a school system. Higher education after the Exile. 3. Study of Hebrew. The Jews in the later history of education.

Chapter VIII.

1. Canonical books and studies. 2. Higher studies. Elementary schools. Encyclopedias and newspapers. 3. State support of the schools. The system of examinations. Chinese view of education. Estimate of Chinese education.

III.

GREEK EDUCATION.

Chapter IX.

1. The spirit of Greece is opposed to, but influenced by, the oriental spirit. Pre-Homeric theology contains the first sources of Greek education. 2. Homer is the standard author. 3. Liberal education; language and literature, music, and gymnastics. Correlation of school and life. 4. Philosophy is opposed to Homer. 5. The courses of study outlined by Pythagoras and Plato. 6. The influence of philosophy upon general education. The Sophists. Isocrates. 7. The system of the seven liberal arts comprises both cultural and scientific subjects, and is supplemented by popular literature and miscellaneous studies. Philosophy is the capstone of general education.

Chapter X.

Chapter XI

IV

ROMAN EDUCATION

Chapter XII.

Chapter XIII

Chapter XIV

V.

CHRISTIAN EDUCATION ON ROMAN SOIL.

Chapter XV.

Chapter XVI.

Chapter XVII.

VI.

MEDIEVAL EDUCATION.

Chapter XVIII.

Chapter XIX.

VIII.

THE ENLIGHTENMENT.

Chapter XXV.

Chapter XXVI.

Chapter XXVII.

IX.

MODERN EDUCATION.

Chapter XXVIII.

Chapter XXIX.

Chapter XXX

INTRODUCTION.

I.

1. MAN has ever realized the need of illustrating the abstract by the concrete and of explaining moral events by analogous physical occurrences. An analogy that is very fruitful of thought is the comparison of human society with the living body. The author of the *Rig-Veda* has this comparison in mind when he tells us that not only the elements and the heavenly bodies, but also the castes of Indian society spring from the body of the god Purusha: the Brahman, from his mouth; the Kshatriya, from his arms; the Vaisya, from his thighs; and the Sudra, from his feet.[1] By means of the well-known fable of the dispute between the stomach and the hands, Menenius Agrippa is alleged to have persuaded the plebeians to return from Mons Sacer to Rome.[2] A further and more frequently employed analogy has been found to exist between the organism and the State: the government has been compared to the head; and the subjects, to the members of the body. The Latin language, especially, has led the way for the modern languages to develop this metaphor. The Romans were familiar with such turns of expression as head and body of the State, of the people, of the army; just as we to-day speak of the head, body, and members to denote different parts of a society. Plutarch draws a comparison between the living organism and the State, the family, and the tribe, for the purpose of illustrating how all these, in

---

[1] *Rig-Veda* X, 90.
[2] Liv. II, 32; for a more detailed account, see Dionys. Hal VI, 86.

1

the course of the ages, preserve their nature, and consequently
that the merit as well as the guilt of the forbears may be inherited by their descendants.[1] Seneca goes still further in considering the whole human race as one social organism, of which
the individual men, united by the bonds of nature and by their
common needs and duties, are the members [2]

Just as it was left to Christianity to grasp the full meaning
of the unity and solidarity of the human race, so has the Christian religion also raised the figurative expression of this union
to a higher plane   The penetrating mind of St. Paul saw in
the living body a symbol of the unity existing between all men
baptized in Christ and of the further unity that obtains in the
distribution of gifts, offices, and works   This common bond
made distinctions of race and caste impossible: "For in one
Spirit were we all baptized into one body, whether Jews or
Gentiles, whether bond or free, and in one common Spirit have
we all been made to drink," the one common vocation of all
is "to grow up in Him who is the head, even Christ, from whom
the whole body being compacted and fitly joined together
maketh increase," at the same time, however, Christ has committed to each member of the body a special function, "for as
in one body we have members, but all the members have not
the same office: so we, being many, are one body in Christ, and
every one members of one another, and having different gifts,
according to the grace that is given us "[3] This teaching has
served Christian theology as the basis for developing the doctrine of the mystical body of Christ.   The same idea underlies
the relations existing between the mother church and her daughter churches, between the visible head of the Church and the
faithful, between the different offices in religious communities,
etc.[4]

Plato introduced this biological simile into the political sciences   He uses it to prove that citizens must have many interests in common: the State should be, as far as possible, an object
of personal concern to each individual; its common weal and
woe should be felt by all just as keenly as the members of a
body share pleasure and pain.[5] The keynote of Plato's *Republic* is that the constitution of the whole State, no less than the

[1] Plut *De sera numinis vindicta*, c 15   (*Moralia*, ed Duebner, t I, p 676)
[2] Sen *Ep* 95, 52
[3] I Cor XII, 12-27, Eph IV, 11-16, Rom XII, 4-6 ff
[4] Tert *De virg velandis*, c I, and elsewhere
[5] Plato, *Rep* V, p 462 and 464, Steph

well-being of the individual, must rest on the concerted action of many factors, each component part of the State as well as of the body following the rule, "Every one shall perform his proper duties." But in developing this idea, Plato employed the harmony of the faculties (not of the body but of the soul) as picturing the unity that must prevail among the different forces at work in the State. Aristotle compares the parts composing human society to the different organs of the animal body, and so obtains his principle for distinguishing the forms of government, which can be divided (as in the animal kingdom the combinations of the variously shaped physical organs differentiate the classes) in accordance with the union they establish between the different classes of the population.[1] Aristotle, however, attaches, on the whole, less weight to this comparison, in keeping with his usual practice not to illustrate human life by pictures drawn from the physical world; but, instead, to use moral examples to elucidate the doings of the lower order.[2]

With Hobbes, the comparison is more than a mere analogy, for he demands that the body of the State be made the subject of study, not only in the political sciences, but also in ethics, the latter being, in his opinion, a part of the former; but since the body of the State is thus made an object of inquiry on a par with the natural bodies of the physical sciences, the whole philosophy of Hobbes is reduced to somatology. According to Hobbes, the sovereign of the State, which is the *corpus politicum*, represents the life principle, and is consequently not merely the head, but the soul, of the body. But one step more was needed to consider the organs of this body as mechanical instruments and the whole organism as a machine, and, by not drawing this conclusion, Hobbes failed to perceive the practical results of his theory.

2. Modern sociology has been enabled by the new discoveries made in the natural sciences to disclose new points of similarity in the old comparison, and has thus been enriched by important and novel concepts. What modern biology has borrowed from sociology in concepts and technical terms (*e. g.*, division of labor, economy of organic life, colony of cells, etc.) it has compensated for in ideas and expressions, of which some possess no more than the charm of novelty, while others are of

---

[1] Arist. *Pol.* IV, 3, p. 1290 Bekk.

[2] Cf. Eucken, *Ueber Bilder und Gleichnisse in der Philosophie*, Leipzig, 1880 p. 14.

permanent value. The light thrown upon biological processes has increased the points of contact between social and organic life by revealing hitherto unknown analogies. The philosophers of a former day saw in the organism and in society only the one whole, "consisting of parts, differing in function, so united as to be conjointly responsible for self-preservation and able to produce harmoniously the collective effects" But after natural philosophy had analyzed the organic body, a further analogy, fruitful of new concepts, was discovered: it was recognized that there is in the organism not merely *one* system, but that the whole is based on the union of a variety of interconnected systems—bones, muscles, blood-vessels, nerves—and that, similarly, men have established the State, not merely by forming *one* union, but by uniting a number of diverse unions and thus producing a complex social woof, which includes the national union, the political confederation, the texture of all classes and all professions, community of religion, and the innumerable associations that owe their being to the respective communities of interests, be they economic, social, intellectual, or otherwise. To bring out these facts, however, such terms as people, nation, confederation, and even society are utterly inadequate, since they denote only different modes of union, not the whole complex; and only the terms borrowed from biology, *social body* or *social organism*, convey fully this complex system.

A deeper study of the organic body has disclosed a further point of agreement between organic and social life. The social and the animal body have in common a continual acquisition and a continual discharge of their constituent elements. The living organism discharges matter, whose place it fills with other elements, and thus is ceaselessly engaged in building up and tearing down. Human society with its births and deaths shows an analogous increase and decrease, it, too, continually renews itself, and, as the animal organism remains, despite the changes affecting its component elements, and as it assimilates and elaborates the new matter before it is distributed to the various systems of which the whole is composed, so the social body also preserves its identity while new individuals are arriving and the old are departing; and it is likewise one of its vital functions to assimilate and incorporate the incoming elements in order thereby to insure the continuity of its forces.

This social reconstruction appears generally not as one whole, concerted process. The observer is almost invariably too much taken up with some particular facts, subservient to the whole, and this prevents him from obtaining a complete view of the phenomena that are so vast and embrace such diverse and subordinate phases. Indeed, it is only the comparison drawn from organic nature that leads one to perceive the unity of the whole process. The value of this analogy is not impaired by the fact that the resemblances are less important than the differences, and that one must ever be on guard lest the social phenomena receive through the comparison with the physical order a foreign and naturalistic coloring. We should never forget that the processes brought about in the animal body by the change of organic matter are but natural and physical; whereas the reconstruction of human society, while including physical occurrences, tends rather towards psychical processes and psychical actions, which finally result in conscious and free actions, and therefore transcend all mechanism, whether physical or psychical. In every action and in every phase of social reconstruction we discern the influence of historical development, a trait that is common to all human activity.

3. The first step in the process of social reconstruction is to engender the individuals that are to receive the effects of the assimilating forces, and this very first act, a reproduction, belongs alike to the natural, the ethical, and the historical order. All classes of living beings renew themselves by reproduction. The natural instinct of the individual animal to produce beings of its own kind is, beside that of self-preservation, the strongest motor force in all animal activity. The properties and attributes of the parents are inherited by the young, and so nature conserves the types of life and preserves the successive generations from material change. Man can purify and ennoble by higher motives the primitive instinct of propagation; he can control it by the moral law and convert the sexual union into the family bond, which is the protoplasm of all social organization. Thus a relationship is established between the function of reproduction and the vital activities of the social body, which is so intimate that the latter can, in a certain sense, be held responsible for the former. Nationality, form of government, morality, education, wealth, historical events, and similar factors influence not only the birth-rate, but likewise the type, qualities, and faculties of the children. Even with the brutes, it is not only the congenital characters, *i. e.*, those inherited from ancestors, but also those acquired by the individual that pass to the young. The same is true, only in much greater diversity, of the human race, for the accomplishments and ac-

quired habits of parents can be transmitted to their children. Not only physical qualities, but properties of the mind and such as are the result of education and culture are handed down from generation to generation; the experiences and achievements of former generations, their progress or retrogression, are all transmitted to their descendants as so many dispositions for good or bad. "By the wonderful power of the seed given to the bodies of men, the inherited good and the inherited evil pass down the stream of human generations "[1] The children receive by inheritance the national type, which, though it is not yet the fixed nationality, is, undoubtedly, the basis for all those influences that tend to create the national spirit By heredity all the types are transmitted that have been formed by the living conditions and various habits of the forbears, and which often assert themselves even where the descendants grow up in an entirely different atmosphere The fact that in the civilizing of primitive peoples, several generations must be brought under the influence of culture before the first fruits of civilization appear, shows how the third and fourth generations are affected by the sum total of the influences that have been exerted upon the present and preceding generations.[2] The caste system has demonstrated that intellectual as well as technical attainments become, as it were, the capital of the successive generations who have devoted themselves to one special field of activity, and thus the children reap the fruits of the labors of their ancestors in the form of increased efficiency[3] Thus nature transmits by physical inheritance the greatest gifts of previous civilization, and the physical solidarity of mankind assumes a historical character long before any psychic influences come into play

Animal life shows another instinct, related closely to the sexual and, like it, tending to preserve the species: namely, the instinct to preserve, nourish, and watch over the young, in a word, to provide them with the necessaries of life In man as well as beast the manifestations of these two instincts are intimately connected, as can readily be seen from the employment of identical, or at least similar, terms for both functions For example, the root of the English word "educate" is the Latin *educare*, which means to rear, to nourish, to bring up, the term "parents," from the Latin *parentes*, seems to support the view

---

[1] Augustine, *De civitate Dei*, XXII, 24, 1
[2] Th Waitz, *Anthropologie der Naturvolker*, I, 81
[3] Ribot, *Heredity*, New York, 1895, pp 364 ff

that the process of life-giving is continued after birth; the Latin terms for child, *proles* and *suboles*, are both derived from *alere*, to rear, to nourish, to bring up; τεκνογονία meant to the Greek as much as to have, *i. e.*, to beget and rear, children.[1] The German words *zeugen* (to beget), *ziehen, aufziehen, auferziehen* (to educate), have a common root, and the two meanings are brought out in *Zucht* and *züchten*. Aristotle attributed to the ψυχὴ θρεπτική, the nourishing soul, all the activity of reproduction;[2] the primary meaning of the Spanish *criar* is to create, to give birth to, but this meaning is now blended with "to rear, to bring up." An old view, occurring in Hindu and Greek literature, has it, that the child's education begins during its embryonic life, and that the mother is only the nurse of even the unborn child.[3] Yet, notwithstanding this close relation between reproduction and education, it is only the latter that can establish conscious relations between parent and child. In the animal world, the relations between parent and offspring, though very close, are of brief duration, whereas with the human race they involve long and eventful cohabitation. The long period of utter helplessness has rightly been considered an advantage to the child because it renders its development both broad and deep; and, by necessitating much tender and loving care, it improves the character of the parents.[4] By contrasting the development of children among primitive and civilized peoples, it has been discovered that the period of helplessness and infancy lasts the longer, the more care is given to the rearing of the young; and thus the greater care of children is not only an indispensable condition for, but also a product of civilization and historical development.[5] The public care of orphans, which we find even among primitive peoples, represents an effort made by society at large. This effort, though determined primarily by individual motives and means, is invariably dependent upon social factors, so that it may truly be said that the methods employed in edu-

---

[1] Cf. I. Tim., II, 15.

[2] Aristotle, *de an.*, II, 4, 2.

[3] *Rig-Veda*, V, 78. — Aeschylus, *Eum.*, 615.—Cf. Lucas, *Traité de l'hérédité naturelle*, II, 67 ff.

[4] Lucretius, V, 1016, considers the intercourse between parent and child as tending to refine the nature of man and as leading him to adopt principles like the following: "Imbecillorum esse æquum misereri omnium."—In *The Luck of Roaring Camp*, Bret Harte relates how the coarse brutality rampant in a mining camp slowly gave way to noble impulses, after the men had adopted a poor orphan.—George Eliot's *Silas Marner* treats a somewhat similar theme.

[5] Caspari, *Urgeschichte der Menschheit*, I, 108.

cating the children of a nation reflect that nation's general morality, and are shaped by its moral and religious views as well as by its social and political institutions.

4. The community of life made necessary by the helplessness of infants, and confirmed by higher motives, marks the beginning of the influence exercised by the souls of the parents on their offspring and of the increasing mental and moral assimilation of the younger to the older generation. These beginnings of assimilation have no conscious purpose or definite end; they are not so much activities of the soul as natural processes by which the existing physical homogeneity is extended into the mental and moral field   Among nations of the savage or barbarous stage, where the influences deliberately brought to bear upon youth are few, the child nevertheless assumes the manners and habits of its parents, adopts their language and customs, makes their interests and memories its own, becomes, in fact, like its elders, solely by virtue of the involuntary assimilation effected by the mutual intercourse and a common life. Similarly, among civilized nations, where education is conscious and carefully mapped out, the involuntary influences will not fail to prepare for the formal training, they will assist it, and frequently also thwart its results   The environment of the child will have its sway, and all that comes to the child by the process of nature will settle upon it, as though it were a precipitation from the surrounding atmosphere, and must consequently be taken into account as the broad and indispensable basis for instruction and discipline   Thus is the mother-tongue handed down to, and acquired by the children   Its very name signifies that it grows out of the intercourse between mother and child   This is an important step in mental assimilation, for language is not a mere soulless form, unconnected with its content, but rather a rich storehouse of thought   The words, forms, constructions, and inflections of a language contain the germs of a definite conception of the universe,[1] which is transmitted to the young along with language   What we call the mother-tongue is the first consciously imparted gift of one generation to the next   Speech and intercourse are, furthermore, vehicles for the quick and natural transmission of experiences, memories, views, and evaluations, and this process of transmission grows more effective as the eye corroborates the ear   The most efficient

---

[1] W v Humboldt, *Die Verschiedenheit des menschlichen Sprachbaues*, 38 —Cf Adler, *Wilhelm von Humboldt's Linguistical Studies*, New York, 1866

force of assimilation in the sphere of conduct is example. Arts and customs, too, are to a great extent transmitted without special effort by the spontaneous tendency of the human mind to imitate and copy; it is thus that many interests, desires, inclinations, and determinations of the will are passed on from generation to generation.

This process gains in fullness and breadth, though not always in strength, by the child's coming in contact with its environment, the main furtherance being obtained from the multitudinous forms of civilized life. It is these forms that generally call forth the first questions asked by a child, and thus the first steps toward education and culture are taken long before formal instruction begins. The habits formed under the influence of the atmosphere of culture which "the young savages in our midst" are compelled to breathe, contribute more to their refinement than discipline and formal teaching. The products of civilization and the results of technical skill eloquently embody ideas and purposes; they can be said to hold in bondage thoughts[1] which are set free by him who inquires into their deeper meaning; for to understand fully any created thing, requires that we, in a certain sense, recreate it; and every article that is the result of mental efforts presupposes mental activity. Consequently, the property of the parents, the furnishings of the house, and the thousand and one articles in a cultured home encourage the process of assimilation, because the ideas associated with them are transmitted to the children, who grow up among these things. This psychological process is an argument for the hereditary transmission of goods; for after the property of father and mother has, in this way, proved a helpful agency of education and culture to the children, it is appropriate that it should remain in their hands.

The hereditary transmission of property, as regulated by law, is a strong bond connecting the generations which succeed one another and preserving the continuity of social labor.[2] By inheritance, we may say, the new generation receives the *fundus instructus* of civilized life, the material basis spiritually assimilated and improved by successive generations, for continuing the work of the human race. The laws governing inheritance affect only one part of this relationship, namely, the trans-

---

[1] "Condensed thought" (verdichtetes Denken); cf. Lazarus, *Leben der Seele*, 2nd ed., II, 213 ff.

[2] Roscher, *Ansichten der Volkswirtschaft*, 42.

mission of private property, but they do not affect the transmission of public and collective possessions; for the property
belonging to the State, its rights and privileges, monuments of
religion, works of art, are likewise handed down to the succeeding generations [1] Lest we miss the psychological import of
this nation-wide transmission we must bear in mind that it is
not a mere transfer of material property, but a link in a chain
that connects various psychical activities. Hopes and memories, traditions and duties, views and intentions, attach even
to private property. To the nation, its public and collective
possessions convey a still deeper meaning: national shrines and
monuments are handed down to future generations, not as
chattels, but as solemn pledges and trusts When taking over
the Acropolis, the youth of Athens entered upon the rich heir-
loom of their country's history

5. The psychic agencies which are subject to the will also
assist in the transmission of those intellectual and moral gifts
which, as we have seen, are so closely connected with a nation's
material possessions Alongside of that spontaneous assimilation, which we have called a psychic process, run the varied
conscious influences of society upon the young

There is no single term that covers the totality of these
conscious efforts, and hence compound phrases have been generally employed. Thus the Greeks joined: ἀσκεῖν καὶ διδάσκειν, to practice and to teach, παιδεύειν καί ἀσκεῖν, to educate and practice; or, with a different shade of meaning, ἄγειν
καὶ πάιδεύειν, to lead and to educate; or placed together such
expressions as: μαθεῖν and παθεῖν, to learn and to experience,
ἔθος and λόγος, habit and teaching; ἐθίζεσθαι and ἀκούειν to
habituate and to hear, or, in a more extensive enumeration:
ἔθη καὶ παιδεῖαι καὶ διδασκαλίαι καὶ βίων ἀγωγαί, habits,
education, instructions, and directions.[2] The Romans joined
together: *studia* and *artes; doctrina, disciplina,* and *institutio*
The Germans say *Lernen und Ueben, Lehre und Leitung; Unter-
weisung und Uebung; Unterricht und Zucht.* The following expressions are familiar to English ears: theory and practice,
lesson and exercise, schooling and training, instruction and discipline. These pairs of terms either contrast intellectual and
moral training, or distinguish between theoretical knowledge
and practical skill, or combine the concepts of intellectual pro-

---

[1] Schaffle, *Bau und Leben des sozialen Korpers,* II, 102
[2] Pseudoplutarch, *De Educatione Puerorum,* c 4

ficiency and moral perfection. None of them, however, embraces all the activities belonging to the subject. Still usage justifies us in letting the terms teaching and discipline (*Lehre und Zucht*) denote the two principal categories and in enlarging the scope of their meaning so as to embrace practice, training of habits, schooling, direction and instruction, guiding and moral improvement, etc. The element of teaching transmits to the young the intellectual content of education (knowledge and skill, teachings of philosophy and doctrines of faith) and renders intellectual assimilation a conscious process. The element of discipline introduces the young into the moral life of the community, admits them to full membership in society, and lets them share its moral interests.

All associations and classes of the social organism are continuously engaged in the work of incorporating their new elements by teaching and discipline; and not only the pupil, but also the apprentice and the recruit, the novice and the neophyte, the tyro and the beginner in any field, must be intellectually and morally assimilated to the respective social bodies into whose sphere they have entered.

6. Reproduction and heredity, the care of the young, the spontaneous assimilation of child to parent, the hereditary transmission of property, the conscious and more or less systematic influences exercised by teaching and discipline,—these are the essential stages of the process by which the reconstruction of social life is wrought. Upon closer examination, however, we perceive that reproduction and heredity alone are the peculiar and characteristic attributes of this process, since the others, though in a modified form, occur also in other fields of social life. It is not only in behalf of the young that efforts are made to provide the necessaries of physical life. No stage of civilization neglects the erection of hospitals and homes for the aged and feeble. The opinions, maxims, and practices of medical science influence the care of children, and with the development of medical science grows its influence in the nursery. The spontaneous assimilation by which the child, as it were, grows into its environment, has a counterpart in the phenomenon that association and intercourse everywhere produce similar results. Adults, like children, adopt without special effort the opinions and sympathies, the style and manner of those with whom they associate. Young and old become refined by moving in polite society; among the rude, they develop into boors; savages become civilized if thrown into intimate companionship with

Europeans; the white man of refinement will lose his delicate
breeding if doomed to a life among savages. Individuals are
not alone in being susceptible to the transforming influences
emanating from communities, for whole classes of society assimilate one another either by mutually exchanging customs
and practices, or by effacing the characters that are less strong,
and offer, therefore, less resistance. Even nationality may be
transmitted, if not without the aid of compelling forces, yet in
a perfectly natural way And thus the assimilation of the
young to the old is but an exemplification of a broad psychological and sociological law that has no particular bearing on
the reconstruction of society. Similarly, the transfer of material property, though an important factor in the solidarity
between successive generations, has nevertheless no direct bearing on social reconstruction. Property changes hands not only
through inheritance; sales, whether free or forced, and donations
must also be considered beside the fact that even hereditary
transmission is not confined to the descendants, but can extend
to the collateral relations.

Teaching and discipline can both be traced back to the
general functions of society, and offer the best opportunity for
studying the reconstruction of social life Teaching, in general,
transmits an intellectual content from one mind to another, and
in so doing, not only reproduces but enlarges the matter transmitted But there is a form of teaching which either goes
beyond the intellectual assimilation of the new generation, or
is not at all concerned with it. Missions, sermons, religious
propaganda are forms of teaching with which the instruction
and education of children can well be associated, but which are
primarily addressed to adults, to "the men of every nation
under heaven," to employ a Scriptural term Science needs
teaching as a vital element, because the purpose of all science
is to extend the boundaries of knowledge, not only for him who
is in possession, but also for him who is in search of it The
research worker is not satisfied unless he can communicate his
discoveries to others, what has been thought out in solitude,
becomes a vital force only when brought into contact with an
outside consciousness He who communicates the results of his
inquiry or speculation to others, teaches; and the great men of
science are the teachers of their age, if not of all future time,
the circles that gather about such leaders are known by the
same name as the lecture halls and laboratory buildings, for
they are called a "school" The artist, too, who sets the fash-

ion for his contemporaries, is known as their teacher; and the disciples who recognize him as such are called his "school". The term "master" connotes both production and teaching; and the disciple as well as the apprentice is a "learner". Mechanical and technical skill presupposes learning and imitation — the showing of models frequently taking the place of teaching. Civilized life abounds in sources of knowledge which no individual can ever outgrow; yea, we only grow up to them when we have completed our course of schoolroom study. Books can, for purposes of teaching, be called the eternal fountain-head of knowledge, for they give visible and permanent form to the intellectual content, and conserve the spoken word as a teaching voice—an achievement which appeared to the ancients little short of divine. The influence of the book is not limited by time and space, as is teaching by word of mouth; though its teaching be mute, its voice is louder than that of any living man, and it will be a teacher and guide to generations yet unborn.

From this point of view, the teaching that serves as a means in the intellectual assimilation of the young appears but as a specific instance of a general function of intellectual life. The same is true of discipline, which is its complement. As no man can outgrow the work of learning and the broadening and correcting of his views, so none can escape the checking and directing influences that proceed from social institutions. All social organizations exert a disciplinary influence upon their members, and that, not only upon the newcomers, who must be trained to live up to existing conditions, but also upon the veterans, keeping their conduct in harmony with the ruling standards. We speak of ecclesiastical discipline, military discipline, police discipline—of the discipline, in fact, of social bodies of every description. The penal code of a State represents the efforts of public authority to maintain its laws by rigorous discipline. Besides the forces which are at work for the training of our young people in morality, there are others aiming at the uplift of the masses; and the care for the perpetuation of morality is closely bound up with the task of preserving its existence in the present. History even records instances where the purposes of both functions overlap; thus, in the patriarchal system of ancient China, the education of the young was entrusted entirely to the police, while the pedagogy of Sparta knew no higher aim than to train future soldiers.

7. Considering the agencies, then, which serve the process of social reconstruction, we must admit that individually they

possess no specific relation to the new elements, but spread out, as it were, in a collateral direction. This, however, militates in no way against the harmony and unity of the process, nor against its being recognized as a distinctive vital function of the social organism. The relation between the one generation in its maturity and the other in its growth and development is too specific, and its ends are outlined too clearly to preclude the creation of spheres, complete in themselves, of activities, laws, and institutions   The system of moral education and the system of intellectual education (*Erziehungswesen und Bildungswesen*) are such spheres, both rest on the broad foundation of civilized life, are interrelated with each other and other fields besides, and yet possess, by reason of their own purposes and problems, a sufficiently distinct character.

"Education" is etymologically derived from the process of rearing children (*educere,* to lead forth, bring up a child) At first it was regarded as a continuation or intensification of the work directed toward the bodily well-being and growth of the child; but since the terms employed for the latter work are related to the expressions in use for the process of generation,[1] education is looked upon, not merely as furtherance of life, but as a life-giving process. Like the person entrusted with the upbringing of a child, the educator watches over the development of a life that stands in need of protection, assistance, and direction from others. his task is analogous to generation in that he reproduces, not a bodily and external, but an inner, moral form   The work of rearing as well as of educating is begun in the home and within the family circle. There physical life is produced and there the moral life also finds the most congenial environment for its first tender growth; and as the mother-tongue marks the beginning of intellectual training, so the manners and customs of the home are the first aids to the moral development of the child. Mere rearing is converted into education as soon as the instinctive impulses of the child become an object of care; to control these, to suppress those that make for evil, to encourage those that exert a favorable influence, to assist the mind wavering between good and bad, to strengthen it until good habits are formed,—this is the first and most obvious purpose of education   Its main support is the relation between authority and obedience, and in this respect education coincides with discipline; but it has a vastly richer content than

[1] Cf *supra,* p 6

the exercise of mere discipline, as its activity is directed toward
the future and its aim is to provide well for the child. Taking
the place of a Reason as yet immature, the educator makes
such preparations as his charge, when arrived at maturity, may
be expected to approve and continue. The educator is not
satisfied with inculcating good manners, he wishes to improve
the moral side also; and hence he does not confine himself to
regulating the present impulses and actions of the child, but
inspires new motives and higher impulses, thus grafting a noble
scion upon wild stock. To accomplish this, he must employ
intellectual agencies; and hence education, by teaching, instructing, and intellectually stimulating, enters into the domain of
doctrine. Instruction, which may be defined as a systematic
inculcation of doctrines adapted to promote the assimilation of
knowledge, is one of the most powerful forces in education. On
the one hand it gives the young, who are drawn hither and
thither by diverse aspirations, an opportunity for well-regulated
activity and exercise of faculties; while on the other hand it
broadens and enriches their mental horizon by awaking interests
which engender new impulses and fresh efforts. Like discipline,
instruction, to be truly educative, must not content itself with
a momentary and partial growth in knowledge; but, with an eye
to the future, must adapt its purpose and methods to mental
development.

Education is a moral, and therefore conscious, activity. It
proceeds from one person and enters another, the latter being
in a developmental stage. It is neither that unconscious (or
semi-conscious) assimilation by which the young are made like
the old, nor a process for merely controlling the actions of the
young, without ever asking whether the influences exerted upon
the child penetrate its soul and there unite in one harmonious
total effect. Education is not a mere giving forth of knowledge,
nor does it consist in sowing seed without regard as to whether
it will sprout and grow. This does not mean, however, that
education can dispense with the unconscious and semi-conscious
influences that spring from the mutual intercourse of men. The
purposive influences which it brings to bear would remain a
mere aggregate, an incoherent mass, if they lacked the subtle
and spontaneous emanations of community life, because it is
these which give a basis and continuity to education. With the
influences of the environment hostile, these influences could
never strike root. Unconscious assimilation is an important
factor which must be taken into account by the educator. It

is like an elemental force, which, if rightly directed, assists the work of the mind, but, if ignored or unchecked, destroys the results of weary labors.

8. In as far as education provides for the development of the growing generation, it may be said to be looking into the future, but, like the head of Janus, it has two faces, one of which constantly looks backward upon the chain of past generations, to which it is adding a new link, and upon the treasures of civilization, which it must conserve and transmit   Education is, then, the fulfillment of a double duty : of charity towards the new generation and of a social duty towards the organisms and individual representatives of culture, to whom it commits the young in order that the State may have citizens, society, workers, the nation, people, and the religious bodies, communicants. The individual *ethos* of education is inseparable from the social; parental authority reflects the State; the customs of the family, the morals of the nation; and the intellectual content, which furnishes the basis of instruction and the guiding principles of discipline, is derived from the very life of society   Despite the liberty granted the individual teacher, therefore, education is after all a homologous activity, and, (as history, especially ancient history shows) it may be made collective by treating it as a public concern with the State as chief educator   But even where no such collective activity has resulted, we may speak of education as a system embracing all educational forces, measures, means, and institutions, though they may not assume the form of a separate and definite organ of the social body.

Education occupies a middle position in the work of reconstructing the social life. The reproduction and rearing of the young precede education, while the incorporation of the new elements into the various classes of society and their training for the special tasks assigned to them there, as a rule presuppose education in the general sense, for education in that sense moves in the general and basic realm, and is therefore rightly considered as opposed to the vocational training required for particular walks in life and acquired, in great measure, only in the respective profession. Professional training may, nay in some instances, *e. g*, in the training of apprentices, must admit certain pedagogical elements, whereas, on the other hand, vocational training may have to begin in the cradle, as with princes. Yet the educational *ethos* is entirely distinct from the tendency to enable a man to enter a particular profession   Education attends mainly to the individual, its principles are the general and basic principles of morality; and it prepares for practical efficiency only in as far as the moral assimilation which it effects is a prime requisite for all social achievement. In professional training, on the contrary, special interests and professional needs are of first importance, and the development of personality is a purely secondary consideration.

Hence education may be described as the homologous activity of the adult generation in watching over and directing the aspirations of the young, in order to make them moral by transmitting to them the foundations of its own moral and intellectual life.

9. It is far more difficult to determine the precise import of the term intellectual education (*Bildung*).[1] Intellectual education implies in the first place an internal, mental form, in contradistinction to the mechanical acquisition of knowledge. In imparting intellectual education we do more than impart knowledge; we convert the matter imparted into a dynamic force, into an intellectually productive content. Materially education means an increase in knowledge; intellectually it means an increase in the plastic power of the mind. What has been learned by heart or acquired by dint of exercise and practice, may be lost in course of time; but the degree of intellectual education once attained will ever remain the pupil's property, though the means employed in imparting it may have been lost. The intellectual culture acquired develops into a habit of the soul modifying the whole personality.

Intellectual education is a co-factor along with temperament, natural disposition, talents and faculties, in the development of the individual; but being a product of free will, it is opposed to what are mere factors of nature. Intellectual education is the fruit of work, work performed by the subject himself and by others. To acquire an intellectual education, the pupil must of his own free will grasp a body of intellectual truths. In this sense we speak of striving for culture, of the sources of culture, etc. But beside the efforts of the individual, other (social) factors, more or less organized, must also be active; and these constitute intellectual education as a system. The process of intellectual education is both individual and social. The intel-

---

[1] *Intellectual education* is the nearest approach, in our opinion, to the German *Bildung*. Among the Germans themselves so exact a writer as Kant used *Kultur* instead of the modern term *Bildung*. To Winkelmann, Göthe, and Schiller, *Bildung* signified more the material action of forming and the resulting form. The perfection of intellectual training they designated as *Aufklärung* (enlightenment).

lectual education possessed by an individual is his property, but
not exclusively his   To be an educated man is merely to belong
to the class of the educated. It is not the individual, however,
but the whole circle of the educated that are the representatives
of education. They represent a community, and it is in this
sense that we speak of general education as being an intellectual
property common to all   However, we should not conceive
this generality of intellectual education too narrowly, as
there are both social limits and social grades.   Intellectual education, in fact, admits of different degrees and is of different
kinds. we distinguish between the education of the scholar and
that of the gentleman, between the education of the higher
classes and that of the masses   By a rigorous use, the term
intellectual education might even be made to exclude entirely
the masses from the educated class   But this would be a misuse
of the word because the lower classes are not outside the pale
of intellectual education, and in highly civilized communities are
generally quite active in its behalf.

The intellectual content which must be assimilated before
one can attain to any particular stage of intellectual education,
is not always the same; but it has one feature in common, viz ,
that the knowledge and skill required is general and basic for
all stages.   By reason of this common content, which is generally received and generally useful, intellectual education is
called *general*,[1] and as such differs from the intellectual education belonging to a class or a special profession   The so-
called cultural studies are concerned principally with the general
elements of knowledge.   Intellectual education demands more
than merely vocational skill, and only cultural studies can produce a harmonious whole— a thing impossible of attainment by
specialized and one-sided vocational training   But the very
generality which is the characteristic trait of cultural studies,
frequently leads to the reception of counterfeits of intellectual
education as current gold coin.   From superficial knowledge
nought but superficial culture can result, when the lower classes
ape a culture other than their own, vulgarity is the inevitable
outcome; and the fashions of the passing hour can never supersede the eternal foundations of true and tried culture.

10 To discover the relation between moral and intellectual

---

[1] The Greek terminology shows a like change in meaning as the modern languages The ἐγκύκλια παιδεύματα or μαθήματα denoted originally the studies common
to the educated, but later they signified the course of study embracing the general elements of knowledge

education we must consider, their respective foundations. The elements that make up the matter of intellectual education reach over into the foundations of the intellectual and moral content of life which moral education transmits to the young. The two-fold purpose of moral education——namely the ethical formation of the developing life and the transmission of the treasures of civilization——has a counterpart in intellectual education, for the latter must also be something more than a mere accomplishment or ornament. The inner form which it imparts to human personality should also be a moral support; and intellectual education is likewise concerned with the conservation and transmission of intellectual treasures. Moral education and intellectual education, nevertheless, present some marked differences, the former being concerned primarily with the appetencies and the will, the latter, with the intellect. The former is moral assimilation; the latter, intellectual. The mainstays of moral education are authority and obedience, whereas intellectual education requires, besides subjection to authority, free and spontaneous co-operation on the part of the subject. The work of moral education ends with the maturity of reason, whereas intellectual education must be continued beyond that period and may well occupy the whole life. Moral education derives its character from the *ethos* and the forms of domestic and public life, from the organism and morals of society; whereas intellectual education depends mainly on the intellectual activity evinced in the language and beliefs, the arts and sciences of a nation. Moral education is satisfied with shaping the educational activities according to a well-defined plan, while intellectual education busies itself with collecting and organizing, develops into an organ of society destined to control the transmission of intellectual treasures in a manner somewhat analogous to the exchange of material goods in our markets.

To summarize, we may define a country's system of intellectual education as the sum total of the institutions, means and helps which enable individuals to master the elements of general knowledge as well as to acquire a certain general facility of doing things, both this knowledge and this facility being freely attainable and fecund elements of intellectual life, which serve as stepping stones for reaching certain degrees of intellectual and moral proficiency.[1]

---

[1] In the present work we shall use the term education in this sense, *i. e.*, to signify *mental and intellectual, not moral, training.* (Tr.)

II.

1. Plato reports Socrates as saying that astonishment is an emotion worthy of the philosopher, because it marks the first stage of speculation. Aristotle contends that men have at all times proceeded from astonishment to philosophy [1] In matter of fact, nothing truly scientific is undertaken except on the spur of surprise and wonderment at some unexplained marvel The scholar begins by marvelling at some strange object that baffles explanation; by and by he is completely taken up with the mystery, and finally he determines to examine it from all sides, to scrutinize it, to fathom it in all its bearings. This is scientific research in its perfect form, carried out independently of utilitarian advantages The questions put by children and the nature myths of primitive nations reveal at first hand the charm exercised upon the mind by new and strange objects. The same charm is potent in research work, even when this is directed towards a practical purpose, it is, however, most active in purely theoretical speculation

The different sciences did not pass simultaneously from the field of practical utility into the higher realm of theoretical speculation, whose threshold is marked by surprise and wonderment Astronomy is one of the few which deal with the marvelous in their very first stages and are subservient to scarcely any practical demands, but soar aloft into the empyrean of pure science Most sciences must first assimilate and reproduce the facts and objects before they can indulge in speculation. Historically, the first object of science was not the discovery of facts but a problem to be solved, problems, not ready knowledge, first stimulated the human mind. The natural sciences were the first to ascend to the stage of pure theory, next came the sciences that deal with man and the moral order. Of the moral sciences, those dealing with general institutions lying beyond the individual, preceded those whose objects were more changeable and that depend on the individual and his whims, or extend into everyday life; for as "use lessens marvel," so the objects of our daily environment are ill adapted to inspire that speculative spirit which proceeds from wonderment.

[1] Plato, *Theæt*, p 155 Aristotle, *Met*, I, 2, *Rhet* I, 11 The sentiment would seem to have been familiar to the ancient mind cf Olympiodor, Εις τὸν Πλάτωνος πρῶτον Ἀλκιβιάδην ed Creuzer p 24, and .Proclos in the work bearing the same title, Creuzer, p 46

Education is affected more than any other science by this disadvantage. Its object is not large, like that of political science or that of jurisprudence. The activity which it investigates is concerned primarily with the individual only; it descends to small, and even minute, particulars; it leaves much to discretion, temperament, and individual interests; and consequently often seeks advice and regulation. The final aims of education are of an ideal nature, and, considered from this point of view, pedagogy and didactic must be regarded as the most ideal forms of artistic instruction. Yet, by very reason of this ideal mission, education is prevented from regarding its objects as concrete facts and looking upon them with the interest of a research worker. Thus education appears as a chaos of contradictory views, or at best as a system of principles, rules, and suggestions abounding in counsel but poor in observations and facts. It cannot be denied that much educational literature is scientific in treatment; but this is owing to the accidental circumstance that the writers were at home in some other science — theology, philology, philosophy, history—and that their educational treatises derive an advantage from the proficiency there acquired rather than to any light they derive from the topic of education itself. Eminent educationists have not scrupled to deny to education the character of a science; and some have even declared the popular essay, the very reverse of scientific research, to be its proper element. A witty teacher ventured the opinion that "Pedagogy teaches partly what we all know and partly what no one can know."

And yet it is only necessary to take the right viewpoint to be persuaded that the subject of education is by no means destitute of that which must elicit scientific thought and which assures a rich harvest for all scientific work spent on it. If we examine our subject at close range, we shall perceive that it includes much that is wonderful ($\theta\alpha\upsilon\mu\alpha\sigma\tau\acute{o}\nu$), a large complex of facts, independent and comprehensive enough to invite the marvelling contemplation of the scholar. Do not the phenomena described above invite scientific research? Undoubtedly it is worthy of scientific scholarship to inquire into the wonderful solidarity of succeeding generations of men, by which the creations and acquisitions of the race are conserved despite the continual change of the agencies entrusted with their care, to discover by what happy coincidence it comes to pass that what has been acquired and conserved by preceding generations, what has made them civilized and cultured, that this is transmitted to one generation after another without a break in the educative process; and to examine how this process of rejuvenation combines and interlaces with the vital functions of the social body, creating at the same time its own proper course and evolving its special organs

2. Education is a science because its field extends to the great collective phenomena wherein the educative and cultural activity of the race has taken shape, and because it thereby gets in contact with the phenomena, both collective and individual, of the social world

The demand that education be treated as a part of sociology is not new, but ancient—in fact, the science of education is an offspring of sociology. Whenever the ancients treated education systematically, they had practical ends in view, but they always dealt with the subject in connection with political and sociological studies, witness Plato's *Republic* In this work, which stands at the head of political and sociological as well as educational literature, Plato treats of education twice first, as the aggregate of all those agencies by which the citizens of the ideal State are to be imbued with the moral principles upon which the commonwealth is based;[1] second, as the power which is to raise the State to ideal perfection by training the future philosopher-kings and directing their minds towards eternity and the Great Beyond [2] In Plato's *Laws* the basic principle of the prospective colonial state is the norm for controlling the propagation and training of children, their teaching and discipline, nay even their games [3] The same work furthermore contains a sort of comparative pedagogy, a description and appreciation of the relative merits of various educational systems among Greeks and barbarians [4] In several passages characterized by depth and beauty education is described as a new life, as a social and religious duty, as a transmission of the treasures of civilization from generation to generation. We quote but one sentence, which recalls a thought already expressed by Pythagoras: "We must have and train children, transmitting to them the torch of life, so that generation may succeed generation, serving the gods in accordance with law and tradition."[5]

---

[1] *Republic*, II, p 376 to III, p 412

[2] Ib VI, pp 503-541   [3] *Laws*, VII, p 798

[4] Spartan education especially II, p 666, Persian III, p 694, ancient Attic III, p 700, Egyptian VII, p 798 and 819

[5] Ib VI, p 776, cf Jambl *Vit. Pyth*, 85, see also *Legg*, II, p 659, III, p 681, and X, p 887

Aristotle's pedagogical system also is essentially sociological. Education in a State is determined by the constitution and is its preserving element; every constitution is an outgrowth of the *ethos* of the nation, is safeguarded by the preservation of that *ethos*, and improved by its elevation, both of which functions (preservation and elevation of the national *ethos*) belong to education.[1] Home education likewise requires that the attention be focussed upon the whole nation: to instruct even a few in virtue, one must be endowed with the gifts of the legislator.[2]

The pioneers of pedagogy as a science built it upon a social foundation. Similarly, their successors never lost sight of its relations to society and the State. The *Didactica* which took its rise in the 17th century, endeavored not only to make teaching and learning less onerous and more profitable, but also to regenerate education in all its branches and thereby to advance the welfare and prosperity of the Christian State. Wolfgang Ratke (d. 1635) with his reforms aimed at nothing less than to establish and preserve one language, one government, and one religion throughout the whole empire. Cristoph Helwig (d. 1617) and Joachim Jung (d. 1657) in their report on Ratke's suggestions declare that the art of teaching is "more necessary and more useful to the art of government than all other arts, because it is by teaching, as all philosophers and political economists admit, that the highest and final end of governing must be obtained."[3] This tendency is still more evident in the writings of Amos Comenius (1592-1670), who describes "Didactica" as *artificium omnes omnia docendi* and as the "universal art to found schools for the teaching of all things." As workshops encourage the trades, as churches foster religion, as courts of justice safeguard the law, so schools should engender, enlighten, increase education—"the light of wisdom"—and "transmit it to the whole body of the race", thus performing their share of the work that results from a mutual relationship analogous to that existing between the members of the living body.[4] What the stomach is for the body, says Comenius, that the "*collegium didacticum*" (a board of scholars who are supposed to watch over the curriculum of the schools) is for the educational or-

---

[1] Aristotle, *Pol.*, VIII, 1, p. 1336.
[2] *Eth. Nic.*, X, 10, p. 1180.
[3] Cf. Guhrauer, *Joachim Jungius und sein Zeitalter*, 1850.
[4] *Didactica magna*, 8, 8.

ganism [1] The same writer repeatedly compares the school system with a printing shop, that is, he conceives instruction as a process of reproducing souls and the art of teaching as a sort of intellectual typography, he even coined a new term, *didachographia*, to express this idea.[2] Still, he recognized that the schools represent but a fraction of the educational and cultural agencies, and that education is not completed in school. He pays due attention to the *"schola materna,"* by which the child receives its first informal instruction at home [3] Nor does he lose sight of the instruction given in workshops and artists' studios, but rather chooses the old and tried traditions living in these institutions as a norm for the formal instruction of the schools.[4] Comenius also devised a system of self-education, a "pansophic library," which was to constitute a *"seminarium eruditionis universalis."* [5]

3. The ambitious dreams of Comenius and his school could not be realized, because these writers, despite the breadth of their view, failed to recognize the importance of history and psychology in education. The rationalists of that period were too subjective, they limited their studies to the individual as such and disregarded his relations to society, present and past, and consequently conceived of education as a discipline concerned only with individuals They never went beyond the relation of teacher and pupil to examine the larger social factors of education Though solitary voices clamored for a public, in opposition to exclusively private education then in vogue, and though the 18th century really gave birth to the view that the education of the lower classes is a matter of public concern, yet not even this novel departure was an adequate corrective of the extremely individualistic conception of education, for the resulting State System of education recognized no public or collective educational activity beside that of the State Now, the social character of education cannot be understood from the political viewpoint alone While it would be unfair to find fault with the Greeks for having failed to distinguish between the social and the political aspect of education because their national customs, their religious institutions and various forms of social organization appeared to them as inseparably united

[1] Ib 31, 15
[2] Ib 32 and *Opera didactica omnia*, Amstelodami, 1657, IV, p 85 ff
[3] *Didactica Magna*, 28
[4] *Didactica Magna*, 21, 21, *Meth ling nov*, *Opp D O*, II, p 103-129 et al.
[5] *Prodramus Pansophiae*, *Opp D O*, I, p 404 ff

with the political commonwealth, we must admit that the political educationists of the 18th and 19th centuries were guilty
of onesidedness when they regarded education as the business
of the State, and entirely ignored those other social and historical forces—the Church, society, and custom—to which systematized education really owed its being. The renewal of the life
of the social organism cannot be properly understood from the
viewpoint exclusively of the State, because the latter is but one
of the factors that constitute the social organism. The ideals
of education owe their existence to the treasures of civilization,
which are safeguarded, or at most controlled, but not in any
sense created, by the State. The State can organize, but the
materials necessary for this process are derived from sources
entirely beyond governmental sway. But the age of rationalism, which recognized only the dictates of reason, which held
society to be the product of a contract, which believed that
faith and morality were the invention of wise men, was obviously not equal to this exalted conception of education and
consequently ignored that part of the educational field which,
while it transcends the individual, yet does not come within
the purview of the State.

The social view of education having been narrowed down to
a purely political view, it was no longer able to supplement the
individual view, and the science of education showed a glaring
defect, which had to be supplied, especially since the political
sciences, with the aid of corrected principles gained from historical studies, began to deal with education. The theory of
Lorenz von Stein, in his *Verwaltungslehre*, which is far more
comprehensive and profound than those of earlier writers, as
Pœlitz, Aretin, and Mohl, may serve to remind pedagogy of
its deficiencies. Stein's starting-point is the concept of intellectual good, which he defines as "knowledge and skill in as
much as they are a product of mental work and economic utili-
zation, and an element in the production of new goods."[1] This
process of production Stein calls education—a concept which is
at first restricted to the individual, but soon transcends this
limit, because every individual needs the co-operation of others
in acquiring an education. The collective activity devoted to
the educative process is termed the system of education.[2] It
is an organic element of the national life of a people which comes

[1] *Verwaltungslehre*, 1868, Vol. V, p. xix.
[2] Ib., p. 8.

into being and asserts itself by its own power. The State does not create it, but finds it ready made. The need, however, of directing the stream of intellectual life along definite channels brings about an active interference by the conscious will of the community as a whole as expressed in the State. In other words, the State takes hold of, and applies its own principles to, education, and we have a public system of educational agencies governed by well-defined laws and regulations.[1] In this public system Stein recognizes three distinct departments: 1. The primary or common school system, 2. Preparatory, professional, and special schools for vocational training, and 3 The agencies for the general education of the people, which embrace the internal momenta connecting the various professions. Such institutions are: academies, libraries, museums, theatres, and their common organ—the press. Stein traces each of these departments in their course of development and describes their organization in the principal countries of Europe. Stein steers free of the superficial view of his predecessors that education and its organs are the creation of the State, and acknowledges that the work of education is autonomous. He also avoids the error of subordinating the science of education to political science, but assigns to it its own proper field of research, which he defines as the establishment of "the principles and laws that govern the transmission of knowledge to the individual through the co-operation of others " Political science, in his opinion, is limited "to controlling the external form and order of the various branches, organs, and agencies of education, by means of which government fulfills the duties incumbent upon the community to provide for the education of its citizens "[2]

It is not our purpose to inquire in how far these views of Stein must be modified before they can be accepted as the groundwork of a satisfactory system of education. One thing is quite obvious· his division of the educational field cannot be accepted as definitive. Were we to accept Stein's definition, we should have to postulate a medium by which the science of education is enabled to enter into proper relations with political science, for it is necessary to ascertain how the individual pursuit of knowledge becomes the business of the whole community, how a system of public education can grow out of united individual efforts, and what is the nature of the influence exercised upon

[1] Ib , p· 12 and p XIX
[2] Ib , pp XIX and xx.

it by national, social, literary, scientific, and religious factors, before it is sufficiently developed to receive a fixed form at the hands of the State. Stein admits that such an inquiry is necessary, but fails to assign to it its proper place. Evidently this function belongs to the science of education, not to political science; and Stein rendered a signal service by showing how far the former must extend its scope before it approaches the domain of politics and jurisprudence and is in a position to cooperate with these sciences.

4. While the science of education is correlated to other and larger fields, we do not mean to force upon it the political point of view, for this were tantamount to neglecting a great part of its sphere. Nor do we intend so to extend its scope as to render it shallow and to create the belief that education, though it brings great numbers under its influence, lacks a subject and an object as well as a particular aim. This naive view is entertained by those who consider it education to keep the children, by fair means or foul, in a tolerable state of order; or by those who consider it real culture to force intellectual data down the pupil's throat. The sophist whom Plato cites in his *Protagoras* gives expression to this ingenuous view when he says that a single individual can no more be held responsible for training others to virtue than a single teacher may be credited with teaching boys how to speak Greek, or a single master-mechanic may be regarded as an instructor of the young generation in the trades.[1] This conception of education is so vague that it assigns even to impersonal agencies the work of educating the young: if the boy is a failure in school and appears to his teachers a good-for-nothing fellow, then some parents will console themselves with the thought, "Life will teach him," or, "necessity and want have educated many who were the despair of both teachers and parents." In opposing these vague notions, the educationists of the so-called Era of Enlightenment (Rationalism), headed by Locke, rendered a valuable service to education. Locke demanded that education be individual and personal, that its end and object is "a sound mind in a sound body"; that the teacher must be left free to employ educational means and agencies in accordance with the needs of his pupils; that he must respect the individual character of each. Quite naturally Locke was an opponent of public school education. Rousseau developed this theory into a stubborn individualism, which de-

[1] Plato, *Protag.*, p. 337.

stroys the bonds connecting the individual with the community, present and past, and isolates education in a manner that runs counter to nature and historical development. His revolutionary doctrines throw a new and glaring light on the subjective and individual factors of education Some of his demands—for instance, to study the child's nature, to train his senses, to make his childish experiences the starting-point of his own co-operation with his teachers, to distinguish between the scientific and the didactic method—revealed a deep psychological insight, and, while pointing out specific problems, encouraged the discovery of new methods [1]

Of the followers of Locke and Rousseau, Trapp was the first to suggest, in his *Versuch einer Pädagogik* (1780), that psychology be made the main source for pedagogical knowledge   Though he himself did not enter deeply into the subject, he pointed out the connection existing between psychology and pedagogy. To have fused these two sciences is the glory of Herbart, who added ethics (though of a purely individualistic character), as another fundamental science, and treated pedagogy systematically according to the deductive method   According to Herbart the fundamental relation is the mutual relation existing between teacher and pupil.[2] His immediate purpose is to perfect education by the aid of science so as to make it an art   His final end is to make the pupil virtuous, to enkindle in his soul varied interests, and to ground his moral life on a strong character   Herbart warns the teacher expressly against fitting his pupil for any special profession or social task [3] His categories are: government, instruction, and discipline. He gives definite rules concerning the method, content, and course of instruction, and the use and method of discipline. Psychology being his auxiliary science, he devotes special care, on the one hand, to the intermediate steps connecting knowledge and volition—interest, sympathy, attention, etc —and, on the other hand, to the means

[1] We agree with Herbart when he says (*Pädagogische Schriften*, ed by Willmann, 1873-75. II, 240), of the educational systems of Locke and Rousseau "This point of view was necessary for differentiating properly between ethics and pedagogy," but we must protest against his assertion that, "Had this not been done, the true nature of pedagogy would never have been revealed " This is an exaggerated estimate of the importance of the new doctrine   In his earlier years, Herbart had more correct views of Locke and Rousseau Cf *Pädagogische Schriften*, I, 336, 506, and II, 241, 258
[2] Cf *The Science of Education*, Translated by H M and E Felkin, London, 1892, p 92, *Pädagogische Schriften*, I, 349 and II, 208
[3] Cf the résumé in my edition of Herbart's educational writings, II, 671-688

by which these manifold influences and impulses are fused into
one harmonious whole.[1] Besides his psychological treatises,
which deal with the conditions and means for raising pedagogy
to a higher scientific plane, Herbart has written others of a
purely theoretical character treating of the individual receptivity of different pupils, the educational content of various
studies, and the efficiency of educational institutions.[2] What
he says on the subject of studying and developing character is
very stimulating and instructive.[3]

Herbart's pedagogy marks the highest point reached by that
school which regards education from the standpoint of individualistic (in opposition to social) ethics. Theodor Waitz neglects
the ethical point of view in favor of the psychological.[4] Fr.
Ed. Beneke has no adequate conception of the significant relations established by education between man and man, to
which Herbart devoted such close attention.[5] In England the
science of education has not developed in the same measure as
in Germany. Herbert Spencer never got beyond a sort of modernized Philanthropinism. Alexander Bain offers a few helpful remarks, but conceives the idea of personality too narrowly
to recompense us for his extreme individualism.[6] His strictures
passed on John Stuart Mill's definition of education show how
little he understood the sociological method. In an address delivered at his inauguration as Rector of St. Andrew's University,
Mill had said: "Education is the culture which each generation
purposely gives to those who are to be its successors, in order
to qualify them for at least keeping up, and if possible, for
raising, the level of improvement which has been attained."[7]
Bain says of this definition, that it is "grandiose rather than
scientific" and that "nothing is to be got out of it".[8] He regards Mill's fruitful idea as over-scientific. We on our part
must confess that Bain's definition of education as "The arts
and methods employed by the schoolmaster,"[9] appears to us
as under-scientific.

---

[1] *The Science of Education*, p. 84 ff., and *The Application of Psychology to the
Science of Education*, translated by B.C. Mulliner, New York, 1898.

[2] In *The Application of Psychology to Education.*

[3] *The Science of Education.*

[4] *Erziehungs- und Unterrichtslehre*, 1835 (new ed. Berlin, 1876).

[5] *Education: Intellectual, Moral, Physical*, 1861.

[6] *Education as a Science.* New York, 1879.

[7] *Dissertations and Discussions: Political, Philosophical, and Historical.* New
York, 1874, Vol. IV, p. 333.

[8] *Education as a Science*, p. 6.   [9] Ibid.

5. The concepts of education have gained much, particularly in depth, by studying pedagogy from the standpoint of the individual; and as we enter the social field, we 'must be careful lest we forfeit this gain. The path leading to this larger field must pass through the field of individual pedagogy; and as our view becomes enlarged and takes in the vast complex of collective educational efforts, we must not overlook the individual-ethical and psychological conditions underlying them.

If anyone doubts the need of studying the social forces in education and of enlarging the view to embrace the collective efforts made in its behalf, let him consider that even so comprehensive an individualism as Herbart's cannot take in all the facts. True, the final end of education is to produce a certain inner state, but what constitutes this state and co-operates in creating it cannot be compressed into an abstract formula. Education always involves a transmission and an assimilation of ideas and principles and presupposes an intellectual and moral vital content as well as certain collective agencies that are the bearers of this content and possess the power to bring about its assimilation The knowledge that forms the object of educational activity is not a mere instrument to be employed at will, but a treasure, which has been handed down the ages and must be scrupulously guarded The forms, too, which the educative process assumes, are closely interwoven with other social and historical agencies, so that no deductive process can hope to draw forth more than a few of the many interlacing threads, leaving the rest of the web a mess so much the more hopeless of disentanglement because of the wrong attempts made to that end. The art of education may mark one of the highest points of pedagogical activity, but it by no means includes the whole field. Wherever one generation is engaged in raising another to its own level, wherever a father faithfully labors to train his boy, wherever a mother prays for life, health and purity for her children, there is education; and often its half-unconscious strength transcends all art The relation between two individuals is indeed basic, so far as education is concerned, but not more so, be it remembered, than the relation between two generations. In order fully to grasp the scope of education as a science, it is necessary to combine the individual and the social views, for only in this way can we realize the richness and depth of the personal relation without losing sight of the various social and historical interrelations. The nature of the problem may be stated, somewhat paradoxically, thus:

Without understanding education in all its aspects we cannot understand the nature of education; and, conversely, the latter is the key for understanding the former. The processes and activities occurring between individuals can be understood only in the light of the general process of assimilation of the young to their elders, which collective activity in its turn must be viewed as the product of a fusion of innumerable individual processes and activities. The science of education may with equal propriety be defined as a science dealing with the whole system of education, or as a science dealing with the acquisition of an education by the individual. If we adopt the latter definition, we must bear in mind that the acquisition of an education is always conditioned by the existing system, in which it has, so to say, taken substantive form, and that neither the ends nor the subject-matter nor the means of instruction can ever be autonomously determined by the individual. If we adopt the former definition of education, as coextensive with the system of educational agencies, then we must not forget that it is not a matter of merely describing the shell or case that has been erected around the work of education, but likewise of appraising the forces active within this system—which in their last analysis, are traceable to individual endeavor. We must in the first case proceed synthetically until we arrive at an understanding of the collective agencies; and in the second case, we must follow the analytical method till we arrive at the individual processes. To express the twofold problem involved, the definition ought really to read: Education is the science treating of all the activities that are directed toward the moral and intellectual assimilation of the young, as performed by and upon individuals, upon the basis of an existing system.

6. The fact that neither the individual nor the social principle is in itself sufficient to supply a starting-point and coign of vantage, because each continually points to, and, as it were, conceals itself behind the other, is a distinct difficulty, but it is one that is not peculiar to the science of education, but common to all the sciences that concern themselves with the moral order both in general and in particular. The State rests on the political consciousness of its subjects—the ethos of its citizens—and must be explained in the light of the same; but the ethos of the citizens is itself a product of the national life—both its root and its blossom. The public market is an immense mechanism whose motor forces (and therefore also the reasons for its existence) lie in the different economic needs of individual men;

but take away the market, and you will have neither business
nor business needs, for the father of these is commerce, which
takes shape and form in the market. ᵛTo solve the problem of
language you must study man, who employs it, but what is
man without language, which is furnished him by society, and
how could he be understood unless considered as a partaker in
the common gift which itself must be explained by his individual soul activity? Customs and institutions, the spirit of the
age and of a nation, are objective forces that impress upon the
individual a stamp that cannot be deciphered without these
same factors; and still, upon closer view, we discover that they
are little more than phenomena of consciousness and exist nowhere outside of the consciousness of individuals, and what
was to have been explained by them must be accepted as the
principle for their own explanation

The two-sided nature of these problems forces itself upon
both classes of thinkers—those who by their philosophical pre-
possessions are inclined to study the collective forces, as well as
those who by preference study the individual. In studying the
fitness of things, which he considered the main purpose of his
ideal State, Plato proceeds from the fitness discovered in the
common life of the race, hoping that this fitness proper to the
larger field would assist in explaining the fitness of the mind
and actions of the individual.[1] But in the course of his inquiry
he recognized that society and the individual must mutually
explain each other, and in this sense compares them to two
pieces of wood, which must be rubbed together in order to produce a spark.[2] Herbart arrives at the same conclusion from
the opposite direction His individualistic psychology leads him
to confess that man cannot be understood except in connection
with society and history, though these two factors themselves
are products of the joint efforts of individuals, so that it is "not
the straight and direct road, but the zigzag path, running this
way and that, in a slow onward course, that will lead to the
correct interpretation of psychological facts".[3] Had Herbart applied this truth to ethics and pedagogy, he would have found
himself compelled to give to these sciences a form differing from
the one they hold in his system [4]

---

[1] *Rep* , II, p 368
[2] Ib , IV, p 435.
[3] *Gesammelte Werke*, edited by Hartenstein, VI, 21, cf IX, 185
[4] In my edition of Herbart's educational writings, I have indicated the passages where it is necessary to go beyond the individualistic conception, and take

7. Modern research has adopted the methods recommended by Plato and Herbart: by employing Plato's rubbing process, it has thrown new light on old problems, and by following Herbart's zigzag path it has come closer to an understanding of the moral world. The demand that the individual and society, the microcosm of personal and the macrocosm of social and historical life, should be made to explain each other, has come to be recognized, at least among German scholars, as a methodological principle. This principle has a twofold importance for the development of the science of education; it supplies it with models showing how the individual and social views are to be carried out, and furnishes a large number of new and valuable data, the result of the researches in allied sciences.

This new principle has been successfully applied in the ethnological field by M. Lazarus and H. Steinthal, who have established a mutual relationship between psychology on the one hand and philology, ethnology, and history on the other. Psychology has thus broadened its horizon, while the other three sciences and the moral sciences in general have acquired a deeper and more exact understanding of their respective problems and much valuable stimulation. Education should establish similar relations to psychology and ethnology, for the fields of the two sciences are practically inseparable: the former examines into the psychological processes of education and the latter into the historico-social forms of these processes; and beside this formal analogy, there is a connecting bond in the very content of the two disciplines. Of the organizations that together make up the social organism, the nation is the first and the strongest, as it is prepared directly by nature; and when there is question of reconstructing the social life, the nation is the first fact to be considered. The national type is transmitted by heredity, and the intellectual possessions of the nation—its language, literature, customs, and beliefs—are the principal means of conscious and unconscious assimilation on the part of the young. Nay, we may say that the youth of a country belong to the nation. The family speaks of *its* children, society of *its* members, but

regard to the two-sided nature of the problem. Cf. *Pädagogische Schriften*, I, XXXV and II, 287. The practical philosophy of Waitz underwent a similar change. Waitz had originally based his system, in an abstract way, on the individual, but by and by he allowed more importance to sociological principles, and finally arrived at the study of anthropology, which he undertook for the purpose of obtaining an empirical and social basis for his system of ethics. Cf. my edition of Waitz's *Pädagogik*, p. LX ff.

the young people bear the name of the nation to which they
belong—Greek, Roman, etc. Many agencies co-operate with
the national spirit in impressing upon the educational system
of each country a distinctive type; but the spirit of the respective nation is always the most powerful. Each nation has its
own peculiar system of education, and if the education of certain classes of society is somewhat the same in all countries,
yet there are always clearly pronounced national differences.
The truth of this observation is borne out by the comparative
study of different national systems of education. Thus Wiese's
Deutsche Briefe über englische Erziehung show that the character
of the English people asserts itself, often in an astounding way,
in their schools, from the principles underlying the system itself
down to the daily routine of the schoolroom and the customs,
good and bad, of the pupils.

The psychological analysis of the soul of nations, the study
of their psychic types, the investigation of the factors that
constitute nationality and their mutual relations—all of which
tasks modern ethnography has undertaken with considerable
success—greatly benefit the science of education; and even an
only occasional ray of light falling thence on cognate subjects
is of some service. In return for this service education assists
the researches of ethnology. To solve the problem of the origin
of language and popular customs it is helpful to observe the
child's awakening to the consciousness of language and morality.
Scholars have not been blind to this fact, but they cannot arrive
at satisfactory results until the educationists have elaborated
and organized the materials belonging to this field. The science
of education must furnish what Francis Bacon would call the
"*instantiæ ostensivæ*" for the immense field of psychical agencies, which we have described (p. 19) as involuntary assimilation,
and which are of far-reaching influence upon a nation's life. It
was left to education to draw the line of strict demarcation
between conscious and unconscious influences and to make of
the former a field of special investigation.

The science of education, if its scope is sufficiently broadened, can furnish ethnology with a new category, the category
of education itself. The educational system of a nation, comprising all that makes for general knowledge and skill, is a special department and the manner of its cultivation bears testi-
mony to a nation's creative genius. Though education depends
on language, literature, science, art, religion, and other factors,
it is coextensive with none of these. The genius of the Greek

nation appears in its *paideia* no less than in its literature, science, and art; and *paideia* implies more than merely the form for sharing these intellectual treasures, for, though it derives its content from them, it has a principle of its own for converting multitudinous knowledge into a harmonious whole, and this principle is independent of the content.

The Humanism of the 15th century, which was at first a purely intellectual movement, but subsequently became a powerful vital force in Italy and the other countries of Europe, was identical neither with science, nor with poetry and art, though its representatives appeared alternately as scholars, poets, or artists. It was a thing of protean shape, as Burckhardt has described it so masterfully,[1] which, after passing through various modifications, became firmly fixed in modern education. These two examples (Humanism and the *paideia* of the Greeks) show that ethnology would do well to include education among such creations of the national spirit as language, mythology, poetry, art, and science.

8. The science of education must furthermore take cognizance of the researches in moral statistics, which received a new impetus when Alexander von Öttingen made social ethics the basis for his statistical studies, trying to prove that a harmony exists between the collective movements of a community and individual liberty.[2] The statistics dealing with the polarity and equilibrium of the sexes, with marriages and births, furnish a broad empirical basis for the study of the process of social reconstruction, and they are particularly well adapted to drive home the idea of the solidarity of society and the succeeding generations of the human race, for they demonstrate the wonderful harmony existing between the natural and the moral order, between necessity and liberty. It has been observed that after wars or other catastrophes causing a great loss of men, the births of male children increase beyond the normal number, whereas their death rate decreases, as though all forces of the social body set to work to supply the wounded organ with what it needs. This phenomenon, known as "the law of compensation" is a veritable marvel, a θαυμαστόν, which gives us a glimpse, though faint, of the natural forces engaged in the reconstruction of the social body.

---

[1] J. Burckhardt, *The Civilization of the Renaissance in Italy*, translated by Middlemore, London, 1898.

[2] A. v. Öttingen, *Die Moralstatistik und die christliche Sittenlehre*, Erlangen, 1868.

The mortality statistics for the different ages enable us to obtain an idea of the numerical strength of a generation in its successive stages. The process may be illustrated by the simile of a tree, broad at the base, but narrowing down immediately to three-fourths of its thickness—one-fourth of the children dying in their first year—growing thinner gradually after the first year, till after twenty years the proper thickness is one-half of that at the base. This is not a perfect picture of the reconstruction of social life, still it will serve as an outline. To supply the material needed for a complete study, we should lay under tribute the school statistics, for they show the paths which a generation follows in acquiring an education, and allow us to follow a generation up to certain stages of its development. But as yet we lack a complete picture portraying all the differentiations in education and the professions and representing all the forces, great and small, that furnish new blood to the social organism.

A further gain for the science of education may be expected from the attempts of statisticians to measure the intellectual activity of communities. Their figures are the ranging-poles for measuring these large fields, which without some positive data are so easily misjudged. The figures for school attendance, literacy of adults (recruits, or persons contracting marriage), frequency of letter-writing, bookproduction and sale, etc., are useful in estimating the degree of a nation's education and the exchange carried on in intellectual treasures; but we cannot base our judgments exclusively upon them, because the things of the mind are contingent upon many other factors which by their very nature do not admit of computation.

Joining hands with the criminologists, the moral statisticians have investigated the influence of education upon national morality, and thereby helped to solve problems that are of the greatest importance for the science of education as well as for ethics. False conclusions have, indeed, been set down by some investigators. Thus Perdonnet's dictum, "Instruction is moral improvement," is the result of ignoring the difference between knowledge and conscience, intellect and will. But it is not the statistics which are at fault; it is the wrong moral standard of the men who draw conclusions from them. Individualism and its near relative, intellectualism, had, since the 18th century, treated ethics so entirely apart from social science that these men were unable to interpret aright the collective phenomena presented by statistics. Öttingen deserves credit for demanding that personal ethics be developed into social ethics, for the science was thereby qualified to digest statistical facts. Some have considered it a whim of the theologian that Öttingen conceded to Christianity its constitutive influence upon morality, but he did this because he felt that no other movement in the history of the world can better explain and more fully harmonize the opposition between the individual and the community, between the rights of an individual and his duties as a member of society, between the liberty of man as a moral agent and the limitations of free will resulting from natural and historical development. Our chief regret is that Öttingen's Lutheran point of view did not permit him to look with an unbiased mind upon the great social and ethical institutions of the Christian world.

9. Auguste Comte's sociology has been vastly overrated, and it needs but a cursory examination to realize that his views throw no light upon the mutual relations existing between the individual and the community. Comte treats psychology as a branch of biology with phrenology as its scientific basis, and consequently cannot be expected to examine seriously into the soul-life of the individual. His moral philosophy is crudely materialistic, and its sensualistic tendency is not corrected by the attempted inoculation of higher and purer elements. His sociology never attains to the level of social ethics, but remains merely social physics and obscures the great problems of moral philosophy by applying the notion of law, as abstracted from nature, to the moral order. Neither will the principles of Comte's philosophy of history bear a close scrutiny. His supreme thesis, reiterated *ad nauseam*, that humanity passed from the stage of childhood, where faith and theology were its guides, into adolescence and youth, where abstract thinking and metaphysics prevailed, and ultimately attained to manhood—the age of Positivism—where, for the first time, facts, and not dreams, are perceived and understood—this thesis, I say, does not explain the development of the human mind. Comte has actually inverted the order in which the principles governing his three epochs should, by reason of their respective value, be considered. Occupation with material things marks the lowest stage of philosophy; then the mind proceeds from appearances to the study of the nature of objects, which denotes a higher step; the highest stage is reached when man recognizes that he is unequal to understanding everything, and that there is a reality to which he can attain only in the light of faith. Comte's

views on education are of very unequal merit; they are purely
fantastic when he describes education as the mainstay of the
new Positivistic age, which is to be ruled by a "hierarchy of
intelligence" devoid of anything smacking of the ἱερόν or of the
things of the mind.   But when Comte tells us that education is
to be sought in the "consensus" of social phenomena, and that
it cannot be understood except by passing beyond abstract
psychological concepts and examining into the ever-changing
state of civilization, he displays fine discrimination.[1] By proving
the solidarity and interrelation of the forces at work in society,
which are the proper subjects of social statics, Comte has rendered a great service to sociology, which gives him a place of
honor among its pioneers, for to inquire into the totality of the
social phenomena will ever remain the starting-point of social
science.

In establishing this same view Lilienfeld and Schäffle have
laid the natural sciences, especially evolution, under tribute and
have gone so far as to divest the time-honored analogy between
the social and the organic body of its purely figurative meaning
and to treat it as a reality, for they consider both society and
the animal body as compounds of forces: the former of intellectual; the latter, of physical forces.   Lilienfeld's method and
presentment are terse and compendious, whereas Schäffle first
sketches the outline of the social cosmos and then fills it out
with the products of his immense erudition.   Schäffle's encyclopedia of sociology marks, as it were, the *terminus ad quem* of
education, *i. e.*, the position which, developing along sociological
lines, it must occupy in the structure of the social world.   This
is a fruitful conception and we have utilized it in the first part
of this Introduction.

We must, however, guard against overestimating the importance of this system of sociology based on the natural sciences.
Though its field is more extensive than that of any of the other
systems discussed, it cannot explain all the phenomena of the
social world.   Thus it has no key wherewith to unlock the prob-

---

[1] Cf. *Cours de philosophie positive*, IV, 349. La vicieuse prépondérance des
considérations biologiques et l'irrational dédain des notions historiques ont par-
eillement conduit à méconnaître profondément la véritable évolution sociale et à
supposer une fixité chimérique à des dispositions essentiellement variables. Cette
influence nuisible est surtout très marquée dans la plupart des théories relatives à
l'éducation, presque toujours considérée ainsi à la manière théologico-métaphysique,
abstraction faite de l'état corrélatif de la civilisation humaine. Cf. *Catholic Encyclopedia*, *Positivism*.

lem of the mutual relationship existing between the individual and society, because it applies concepts derived from the natural order to the intellectual order, regardless of the generic difference between the two.   Lilienfeld and his school perceive in the analogy between the living body and the social organism more than a simile fruitful in thoughts and suggestions, and make it the first principle of inquiry, since they assume a real conformity, almost identity, in the operations of the two essentially different fields.   Society is not a compound of ideal forces; it is rather an ideal compound of forces.   Masses of men, though one in language, customs, and interests, do not constitute a nation; they must be conscious of being bound together by the ties of a common nationhood.   A number of men imbued with the same ideas on religion do not constitute a religious body; to be a religious body, they must be conscious of being united by a common faith.   The animal organism needs but a union of forces to be a reality; but social forces must produce an act of consciousness, before the social organism can be said to possess reality; without this act—which is an act of the free will—no social organism exists.   Therefore consciousness is of vastly greater importance for the social organism than the organic individual, the cell, is for the living body.   The cell is but a part of the animal organism, whereas the consciousness of the individual is not only a part of the social organism, but the source of its continued existence.   Compared with the organism, the cell is a unit of a lower order: the organism is its end; but in the relation between the individual and the community, the latter is not superior to the individual: both are complements of each other, and neither of them is merely a means for the other.   There are two *termini* in the moral world: the one is the personality of the individual, the other is the intellectual and moral community; the structure of the physical universe here makes way for a new architectonic principle.

The deep, yet simple, wisdom of Christianity is our safest guide also in this matter, and it alone furnishes the true standard by which we can correct the errors of the naturalists.   The Church has ever considered the simile of the living body as of basic significance for her own teachings, and no mechanistic or individualistic system of philosophy has ever made her doubt of her own organic character.   But, though intent on incorporating the individual with her mystical body, the Church never denied the absolute value of the individual soul, but has ever regarded, next to God's glory, the care for the individual as the chief function of her divine mission among men.

III.

1. If we insist that the science of education embrace the social and collective phenomena belonging to its field, then we must demand that history also enter into the scope of the educationist, for it is one and the same principle that requires the study of the social and the historical aspects of education. To assign to education its proper place in the process of social reconstruction is synonymous with determining its position in the course of historical development and inquiring into its influence upon the continuity of human affairs. To consider education as a bond between different generations, as a heritage and an assimilation, is to view it from the standpoint of history, for all that has been transmitted and all that produces the assimilation—intellectual treasures and human organizations—have developed in the course of time and can be understood only in the light of history. To follow up the forces and agencies that together constitute the system of education, means to deal with historical movements and historical values, for, though they can all be traced back to human nature, they have assumed various forms in the course of historical development.

Educationists have ever evinced a certain unwillingness to study the historical development of education, and, despite the intimate connection between the social and the historical side of the subject, some have studied the former but ignored the latter. The reason is that educational movements as a rule owe their existence to a desire to reform, if not to reorganize, the existing system, and hence direct attention to the future rather than the past. Reformers never do full justice to the achievements of the past; intent upon changing prevailing conditions, they are too prejudiced to appraise them at their true value and to appreciate the actual work embodied in existing institutions.

Plato, it must be admitted, in devising an educational system for his philosopher-kings, did not reject all points of contact with the past, but adopted some of the national customs and some of the educational views of Pythagoras. Yet he did not understand the importance of historical development for education, for he demands that the child be brought up outside the family circle, learn nothing of the nation's poetry and traditions, and be kept aloof, at least during its early years, from the company of its elders, whom the philosopher thought hopelessly corrupt. Even in his *Laws*, where he adheres more closely to the conditions obtaining in his day, and where he expresses such a sublime conception of education, describing it as the transmission of intellectual treasures, even there we miss a broad outlook upon the forces and agencies of history, upon which all public institutions depend, and which cannot be supplied by abstract principles. No system of state pedagogy but will reveal the same defect: the various organizing activities of the State are dealt with, but the historical forces and agencies that created a system of education before the State ever concerned itself with the matter, are simply ignored.

The pedagogical systems of the 17th century, which also ventured upon the dangerous ground of state pedagogy, are aptly characterized by the motto which Wolfgang Ratke, their pioneer, chose for his writings: "*Vetustas cessit, ratio vicit.*" Comenius, the most important representative of the new educational thought, did not express himself in equally strong terms, but he nevertheless failed to explain whether and where his far-reaching reforms had a support in history.[1] These earlier didacticians had some sort of a historical basis, in as much as they held fast to the philological and theological element of the older education; but the later pedagogy of the Enlightenment discarded this also. Rousseau made it his principle to repudiate the past: "Always do the opposite of the traditional, and you will do the right thing." Though his followers modified this maxim somewhat, yet they too distrusted whatever had been handed down from the past, and contended that pedagogy had to be made all over. The leaders of the rationalistic era held that the arts and sciences, pedagogy included, could be raised to an eminence undreamt of in the "Dark Ages," if only new methods superseded the antiquated fashions—never once real-

[1] Comenius mentions his immediate predecessors, Ratke, Bodinus, Fortius, Bateus, etc. (Cf. *Didactica magna*, introduction, §10 and *Methodus linguarum novissima*, cap. 8); but he knows nothing of the great encyclopedias of the Middle Ages, the remote forerunners of his pansophical undertakings, nor of such textbooks as had formerly been in wide use, e. g., J. Murmelius' *Pappa*, which followed the principles of the *Janua* in arranging the vocables according to their meaning. He likewise failed to appreciate the system of the seven liberal arts, although it embraced the mathematical studies demanded by Comenius; and his connection with the whole system is, at best, only external (*Didactica magna*, cap. 30).

izing that they were carrying on their work of destruction, by means of the very instruments they had inherited from preceding generations, and that they were entirely dependent in their own efforts upon the views, the endeavors, and the achievements of the past.

2. Pestalozzi presents a curious amalgam of the *Zeitgeist* and the opposite tendency to adopt all that had proved its value in the past and must, therefore, be regarded as a basis for all future attempts. It is this contradiction that makes Pestalozzi's system so difficult to understand. He contends, especially in his early writings, that education should not cast about for new-fangled theories, but follow the wise and simple methods handed down from past ages, and that all attempts at reform should embody the "venerable remains of the superior educational system of our ancestors".[1] But his own system of education was launched in direct opposition to this view, as entirely new and well-nigh perfect. In devising it, Pestalozzi failed to appreciate the most obvious truths of the old education. When he established language, form, and number as the three instruments of education, he forgot that these have been the foundation of all schooling from time immemorial. The Pythagoreans considered number and measure the basis of wisdom, and highly regarded the mental power that gave things their names. These three factors had been employed as fundamental principles of education thousands of years before Pestalozzi. What need for him, moreover, to search, as he did, for a core around which the elementary branches might be grouped, when religious instruction had long before established itself as such!

Though Herbart was clearer and more definite in his aims than Pestalozzi, he failed, like the latter, in trying to bridge the chasm between a shallow, unhistorical *Zeitgeist* and the deeper and more comprehensive view of education. Herbart's principles and methods are individualistic, and therefore his pedagogy is too narrow to embrace the historical factors of education. He holds that the true nature of education was revealed only after Locke had given the impetus to examining the personality of each individual pupil,[2] and merely insists that "since Locke the science of education has made constant progress".[3] In his

---

[1] *Schweizerblatt*, 1782; *Complete Works*, edited by Seyffarth, VII, pp. 273, 294, et al.

[2] *Pädagogische Schriften*, II, p. 240 and p. 233.

[3] *Application of Psychology to the Science of Education*, tr. by B. C. Mulliner, London, 1898, p. 9.

review of Schwarz's *Erziehungslehre* he describes the author's
notes on medieval education as "unpleasant parerga which are of
purely historic interest, but may serve to give us some satisfaction as showing the superiority of present educational methods."
Schwarz's account of the Humanist movement is of less interest
to him than the question, what methods Sturm would adopt
under present-day conditions.[1] This attitude is convincing proof
that Herbart never realized that our modern universities had
their beginnings in the Middle Ages, that our colleges are a result of the Renaissance, and that the essence of modern education cannot be understood except in the light of the Middle
Ages. Occasionally, however, Herbart makes a statement which
proves that his view was not entirely hemmed in by the exi-
gencies of his system.   In his *Allgemeine Pädagogik*, published
in 1806, he avers that "the true and right educator is the power
of what men have at any time felt, experienced, and thought,"
and that "to present to the young the whole treasure of ac-
cumulated research in concentrated form is the highest service
which mankind can render at any period of its existence to its
successors."[2] Seven years later, when engaged on problems of
psychology, he was even more emphatic in asserting that human
progress depends entirely on historical development, because
each generation transmits to its offspring those ideas that have
been most fully developed, besides its language, its inventions,
arts, and social institutions, so that the whole past lives in each
one of us, and empirical psychology cannot be universal in its
scope unless it remains under the influence and inspiration of
history.[3]

This change in Herbart's views was, no doubt, induced by
the general revival of historical studies at the beginning of the
19th century.   The individualistic philosophy of the Enlightenment had given way to a healthy reaction: men turned to study
the inheritances of the past and found among them the counter-
parts as well as the reason for existing conditions.   This change
affected all sciences; for philosophy and jurisprudence it proved
epochal; economics, too, received a fresh impetus in all its departments; and educationists took up again the study of what
had been neglected for a full century—the continuity of educational history.   This revived interest in the history of educa-

---

[1] *Pädagogische Schriften*, II, pp. 233, 237.
[2] *The Science of Education*, tr. by H.M. and E. Felkin, London, 1892, p. 81.
[3] *Lehrbuch zur Einleitung in die Philosophie*, 1813. *Gesammelte Werke*, edited
by Hartenstein, I, p. 302.

tion as well as that of the other sciences, owed not a little to
the teachings of Hegel and Schelling. Schwarz, a disciple of
Schelling, was the first to write a general history of education,
*Geschichte der Erziehung nach ihrem Zusammenhang unter den
Völkern* (1813 and 1829). Of Hegel's scholars, Fr. Cramer,
Alex. Kapp, G. Thaulow and others produced valuable historical works. The re-introduction of the Christian element was
of even greater importance, for Christianity, along with the national and ancient elements, not only constitutes the real content of history, but it is the golden thread which unites the
different ages, binding them to the supernatural element that
is eternal and indestructible. It is significant that Karl von
Raumer's history of education, the first to draw upon original
sources, and of permanent value despite its partisan spirit in
religion, is based on Christian principles. The same is true of
K. A. Schmid's monumental *Enzyklopädie des gesamten Er-
ziehungs- und Unterrichtswesens* as well as of the same author's
scholarly *Geschichte der Erziehung.*[1] The history of education
has since been cultivated with good success, K. Kehrbach's
Monumenta Germaniae paedagogica being the most striking case
in point. The history of education is to-day rightly considered
to be the best safeguard against superficiality, vagueness, and
subjectivism. Many educationists perceive that numerous and
diversified relations exist between history and the science of
education, and it needs but one step further to prove that some
of these relations are intrinsic and essential.

3. What, then, were the reasons that have led modern educationists to take up the study of history, and what positive
gain can they expect from historical studies? In the first place,
they can expect the gain obtainable by all the sciences, natural
as well as moral, whether relatively complete or still in an embryonic state, when they study their own development in the
light of history. To progress securely, every science must know
whence it has come; to increase its stock of knowledge, it must
join what it has acquired to what it has received from tradition;
in order not to overestimate the new, it must be able to recognize the old in the new; and in order not to underestimate the
new, it must never lose sight of the problems that have for ages
baffled a satisfactory solution. Education has more reasons than
most other sciences for accepting historic continuity as a princi-

[1] K. A. Schmid's *Geschichte der Erziehung* was continued by G. Schmid; the
fifth and last volume appeared in 1902.

ple for all its researches, because all educational systems are, by their very nature, directed more towards the future than the past, and are ever flushed with the hope of making new and startling discoveries, so that educationists are, as a rule, loath to recognize the achievements of the past and slow to combine them with the endeavors of the present.

The history of education as a science is not directly concerned with education as such; its proper end is to record educational views, theories, and systems, to tell about the men who propagated them and the books they wrote. It is a part of the larger history of the sciences; it is intimately connected with the history of philosophy, since all advanced educational thought is influenced by the trend of speculation; but it is also related to the history of religion, of language, and of the art of language, because theology, philology, and literature are of fundamental importance in education. The history of the science of education must follow up, with some attention to detail, the history of these related sciences and of the other sources of educational thought; it must throw light upon all phases of educational speculation; must trace the lines of contact and divergence between the various educational theories; must show where one system complements another; and must, finally, show how the educational conditions of the present may be improved.

While engaged in such studies we cannot but note that the very object of whose speculative treatment we are tracing the history, is itself a matter of history: the educational theories of the past presuppose existing (and therefore changing) conditions. Educationists, whether they wished to reform or to throw light upon the traditional views, always had an eye on the educational practices of their age. This alone would make it necessary for us to consider, not only their theories, but also the educational systems in vogue at their time. But over and above this consideration, the various educational practices and institutions are in themselves of paramount importance for obtaining a clear view of the nature of the educative process. Human nature remains, indeed, essentially the same, and has ever been the basis for all educational endeavor; yet it does not supply all that is needed to explain the categories, the aims, the problems, and phenomena of education. To explain these we must analyze and compare the various institutions that have taken shape in the course of time. Any purely theoretical explanation will ever be exposed to the danger of looking on the merely transient as of permanent value, of confounding the particular with

the general, of establishing its general principles on a too narrow
basis of facts, and of underestimating the interrelation and interdependence of existing systems of education.   To remove
these pitfalls and to supply a comprehensive and illustrative
supply of historical material, is the aim of the history of educational systems. Its relation to the history of the science of education is analogous to the relation between the history of the
Church and the history of dogma, between the history of law
and the history of jurisprudence, between the history of poetry
and the history of poetics. In the one the content of the art or
science is the object of inquiry, whilst the various methods
adopted to explain and to systematize this content are treated
in the history of the respective systems. Considered from the
viewpoint of historical science, the history of the systems of
education is a department of the history of civilization, closely
related to the history of morals, of religion, and of social and
political institutions. Like all departments of the history of
civilization, it must turn to diverse sources for its material. In
former times the principles, institutions, and customs belonging
to this field were rarely made the subject of special and detailed
accounts; and to obtain any knowledge of them we must consult law and statute books, search in larger histories for an occasional reference to educational conditions, and, in general,
trace existing institutions in a roundabout way to their beginnings. Even professedly educational writings, as they mostly
aim at reform, are not reliable guides to a knowledge of actual
conditions; and school laws are subject to the same limitation.
The study of modern educational systems is rendered less difficult by the fact that trustworthy sources and original documents
are generally accessible. The aid rendered by statistics, aptly
described as "history halting on its onward rush," is invaluable
in connection with the study of present-day systems; and to
understand these is of essential importance to the historian of
educational systems. Political history may refuse to regard as
historical such movements as are still in process of development,
but the history of civilization is real history in the sense of the
ἱστορία of the ancients, *i.e.*, it is concerned with movements and
events both past and present. Even if there be a difference in
tone and manner between the history of the past and that of
the present, they are parts of one whole and may not be separated. To explain existing conditions historically, we must describe their present status; to describe the institutions of the
present, we must inquire into their origin and development.

4. To trace existing institutions to their beginnings, *i.e.*, to look back upon the history of the forces at work to-day, is the most interesting part and the most profitable task of the history of education. This history will show the genealogical tree of our educational views, ideals, and customs, and of our cultural tendencies, instruments, and institutions; it will, furthermore, show the concentric layers formed in the trunk of the tree, as the ages rolled on; it will indicate the points whence branches and twigs issued, and will open up to view the intricate roots that supply the nourishment. Such an inquiry must extend far back into the past, because our complex civilization and culture comprise elements brought from distant climes and ages. Our alphabet is an invention of the Phenicians. Our calendar is the joint work of the Egyptians and Babylonians; to the Egyptians we probably owe also the animal fable and elementary mathematics. To India we are indebted for our system of notation and for certain exotic elements in our tales, while the indigenous elements can be traced to Celtic, Germanic, and Slavic sources. The Greek and Roman classics equip our youth for higher studies, but the ancients are in a still larger sense the teachers of the modern world: their grammar, perfected in Alexandria, is the foundation of all our language studies; the mathematics taught in our schools is based upon Euclid's elements, and our advanced mathematicians have but just begun to break the ancient fetters; our rhetoric, prosody, science of music, all follow ancient models. It would not be difficult to show traces in modern education of the ancient system of the seven liberal arts. Thus not only the content, but the forms and methods of our education are, in great measure, inherited from the ancients; our educational aims, too, are deeply influenced by their cultural ideals—the *paideia* of Greece and the *humanitas* of Rome. About one-half of the world's leading universities and a great number of the world's best secondary schools can be traced back to the Middle Ages; the medieval *Origines* and *Specula* are the prototypes of the modern encyclopedia, and *The Soul's Balm* and *Jewel* of the Middle Ages are the patterns of our juvenile literature; the youth of our day are still enjoying many of the verses, sayings, riddles, and games that entertained the lads and lasses of the Middle Ages. Modern culture conserves more of this inheritance than modern education, since the latter is so intimately interwoven with the daily ever-changing life of the masses; but even customs and manners are often more closely connected with tradition than would seem, at first sight, to be the case.

There is a certain pleasure in tracing the beginnings of existing conditions and in throwing light upon them by disclosing
the history of their gradual development; but this pleasure is
not the only incentive for historical research, for there are joys
and rewards in the work irrespective of its connection with the
present. At first, it is perhaps a sort of what Carlyle would
term "divine curiosity" that leads men to these researches; yet
the savant will eventually discover a thought and a soul in the
raw-material of experiences and facts, though to the layman it
might well seem destitute of meaning. No fact is too insignificant, too remote from human interest, but the savant will find
in it material that will serve either for a point of comparison or
as a link in the chain of some general reasoning. Hence a further
advantage accruing from the study of history: history teaches
not only the dependence of human agencies on other factors,
but also their mutability; it discloses not only the hidden springs
of our actions, but also their analogues in conditions of life other
than our own It supplies the empirical material which must
form the basis of all speculation tending toward the establishment of general principles and without which speculation is
wild and untrustworthy. Because the viewpoint of education
is generally narrow and its generalizations therefore lack breadth,
this science stands in special need of having its theoretical speculations rectified in the light of historical events. Too many
teachers consider the aims, the content, and the methods of
their professional work as implied in education itself, and frown
on any suggested change as revolutionary and subversive of
educational ideals. Many modern educationists create the im-
pression that the public school system enjoys the monopoly of
education, and that any other system, no matter of what age
or country, lags woefully behind But when some prominent
educational leader opens their eyes to the defects of the system
and the superiority of others, then the former panegyrists of
the public school are likely to become its fiercest foes; narrow
and provincial before, they are broadly generalizing cosmopoli-
tans now; they pass from one extreme to another: seeing no
longer any redeeming features in the public schools, they would
transplant the German system to American soil, and, unmindful
of the modifications necessitated by a different environment,
they would produce but a parody and caricature of a foreign
system. But the history of education will both broaden and
deepen the views of educators, and so will prove a corrective

as well for a narrow provincialism as for too broad a cosmopolitanism.

5. The relation, therefore, between the history of education and the study of the nature of education is of an intrinsic and essential character. To examine into the origin and the changes of systems of education, is not a mere complement, but a basic part of the science of education. Research and speculation, elaboration of the historical and empirical data and strict evolving of principles, *i.e.*, a historical and philosophical treatment, belong together and must be employed together to attain their end. This need of combining the two methods is not confined to education, but is common to all the moral sciences, because they are at once historical and philosophical. To ascertain the nature of law, we must inquire into its historical forms and see what laws have existed in various ages and among different peoples, else we shall never arrive at reliable conclusions concerning its source and nature. To be successful, then, in this field, we must combine the historical with the speculative method. Pure speculation, though productive of good results, could never have solved the problem of the beautiful; neither could the exclusively historical study of taste and the arts accomplish this; a real science of art was made possible only after the study of æsthetics was joined to that of the history of art. Similarly, ethics must unite history with speculation; it must, as its name implies, treat of morals, of the forms and rules of life, and record their changes in the course of history; but it may not sink down to the level of a merely empirical science, it may not neglect its high mission to prove that human nature is the basis of morality and that the destiny of man is its end. What Trendelenburg has so well said of ethics is true of all the sciences that deal with human actions: "The principle of this science is human nature, both in the depth of its idea and in the wealth of its historical development. Both belong together, for the history alone would dull the vision, and the ideal alone would lead to empty and hollow views. True progress consists in permeating the historical method with the ideal, and in joining the ideal to the study of historical facts." [1]

The historical method, if rightly applied to the moral sciences, affects neither their speculative nor their normative character; they will still fulfill their twofold purpose of ascertaining facts as well as setting up ideals. True, the pioneers of a science,

---

[1] *Naturrecht auf dem Grunde der Ethik*, 2nd ed., 1868, p. 45.

4

when first applying the historical method, are usually tempted to lose themselves in the labyrinth of historical development and to relegate to the background the question how this new information is to shape the policy of the present and future, or what benefits are to accrue from historical discoveries to living science. Savigny, the founder of the historical school of jurisprudence, was accustomed to trace the organic growth and development of law, and felt but little attraction for the legislative problems of his own day.[1] His great pupil, Jacob Grimm, who created the historical grammar of the German language, so loved "to trace the origins of the simple and wonderful elements of the language to dark and immemorial ages," that he indignantly refused to lay down rules for its correct use and considered the analysis of the rules of grammar the driest of drudgery.[2] And when we consider the activity of modern governments, fabricating law upon law to meet the most trivial contingencies, we may well appreciate Savigny's dislike of pressing into the service of the State the genius of his science, which had but just begun to draw strength from the past; and we shall likewise understand Grimm's refusal to furnish every mediocre pedant with the gold he had unearthed from the rich mines of language development. Yet science must not hold aloof from the problems of everyday life. Jurisprudence may not refuse to serve as a luminary both for legislation and the practice of law, because it is by practice that theoretical principles and methods must be tested. Neither may the science of philology prove disloyal to its time-honored name of *ars grammatica;* it must prove not only an explorer of the past, but a teacher of the living present. Science may not in the long run eschew the practical problems of the day, and as a matter of fact never does. Though it is sometimes wrapt in deep thought and reflection, these but presage a period of intense activity. In the face of a vast mass of new materials, science may well seem impatient of using the imperative form and content itself with the indicative; but the final goal of human endeavor is the imperative, the categorical imperative, as Kant called it, to which is joined a system of hypothetical imperatives, which must be formulated and explained by science.

It was only in this sense that we demanded above (p. 21 ff.) that the science of education, before drawing up rules and regu-

[1] Savigny, *Vom Berufe unserer Zeit zur Gesetzgebung und Rechtswissenschaft,* 1814.
[2] Jacob Grimm, *Deutsche Grammatik,* 1st edition, I, Preface.

lations, should devote itself to the study of actual conditions.
In doing so, of course, it should not set aside all practical and
ethical tendencies, but merely halt the shortsighted and ill-
advised haste of those who wish to regulate and direct before
they have obtained a clear view and thorough knowledge of the
subject. The human activities to which education is devoted
are concerned largely with the solution of problems and the performance of duties, and are too closely interwoven with the
highest interests of man to admit of being studied with that
coolness and objectivity with which we observe natural phenomena. The search after truth and the search after justice are
here inseparable. The question, What is education? is synonymous with another, namely, What sense is there in these
doings? What ideas underlie them, and what standards are
derived therefrom? All these questions inevitably culminate in
this: What is the end and object of education? If we begin our
study by first trying to ask this last-mentioned question, we
might be tempted to confine ourselves to the problems of the
here and *now*, and to employ too narrow a standard in laying
down laws and regulations. If, on the other hand, we begin by
studying actual facts and conditions and survey the immense
field, as it were, from the summit of a mountain, we shall avoid
that danger, without, however, neglecting the important task
of fixing norms and standards. We must study the history of
education in order to get at the rational basis of its various
phases, to become acquainted with the ideas underlying and
inspiring educational movements; and such a historical inquiry
will naturally lead up to the practical and moral question, In
how far are present-day educational aims, methods, and conditions in conformity with the dictates of right reason? and,
By what ideas is our age guided?

A scientific inquiry following the lines just described, will
quite naturally differ from a book of practical instructions.
Theoretical and practical pedagogy are not co-extensive. The
former is philosophical in character and deals with general
conditions, while the latter is concerned with particular cases;
the former treats of the true and the right, the latter discusses
the means and instruments of realizing what is true and right.
Theoretical pedagogy furnishes the major premise; practical
pedagogy, the minor and draws the conclusions that govern
educational activity. Theory is ever striving for broad and
deep views, while applied science gives practical and definite
directions, which must allow full play to the tact of the indi-

vidual and yet serve him as guides. Yet theory and art are not heterogeneous. They are drawn from the same point of view, and Herbart is evidently mistaken when he considers the chief difference between theoretical and practical pedagogy to be that the former considers merely the conditions of education (p. 28), whereas the latter proceeds from the concepts of purpose and aim. We cannot determine the purpose of a science without research and theorizing, and the aim of a science can therefore not be considered the starting-point of speculation; neither can we, on the other hand, establish the conditions on which an action depends without looking into the action itself and examining into its special purpose; theory and practice are related to each other not as fact and ideal, but as inquiry and rule; but inquiry into facts must take cognizance of the ideal, facts and ideals being inseparable.

6. The relation described above as existing between history and the science of education is common to all the moral sciences. But there is one relation which is proper to the science of education alone. In as far as the system of education represents a field of human activity, it has its own history; but at the same time it is related to general history, as being a phase of the reconstruction of social life, which is a condition of all historical movements. All activity directed toward the intellectual and moral assimilation of the young makes history and operates by means of history; it makes history, for it bridges over the gulf between the present and the past and adds new links to the chain of successive generations; it operates by means of history, for its instruments, the things which it transmits, the institutions which it restores, are all products of previous development. Thus we have in educational science both a motor of the future and a condenser of past forces.

Educationists have generally overlooked the last-named fact; and, giving more attention to the influences that education exerts upon the men and women of to-morrow, they regard the education of the young as the arm of the lever with which the generations of the future are to be raised to a higher plane. Plato hoped to realize his social ideals by changing the ways of the growing generation; and Rousseau and Fichte shared his view. Cristopher von Uttenheim, Bishop of Bâle, demanded that the reformation of the Church begin with the young; and Leibniz' saying, "*Si l'on réformait l'éducation, l'on réformerait le genre humain*," is a commonplace. But a critical and dispassionate study of the great revolutions of the past—political, religious, and otherwise—does not warrant such exaggerated hopes. Momentous changes have always been wrought by adults,-for new principles must first change the life of a nation before they can modify its schools. The Gospel was preached first to men and women, and it was only after society had been Christianized that a system of Christian education was established. Humanism was received first by scholars, artists, and men of the world, before it conquered the schools. The Reformers of the 16th century first transformed religion and society before they affected the educational systems. Upon closer study we shall find that the great revolutions of the past were wrought, not by, but in direct opposition to, the educational systems prevailing at the time: the first Christians had been educated as Jews or heathens; the Humanists, as Schoolmen; and the Reformers, as Catholics. Life is a power that effaces the impressions of youthful days, because the forces present to the adult man are more powerful than the influences which would assimilate the young to the types of a past age. Even in spheres that are more secluded, and where we should expect a more continuous development, *e. g.*, in art, literature, and science, the influence of education upon the process is surprisingly small. The great masters attain their eminence despite the deficient education received during the period when their genius was still growing; the epigoni remain small in the face of all the wealth and inspiration drawn from the models of their predecessors. In the springtime of genius great talents spring up on all sides, and draw their nourishment from the poorest of soils; but when the time of plenty has come, when the field is saturated with the richest of elements, there ensues satiety, the zest for labor passes away, and inspiration dies of surfeit.

Yet education will ever remain a powerful force in history, even though mightier powers seem to undo much of its work. The results of education are often hid from view, but they are there—a mighty power—for modifying the larger movements, for intensifying some of their phases, and for extending their effects over wider areas. The man who changes the current of his country's course of thought or action is of necessity the creature of an older system. The impressions received in youth always influence the activity of manhood, either by unconsciously influencing conduct or by acting as a brake in some direction or other. Education is, then, a determining factor even with a generation that launches a new movement. But its chief influence is exercised when there is question of transplanting the

new principles permanently into the minds and lives of men.
The life of the race will never be guided by new views until a
whole series of generations has been imbued with them. If the
new principles be powerful enough to direct education into new
channels, they have stood the test; if they succeed in this, the
new movement will prove a thing of permanence in the world's
history; but if they fail, the new movement will eventually
prove but an episode and a ripple in the onrushing stream of
events.   While the sober view of education should thus preserve
us from exaggerated notions of its influence, we still have reasons
enough to work strongly and unremittingly to shape education
along the right lines.   Though the direct influence of education
upon artistic and kindred activities be small, its indirect influence is great.   No teacher would attempt to create a genius
out of mediocre material; but it is the teacher's duty to make
the world's masterpieces the common property of all, to purify
and correct the taste of the public, to bring hidden talents to
light, and in this way be instrumental in preparing the way for
a new spring of art and literature.

These and similar considerations reveal the debt that the
science of education owes to pragmatic history: the latter furnishes a standard for the assimilation of the young; it corrects
the exaggerated notions of the importance of education, yet safeguards us against underestimating its influence.

7. The other side of the twofold relation between history
and education is that of history co-operating with education.
Of this the ancients did not, indeed, lose sight, but as all their
educational activity was based upon historical traditions, they
speculated but little about the service rendered to it by history.
Modern pedagogy, in endeavoring to correct unhistorical and
individualistic tendencies, has given special attention to this
side of the subject.   Education employs the forces of history,
for it makes the growing child a historical being, raises it to the
level of the present, and allows it, in a certain sense, to run
during the short years of its youthful plasticity the laborious
course that mankind has run throughout the long ages of history.   There is a special pleasure in speculating along these
lines, in discovering the analogies between the development of
the race and of the individual, in order to ascertain principles
apt to throw new light on the educative process.   Pestalozzi
was much given to such reflections, but his system would not
admit of them.   Herbart was influenced by them when he
compares the heroic age of Greece to the early years of a boy

and suggests that education begin with the reading of the *Odyssey*, whose heroes represent a world akin to the dreams of a boy's fancy, proceed with the naïve narrative of Herodotus to the glories of Greek literature, and take up the disputes of Rome's constitutional history when the mind of the young man turns to serious tasks and problems.[1] Modern evolution introduced a new viewpoint. It holds that the human embryo passes through all the stages of lower animal life before it finally arrives at the human form; and, analogously, looks on the development of the child and youth as a successive passing through all the types of man represented by historical development, and completed in the present. The evolutionists think that it is natural for a boy to pass through antiquity as the period when the human race most enjoyed the contemplation of beauty, and that a defective development would result from making the study of the natural sciences precede that of the classics.[2] The evolutionist methods of teaching are modelled along genetic lines, so as to embrace successively all the stages which knowledge has passed through in the history of the world. Thus, the pupils are first taught to assume the shape of the earth to answer Homer's description, later to adopt Ptolemy's views, and finally the Copernican system. In geometry they would, with the predecessors of Pythagoras, first compare the squares of the sides of certain triangles before taking up the theorem of Pythagoras. In natural science they first study the facts of nature with regard to man's needs and advantages, but at a more mature period they discard all considerations of relativity and study facts and events objectively and independently of any particular point of view.

The science of education will profit by the study of the interrelations between education and history, provided the essential differences existing between the development of the race and that of the individual are duly emphasized. The path along which we lead the young is not so firmly fixed within the lines that mark the way humanity has taken in its course, that we are unable to bend it this way or that by our own views and principles. If it is true that education is a compendious repetition of universal history, it is equally true that we teachers

---

[1] *Herbart's A B C of Sense-Perception and Introductory Works*, transl. by Eckoff, New York, 1896, p. 84; *Science of Education*, transl. by H.M. and E. Felkin, London, 1892, p. 74; *Outlines of Educational Doctrine*, transl. by A. F. Lange with annotations by Charles de Garmo, New York, 1901, pp. 262 ff.

[2] Lilienfeld, *Gedanken über die Sozialwissenschaft der Zukunft*, 1873, I, 274.

make the compendium in the light of our own ideals. A knowledge of the development of the race is not sufficient to enable us to interpret the development of the individual, for the former requires to be interpreted no less than the latter. The philosophy of history, in attempting to interpret the evolution of the human race, must necessarily take its stand on certain religious and ethical principles, and consequently is on the same level with pedagogy, not superior to it. The naturalistic view, which is too ready to attribute the works of free will to nature, may throw some light on the problems involved, but can never solve them.

IV.

1. In the preceding pages we attempted to sketch the lines which the science of education must follow in order that it may be raised to the level of the allied sciences that deal with human actions. Most of what has been said refers to pedagogy as well as to what the Germans call *Didaktik*, but, as we purpose to treat in the present work only of the latter, *i.e.*, the science of education in its sociological and historical aspects,[1] it will not be out of place to indicate, briefly, in how far its subject-matter differs from that of pedagogy in general.

An erroneous conception of the union that ought to exist between the social and the individualistic view of education results, as a general rule, in the curtailing of either the social or the individual field of labor. If interest in social institutions preponderates, men are likely to ascribe undue importance to the existing educational apparatus, which represents the fruits of organized efforts, to look on education as a mere complement to culture, and to treat pedagogy as an appendix to the science of education. If the viewpoint be individualistic, and education be considered as consisting in forming the individual according to a preconceived ideal, then there is danger of ignoring the broad and diversified elements of education, and the science of education will become a part of pedagogy and receive inadequate treatment. The first of these errors we meet in the 17th cen-

---

[1] The term "didactics" has in English pedagogy taken on an unfavorable meaning, referring to cut and dried methods, as opposed to organic education; whereas, in Willmann's use of it, it has quite another connotation. And so, for want of a better term, we shall substitute for the German *Didaktik* the English *science of education*. (Tr.)

tury, to which age we owe the idea of a *Didactica*,[1] or "Art of Teaching" (*Lehrkunst*).

It was not merely their taste for euphonious and novel terms that led the educational reformers of the age to invent a new name for their science, but rather the fact that their efforts went beyond the labors of the past and tried to embrace the entire system of education as one harmonious whole. This one whole embraces, as may be seen from the systematic presentation of the new ideas by Comenius in his *Didactica Magna*, the work of moral training. Comenius' concept of teaching includes training in morality and virtue,[2] the educational influences of the home,[3] and care for the body, as important factors in sucessful schooling.[4] Thus the *Great Didactic* really presents a complete system of pedagogy, though its specific functions are not all developed.

The same mistake was made, on a larger scale, by the contemporary exponents of political science when dealing with matters educational. To them the school system is the main thing; education is either treated under that head or lost among the measures governing the discipline and morality of the commonwealth. Robert von Mohl adopts the latter policy; Lorenz von Stein, the former. Stein's treatment lacks clearness because he neglects to distinguish properly between refinement (*Gesittung*) and education, between moral and intellectual assimilation, and fails to assign to pedagogy a special field of activity. His definition of pedagogy as the science of the acquisition of education by the individual, is in reality a definition of what we call *Didaktik*, or rather of that part of it which treats of the individual. The science Stein postulates would be a complete *Didaktik*, but not a complete pedagogy.

2. Herbart's teachings will show how difficult it is to determine from the individualistic viewpoint the mutual relationship between pedagogy and *Didaktik*. Herbart considers pedagogy

---

[1] Wolfgang Ratke is probably the author of this term, as he assumed the surname of *didacticus*. At all events the term came into general use in course of the disputations waged about Ratke's educational reforms. It is an abbreviation for *Methodus Didactica*, this complete form also being in use. The 17th century also coined the terms mnemonics, cyclopedia or encyclopedia, polymathy, polyhistory, pansophy, all of which denote undertakings connected with current educational reforms. The terms anthropology and psychology may also be traced to this age of polymathic realism.

[2] *Didactica magna*, IV, 6; XXIII ff.

[3] Ib., XXVIII.

[4] Ib., XIV, 4 and XV.

as the superior science and *Didaktik* as one of its parts, co-ordinate with the science of government and discipline. The first principle of his *Didaktik* is the concept of many-sided interest to be evolved from the idea of virtue. Its subject-matter is limited to "educative instruction," *i. e.*, such instruction as renders the individual conformable to the ideal of virtue. Pedagogy is not—and therefore its didactic part much less—concerned with purposes and motives that lie beyond the individual. The social arguments advanced in favor of the classical studies— the culture of the higher classes of society, the conservation of venerable and time-honored treasures of art and science—receive scant favor at Herbart's hands. He describes them as "just as unpedagogical as would be the policy of giving a crowd of boys a sound trouncing as soon as the new fence has been put up, so that they might better remember the boundaries."[1] He describes as unpedagogical and, therefore, as outside the sphere of the *Didaktik*, all those studies "for which acquisition of wealth and external success or strong personal preferences supply the motives"; and he avers the same of those studies whose only concern is the *tuto, cito, jucunde*.[2] Consequently he entirely excludes the school system from his *Didaktik*, saying that it is "a vast and difficult subject involving not merely pedagogical principles but also the maintenance of learning, the dissemination of useful information, and the practice of indispensable arts."[3] From this last point of view he assigns the system of education to that department of practical philosophy which deals with the "system of civilization," which is but one of a series of "social ideas."[4]

An unprejudiced examination of these teachings will reveal their untenable elements: they unduly narrow the sphere of *Didaktik* by considering the subject of teaching from one point of view only and by excluding the educative process as a whole. But to detach from this whole the training in morality and virtue is a dangerous proceeding, for it breaks many of the bonds that join elements which belong together. The aim to make the young moral and virtuous by means of studies and practice, is lacking in none of the historical systems of education; but nowhere was it ever isolated or regarded as the

---

[1] *Pädagogische Schriften*, II, 470.

[2] *Outlines of Educational Doctrine*, p. 40.

[3] Ib., p. 321.

[4] *Outlines of Educational Doctrine*, pp. 11 ff.; *Gesammelte Werke*, edited by Hartenstein, VIII, 96; IX, 424.

only legitimate end. It was always joined to other aims, such as to impart knowledge, to train the faculties, to equip the young for the battle of life or for special professions; and inseparably connected with all these diversified, subjective, and changing aims is the objective and impersonal end: to conserve by teaching and learning the content of education to future ages and to fit the young for transmitting the intellectual property of the race to their descendants. To ignore this end and to consider all aims except the training to virtue—which is made the moral end κατ᾽ ἐξοχήν—as heteronomous, is certainly improper; for to develop the faculties of the young, to prepare them for fulfilling the universal law of work, is undoubtedly a moral action; and it is no less moral to conserve the intellectual inheritance of our ancestors by transmitting it to our descendants. Herbart, consequently, despite his laudable ethical tendency, fails to meet the moral requirements of educational work, and to recognize the interrelation of moral obligations as observed in history and daily life. Neither can the materials of teaching be divided into such as serve moral ends and such as serve external purposes. All studies and exercises may serve a moral purpose, and all are related somehow to external circumstances and conditions.

Thus the very subject of education compels us to extend the boundaries of this science on all sides; but even if we extended it. beyond the individualistic conception of Herbart, it would not be sufficient to cover the subject-matter of *Didaktik*. From the standpoint of the moral assimilation of the young we cannot obtain a complete view of the acquisition of education (*Bildungserwerb*) and the organization devoted to it; and it was this consideration which led Herbart to incorporate this discipline into his "system of civilization." But he fails to show that this "system of civilization" has any basic relationship to education, and to compare the collective agencies dealt with by the former with the educative activities and processes that form the subject-matter of the latter. Had Herbart succeeded in doing this—he made several attempts[1]—his theory would have found a support outside of pedagogy and the problem of the *Didaktik*, viz., education in its social and individual aspects, would have been adequately solved.

3. Schleiermacher's ethics aims to do justice to the great organisms of the moral world, and is directly opposed to the

---

[1] Especially in his *Erziehungskunst* in the *Enzyklopädie der Philosophie; Pädagogische Schriften*, II, 452 ff.

individualistic trend of Herbart's philosophy—a fact which renders much of what Schleiermacher has written on education of particular value. He considers pedagogy one of the "technical disciplines" which branch out from ethics, and says that it occupies itself with answering the questions: What does the older generation wish to do with the young? How do its activities correspond with its aims? Are the results proportionate to the labor expended? Pedagogy, he teaches, is co-ordinate and partly coextensive with political science, which is engaged in conserving and strengthening the State in the midst of the changes arising from the succession of generations. And as it belongs to the general problem of morals to conserve the life of the Church, pedagogy joins hands with the science of religious organization, which is a part of ethics.[1] The standpoint for the *Didaktik* is furnished by a third ethical organism, *viz.*, "community of language and knowledge." This community is grounded on the intellectual interrelation between the consciousness of the individual and that of the commonwealth. Its basic relation is that between teaching and learning, and consists in the transmission of thoughts from mind to mind. The ethical process is carried out by the co-operation of invention and communication, by the concurrence of intellectual superiority on the one hand with the possession of common intellectual treasures on the other. The medium of all these activities is the school, in the broadest sense of the term, including the school proper, the university, and the academy of sciences. The school, thus understood, is the agency for imparting knowledge to the individual as well as to the community, in other words, for imparting individuality and nationality.[2]

The organization of this moral community is the object of the *Didaktik*, which, as Schleiermacher says, "deserves to receive a fuller and larger treatment and should make a thorough study of the peculiarities of the different nations and their methods of imparting knowledge."[3]

Schleiermacher carried out only part of his plan. In his *Erziehungslehre* he assigns to education an even broader basis than in the methodological discussions just quoted, by bringing it into relationship, on the one hand, with the Church and the State, and, on the other, with the community of language and of morals, and thus establishes a relation between education and

[1] *Erziehungslehre*, edited by Platz, 1846, 7, 12 ff.
[2] *Entwurf eines Systems der Sittenlehre*, edited by Schweizer, 1835, § 179.
[3] Ib., § 282.

the "totality of intellectual activities."[1] Schleiermacher never developed his *Didaktik*, either because he thought the historical material not sufficiently prepared, or because he distrusted the adaptability of the ethical categories which he had arbitrarily deduced from his metaphysical principles.

The *Didaktik*, if developed along the lines traced by Schleiermacher, would not be wanting in breadth, but its problems would lack definiteness. Dealing *ex professo* with the imparting of knowledge, this science would naturally have to embrace all that is implied in teaching and learning as well as in tradition and the interchange and exchange of thoughts and ideas, including the science of language, as being the most important means of communication, and the sciences that deal with the use of language, *i. e.*, rhetoric, poetics, etc. And in as far as it would cover not only the institutions where instruction is imparted, but also those engaged in scientific research, it could not confine itself to the subject of thought-transmission, but would have to treat, besides, of the creation of thought; and so a science of unlimited compass would be the result.

In spite of these objections, Schleiermacher's ideas are highly stimulative and prolific. Many of his views on pedagogy are essentially correct, and his false notions result from indefinite and excessively rigid principles rather than from any essential error inherent in his system.

4. The relation between pedagogy and *Didaktik* is determined by the respective objects of the two sciences: the system of moral education and the system of intellectual education (*Erziehungswesen und Bildungswesen*) in their mutual relations. Both belong to the same sphere, both are parts of the one great movement which tends to reconstruct the social organism; but within this sphere they appear as separate and co-ordinate disciplines. The system of moral education is not subject nor supplementary to the system of intellectual education. The purpose of the former is to watch over the moral life that is gradually developing, and it must therefore possess its own ethos, its own motives, aims, instruments, institutions; and all this is essentially different from the aim of the system of intellectual education: to make certain intellectual treasures the common property of all. The system of intellectual education is likewise more than a series of educational agencies; the forces of the community co-operating for cultural purposes create an

---

[1] *Erziehungslehre*, pp. 40, 108, 607.

organism which cannot be understood from the viewpoint of
moral assimilation alone.

If it were a question of merely describing the place which
these two sciences occupy in the national life, there could be no
question that they occupy entirely different positions. The
methods adopted by a nation in the moral education of its
children must be treated in connection with the study of its
political and social institutions, its public and private morality,
and its religious and philosophical views. But the content of
the nation's culture, all that which is considered its intellectual
possession, and what is transmitted in the schoolroom and elsewhere, must, along with the cultural agencies, be dealt with in
connection with the study of the nation's intellectual interests,
its literature, its arts and sciences. This difference becomes
even more marked when we consider the historical presentation
of the two disciplines. The history of a nation's system of
moral education is intimately connected with the history of its
civilization, the history of its manners and its social orders; its
viewpoint is mainly ethnological, because it must show how the
spirit of the age and of the nation have influenced the provisions
made for the care of the young. The history of intellectual
education, on the other hand, depends, in the first place, on the
history of a nation's intellectual life. Its principal source is the
history of literature, for this reveals most directly the development of national culture; and when the history of intellectual
education chronicles the history of textbooks, encyclopedias,
and all writings pertaining to culture, it will itself be a history
of literature in the broadest sense. It will approach a history
of the sciences when it treats historically the various methods
of teaching employed at different times in the schools. But it
is only when treating of the institutions of general education,
especially the schools, that the history of intellectual education
draws upon the history of political and social development.
The history of the system of intellectual education must also be
studied from the viewpoint of ethnology, for it must trace the
relations between the character of the age and the nation, between the ideals of, and efforts for, intellectual education; at
the same time it must study the process of hereditary transmission, so wonderful at times, by which the elements of intellectual education are passed from one nation to another, from
one age to another, where they assemble and assume new and
entirely different forms, a process which is without a parallel in
the system of moral education.

This difference between the systems of moral education and intellectual education, so clearly marked in the descriptive and historical treatment of the two subjects, should not be ignored when studying them philosophically, especially since good results will flow therefrom for deeper speculation. Not only are these sciences entirely different from each other in scope, but their individual problems require different methods of investigation. It is true that both pedagogy and *Didaktik* depend in a similar way on psychology, whether the latter be conceived as treating the functions of the soul, or as the (not yet fully developed) science of racial types, called by some ethnology (J. Stuart Mill), by others *Charakterologie* (Bahnsen), while some consider it a part of anthropology. But the parts of psychology that lend support to pedagogy and *Didaktik* respectively are not the same. Pedagogy is chiefly concerned with the higher and lower appetites of man, with the will, the feelings, the moral type or character; whereas *Didaktik* deals with his intellectual faculties, understanding and reason, intellectual types, talents, and abilities. Whereas the former is mainly concerned with obtaining a psychological view of man's different interests and strives to ascertain their sources and the causes for individual differences, the latter is taken up with the study of the mental horizon and the psychical activities that constitute it, with the special abilities and the special trend of mind that are responsible for its individuality.

The relation of the two sciences to ethics is likewise different, the relation between ethics and pedagogy being close, while that between ethics and *Didaktik* is remote. Both deal with evaluations, with motives, problems, and intellectual treasures as well as with the elements of the moral personality. But pedagogy follows the development of the moral personality in all its points and relations and explains one of the fundamental conditions for the conservation and (indirectly) the production of all moral treasures, thus throwing light on the problems of duty. The *Didaktik*, however, contents itself with considering the moral ends of life as completing and safeguarding the intellectual endeavors with which it is concerned. But it is related to other philosophical disciplines that are foreign to the domain of pedagogy: to logic as being the canon of thought, and to epistemology, the science of the method and grounds of knowledge—a relationship which is desirable indeed, but, at present, not yet fully realized.

5. In attempting to raise *Didaktik* to the position of a science complete in itself, we meet still greater difficulties than those resulting from its dependence on pedagogy, which we have treated in the preceding pages. These difficulties regard not so much the independence of our science as the feasibility of developing it according to some adequate standard of unity.

The very nature of general education implies that its content is drawn from various arts and sciences. Education comprises, in its more developed forms, a whole series of elements, each of which represents a more or less extensive field of research or achievement. Modern higher education is particularly rich in the diversity of its contents: besides the historically transmitted elements—the philological material embodied in languages, together with theology, philosophy, and mathematics—it comprises the divers elements of knowledge belonging to the historical, geographical, and natural sciences and, finally, technology, music, and gymnastics. But this universal tendency of modern education precludes the possibility of attaining, in fields so numerous and so diverse, anything approaching the knowledge and mastery demanded of a specialist. The man of culture is content with a general knowledge of the various subjects; he lays claim merely to have an open mind for the various arts and sciences, without professing to be a specialist or a virtuoso. And similarly, general education rests satisfied with removing only the elementary difficulties and with laying a foundation of universal knowledge; it fits the pupil for extending and intensifying his knowledge and makes his mind and heart alive to the charms of the various studies.

While the course of general studies may be pardoned for limiting itself to the elementary and popular, the same may not be allowed to him who would treat professedly of education itself, in order to establish a science of general education. It seems indispensable that such a one be perfectly acquainted with the cultural side of the arts and sciences, and the undertaking, therefore, postulates a thorough acquaintance with the arts and sciences, so that not only the fruits of education be known, but the trees that produced them. He who would pass judgment on the cultural content of studies, on the methods to be followed in selecting, ordering, and treating the subject-matter of the various studies, must be at home in all the arts and sciences, and his knowledge must possess the universality of culture and the thoroughness of science.

These demands could be satisfied, in some degree, in the age that produced the idea and the beginnings of our science of education. In the 17th century it was the order of the day to strive after encyclopedic knowledge; the terms polyhistory, polymathy, panmathy, pansophy, cyclopedia had a great vogue, and of the didacticians at least a few—such as Joachim Jung, Amos Comenius, J. J. Becher—commanded vast stores of erudition, both general and special. And in the 18th century Johann Mathias Gesner, in his celebrated Göttingen lecture, *Isagoge in eruditionem universalem*, laid down general directions for studying which are as remarkable for exact knowledge as for depth. In the same century Johann August Ernesti, theologian and philologist, in his *Initia doctrinæ solidioris* (first edition, 1734) dealt ably with the philosophical disciplines as well as with mathematics and physics. To-day science has pushed out its boundaries so far and its various departments require so many special methods of research, that it is obviously impossible for any individual to encompass the domain of knowledge in its entirety. To speak of universal scholarship or of encyclopedic research is to-day a contradiction in terms, as we consider the labors of a scholar to be confined to a special field of research, and refuse to regard as science any attempt at covering the whole "orbis doctrinæ." We consider "polymathy" as necessarily connected with shallowness and incoherency. The man professing to have universal knowledge is to the modern mind the very personification of vain superficiality. To attempt to create an art of teaching everything to everybody, in imitation of the Renaissance, would appear to most people to-day as building a castle in the air, and any such undertaking would speedily incur condemnation of modern scholarship.

Modern scholars are quite generally of the opinion that the specialist, being conversant with the matter and method of his science, should also determine the matter and method for its pursuit in the schoolroom. They contend that the specialist alone can be a safe guide in this regard, and that the theorist, if he forsake his directions and speculate along general lines, is inevitably doomed to grave mistakes and final failure. Hence the only science of education that could make any pretensions to scientific reliability should be the result of the combined efforts of a large number of specialists, each a master in his chosen field. Anything beyond this would merely be an airy nothing, a something subject to continual changes by the specialists, which would make it impossible to establish a harmoni-

ous science of education, one that might assign to each science
its share in the educative process.   Ever since the training of a
specialist has been demanded of the prospective teacher, these
ideas have found acceptance among educationists, and many of
the latter look askance at a science of general education, even
though it be fathered by authorities as eminent as Herbart or
Schleiermacher; and they defend their position by contending
that any such science would require the teacher to dabble in
subjects foreign to his profession.   Educationists, likewise, are
learning to specialize each in his own subject. The general principles of education are left to writers on pedagogy, and its special problems, *i. e.*, such as deal with particular methods of
teaching or individual branches, are handled by writers in special fields; and so the science of education, hedged in between
the adjoining field and the ground intersected by special studies,
seems to be denied the room necessary for it to grow and to
expand.

6. Yet we cannot allow the educational problems that are
interrelated with one another to be simply ignored.   It is assuredly necessary in education and in the science of education,
if anywhere, to keep a firm hold on the bond that joins the
parts together into one harmonious whole.   In this field, no
work, be it ever so specialized, can forego the application of
general principles; it must take into consideration the end of
education, the relation of one subject to others, the stages of
the pupil's development, the general agencies of education, the
prevailing customs of the schools, the intellectual interests of
the age; and hence the work of the specialist is never independent of general educational principles, and the value of his work
depends as much on his familiarity with the above conditions
as on his mastery of his special field.   Unless there is unity and
harmony in fundamental principles, the combined efforts of ever
so many specialists cannot produce one harmonious whole; but
these fundamental principles can be arrived at only by a speculation that takes into account the whole, and not merely a part,
of education.   The most pressing problems of our present-day
education do not call for the ability of the specialist, but rather
for the broadmindedness of such a scholar as will be able to
survey the whole field.   It is at present more necessary to
show how the various sciences are interrelated to one another and to the whole of education, to assign to each its own
function in regard to what is expected of the whole, than
to reform the methods of teaching individual subjects.   The

curricula of our schools cannot be charged with not being sufficiently scientific; neither are our teachers, on the whole, poorly
equipped in their own special branches. The defect lies rather in
this, that our curricula do not represent an organic whole, but a
disjointed mass of what is in its parts excellent enough; and our
teachers, though they be trained specialists, are ignorant of the
functions of the college or university as a whole; they have an
eye only for their own narrow field and know nothing of the
valuable work performed by the professors of sciences other
than their own. The remedy for this state of affairs obviously
does not consist in more specialization, nor in improving the
methods of teaching individual subjects, but rather in empha-
sizing and applying the general principles of the science of
education.

There is a widely spread opinion that the science of education, because of its general tendency and indefinite scope, is
bound to be flabby and vague, satisfied with dreamy speculations out of touch with actual conditions. When we contrast
the clear-cut and practical directions given by certain specialists with the vaporings of some educational theorists, we must
confess that this opinion is not entirely groundless. It is re-
freshing to turn from the glittering generalities of Basedow and
Trapp to F. A. Wolf's *Consilia scholastica*, which have a solid
foundation in the wisdom of past ages. The principles laid
down by Jacob Grimm and Philip Wackernagel for the teaching
of German dealt a deathblow to the formalism of the doctrin-
aires, who had carried out Pestalozzi's ideas on language teaching. Even the subtle distinctions of Herbart, which overlook
the specific character of individual branches and do not attend
sufficiently to the practical imparting of knowledge, must give
way to the wise suggestions of Nägelsbach, Roth, Palmer, etc.
It has been observed that the science of education generally
gained in strength and definiteness when it came in touch with
any special science—philology, theology, history, etc.—and it is
therefore but natural to expect that such intercourse will prove
helpful for its future development.

It would, however, be wrong to conclude that a systematic
study of general education is unprofitable. To illustrate: to
pass judgment on Philanthropinism, we must regard not only
its results, but also its aims and objects. It was undoubtedly a
great achievement of the Philanthropinists to have brought out
the fact that to obtain perfect results in the school it is necessary to correlate the various branches, and also to adapt them,

as far as possible, to the natural inclinations of the pupils. In this the Philanthropinists were instrumental in banishing from the schoolroom many of the violent, and even brutal, practices of former ages; and their very errors have stimulated their followers to search more deeply, and thus proved the occasion of improved methods of teaching.

The same may be said of Pestalozzi's system, though it largely culminated in formalism. Pestalozzi's aim was to discover the basic elements of the elementary school branches, with the elementary mental activities corresponding to them, and to shape the content of education in such a way as to bring about the closest possible correlation between the elements of instruction and the activities of the mind, the mind acquiring the mastery of the materials of education by a process of psychic activities that succeed one another with internal necessity. Pestalozzi here attained a depth beyond that attained by any scientific specialist in outlining methods of teaching. And his conception has not only been a gain to the science of education, but has produced results of far-reaching importance for the various subjects. The object-lessons introduced into the teaching of geometry, which supply a defect of Euclid's system, are one result; mental arithmetic, and the reform of the teaching of drawing and geography are other results. But his theory has accomplished still more; it has deeply influenced the scientific study of geography, for Karl Ritter, the father of modern geography, conceived the idea for his system, which established the treatment of geography as a study and a science, from his intercourse with Pestalozzi and the application of his method. Though this is a solitary case in history where the science of education has proved the inspiration of scientific research, it is proof sufficient that this science is at times in a position to make return in its own ideas for what it receives from the scientific research workers.[1]

---

[1] Kramer, *Karl Ritter, Ein Lebensbild*, I, 307, quotes the following passage from one of Ritter's letters concerning his geography: "What first prompted me to undertake this work was the desire to fulfill a promise I had made to Pestalozzi, to apply his methods in writing a textbook of geography, which was to be introduced into his Institute; but upon beginning to do so, I found that all the attempts previously made in this field were but patchwork, depending on chance instead of science. Imbued with the spirit of the method (the methodists themselves know nothing of geography) which disdains arbitrariness, I sought what was necessary, and found it in the midst of the geographical chaos, and once I had caught the thread, the whole skein unravelled itself." See the quotation (ibid., II, 146*) from Vulliemin, *Le Chrétien évangélique*, 1869, p. 24: "C'est à Pestalozzi que Ritter fait

Herbart's science of education is similarly fruitful in results, even though the impartial critic will discover deficiencies in the theory itself and in the treatment of individual sciences. Let every one who is tempted to apply too exacting a standard to Herbart's efforts, remember Goethe's words, which may well be applied to all sweeping condemnations of great works:"Descendants should beware of nibbling fastidiously at the great works of their teachers and masters, and of making demands of which they themselves would never have dreamed if these great men had not 'accomplished so much as to tempt those coming after them to demand still more."[1] No specialist could furnish all that Herbart supplies: the farsighted view of the objects of education; the insistent demand that all educational influences converge in the pupil's circle of thought and there blend into one harmonious result, which shall be, not only intellectual, but also ethical. Herbart has revealed the sorest spot in modern education, and if his scalpel now has to be exchanged for one of a more recent make, or if the operation must be performed in a different way, it cannot be denied that Herbart did humanity a great service in demonstrating the urgent need for a radical cure.

7. There are certain permanent problems and ever-recurring questions that constitute the fixed centre of the science of education and form its proper field of research; but along the periphery of the circle this science touches the boundaries of many other sciences, and thus it will never lack opportunities for specializing. To ignore this promising field in order to consider the centre alone, would be as foolish as to ignore the central problems for the sake of devoting exclusive attention to special features. Every human problem requires the co-operation of many hands and many heads, and no problem, especially in the field of education, can be solved without being viewed from different angles. The specialist has a right to be heard; but if he wishes to serve the whole, he must be well versed in

remonter l'impulsion première à son esprit et la principale part de ce qui'l y a de meilleur dans son œuvre. Quarante ans après son séjour à Yverdon nous l'avons entendu le déclarer avec bonheur: 'Pestalozzi,' nous disait-il, 'ne savait pas en géographie ce qu'en sait un enfant de nos écoles primaires; ce n'en est pas moins de lui que j'ai le plus appris en cette science; car c'est en l'écoutant, que j'ai senti s'éveiller en moi l'instinct des méthodes naturelles; c'est lui qui m'a ouvert la voie et ce qu'il m'a été donné de faire, je me plais à le lui rapporter comme lui appartenant,'" Cf. *ibid.*, I, 275, and Ritter's *Erdkunde*, Vol. I, Introduction.

[1] *Werke Ausg. letzter Hand*, 1830, XXXVII, p. 62.

the science of education, *i.e.*, be familiar with the principles that
govern the work of education as a whole.

It seems but natural to demand in turn of the educationist
that he have a general knowledge of the sciences; but the un-
precedented development of modern science renders this impossible, and, really, in our conception of the science of education it is not necessary. The educationists of the Renaissance
defined *Didactica* as the art of teaching, and undertook to outline general and detailed methods for all the subjects taught in
the schools. From this point of view it was perfectly legitimate
to demand that every teacher should be a master of all branches
of his science. We take a different view. We define *Didaktik*
as the science of general education and as such it need make no
pretensions to master all the practical features of the organized
work of teaching, but may be satisfied with something less.
The science of education must undoubtedly be equal to the
solution of far-reaching problems; it must be able to show how
science becomes transformed into education, how its content
can be made the property of the mind, and what conditions
must obtain to make the work of teaching fruitful of results.
But these and similar problems can fortunately be solved without an encyclopedic knowledge, which is impossible for any one
man to acquire. A limited knowledge of the different sciences
will suffice, if it be but rightly applied. To understand how
science becomes education, it is necessary to regard the process
from the viewpoint of the former; but the main requisite is to
examine the process closely in one field in order to enable the
mind to grasp analogous processes as described by specialists as
happening in other fields. The educative agencies should furthermore be studied concretely as operative in a particular
field, not to serve as a rigid schema to the mind, but rather as
a key for unlocking other gates. The methods to be followed in
imparting the contents of the various sciences will be discovered
in the same way: we begin our inquiry at one special point,
follow up, to the best of our ability, the divers ramifications of
the subject, not neglecting to call upon the specialists for assistance whenever we find ourselves unequal to the task. The
science of education does not require the investigator to experiment in all fields, but insists that, while working in a limited
field, he should acquire the habit of putting the right questions,
first, in regard to the nature of the object, secondly, in regard
to the phenomena that constitute the general problems, and,
thirdly, inquiring of the specialists whenever his own knowledge

proves inadequate. Hence the objection that *Didaktik* demands two incompatible prerequisites—a universal mastery of the sciences and profound scientific research—may be solved by saying that only the latter is strictly required, whereas the universal mastery implies no more than that the mind be receptive towards all the sciences and ready to fill in the lacunæ in its own knowledge with the information supplied by specialists. The educationist, then, may safely adopt the well-known principle of scientific research: "*In uno habitandum, in ceteris versandum.*"

But is this demanded receptivity a remnant of universalism, a spur driving the mind beyond the bounds assigned, and therefore a serious menace to scientific progress, since it is precisely the demarcation of sciences that has proved such a valuable principle of modern scholarship, making possible the division of labor? This question may be answered by another, *viz.*: Does modern science owe its success to this principle of the division of labor alone, or is that great success due in part to such principles as stand in direct contrast to the division of labor, and practically negative it? Recent scientific research has, indeed, accomplished much by dividing previously whole and undivided circles of knowledge, into sectors and segments; but it has at the same time drawn new circles and has joined such as were formerly separate, gaining new light from the points of intersection. We have in the course of these discussions mentioned several sciences that owe their existence to the joining together of departments of knowledge, which were formerly foreign to one another, and which have for their methodological principle the combination of different kinds of knowledge. Sociology, for instance, obtains its general view of social phenomena by combining the findings of the political sciences with those of the history of civilization, anthropology, psychology, ethics, and even the natural sciences; and if we insisted that the sociologist should confine his researches to one of these fields—because he can never expect to become proficient in more than one—it would mean the end of his study of sociology. Ethnological psychology consists entirely in combining the matter and the findings of sciences foreign to one another (philology, linguistics, ethnography, psychology, history of civilization, etc.) in such a way that all the various data are considered from viewpoints that tend to harmonize them. The modern science of individual psychology also has its basis and source of material in heterogeneous fields, in the natural sciences and in the moral sciences, and must draw especially upon the latter, because it is they that seek in the activities of the community the causes of individual psychical phenomena (*vide supra*, pp. 31 ff.). The characteristic feature of modern geography, as established by Karl Ritter, is that it is neither a purely historical, nor a purely natural science, but partakes of the character of both; Ritter presented the earth's surface in its relations to nature and man, and as the foundation of the study of the physical and historical sciences.

No one would charge these sciences, which have compassed so many different fields of research, with having attempted too ambitious a task. The science of education may consequently claim the same liberty, and with even more reasons than the sciences mentioned, because it contents itself with a more limited mastery of topics lying outside its own special range of inquiry.

---

8. Having established the independence and the unity of the science of education, it remains to indicate briefly the plan we have adopted in dealing with it in accordance with the methodological principles laid down above.

The object of this science is the process of education as it appears both in the systems of education which represent the joint efforts of a community, and in the acquiring of an education which represents the efforts of the individual.

The system of education may be viewed both as an organism and as an organ. It is an organism in so far as it is a relatively complete whole of institutions and agencies for imparting education. It is an organ in respect to the social body of which it performs a function. We must study the system of education, first, from the viewpoint of the variety of agencies which it joins in one whole; and, secondly, from the viewpoint of the historical agencies responsible for this variety, *i. e.*, in respect to the changes it has undergone in course of time.

The acquiring of an education is essentially a conscious and free act, vitalized by its own special end in the light of which it must be judged. Materially the acquiring of an education appears as varied as the sources whence the educational content is derived, and hence it will be our aim to discover the sources of the material elements of education. Further points of study are, first, the form, which the subject-matter assumes, in keeping with its own nature and with the purpose of the educative process; then, the various didactic aids determined by the faculties of the soul and the psychical functions as well as ethnological factors—differences in the adaptability to education and the stages of development. Thus our method of treatment may follow the topics indicated by the four principles of Aristotle, though we must change the order in which he enumerates them.

In determining the order of our treatment of these four points (end, matter, form, means) we shall have to bear in mind that we cannot separate education as a system from the acquiring of an education, because the two are mutually interdependent (*supra*, pp. 31 ff.). To bring out this fact, we shall insert the part dealing with the acquiring of an education (*Bildungserwerb*) in the middle of the treatment given to the system of education: the historical treatment of the system of education will come first; and the sketch of the whole system of education, showing at the same time its ramifications into the whole of social activity, will come last. In this way we hope to bring out clearly the social character of education, as well as the fact that it is the result of uniting individual efforts and activities.

To understand the terms we have chosen for these portions of our work, the reader will note that the historical section is not intended to give a history of education; this being the province of another science. What is intended is to describe only the typical forms of education as they have appeared at different times. Our treatment of these historical types will furnish a basis for the subsequent inquiries, but it will not attempt to be exhaustive.

That portion of our treatise which deals with the purpose of education pays due attention also to those motives that do not enter directly into human consciousness, or at least not with sufficient definiteness to be called ends. We shall therefore treat more generally of the motives and aims of education.

The following part can be described more adequately as dealing with the content of education rather than with its subject-matter. The caption we have chosen more clearly indicates the one aim that holds together the heterogeneous matter contained in education, and connotes careful examination of all parts to discover their bearing upon, and exact relation to, education. Since the forms and agencies (*Vermittelungen*) employed in acquiring an education frequently overlap, it will be best to combine the treatment of the two subjects. But we shall have to separate the part giving a complete view of the system of education from the part that assigns to the work of

education its proper place in the whole of the duties of human
life. The wording "education in its relation to the sum total
of life's duties" expresses both the ethical and the sociological
side of the matter.

We have outlined the path we intend to pursue, and the aim
we mean to reach, but we have done so with a mind more to
the problems suggested by the subject itself than to the actual
means at our disposal for solving them. Were we to consider
merely the latter, we should certainly not be inclined to attempt more than to follow the beaten paths. But the problems
which our subject raises must not be minimized, even though
they transcend our knowledge and ability. The present work,
which was inspired by just such a problem, may not furnish a
satisfactory solution, but the author will be content if he has at
least stated its terms more clearly and encouraged others to
supply what is still missing in order that the problem may be
solved.

PART I.

~~~~~

THE HISTORICAL TYPES OF EDUCATION.

I.

EDUCATION IN ITS RELATION TO CULTURE, CIVILIZATION, AND MORAL REFINEMENT.

CHAPTER I.

Civilization—Culture; Moral Refinement—Education.

1. The terms *civilization* and *culture* are used to denote all those institutions, activities, and objects that humanize life and ennoble and elevate existence, or, as the ancients put it, raise the ζῆν to εὐ ζῆν, καλῶς ζῆν. The term civilization is, in accordance with its etymology, generally understood to embrace the institutions and forms of life that make man a member of a community, and consequently comprises all the forces making for a social and common life in opposition to the egotistic instincts of the solitary savage. The term culture has also retained some part of its primary meaning, for it signifies the cultivation of those fields of labor that present themselves to the human mind after it has emerged from the indolence of the primitive stage and reward the labor bestowed upon them by objects that lend dignity and happiness to life.

Civilization is based on religious and civil laws, on manners, customs, and the social order; *culture*, on faith, knowledge, ability, labor, and social intercourse, artistic and creative activities of all kinds. Civilization comprises the foundations of life, which the ancients regarded as blessings accruing from what such kindly deities as Osiris and Isis, Dionysos and Demeter, had taught the children of men; culture comprises the gifts committed to man when, according to Greek mythology, Prometheus breathed life into the sluggish and brooding race of men, not without warning them against restless and immoderate striving.[1]

---

[1] Arist., *Pol.* I, 2, III, 9. Diod., XII, 13, and elsewhere.

Civilization humanizes by joining together; culture, by vivifying. The strength of the former lies in the solidity of its foundations and the firmness of its structure; the glory of culture, in its breadth and depth. We are wont to regard civilization as the everywhere recurring foundation of humanity, untouched by differences in the spirit of the nations: we speak of civilized nations, not of national civilizations. But we are in the habit of considering culture as influenced by, and dependent on, the creative genius of each nation, and we even name it after the different nations, thus referring it to the nation as such, and this despite the fact that humanity always plays an important rule in making for points of similarity in the culture of even the most diverse nations.

2. The relation between civilization and culture will come out still more clearly if we contrast the kindred terms: *moral refinement* and *education*. The term *moral refinement* stresses the subjective element not expressed by civilization, denoting a bent of mind corresponding to the dictates of civilization; it expresses the internal effects of civilization in the individual, and is akin in this regard to the Greek ἦθος, which signifies, beside the objective content, the subjective state of the soul. To be refined is to be more than merely civilized; it expresses that the external forms of civilization have been received by the soul, that the heart and mind have been raised above the standard of primitive man. We may speak of sham civilization, *i. e.*, civilization that is purely a matter of external forms, but we cannot correctly speak of counterfeit refinement or of purely external forms of refinement, since refinement presupposes that the soul, or the inner man, has become truly ennobled. As soon as civilization has entered into the flesh and bone of the individual, he has refinement.

Analogously, there is a subjective, individual element implied in education. Education certainly signifies something more than that the creative forces of nature have been called into play, for when we speak of an educated person, we wish to say that the creative forces of nature have been active in his mind and soul spontaneously building on the foundation of his natural endowments. Similarly, when we speak of an educated nation, we wish to say that the nation has not only acquired the treasures of education, but is able to hold and to impart them to individuals, so that they become for the latter the sources of such mental qualities as an open and receptive mind, a refined taste, and nobility of soul. No great receptivity is needed to share in the blessings of culture; but great efforts are required to obtain a real education, and these endeavors must be continuous if the education is to be permanent. Before a man can be considered to be truly educated, it is necessary that he correctly join together and incorporate in his personality the various elements of culture. It is not an easy task, though it is essential for the man of education to harmonize into one whole the parts which together form the content of education and to express this in all the activities of his soul.

3. Education is not co-extensive with the whole of language, literature, faith, science, religious worship, art, technology, economics, but is placed beside and among these fields; it is in touch with each and all, but is not co-extensive with any single field, but transcends beyond all. Its content is, indeed, related to all these fields, but its proper function is not to reproduce any of them in their entirety, but to make a wise and prudent selection of their choicest elements. The work of cultural education is taken up with general and basic knowledge and arts (*Fertigkeiten*), which have about the same relation to the whole of the vast field of culture as a smaller circle to a larger concentric circle. The system of education is the tangible form for the whole of the joint efforts and agencies devoted to the acquiring and imparting of a general education. But the work of culture can not, by reason of its universality and all the branches spreading out from its boundaries, be comprised in any similar single institution; but the nation, or rather the social organism, embracing all professions and all classes of society, must be said to be the representative of a certain culture.

CHAPTER II.

Interdependence of Education and Culture.

1. Among the four socio-psychological concepts that we considered, the concept of education shows the smallest compass, and hence we may expect that it will also be the most conditioned; and, in point of fact, there are presuppositions (*Voraussetzungen*) in culture, as well as in civilization and refinement, which produce, according to their modification, various types of education.

The culture of a nation is an important factor in shaping its education. Nations possessing an indigenous culture have the sources and monuments of their education on their own soil and in their own past; the content of education transmitted to the descendants is the property of the nation, the language in which it is couched may have a strange and unfamiliar sound, but it is the language of the forefathers and will, upon closer inspection, reveal its kinship to the living language of the day. But a nation with a foreign and borrowed culture is forced to look in foreign lands for the sources of its education, and must master one, or perhaps several foreign languages before the path leading to these sources will be clear, and consequently education is the exclusive privilege of certain classes of the population. The education of such a nation is like an exotic plant, whose care requires much labor and which, moreover, remains restricted to a very limited territory. Yet this very disadvantage may be productive of good results in stimulating men to such redoubled activities as may succeed, finally, in assimilating fully all the foreign elements and in creating out of the union of native and foreign materials a second education that is truly national in spirit. In this process the two opposed factors may produce happier results than are possible to a nation whose educational system received no foreign influences, and which, by being limited to the continuous reproduction of the same content, may easily degenerate into a dead and soulless thing—a fossil.

2. While the starting-point of a nation's culture is thus an important factor in developing a specific character in education, an influence equally strong is exerted in the same regard by the direction of the nation's cultural activities. If the religious element is the chief influence in the national life, the foundation of the national education will also be religious in character. The principal purpose of all schooling will be the preservation of the sacred traditions; the intellectual interests will be committed to the priests, and their education will mark the highest stage of artistic and scientific achievement, and even if a popular education should develop and exist side by side with the education of the clergy, the latter will remain the model in content as well as in form. The system of education will present hard and fast distinctions in forms and grades, and these distinctions will be jealously guarded against any and all innovations; teaching will be considered more as an imparting of positive knowledge than as an awakening of the pupil's mental

powers; but the relations between teacher and pupil will bear so sacred and reverential a character that the knowledge imparted will prove a strong moral force.

The opposite of this type of education is developed by a culture with a predominantly æsthetical tendency. Here the poet has charge of the subject-matter of teaching, which is held in high esteem not merely for its content but also for its perfect form; here the artist and the master of language are ever discovering and making accessible new sources of education. The man of education is he who can not only enjoy the works of art, but also interpret their message and meaning. This latter ability raises him above the masses, who can only look on, or listen to, the creations of genius. Whosoever has a message of general interest is considered a teacher; circles of pupils gather about him, and a school is established. Education is prized not for its content (sacred in having been handed down from the forbears), but for its inherent grace and charm; it is looked upon as the means for perfecting and rounding off the personality of man.

Again, the educational system of a nation will be more fixed and stable in form, if the national life is deeply influenced by an abiding interest in science and research. Such a nation will distinguish very carefully between scientific and purely cultural studies, and between the work of scientific research and the elementary or propædeutic study of the sciences. There will be a twofold conception of the school: one as comprising the scholars engaged in scientific research, and the other as representing the institution where knowledge is imparted to the young. In as much as the school in the latter conception must prepare for higher studies, it may be called a school of science and may become the fixed centre of the educational system. The general education of the masses will pursue a different course than the education of the scholar, but the findings of scholars are a deep influence in popular education. The popular essay, the encyclopedia, polite literature, the newspaper, the magazine—all join in popularizing the discoveries made by scholars; and though this popularizing activity does not always promote scientific progress, yet the process itself is due to the expansive force of science, which will out, "like the water which, once it is set free from its source, will continue to flow on its endless course; and like the flame which, when once enkindled, will emit both light and heat."[1]

---

[1] J. Grimm, *Ueber Schule, Universität, Akademie.*

On the other hand, the idealism, which is characteristic of
the education fostered by the devotion to the arts or to scientific research, will wane if a nation permits its national life to
be absorbed in economic and utilitarian interests These interests will establish the bread-and-butter standard for evaluating
the work of the school; they will make the practical efficiency
of the pupils rather than the development of their intellectual
and moral faculties the end of education. These losses, however, are counterbalanced by positive gains in other directions.
There is in this education, aiming, as it does, at practical efficiency and practical results, less danger of resting satisfied with
selfish enjoyment or idle speculation, which is too frequently
the fruit of the purely æsthetical tendency in education: by
attaching special importance to work, the moral value of the
latter will be enhanc d, and this will in turn assist in improving
the living conditions of the workers of all classes. Technical
and practical training as well as the education of the masses will
be assured a place in the national system of education The
technical sciences will multiply and improve the vehicles for
human intercourse, and some of these improvements, though
they be only technical, may, as is seen in the history of the art
of printing, turn education into an entirely new channel the
education of the nations who have adopted the printed book is,
in some respects, of a higher type than that of the nations who
are confined to script.

3 In establishing the community of life, which is the necessary condition for a system of education, civilization is a more
remote, but not a less important, factor than culture. Man
must first settle down to fixed habits of life, his relations with
his fellowmen must be firmly established and well-regulated, ere
a mutual influence of the more delicate psychical effects can be
exerted The forces of civilization are thus the foundations of
education and, though they do not create the latter, their influence in this regard is powerful and manifold Laws and
customs determine when the individual is of age, and this fact
is of great importance in education, as it is in great part responsible for the grading and the completion of the individual's
period of school life. Laws and customs also regulate the relations between the various social classes, and thus determine
whether the national education belongs to one or more classes.
The prevailing views on what is just and right will decide whether and how far women are to share in the intellectual gifts, and
thereby modify not a little the work of cultural education. The

system of education depends most upon the power of the State when it has grown to such dimensions as to necessitate its legal organization.   The nature and spirit of the constitution of the State, its relations to the other social organisms—the family, society, the Church, the people at large—will then shape, in great measure, the legal form of the system of education; and this legal form will eventually prove a powerful factor in determining even the most minute details of school work.   But even before this direct influence of the State is felt, there is a continuous influence proceeding from the public life of the nation. A great world power exerts an entirely different influence than the government of a petty prince; a monarchy exerts a different influence than a republic; and a nation conservative in spirit and another given to perpetual changing will again exert different influences.   One government favors more a solid and stable form of education, while the other encourages the moveable and individual type of school; and this respective policy is followed even without the direct intervention of the State, solely as a result of the spontaneous tendencies of human activity.

4. If customs and laws are the chief factors in modifying the forms and institutions of education, refinement is responsible for the endeavor to make all the educational work one harmonious whole.   The ideals of education, be they ever so varied in form, can always be traced to moral views and principles, which are formulated when a nation becomes conscious of its refinement. Among the motives encouraging us to strive for an education is the sincere persuasion that it is proper for a man to receive some intellectual content, to make it part of his nature, and thus to become a member of a select circle.   Even the crudest reasoning must discover the relation existing between education and refinement.   The ideal of the wise man preceded the ideal of the man of education.   Long before the idea of a common intellectual property, refining in influence, had been conceived, men had looked up with veneration to the wise man, who was by the bounty of the gods in full possession of the highest of intellectual gifts, and whose life was a model and an inspiration to all. Aristotle enumerates the following traits noted universally in the wise man: his knowledge covers all fields, though he is wise enough not to attach too much importance to the details and the individual; he finds no difficulty in solving problems that are difficult to others; he knows the causes of all things; he possesses a rare skill in instructing and directing his fellow-

/men [1] All these features are common to our ideal of the educated man: his education, too, should be universal and thorough; he should be endowed with the power of expression; and
should make practical use of his knowledge and educational
attainments.   The man of education is, in a certain sense, an
epigonus of the wise man of antiquity; he is the incarnation of
the idealized vision of the ancients.   He is the incarnation,
moreover, of the ancient ideal on a large and ever increasing
scale; what had been the prerogative of a few select and highly
gifted mortals, has come to be the common property of the
multitude; the intellectual life has come down from the highest
heights into the valleys of the plain and homely folk.

CHAPTER III

Education and the Stages of Culture

1 Order and a worthy content of life appear, therefore, as
the basis of that refinement and assimilation of men, upon
which education is founded, and hence a nation that lacks in
its national life these elements, cannot be said to possess education   Primitive peoples, whose life is destitute of system and
law and order and regular activity, have no education   Still
we would not deny that every stage of development of a race,
no matter how primitive, is in possession of some ideas, of some
knowledge, of some arts, and that a certain mental growth may
be observed in the individual's mastery of these elements.   The
very language is the vehicle of much thought, a valuable asset,
and the languages of "nature peoples" (*Naturvolker*), even if
primitive, are often strangely ingenious in structure, and disclose in their vocabulary a surprising wealth of ideas gained
from communing with nature.   The traditions of the Golden
Age. of the destruction and restoration of the human race, of
the Deluge, which we find among almost all peoples, and which
extend back into time immemorial, are only a fraction of the
intellectual treasures of primitive peoples, which can not but
exert an elevating influence upon these children of nature
Their feelings, both of sadness and joy, they express in songs
and music; wise and witty sayings, the proverbs and adages,
which they transmit to the succeeding generations, are the

1 Aristotle, *Met*, I, 2

vehicles of much homely wisdom. They cultivate the arts of dancing and of military drills, not merely because they are pleasant or useful, but because they develop physical charms and graces. Nations destined to become truly cultured show even in the first stages of their development the characteristic features of their later education. The heroes of Homer can not be expected to bring out in full the culture that was the glory of a later Greece, and that actually grew out of Homer's poetry; but what Phoinix, the teacher of Achilles, describes as the end of his training, "to shine in councils, and in camps to dare," [1] is not essentially different from the educational ideal of a later age. Similarly, the education given by the Aesir Heimdall to Jarl, as described in the *Lay of Rig*, in the *Elder Edda*,[2] is an unmistakable counterpart of the chivalric education of the Middle Ages. But this is, nevertheless, not ground enough to allow even to the more developed of the primitive races a type of education. The possession of education may be denied to them for various reasons: their teaching lacks a substantial and articulated content; the matter of their knowledge and arts is not co-ordinated; their acquiring of an intellectual content wants form and order; and they make no attempt to systematize their pursuit of knowledge. But to the student of education this incipient development of an educational type should prove of particular interest: as the educational life of the nation is not yet fixed, one can observe its elements, as it were, in a fluid state before they are partly chrystallized—a necessary condition for the creation of an educational type; the forces, too, that will continue to operate in a higher stage of culture are already at work and are noted more readily in the primitive than in the advanced stage—*viz.*, the spontaneous assimilation of the young, the spontaneous teaching and learning, and the very fruitful, even if crude and informal, daily intercourse.

2. It is not an easy task to determine the exact point when a "nature people" may be said to have advanced so far in civilization, culture, and refinement as to deserve to be termed an educated people; but it may be safely stated that this stage is reached when the art of writing has come into general use. The art of writing holds fast, like a fixative, the intellectual content of a nation's life; to religious ideas it gives a permanent form in the sacred books; it collects all the knowledge transmitted

---

[1] *Iliad*, IX 445.
[2] *The Elder Eddas*, Transl. by B. Thorpe, Norroena Society, New York, 1906, 81 ff.

from the past, and this knowledge, now stated with precision, is the basis of scientific research; it selects from the legends and poems handed down, by word of mouth, the nation's standard poetry. When written, the reminiscences and memories of the olden days are history; and the customs and manners, when expressed in writing, assume the force of laws. Of the content of a nation's knowledge only that which has been reduced to writing can be made the subject of real teaching, and the art that is the instrument for formulating it, is the subject of systematic practice. Reading and writing are the first subjects of real teaching and learning; and as the alphabet to-day still holds the first place in the schooling of our children, so it also marks the entrance of education into the life of a nation. The beginnings of schools can be traced back to the time when the art of writing was made the subject of systematic study and practice. We find, indeed, that nations who lacked the art of writing would assemble the children together for the purpose of discipline and physical culture, but never for the purpose of common study. Though we may deny that Comenius' definition of the school as the "*officina transfundendæ eruditionis e libris in homines*"[1] is perfectly satisfactory, yet the school and the book are, in matter of fact, mutual complements, and have been mutually related long before there was such a thing as a textbook. But the book is not only the basis of instruction, but also its supplement; "to write is but to speak to the eyes, and to read is but a hearing with the eyes."[2] The written word is heard longer and farther than the spoken word; it travels abroad, through the length and breadth of the whole country; and long before the demand of the reading public had created the supply of a large and extensive literature, the inscription, the page, and the book had become the vehicles of general knowledge, and some of the most powerful means for equalizing the knowledge and ability of men.

The stage of development reached by a nation when it is first introduced to the art of writing, or the matter which is first committed to writing, may determine the future character of the national education. The ease or difficulty with which the written language may be learned, or even the technical matters to be considered in writing, especially the cheap or expensive writing materials—all will influence, favorably or

---

[1] *Opp. Did. O.* II, p. 527
[2] H. Wuttke, *Geschichte der Schrift und des Schrifttums*, Leipzig, 1872, p. 11.

otherwise, the progress of national education. If the first book be a collection of hymns, the effects will be other than if the first matter written down were historical facts, or laws, or manners and customs. The art of writing will likewise fare differently, both in the schoolroom and out, if the national language recognizes but one system of writing instead of permitting two—the sacred and the profane—to co-exist with one another. Nor can we expect the same educational results in the nation that has a system of writing which is so difficult, that its mastery requires the work of the entire period of a child's schooling, as in another nation whose written language is so easy as to be mastered by a lad of seven. Again, there will be different results, if the leaves of trees or bast, or slate and paper, are used for writing materials instead of such materials as are too costly for extensive use.

3. While nations, then, that possess no written language have likewise no education, there is a further point to be settled whether all nations that practise the art of writing possess an education, or whether there be any additional requisites.

When we consider how far superior education is to culture (*Kultur*), we shall realize that education is so choice a flower of humanity that it can be expected even from a civilized nation only under the most favorable circumstances. It may well seem that a special creative force is needed, over and above the forces inherent in culture, to join certain elements of the latter into a harmonious union, and to make them so much a property of the individual person that they shall prove in his life an element of intellectual fructification and of æsthetic and moral enlightenment; and that for this purpose the function of culture must first be set free, in order to fit it for exercising so free and unhampered an influence on the inner life. There are some nations, who have attained a high degree of civilization, but who have evolved the idea of an individual personality so slightly, that there can be no thought with them of centering the work of culture in the development of the individual. Shall these nations then be denied the claim to education, or may it be assumed that the absence of these factors would but indicate that the idea of education is, like every other idea, subject to a long period of successive development, before it can be considered a historical reality?

The answer will decide whether the civilized nations of the East may be called educated or no. There can be no doubt that these nations were highly civilized, but the rigidity and

fixedness of their institutions, and the hard and fast lines binding the individual to the whole and the past, seem to render
educational efforts—which must be free, if anything—impossible   These nations looked upon the regulation of life and the
consequent perfection of it as lying beyond the individual,
though they regarded it as a sacred duty of the individual to
co-operate in attaining this end.   The chief duty of the individual was to fill his place in the whole of the social organism
and to conserve and guard scrupulously all that was entrusted
to him of the highest gifts of civilization.   The ancient civilization of the East recognized no distinction between right doing
(*Rechttun*) and correct acting (*korrekt handeln*); to know something was the same as to have learned it by heart; to be master
in any field meant no more than to be able to do what the forbears had been doing centuries before.   Though we can not
concede that the civilization of the ancient Eastern nations was
mere "barbarism ruled by priestcraft and the darkest of superstition," yet, in point of fact, the social constitution of these
nations and their servile worship of traditions allowed scant
opportunity for the homogeneous development of the intellect
and for the free use of the products of culture for the purposes
of education

However, this is not sufficient ground on which to deny the
existence of a certain type of Oriental education   To do so
would be unfair to all that has been achieved by the Eastern
nations in the field of the higher life of the mind.   The prejudices of a former day, which refused to recognize any education
in the East, should long ago have died a natural death in the
face of facts unearthed by modern scholarship.   Modern research has thrown new light on Eastern conditions, and has
disillusioned the world of the notion of the oriental priests, who,
jealous of their secrets, would withhold from the masses the pursuit of knowledge   The ancient Greeks inform us, that popular
education had in the early days of Egyptian history branched
off from the education that was held sacred, as being the exclusive privilege of the priest; Plato does not hesitate to re-
commend this popular education to his countrymen, as possessing many features worthy of imitation.[1]   It is now a well known
fact that the knowledge of the *Vedas* was not looked upon as
the monopoly of the Brahmans, but that the religious instruction was open alike to the warrior and the merchant   The

---

[1] Plato, *Legg*, VII, p 819

educational system of India, though one of many ramifications, resembles more closely, in form and structure, the organization of the family than of the school; but the school system of ancient Egypt was well organized and well graded. Indian literature is not devoted to science exclusively, for a large portion of it is pure letters, serving not for any purpose of study, but for elegant leisure. Upon a deeper study of oriental education we shall realize that it does not lack altogether the idea of individual education. The Hindu makes a due distinction between the man of learning and the man of education; he has a happy term for designating the latter, taking, as the Germans do for *Bildung*, his conception from the idea of forming man like a vessel; though his word for the man of education, *vidagdha*, is superior to the German *der Gebildete*, because the Indian term expresses that the ware has been well baked in the fire. *Durvidagdha* is the Sanskrit for the half-baked one, the man of superficial education; *viceschadschna* is the man of universal learning, and *adschna* is the ignoramus.[1]

If noble self-respect proves that the content of education has become the property of the soul, then we must allow that the Egyptians also assimilated their knowledge, for Plato has the Egyptian priest make the proud avowal: "Ye Greeks are but children, and a Greek shall never attain the wisdom of old age; ye all have the minds and souls of children, for ye lack the knowledge of the olden days, and have no wisdom come down from the early ages."[2] Does this sentence not give expression to the proud consciousness of possessing a complete personality, and does it not voice perfectly the ethos of Oriental traditions? It were certainly a serious defect in what purports to be a history of educational types to have it begin with the nation of children and ignore the idea of education—however imperfect, yet venerable and deep in meaning—as formulated by those nations of the East, that have been, in a measure, the teachers of the Greeks, and, therefore, of all Western nations.

[1] "Lightly an ignorant boor is made content,
    And lightlier yet a sage,
    But minds by half-way knowledge warped and bent,
    Not Brahma's self their fury may assuage." — P. E. Moore, *A Century of Indian Epigrams*, Boston, 1898, p. 52; Bhartrihari, I, 52, 87.

[2] Plato, *Tim.*, p. 22.

II.

ORIENTAL EDUCATION.

CHAPTER IV

India

1. Some of the great indigenous civilizations of the East date from prehistoric times and flourished for thousands of years However, because of the vast differences between the East and the West and between the ancient and the modern world, the ancient civilizations of the East might well appear strange and unintelligible to us. But the culture of the Indo-Aryans seems to present the fewest difficulties to the modern mind. And it is, indeed, not so very difficult for us to understand the plastic forces at work in the civilization of ancient India, and that for the following reasons. There is, first of all, our kinship with the Indo-Aryan race Next, there are certain points of contact between our culture and that of ancient India, for Western culture, on the one hand, owes some of its most valuable elements to India, while the latter, on the other hand, has received valuable cultural elements from the West Finally, the culture of the Indo-Aryans is still existing and thus allows us a concrete view of at least some of the educational forms produced by the civilization of ancient India.

The collective designation of the sacred literature, which is the foundation of Indian education, is *Veda*, *i. e.*, knowledge At the base of this entire literature of more than one hundred books lie four varieties of metrical compositions known as the four *Vedas* in the narrower sense The *Rig-Veda* contains the invocations addressed to the gods by the priest of Rik. The *Sama-Veda* contains the prayers of the sacrificing priest; these prayers are but repetitions of the verses of the *Rig-Veda* in new combinations. The *Yajur-Veda* contains the blessings pronounced by the Adhvarju. The *Atharva-Veda* is the ritual of a special order of priests, who practised fire worship, but who performed no definite liturgical function. The *Samhita* of each of these four *Vedas* is a purely lyrical collection, to which were added the *Brahmanas* and *Sutras*, *i. e.*, liturgical, dogmatic, and didactic explanations, which are the main content of Vedic theology.[1]

The hymns and the dogmatical and liturgical parts represent, as it were, the inner circles of the *Veda*, and around these all Indian literature and science is grouped. The demarcations between the *Veda* proper and what has grown up around it, or directly out of it, are so shadowy and vague as to make a clearcut distinction impossible.[2] How the *Vedas* influenced the course of studies is clearly seen in the various systems followed in explaining the sacred text. There was one system of *Veda* interpretation which treated etymological, mythical (using tales and legends to illustrate the text), and liturgical matters and also examined into the inner nature and interrelation of things.[3] Another system recognized six *Vedanga*, i. e., six branches of *Veda* interpretation which issued organically from the sacred text: phonetics, poetics, grammar, exegesis, liturgy, and astronomy—the last-named being an important part of the priests' learning, because they had to set the date for the sacrifices.[4] More comprehensive still is the system of the ten sciences, said to have been established "in early times by ten priests who were familiar with the contents of the *Vedas*, and who made this abstract for the purpose of rendering the subject less difficult by teaching the several branches separately." This system comprises, besides the six branches mentioned above, the following: laws, legends, logic, and dogmatic theology.[5] The two *Upavedas*, which treat of music and medicine, also originated in the study of the *Vedas*.

2. In this system of the ten sciences grammar occupies, by virtue of its age and its inherent dignity, a prominent place. The Brahmans worshipped language as a deity; they offered sacrifices and sang hymns in its honor; and with loving care and consummate skill they analyzed the body of language. It is probable that the knowledge of phonetics antedates the completion of the hymnological sections of the *Rig-Veda*. "These (the Ganas)," to quote Max Müller, "supplied the solid basis on which successive generations of scholars erected that astounding structure which reached its perfection in the grammar of

[1] A. Weber, *History of Indian Literature*, Transl. by Mann and Zachariæ, London, 1878, pp. 8 ff.

[2] A. Ludwig, *Der Rigveda*, Vol. III, pp. 15 ff.

[3] Ibid., p. 75.

[4] Ibid., p. 74.

[5] Max Müller, *Rigveda-Pratisakhya*, Leipzig, 1869, p. VIII.

Panini. There is no form, regular or irregular, in the whole Sanskrit language, which is not provided for in the grammar of Panini and his commentators. It is the perfection of a merely empirical analysis of language, unsurpassed, nay even unapproached, by anything in the grammatical literature of other nations."[1] The study of grammar had to grow the more in importance the more the language of daily life departed from the classical language of literature (Sanskrita) and the more difficult the understanding of the sacred and classical texts became. This fact accounts for the exaggerated praises paid to grammar, which is described as the art that leads men to eternal happiness, as having been inspired by the deity, as mastered only by asceticism, etc   Panini's grammar, being obscure because of its conciseness, was ill adapted for the purposes of instruction, and hence special grammars were written for the schools; the *Siddhanta Kaumudi* (*The Moonlight of the Laws of Language*), though of a later date, was used widely, and the abridged edition of this same work. *Laghusiddhanta Kaumudi* (*The Small Moonlight of the Laws of Language*) is to-day still used quite generally [2]

The Indian art of language dates, like the Indian grammar, from the study of the *Vedas* The great Indian epics *Mahabharata* and *Ramajana* are considered as sacred as the *Vedas* and are occasionally called the fifth *Veda* [3] These epics contain historical and didactic elements intermixed, the former, however, received but scant attention at the hands of Indian scholars India has, despite its reverence for the past, developed no interest in history. Either the tendency for phantastic and allegorical conceptions prevented this, or the elegiac-mystical view that all human work is only a fleeting show, led the people to under-

---

[1] Max Muller, *The Science of Language*, New York, 1891, I, 124, 125 — Panini lived in the fourth century B C , and his grammar, consisting of eight books containing 4,000 rules, is the oldest Sanskrit grammar which has been preserved

[2] It is written in Sanskrit, and the Hindus seem thus to find it as easy to learn an unknown tongue through the medium of another unknown language, *ignotum per ignotum*, as did our own ancestors in the Middle Ages, who learned Latin from grammars written in Latin, Its 1,000 *sutras*, or rules, treat of sounds and letters (their various classes are memorized by ingenious abbreviations), euphony, declension (in a poor arrangement), conjugation, and word-building The unabridged *Moonlight* is taken up after the *Small Moonlight*, to be followed by the dictionary of roots (*Dhatupatha*), and the versified list of synonyms (*Amara-koscha, The Immortal Treasure*) The reading of poets is taken up only after all this ground has been covered Cf Ballantyne, *The Pandits and Their Manner of Teaching*, in *The Pandit*, 1867, No 10, and 1868, Nos 21 and 23

[3] Ludwig, l c , p 16

rate the value of historical records. But didactic poetry, especially the fable, flourished all the more. Even before the Macedonian invasion, fables were much in vogue in India and, even before they had been brought together in the collections with which we are familiar, the peoples of Western Asia were drawing upon the stock of Indian tales; and it is to Western Asia that we owe the Indian beast fable common to all modern literatures.[1] The wise saying enjoyed equal popularity with the didactic tale, though it was never introduced in the schools. Songs, however, were cultivated but little, and music, too—though it was used at the religious services and represented in the national mythology by the Gandharvas, and though its theory was made the subject of special studies[2]—never became a vital or educational element. The same must be said of the drama, whose beginnings, closely related to the forms of religious worship, may be seen in the national life, but whose full development is the result of Greek influences.

The study of the art of language is of later origin than the study of grammar, but it, too, was eventually incorporated into the course of general education. The rhetoric and poetics of India, whose beginnings can be traced to the sixth century before Christ, treat of the meaning of words, of the different kinds of poetical compositions, the different kinds of style, and the ornaments of composition.[3]

---

[1] In the introduction to his translation of the *Panschatantra* (Leipzig, 1859, Vol. I.), Benfey deals with the influence of ancient Indian material upon the folklore of Asia and Europe. Cf. Max Müller, *Migration of Fables*, in vol. 3 of his *Chips from a German Workshop*.

[2] Mention is made of a textbook bearing the title *Gandharva-Veda*, *The Science of the Gandharvas*, or celestial musicians. It is to India that we can trace the practice of designating the musical tones according to their first letters; Benfey (*Indien* in Ersch and Gruber's *Enzyklopädie*) is of the opinion that the Indian formula: sa ri ga ma pa dha ni, was first brought to the Persians, next to the Arabians, and finally to the Italians (Guido d'Arezzo). Cf. A. Weber, *History of Indian Literature*, p. 272.

[3] Ballantyne (l.c.) quotes the following from the textbook in use at present: "What is a sentence?" "A sentence is a combination of words, which can be joined together, which are actually related to one another, and are placed together." A few examples are given to illustrate the definition. "He sprinkles with fire," is no sentence, because the words cannot be joined together. "Cow, horse, man, elephant," is no sentence, because no relation is expressed. If I now say "Devatta" and after twenty-four hours, "goes," I have no sentence, because the words are separated from each other.—"What is a word?" "A word is a succession of letters, joined by usage, but not in a logical way (*i.e.*, not in the order as they occur in the system of sounds), and which conveys some meaning." The meaning may

Logic, considered the auxiliary science of dogmatics, remains ever in closest relation to it.   It is the science of the three arguments and their sources: perception, conclusion, and the authority of the sacred writings.   The Greeks report, indeed, of Indian logicians who practiced their art professionally, but the Brahmans looked down upon them as idle chatterers and refused to acknowledge them as teachers.[1]

While only one of the mathematical sciences (astronomy) is numbered with the Vedic sciences, the others may also be traced to theology as to their first source.   The first traces of Indian algebra occur in Pingala's *Treatise on Prosody*, in the last chapter of which the permutations of longs and shorts possible in a metre with a fixed number of syllables are set forth in an enigmatical form.[2]   Notes on geometry occur first in ritualistic writings.   Though mathematics belonged to the priestly sciences, it exerted some influence on the intellectual life of the whole nation. The Hindus are the authors of our system of notation, which is based on the ingenious idea of denoting by the position of a figure what power of 10 is its factor.   This system has been adopted by all civilized peoples, and it has made possible all the progress that has since been made in arithmetic   It could be invented only among such a nation as gave much of its time to numbers and found therein much pleasure; and the invention once made was a potent force in developing the nation's sense and science of numbers.[3]   A further proof of the Hindus' mathematical ability, as given outside the ranks of scholarship, may be seen in the game of chess, which was invented in India, and which is the most ingenious of all games of war and a splendid school for the training of the place-sense and of the faculty of combination.

4   The real representatives of Indian scholarship are the Brahmans, who trace their origin to the head of the god from

be three-fold expressed, suggested, or understood   In kind, the words are either names of gender, names of qualities, names of persons, or names of actions —There are two varieties in poetry, the first deals with what is seen, and the other with what is but heard

[1] Strabo, XV, p 719

[2] A Weber, *History of Indian Literature*, p 256, footnote

[3] The Indian figures 1-9 are abbreviations of the initial letters of the numerals themselves, the zero, the creation of which is the real speculative achievement of the whole system, has arisen out of the first letter of the word *sunya* (empty).   The Arabs were the first to borrow of the Indians the decimal system of notation with its symbols, and they are responsible for its becoming widely known in the West. Cf Chapter XIX, *infra*

whose members all the world has sprung. But the study of the
Vedas was open to all Aryans, *i. e.*, to all members of the Indo-
Iranian race, even if they belonged to the castes of the warriors
or merchants. The ostracized caste of the Sudra is separated
from the rest not only socially, but also ethnographically. The
ceremony of girding the young Aryan with the sacred cord
marks his reception into the national religion; the Brahman boy
is received in his eighth year, the son of the Kshatriya after his
eleventh, and the young Vaisya after his twelfth year. Immediately after their reception, the study of grammar is taken up
in preparation for the study of the *Vedas*. A Brahman is the
teacher; the boys live with him and serve him, and they are
treated as apprentices rather than as pupils. The methods obtaining in the schools are solemn, quaint, and old-fashioned;[1]
but the discipline is mild. To master one *Veda* is the work of
twelve years, and thus 48 years are required for mastering the
four *Vedas*. Religious ceremonies, called the "second birth" of
the pupil, mark the end of his schooling. Most pupils leave
the teacher's house at about the age of twenty; others, however,
remain with the *guru* (the venerable one) for their whole life.

Brahman schools with collegiate forms of instruction are of
later origin and are most probably imitations of the Mohammedan mosque schools (*madrassehs*). As the religion of India is
not centred in certain temples, and as its science, too, is not
centred in the libraries or archives of temples, so its higher
educational system also lacks the collegiate forms of instruction.

---

1) The *Rigveda-Pratisakhya*, edited by Max Müller in 1869, gives the following
directions: "The teacher shall for the recitation observe the following points. He
shall be seated so as to be facing either the east, the north, or the north-east. If
there be but one or two pupils, they shall be seated so as to face the south; if more
pupils be present, they may be seated according to the size of the room. After all
the pupils have embraced the teacher's feet and after they have placed them on
their head, they shall invite the teacher to begin the instruction, 'Master, read'.
The teacher shall reply, 'Om! Let the first prayer—which is both for the teacher
and his pupils the gate leading to heaven—mark the beginning of all study.' . . . .
Complying with their request, the teacher shall begin to recite and he shall recite
every word twice. As soon as the teacher has so recited several words, the first
pupil shall be called upon to repeat the first word. When asking for an explanation
the teacher shall be addressed, *Bho* (Reverend Sir); the assent to the explanation
given shall be expressed thus, *Om Bho*. It shall be the duty of the pupils to memorize a lesson after it has been finished in this way; they shall then continue to
repeat it, being careful to preserve the same high tone, and not to contract words
that are independent of one another, and to indicate by a slight separation compound terms. . . . . After all pupils have then recited in this manner their lessons,
they shall again embrace the feet of the teacher and be dismissed for the day."

The schools for writing and reading are numerous, though they also lack a fixed and settled organization. In most cases the pupils are seated in the open, grouped about their teacher, and write on palm leaves. If their number be very large, the teacher employs the more advanced pupils to instruct the others. Dr. Andrew Bell, superintendent of the Military Male Orphan Asylum in Madras (died 1832), learned this method of the Hindus and introduced it into Europe, where it became known as the monitorial system of instruction. In face of the widespread illiteracy in modern India—92.5% in 1901 for the population over ten years of age[1]—it would seem that the conditions two thousand and more years ago were, if anything, superior: the Macedonians were surprised, when invading the Pundjab, at the sign posts which they met on all sides on the roads, and which gave the place-names as well as the distances.[2]

5. There are many testimonies that go to prove that the Hindus attach great importance to knowledge. "Knowledge," says Bhartrihari, "is man's greatest ornament; it is an undoubted treasure; it assures its possessor of pleasures, glory, and good fortune. It is the teacher of the wise, the friend in a strange land, a power that will never fail, a gem of the purest ray; and it is esteemed of kings. Deprive man of knowledge, and he sinks to the level of the brute."[3] In the *Code of Manu*, the most authoritative of Indian law books, we read. "He who imparts the sacred knowledge of the *Vedas* is deserving of a greater veneration than he who is responsible merely for the existence of the body, because the second birth assures one of immortal life, not only in this world, but also in the next. What the parents produce is the birth of only a mortal being, but the birth given by the teacher of the *Veda* is the birth to a real, never-ending life, which is free from the ravages alike of death and old age. He who imparts the sacred lore, be this great or small, shall be known as *guru*, the venerable sire."[4] The same high esteem for learning inspired the view that man is thrice a debtor: he is first indebted to the wise, as to the authors and fathers of the faith, only in the second place is he indebted to the gods; and in the last place to his parents.[5] These expressions of the high value of learning agree in showing that knowl-

---

[1] *Cyclopedia of Education*, edited by Paul Monroe, s v *Illiteracy*
[2] Megasthenes, frg 34, 3 Schwanb
[3] Bohtlingk, *Sanskrit-Chrestomathie*, St Petersburg, 1845, p 199.
[4] *Manu*, II, 146-149
[5] Max Muller, *Religion und Philosophie, Deutsche Rundschau*, 1879, I, pp 57 ff

edge is prized, not for its own sake, but as a means to an end; it is prized as being the path that leads to mystic perfection. Once this is attained, the treasures of knowledge are valueless; they have been superseded and are neglected and forgotten. The Hindu's pursuit of knowledge presents a strange process: in his boyhood he is eager to acquire the knowledge of the *Veda;* in his manhood he will faithfully observe its minutest regulations; but in his old age he will be rapt in deep speculation, entirely oblivious of the knowledge and laws he had held sacred in the days of his strength. "We may still meet Brahman families whose children will con over, and learn by heart, and recite by rote the old sacred songs, and whose father, too, will not allow one day to pass without the sacred rites and ceremonies, but whose aged grandfather will openly profess supreme contempt for the elaborate ritual; for he holds the gods of the *Vedas* to be but names, vain and meaningless abstractions of what he knows to be beyond the power of expression; and he seeks and finds his satisfaction and peace where alone it can be found, in the highest philosophical speculation; and the latter is to him a religion more sacred than any forms of the national worship; his speculation is the realization of the entire *Veda*: it is *Vedanta,* the end and aim and fulfillment of the *Veda.*"[1] A similar disintegration of knowledge may be found among the one-sided mystics of all ages, but it has been systematized by no other nation. Still, the Hindus accomplished much in science and general education, which is the more surprising as the final end of all their intellectual efforts is the *futura oblivio.*

CHAPTER V.

Egypt.

1. There is an unmistakable analogy between Egyptian and Indian education. In Egypt, as in India, collections of hymns are the basis of theological literature, and the latter is the source and beginning of science and of educational efforts. Again, in Egypt, as in India, the priests are in charge of all learning, and all educational efforts must subserve the ethico-religious interests. Yet there are noteworthy differences between the educational systems of the two countries.

---

[1] Ibid., p. 69.

7

The sacred literature of ancient Egypt consisted of the 42 books whose authorship was ascribed to the god Thoth, whom the Greeks worshipped under the name of Hermes; and hence the 42 books became known as the Hermetic Books. The oldest book and the one held in highest esteem is the book of hymns. It is thought to be identical with the collection of hymns found among the papyri stored in the Egyptian tombs, and published in 1842 by Lepsius as *The Book of the Dead*.[1] The second book treats of the right, or royal, path; along with the book of hymns it was carried at the head of all solemn processions, and its contents were known to the whole nation. The contents of the next four books, the books of the horoscope, may be described as scientific, for they treated of the heavens, the sun, moon, and the motions of the stars. The next ten books contained the learning of the temple scribe, the *Hierogrammateus, i e* , the science of hieroglyphics, geography, the laws of the sun, the moon, and the planets, topography, surveying (especially in its connection with the Nile), and lastly the science of building and ornamenting temples. The next ten books dealt with liturgy, the science of the master of ceremonies, the *Stolist*. The next ten books contained matter reserved to the priests, and treated in full the functions of the high-priest; dealing with the science of the gods and of laws, they may be called compendiums of dogmatics and jurisprudence. The last six books never enjoyed the same authority as the others, and were not considered canonical, they treated of the "qualities of bodies, of bodily diseases and their cure, and of women."[2]

These writings, of which a copy was deposited in the archives of every temple, are the core of a very extensive literature. The Egyptians themselves give 36,525 as the number of all the writings belonging to this class of literature. The number quoted is that of the great Sothic period and is obtained by multiplying the number of days in a year by one hundred.

2. In comparison with the Vedic sciences, the books of Thoth give scant attention to grammar, treating in this regard only of hieroglyphics. More attention was given to mathematics, astronomy, geography, and medicine A striking feature of Egyptian literature is the strong interest in history: the Egyptians recorded in their annals the deeds of their kings;

[1] A translation by Birch has been publish d in Bunsen's *Egypt's Place in Universal History*, V, 66-333

[2] Clemens Alex , *Strom* , VI, 4, p 269 ed Sylburg

inscriptions told all that was noteworthy in the history of the race; the nation was proud of its knowledge of the past, and was eager to communicate it to the foreigner.[1]

The several departments of science were entrusted to the individual orders of priests. They were to know by heart and to be able to quote freely the books of Thoth, but only the highest order of priests were expected to command a universal knowledge. Some knowledge was, despite these restrictions, expected of the people at large. Among the treasures accessible to all were the social gifts granted by Thoth: language, the art of writing, the worship of the deity, the knowledge of the stars, music, and physical culture.[2] Most, if not all, of the inhabitants of ancient Egypt seem to have been able to read and write. "The temples spoke in letters of heroic size; the worship of the gods and the songs sung in praise of princes and kings impressed the teachings of religion and kept alive the memory of the nation's glorious past; the inscriptions were engraved in imperishable marble and porphyry, and would continue for centuries and ages to speak their message to the race."[3] Rolls of parchment were placed beside the dead to cheer them on their mysterious journey. Pious sayings and proverbs were engraved on the articles in daily use. Court trials were transacted in writing, and all contracts had to be made in writing. In fact, everything of any importance was written down; and gods, as well as men, are often represented as engaged in writing. The hieroglyphic characters—there were about 650, of which some represented simple sounds, while the majority represented compound sounds—are by most Egyptologists explained symbolically, but Seyffarth and his followers explain them phonetically. They are the basis of the later development of the hieratic style of writing, and the latter, by changing to a still more simplified form of representation, finally evolved what is known as the demotic or epistolographic style, which comprised about 350 characters.[4] The priests pursued the more advanced study of these various styles,[5] while the lower castes acquired only an elementary knowledge of reading and writing.[6]

[1] Her., II, 3 and 100. Diod., I, 73. Tac., *Ann.*, II, 60.

[2] Diod., I, 16. Cf. Plato, *Phædr.*, p. 213.

[3] Heinrich Wuttke, *Geschichte der Schrift*, Leipzig, 1872, pp. 576 ff.

[4] M. Uhlemann, *Thoth oder die Wissenschaften der alten Aegypter*, Göttingen, 1850, pp. 173 ff.

[5] Diod., I, 81.

[6] Plato, *Legg.*, VII, p. 819.

3 Arithmetic and geometry were also studied by the children of the masses. Plato has naught but praise for the extent to which the knowledge of these branches had spread among the whole nation, but he finds fault with the practice of devoting the knowledge of them to exclusively practical ends instead of employing it, at least in part, for higher and cultural purposes.[1] The two subjects were of great practical benefit for the trades and commerce, especially for architecture and administration The Egyptian yard, the unit of measurement, is remarkable for the exactness of its division, and the still extant ground-plans of tombs agree perfectly with the execution   The practice of having charts of fields and maps of the different sections of the country made, for the purpose of dividing off the castes and of taking up the census, dates back to the earliest times.[2] The Egyptian system of notation lacks the speculative idea of the Indian system,[3] but their theory of numbers as well as their geometry, both of which stimulated Greek philosophers, must have had a philosophical foundation.[4] Astronomy and astrology could not, because of their nature, be cultivated so extensively as arithmetic and geometry; but the mere fact that they are mentioned twice in the sacred books, once as the higher science of the temple scribe and then as the elementary science of the horoscope, demonstrates that the rudiments of them were accessible to the people at large. It is certain that all Egyptians were familiar with the calendar and its mythological-astronomical apparatus, as well as with the horoscope and the observations and superstitions on which it was based The public monuments recorded not only all important events in minute detail, but gave, besides, a description of the constellations visible in the heavens at the time, and it was a general practice to foretell for every newborn child the events of its life

[1] Ibid , VII, p 819 and V, p 747, *Rep* , IV, p 436

[2] M Uhlemann, l c , pp 262 ff

[3] The numbers 1, 10, 100, 1000 were represented by symbols, which, by being placed a certain number of times expressed how many times the number which they represented was to be understood   The use of these symbols never extended beyond Egypt, but the Egyptian symbol for addition, a cross, and the manner of writing fractions (originally the picture of a mouth above which the numerator and below which the denominator was placed) are in universal use. Cf H Brugsch, *Numerorum apud veteres Aegyptios demoticorum doctrina*, Berol , 1839

[4] E Roth, *Geschichte der abendländischen Philosophie*, Mannheim, 1862, II, 586 ff

from the aspect of the heavens at the moment of its birth.[1] Music was closely allied with astronomy; a planet was assigned to each of the seven notes; the three principal notes, the primary, the quint, and the octave, were representative of the seasons: the high note, of summer; the low, of winter; and the middle, of spring.[2] But there was an even closer connection between music and the national religion. The least change in vocal or instrumental music was strictly prohibited, and the priests were the musical censors,[3] which fact, far from indicating a slow development of the art, proves that it was practised so extensively as to threaten a departure from the standards of sacred music. It would seem that the physical culture in vogue among the Egyptians represented a system of national gymnastics, though the Greeks deny this. Yet Thoth-Hermes was considered the inventor of the palæstra, of eurythmy, and of physical culture in general; cleanliness, anointing, and the practice of dietetics were Egyptian customs of old and national standing.

4. The archives and libraries that were connected with the temples, first suggested the establishment of priests' colleges, and these in turn proved the centres of a well organized system of education. The description given by the Egyptologist G. Ebers of the temple schools of Thebes shows them to have been highly organized.[4] These schools were patterned after the older institutions at Heliopolis and Memphis. They were grouped about an institution of higher learning, where all such as were aspiring to the professions of priests, physicians, mathematicians, astronomers, or grammarians could not only secure an adequate training, but were furthermore assured, once they had reached the highest degree of knowledge and had been enrolled among the scribes, of a free home. The savants had access to a large library, which housed thousands of papyri and with which a papyrus factory was connected. Some of the savants taught the younger pupils who were educated in the elementary school

---

[1] The belief in the horoscope is founded on the idea that the soul of the child has come down from the world of the stars. The horoscope itself is the degree of the ecliptic which rises at the hour of birth. The planet next to this is considered the star of life. Cf. Röth, l.c., I, p. 214.

[2] Heinrich Wuttke, l.c., p. 569. Diod., I, 16.

[3] Plato, *Legg.*, II, p. 656 and VII, p. 799.

[4] In the novel *Uarda*, Vol. I, pp. 1 ff., Ebers vouches for the reliability of his description: all the details are drawn from sources contemporary with Ramses II. and his successor Menephthah, *i. e.*, 1324-1230 B. C.

connected with the Seti-House, the name of the whole establishment. This elementary school was open to all sons of free-born citizens, and was attended by more than 100 pupils, who lodged and boarded in the same institution. The pensioners of the temple, the sons of noble families, sometimes even the sons of the king, lived in a separate building. Before advancing from the elementary to the higher school the pupils had to pass an examination. Having passed this examination, the student would select one of the higher teachers as his special teacher, and the latter, being once chosen, had the exclusive charge of his training, and the pupil owed him for life the allegiance of a client to his patron. A second examination had to be passed before the student could be admitted to the office of scribe or any other public office of the State. Those pupils who showed talent for sculpture, architecture, or painting were trained in a special art school; they likewise chose their own teachers In most cases the pupil's choice of a profession was dictated by that of his father. documents have been found in the grave of an architect stating that his family practised this profession for twenty-five successive generations.—All the teachers of these various schools were priests assigned to duty in the Seti-Temple There were more than 800 priests in charge of the teaching; they were divided into five classes, and were governed by the three "Prophets." The rooms of the priests opened on the corridors of the different buildings, whose courtyards (paved and covered with mats) were the "classrooms," and the students lived in the stories overhead. The discipline was severe: "The pupil's ears are found on his back; strike him, and he will lend you his ear," is the opinion of an educational writer of ancient Egypt. Much attention was given to memorizing The authority of the teacher was supreme, and this accounts for the rigorous training of the will The importance attached to memory-work prevented premature philosophizing

The educational system of ancient Egypt shows, in contrast to that of India, a realistic tendency: the Egyptians, though also interested in theological speculations, are interested, besides, in historical and physical realities, they also speculate about number and space, but they turn the knowledge of these matters to practical account, they are not content with satisfying the needs of the mind, but have an open eye for the needs of the body as well; they systematize and organize all that helps to conserve and transmit the treasures of the mind. In ancient Egypt, however, just as in India, religion is the basis of all knowledge and art and science: the earth is "the house of adoration," the worship of the deity is the final end of all human activity, and knowledge is to be sought only as a means for arriving at ethicoreligious perfection; books are to be a "sanatorium of the soul."[1]

CHAPTER VI.

The Nations Employing Cuneiform Writing.

1. The spelling out of the hieroglyphics has revealed much that was previously unknown of ancient Egypt, and similar results may be expected from the decipherment of the cuneiform writings for the nations of the Near East.   Much as the Turanian Chaldeans, the Semitic Babylonians and Ninevites, and the Iranians differ ethnographically, they are one in the use of this writing.   The culture of Egypt antedates, according to the view prevailing at present, the culture of these nations, and so the latter owe the beginning of their educational development to Egypt.   The Chaldeans, having been influenced directly by Egypt, transmitted their civilization to their Semitic conquerors, and these in turn passed on the intellectual heritage to the Medes and Persians.   According to another view, however, the Babylonians were the teachers of the Egyptians.[2]   The decipherment of the cuneiform inscriptions has in the history of the Chaldean and Semitic peoples revealed the case—certainly the earliest known case in the history of education—where the organized culture of an older people was transmitted whole and entire to a younger people.

While excavating at Nineveh, Layard discovered the remains of the royal *brick library*, of which some 30,000 fragments were sent to the British Museum.[3]   The tablets record matter pertaining to mythology, history, geography, statistics, natural history, astronomy, arithmetic, architecture, and grammar; and the different colors of the *bricks* (black, grey, blue, violet, red,

---

[1] Ἰατρεῖον ψυχῆς is the inscription placed by Osymandas on the library which he built at Thebes.   Diod., I, 49.

[2] Hommel, *Die semitischen Völker und Sprachen*, Vol. I, 1887.

[3] For the following cf. Hilprecht, *Explorations in Bible Lands*, Philadelphia, 1903, I, 1-577; Booth, *The Discovery and Decipherment of the Trilingual Cuneiform Inscriptions*, London, 1902; Vigouroux, *La Bible et les découvertes modernes en Palestine, en Egypte et en Assyrie*, Paris, 1896; Kaulen, *Assyrien und Babylonien*, Freiburg, 4th ed., 1891.

yellow, brown, white) signify the different sciences treated. One of the grammar tablets speaks of the origin of the library: "Palace of Asurbanipal, King of the World, King of Assyria, to whom the god Nebo and the goddess of instruction have given ears to hear, and whose eyes they have opened to see the foundation of government. They have revealed to the kings, my predecessors, this style of cuneiform writing. I have written on tablets the revelation of the god Nebo, the lord god of highest knowledge; I have ordered the tablets and have given them a place in my palace for the instruction of my subjects." The royal founder of this library is the fourth of his name, the warlike Sardanapalus of the Greeks, who reigned in Nineveh about the middle of the seventh century before Christ. But the monuments of learning which he collected, are not the work of the Semitic Assyrians, but translations from the older literature of the Chaldeans, who were the inventors of cuneiform writing and the earliest representatives of the civilization of Near Asia. To acquire an education, the Assyrian had to go to the works of the Chaldeans, written in an old-fashioned style of writing and couched in the Ural-Altaic language, of which the Finno-Ugric is a subfamily. It was the study of this language, spoken and written, which occupied the Prophet Daniel and his companions for the three years of their stay at the court of Nabuchodonosor, where "they received knowledge and understanding in every book, and wisdom" (Dan. 1, 4, 5, 17). The grammar tablets prove indirectly that the Assyrians could acquire the higher learning only by way of a tongue that was foreign to them. Out of about 100 of these tablets a reader has been made out, which served the purpose of explaining an older and foreign idiom in the language with which all were familiar. In the reader there are three columns of characters, and the first gives the Assyrian symbol, the second, the symbol for the Turanian-Chaldaic word (which is to be explained), while the last column gives the explanation in Assyrian, *i. e.*, in a Semitic language. This primer is undoubtedly older than Asurbanipal's library, and is, like all the intellectual work of Nineveh, patterned after Babylonian models.

The ancient writers are unanimous in praising the simplicity and thoroughness of Chaldean teaching. "They (the Chaldeans) transmit," says Diodorus, "their wisdom from one generation to the next: the boy is free from all other work and receives all wisdom from his father; and thus, having his own parent as teacher, the boy's instruction is comprehensive; the pupil never lacks attention, nor does he hesitate to give the fullest confidence to his master.   The schooling begins almost at the cradle, and hence with the natural docility of the child and the many years of learning, the best results are obtained."[1]   The higher education of such as had a mother-tongue other than the Chaldean must have been more systematic; what the Prophet Daniel describes is a sort of palace-school for Semitic youths.   The rapidly developing science of Assyriology promises to shed more light on this education, which must have been rich in foreign elements.   The opinion, first expressed by Professor Fr. Delitzsch, in his lectures *Bible and Babel*, in 1902, that the Mosaic Law can be traced back to older Babylonian laws, has given rise to much discussion, but the majority of scholars agree that the monotheism of Moses, the underlying principle of his laws, was not influenced by Babylonian teachings.

2. We lack the data to give an adequate description of Persian culture, which resulted from the mixture of Chaldaic-Assyrian elements with the native Aryan.   Greek writers praise the Persians for training their children to be truth-loving and useful members of the race.   They tell us that the wisest of the nation were chosen for teachers, whose duty it was to acquaint the young, by word and song, with the deeds of the gods and the nation's heroes.   The education of the king's sons was entrusted to the four wisest teachers, and it was their duty to make the princes sincere, just, and manly, and to introduce them to the occult science of Zoroaster.[2]   The Zoroastrian sacred writings, discovered in the 18th century, give an account of this magic as well as of the religion of ancient Persia and the laws based thereon.   From these writings we see that the priests enjoyed in Persia as much esteem as in India; that all classes were instructed in religion; and, incidentally, we learn of some customs obtaining in the Oriental schools.[3]   Yet we cannot

---

[1] Diod., II, 29.

[2] Her., I, 136; Strabo, XV, p. 733; Plut., *Alc.*, I, p. 121.

[3] In the *Zend-Avesta* we find occasionally the catechetical method as well as the use of numbers as aids to the memory.   We quote the following passage as containing these two elements and as giving in the briefest compass the social and moral system of Iranian civilization.   "The speech spoken by Ahura-Mazda contains three principal points and mentions five castes and four masters.   Which are the three principal points?   Good thoughts, good words, and good actions.   Which are the four castes?   Priests, warriors, tillers of the soil, and merchants. The Lord and the Law teach that all that is praiseworthy becomes the possession of him whose thoughts, words, and actions are true.   The deeds of the pure mean for the world an increase in purity.

ascertain whether the knowledge and learning of the Persian priests has, as in India and Egypt, ever given rise to various scientific and cultural studies.   But the ease and quick despatch with which the Greeks---beginning with Alexander the Great— destroyed the national culture, superseding it with their own, may be considered proof enough that Persia never enjoyed the wide-spread and diversified education of India and Egypt. Persian culture had not entered deeply enough into the life of the people and was therefore too weak, as not possessing body enough, to offer an effective resistance to the encroachment of foreign elements.   It fell back along the entire line, and at the time of the Sassanids the ancient spirit of the nation was dead; it had to be recreated entirely, and in this process of recreation the remains of the ancient religion proved the best aid.   It was only at this time, in the third century of the Christian era, that the nation took up the scientific study of its sacred writings, and this study was continued with such success as to go beyond the translation and interpretation of the text and to treat cosmology, natural and universal history.   These various subjects are treated compendiously in the *Bundahish*,[1] which was compiled in the Middle Ages.

CHAPTER VII.

The Hebrews.

1. The Hebrews are connected with the other Eastern nations by many different ties: they are a Semitic people; in early times they were influenced by Egyptian civilization; and later

Which are the masters? The master of the household, the chief of the tribe, the lord of the community, and the ruler of the province; Zarathustra is the fifth master. When is a thought good? When the wisest entertain pure thoughts. What speech is good? Sacred speech. When is an action good? When the purest perform a deed while praising the Lord. Ahura-Mazda has spoken. Whom has he addressed? He has spoken to the pure of heaven and earth. In what capacity has he spoken? He has spoken as the best of kings." *Jacna*, XIX, 44-58.

[1] The book, edited and translated by Ferdinand Justi (1868), treats, in concise form and with continual reference to the *Avesta*, the following subjects: creation of the world, the conflict between the powers of good and evil, the properties of the earth, mountains, seas, rivers, animals, etc., the earliest history of man, generation, resurrection, motions of the planets, mythical stories, chronology, and the succession of dynasties.

by the civilization of the Near East. Still they occupy among the peoples of the East a unique position, as may be seen also from the unique type of education that they developed. Their sacred books, the Sacred Scriptures, revered alike by Jew and Christian, differ from the canonical books of polytheistic peoples: Their core is not a book of hymns, from which the sacred law, sacred history, and sacred science might have grown. Instead, the Bible begins with history and bases the laws upon it, and lets the hymns, the prophecies, and the wisdom of the proverbs follow after. The *gesta Dei* are the foundation of the whole; they are the key to the Law, the perennial inspiration of piety and meditation. The *Pentateuch* lacks the tendency of the *Veda* or of the books of Thoth to encourage speculative and poetic thought. Nor does its doctrine of the one God lead to the study of astronomy, or of magnitude, or of numbers. The theocratic form of government lends little glamor to the deeds of war and of heroes; and a form of worship in which all pictorial representations are forbidden, retards the growth of the fine as well as the mechanical arts. Thus all that is needed for the development of priestly learning no less than for the organization of the work of teaching, was missing with the Hebrews. In content their teaching was restricted to the Law and the history of the nation, but in form it was the more free and varied: the master of the household, the priest, the prophet, one and all, taught the word of God. The word of God was, like the omnipresent Lord, to strike upon the ear at home and in the field, at night and in the morning (V. Moses, VI, 7). It should meet the eye everywhere, and should be expressed in written words and meaningful symbols; and the language of the people should never weary of explaining the worship and the monuments of God's greatness. (II. Moses, XII, 26; XIII, 14; Josue, IV, 6; V. Moses, XXXII, 7.)

The Lord Himself has trained the people of His election "as a man traineth up his son" (V. Moses, VIII, 5), and has taught it "profitable things and led it in the way it should walk" (Is., XLVIII, 17). Thus God Himself sanctifies all teaching and discipline. The instruction of the individual is only a repetition on a small scale of what the Lord has wrought in the generations of His chosen people, and the teacher merely implants anew and protects from the natural temptation of polytheism that higher principle which had been planted and safeguarded by the Lord in the beginning. Thus the teacher's vocation reflects God's activity: "They that are learned shall shine as the brightness of the firmament; and they that instruct many to justice, as stars for all eternity" (Dan., XII, 3). Each individual is, like the whole nation, the object of the loving care and guidance of the Lord, who knew each man "when he was made in secret, and who ordered his days ere one of these was at hand." (Ps. 138, 15; cf. Ps. 21, 10; Jer., I, 7.) Consequently, the value of the individual personality is rated higher among the Hebrews than among the other·ancient peoples of the East; the religious faith of the individual is deepened, and he assumes a higher nature. For instance, no people of the East has produced any individuality that could compare with the clear-cut characters of the Hebrew prophets. With other nations an individual could scarcely—and that but rarely —rise above the rank and file of the caste.

2. Thus the ancient Hebrews were a teaching people, even if they had no organized system of schools. It was the faith in their God that developed their minds to such a degree as is generally attained only with rich and free elements of education. The period before the Exile produced only the beginnings of a system of education. The schools of the prophets, which are frequently mentioned in Scripture,[1] do not invite comparison with the temple schools of ancient Egypt. They have been explained in most diversified ways. The Fathers of the Church looked upon them as predecessors of monastic institutions. The rabbis explained them as academics. Protestant theologians considered them training schools for preachers. The Deists regarded them as schools of free thought and moral philosophy. However, it may now be considered as an established fact that they were circles of disciples who gathered about men eminent for sanctity and divine gifts, for the purpose of conserving the sacred traditions and of cultivating the art of sacred music; these gatherings, however, seem to have lacked the character of permanent organizations.[2]

We have no records of popular education in early Hebrew history. But the art of writing appears to have been generally known, as may be concluded from the law that every Israelite should write the most important of God's precepts "in the entry and on the doors of his house" (V. Moses, VI, 9). It is probable that the Hebrews continued to practice the art of surveying, which they had brought along from Egypt (Jos.,

[1] I. Kings, X, 5 ff.; IV. Kings, II, 3 ff.; IV, 38.
[2] *Catholic Encyclopedia*, s. v., *Prophecy*.

XVIII, 4 ff.). Music, especially liturgical music, in which all present at the divine services joined, was a general accomplishment. (Ps. 67, 26 ff., and elsewhere.)

A system of higher education was organized only after the Exile. The reason was the same as with the Persians: the need of safeguarding what remained of the nation's intellectual property and of restoring what was destroyed. In the day of trial the Law alone had saved the nation from complete destruction, and with the restoration of peace came a zeal for its conscientious observance. This observance, however, necessitated a thorough study of the Law, and such a study was the chief duty of the Sopherim, whose first representative was Esra (about 450 B. C.). The Book of Ecclesiasticus, written in the Alexandrian Period, speaks of the studies of the scribe, or doctor of the Law, who was at that time the representative of a social class (chapter XXXVIII, 25 ff.): "The wisdom of a scribe cometh by his time of leisure; and he that is less in action, shall receive wisdom. With what wisdom shall he be furnished that holdeth the plough and that glorieth in the goad, that driveth the oxen therewith and is occupied in their labors?...He shall give his mind to turn up furrows, and his care is to give the kine fodder. So every craftsman and workmaster that laboreth day and night, he who maketh graven seals, and by his continual diligence varieth the figure: he shall give his mind to the resemblance of the picture, and by his watching shall finish the work... The wise man will seek out the wisdom of all the ancients, and he will be occupied in the prophets. He will keep the sayings of renowned men, and will enter withal into the subtleties of parables. He will search out the hidden meanings of proverbs, and will be conversant in the secrets of parables." But that the knowledge of the doctor of the Law is not confined to Scripture, is evident from the Book of Wisdom, dating from about the same time, where the scribe (ch. VII, 18-21) is said to be versed in "the beginning and ending and midst of the times, the alterations of their courses and the changes of the seasons, the revolutions of the year and the dispositions of the stars, the natures of living creatures and rage of wild beasts, the force of winds and reasonings of men, the diversities of plants and the virtues of roots; and all such things as are hid and not foreseen, I have learned, for wisdom, which is the worker of all things, taught me." Thus the way was open for the development of theology and its auxiliary sciences, which now grew up about Scripture as their centre, and which were later collected in the *Mischna* and the *Talmud*.

3. The changed conditions after the Exile that led to improvements in the higher schools, necessitated a corresponding improvement in the schools of the masses. The language of Scripture was no longer the language of the people, and knowledge could be handed down only through systematic instruction in the home and the school. The highpriest Joshua ben Gamla introduced, about 67 of the Christian era, a system of elementary schools; he ordained that each town, and even each village, should open an elementary school for children. Moses Maimonides says of the Jews of the Middle Ages that they everywhere employed teachers of boys, and that they would curse the town where no such instruction was given, or, if that availed not, even destroy it, "because the world existed solely by the breath of school boys."[1] The deep interest in studies gave rise to the belief that a system of schools was described in the Bible, and that the Jewish system of education dated, therefore, from the earliest times. To the rabbis the patriarchs appeared as the founders of academies; and the tribe of Simeon they regarded as the tribe of teachers and as enjoying, in consequence, a dignity fully equal to that of the tribe Levi, etc. Of the methods of teaching, that of interpretation or exegesis was cultivated most. The need of harmonizing different interpretations gave rise to the disputation, which is a method of teaching peculiar to the Jews. Language teaching, however, did not develop beyond the primitive stage; and the first systematic study of Hebrew grammar was made as late as the 11th century by Rabbi Jona, who followed the methods of Arabian grammarians.

The old method, still in vogue to-day, for introducing the child to the language of the Thora, consists in having the teacher first speak the words and sentences of the text, next translate them, and finally let the pupil memorize all. Thus the text is read, explained, and memorized without one single word of grammatical analysis.[2] This method was followed by the Hebrew teachers of Reuchlin, Trotzendorf, and A. H. Francke; and Esra Ezardi, Francke's teacher, defended it as embodying the first principle of language instruction: "*Lege biblia, relege biblia, repete biblia.*" Wolfgang Ratke and others adopted it in the 17th century for the teaching of the classical languages, and it

---

[1] Schwarz, *Erziehungslehre*, Leipzig, 1829, I, I, p. 204.
[2] Jost, Brzoska's *Zentralbibliothek*, 1839, Feb. issue, pp. 49 ff.

was useful in offsetting the evil effects of the one-sided grammatical method.

The Jews of later days have repeatedly rendered special services to Western education by being the intermediaries in transmitting certain educational elements from the East. In the Middle Ages they played an important rôle as the connecting link between Moslemin and Christians; to the latter their philosophical and medical works were particularly helpful; and it is owing principally to the Jews, that the oriental tales and legends have become so widely known in the West.[1] In the Renaissance the rabbis were in great demand for teaching Hebrew and other oriental languages, and the pantheism of the Kabbalah was a deep influence in the philosophy of the age. Jewish rationalists were an important factor in popularizing the philosophy of the 18th century. However, at the present time the Jewish elements are assimilating more and more with western culture. The specific features of Jewish education are fast disappearing, and represent, in fact, a mere remnant of Hebrew culture, although still an interesting object of study. "With no class of people will you find among the savants so few books and among the lower orders so many books, as among those Jewish elements of our population that have remained faithful to the ancient ideals of their race. Nowhere else will you find anybody taking so much delight in a book as among the Jews, and often, after having driven the most sordid of bargains, they appear to refresh their minds by recurring in their conversation ever and anon to the sublimest of subjects. You will frequently find the wretched dealer in second-hand goods, or the trader in cattle, bending of a Sabbath, or of a winter's evening, over old and venerable tomes, studying the most abstruse casuistry, or revelling in Hebrew history or poetry, or writing for publication."[2]

CHAPTER VIII.

China.

1. Chinese education has been influenced very little by the peoples we have been dealing with, and hence it differs essentially from their educational systems. The education of China

---

[1] Benfey, *Pantschatranta*, I, pp. 10, 26 ff.
[2] Jost, l. c.

lacks the religious foundation. The Chinese mind is fixed upon the things of this world and does not connect them with a higher order. The fine arts, as finding their highest inspiration in religion, are neglected, while the mechanical arts attained early a high degree of excellence. The moral life lacks the ennobling and sanctifying element that might raise it above the trivial and insipid. Science ranges over broad and varied fields, but does so at the expense necessarily of depth, the natural result of the absence of the speculative element. "The life of the Chinese is workaday and profane; the State takes the place of the Church; the laity has crowded out the clergy; the workday supersedes the holyday; memorial halls take the place of temples and shrines."[1] The canonical or classical books, which are the basis of Chinese education, are not regarded as religious or sacred. They are not an inheritance, guarded by priests, but mere compilations of current traditions made for moral and educational purposes by Confucius, "the King of Teachers" (about 550 B. C.). "To the *King*, edited by Confucius, the model of literary form, the acme of philosophic wisdom, is largely due that extraordinary stability of Chinese thought and institutions which is the wonder of the world." The *Five Classics* of Confucius are: *Y-king*, the book of changes, 64 figures, unintelligible even at the time of their first publication, which probably signify some cosmological facts; *She-king*, the book of odes, a collection of 311 moral, political, and lyrical poems; *Shao-king*, the book of history; *Li-ki*, the book of rites; and *Ch'un-ts'ew*, *Spring and Autumn*, the last-named being the only one claiming Confucius as the actual author. To the *King* must be added the *Four Books*: *Lun Lü*, or Analects of Confucius, his views and maxims retailed by his disciples; the *Book of Mencius*; *Ta Hsüeh*, or Great Learning; and *Chung Yung*, or Doctrine of the Mean, a short treatise enlarging upon Confucius' teaching about conduct, and ascribed to his grandson K'ung Chi. These classics occasioned innumerable commentaries and paraphrases, and the whole vast field of Chinese literature, history, didactic works, and poetry, is indirectly connected with them. The polyhistor Chu Hsi (1130-1200) is important in the history of education for having compiled in works, large and small, all that he thought worthy of preservation. For the instruction of the young he compiled the encyclopedia *Siao-hio, i. e., The Small Study*.[2] No

[1] Adolf Wuttke, *Geschichte des Heidentums*, Breslau, 1853, II, p. 68.
[2] Heinrich Wuttke, *Geschichte der Schrift und des Schrifttums*, Leipzig, 1872, p. 353.

science of language developed in connection with the study of these early writings. The Chinese are indifferent to the spoken word, for they regard it as the mere expression of the written characters, which may be read according to different dialects; and thus the study of grammar dwindles down to an explanation of the pictured symbols.[1] The Chinese never lacked the elements of the mathematical sciences: in the 11th century B. C. arithmetic and the calendar were widely known, maps of the empire were drawn on vases, and tables of statistics posted in public places. But it was only in the Middle Ages that they received of the Arabians the rudiments of astronomy and geometry and of the Hindus their system of notation.[2] The Chinese esteem music for its ennobling effects on the young: its function is to produce the harmony of souls, to be the step leading to wisdom, and to prove a type of the order that ought to prevail in a well-organized community. Yet music has not developed in China, neither on its æsthetical nor its theoretical side, and the method of writing music the Chinese learned only of Christian missionaries.

2. The *King*, seven small volumes with many commentaries, are the chief subject in higher education. The pupils copy the text and try to fix in their memory and imagination the characters peculiar to the book studied. The more advanced pupils analyze the text, and practice the use of lists of pictured words. The most important work, however, is the writing of compositions, for which the subjects are taken either from the classics or from encyclopedias.[3] Some attention is also given to the writing of verses and to the acquiring of a business style. Despite the dryness and severity of the instruction—the picture of a hand holding a rod represents the word *kiao* to teach—the pupils leave school with a taste for literature. A man of education will invariably have a library of scientific and literary works, and will also visit the public library quite frequently, besides reading his magazines and newspapers at home.

Elementary instruction is, like the higher education, chiefly a matter of memory and of the skillful use of the brush-pen. It deals, however, only with the common characters, the knowledge of which does not yet fit a person to read the higher literature. The most widely used elementary textbook is the *San-*

---

[1] Ibid., pp. 320 ff., 402 ff.
[2] Ibid., pp. 277, 364 ff.
[3] Ibid., p. 388.

8

tse-king, which was written in the 13th century of the Christian era by the teacher Wang-po-heu. It contains 1068 word-pictures in groups of three, joined by rimes, and touches upon all that is thought most necessary for life. Many books have been written to explain its contents and to suggest the best methods for imparting its material to children.[1] The children's schooling begins at the age of five or six. Several years are spent first in learning to sketch roughly the pictures of words and then in making more exact drawings of them; before the age of fourteen to sixteen, pupils can rarely read and write.[2]

The West has taken a new interest in Chinese encyclopedias since the publication, in 1905, of the great encyclopedia in French and Chinese, comprising twelve volumes and edited by the Jesuit Wieger. This monumental work, honored with the grand prize of the Paris *Académie des inscriptions et belles-lettres,* comprises Chinese grammar, literary as well as colloquial, dialogues, orations, ethics, philosophy, history up to the date of publication, written characters, etymology, dictionary, etc. 40,000 letters had to be cast for the printing of the encyclopedia, and the work was done by Chinese under the direction of lay-brothers.

The Chinese newspapers have had a long history. The *Peking Gazette (Tsching-pao, News of the Capital)* is said to have been founded 911 B. C.; it appeared in print since 1351, has been issued daily since 1800, and is now published three times a day; each issue appearing, according to the time of day, on yellow, white, or green paper.

---

[1] Neumann, who edited it along with a translation and commentary (Munich, 1836), was the first to bring this textbook to the knowledge of the West. The following is a summary of its contents: importance of education, examples of good children, numbers, the three fundamental entities (heaven, earth, man), the three duties (patriotism, piety, conjugal love), the four seasons, the four cardinal points, the five elements (water, fire, wood, metal, earth), the five virtues (humanity, justice, good taste, wisdom, fidelity), the six kinds of grain, the six domestic animals, the seven passions (joy, anger, aversion, fear, love, hatred, lust), the eight tones, the nine generations from the great-great-grandfather to the great-great-grandchild, the ten moral ties (between father and son, between the married, between brothers, king and people, old and young, and friends). This is followed by a list of the canonical books, a survey of the country's history, admonitions to industry, and examples of industry. The popularity of this primer has recently induced Christian missionaries to preserve its form while Christianizing its content, and the attempt is reported to have proved very successful.

[2] H. Wuttke, l. c., pp. 386 ff.

3. The State supervised and assisted the schools in the earliest times. The Emperor Yao, the Chinese Alfred (2205-2198 B. C.), divided the government lands, and apportioned off no small part of them for school purposes.[1] In 1097 B. C. an imperial edict of the Emperor Tscheu decreed the establishment of large and small schools throughout the country.[2] Till 750 B. C. the schools of the country were state institutions. The school of the court, the highest in rank, had its own teachers; but in the provinces the teaching was committed to state officials, regardless of their age or experience.[3] The schools were an integral part of the imperial police system. But the schools of modern China are private, and by supervising the examinations the State provides both for the uniformity and the spreading of knowledge. Because the examinations determine the individual's social and political rank, the interest in education is intense and general. Every village boasts a school, and evening and night schools are numerous in all towns.[4] To be admitted to society or to be classed among the men of education, one must pass the first examination, which consists in writing several compositions on subjects taken generally from the *King;* three prose compositions and one poem must be written on four texts taken from the classics. It is estimated that no more than five per cent of the candidates pass this examination, and, though their number cannot be stated exactly, Chinese authorities confess it to be a full million. To ensure the possession of the title obtained by this examination, the holder must every three years pass a similar test. The next higher examination lasts a full month and admits the candidate to a public office. The third examination is taken to obtain the title of savant and to be eligible to the highest state positions; it lasts thirteen days, consists in writing compositions in elegant style, and can be taken only in the capital of the country. The savants desiring to be members of the Peking Academy of Sciences (founded in the ninth century of the Christian era) must pass a final examination in the imperial palace; this examination is not confined, as the others, to certain periods of time.[5]

[1] Plath, *Ueber Schule, Unterricht und Erziehung bei den alten Chinesen,* Munich, 1868, p. 13.
[2] H. Wuttke, l. c., p. 278.
[3] Plath, l. c., p. 56.
[4] Fr. Müller, *Ethnographie,* 1873, p. 392.
[5] Plath, l. c., p. 6.

By this system education and scholarship obtain a politico-economical importance; knowledge is a social power, yea, an attribute of public power.   Yet the encyclopedic character of knowledge and the value of formal accomplishments are stressed equally in all the various examinations.   It is not professional knowledge that fits a man for public office, but his knowledge of language, and the savant differs from the man of general education, not in possessing a different knowledge, but solely in the greater volume of his learning.   The subject-matter of elementary and higher education is practically identical.   It is, then, but natural that in China the acquisition of knowledge goes hand in hand with spreading it.   It is significant that the symbol for one of the terms for "teaching" (*hoei*) combines the signs for "word" and for "everyman," thus expressing that to teach is "to transmit words for everyman."   Similarly, the terms for the one who knows and for the one who teaches, play, as in the English "master," into each other.[1]   The Chinese proverbs: "To teach and to learn imply a mutual growth," "Teaching is half learning," also voice the idea that the receiving of an intellectual content connotes that it will be transmitted to others.

Chinese institutions and writings embody the view that teaching and learning must be moral in aim.   In the *Li-ki*, (*The Mirror of Morality*), we read, "The righteous scholar should look upon a righteous heart as his chief treasure; honesty should be his best possession; and the enriching of his mind should be his profession."[2]   Chu Hsi, describing the difference between the two grades of education, says, "The lower education teaches moral living and the ways and means of making moral progress.   But it is only the higher education that gives a clear insight into the foundations of morality; it is the highest perfection of all norms and the full development of the mind; it teaches why we are enjoined to lead a moral life and to make progress on the path of virtue."[3]

The educational system of China has frequently been overestimated.   Its admirers praised the Chinese for recruiting the state officials from the ranks of scholars; but they failed to note that by this very privilege the scholar became a mere official. They rejoiced that writers were admitted to high places; but

[1] Ibid., p. 26.
[2] Heinrich Wuttke, l. c., p. 391.
[3] Adolf Wuttke, l. c., II, p. 198.

they overlooked that thus the entire field of writing and literature was left to the mercy of the state functionary. While admiring the industry of the Chinese, they did not note how valueless is the matter thrashed out by this ceaseless activity. The Chinese were congratulated upon the fact that their system of education precludes all friction between Church and State, between religious and secular education. But this advantage was secured at too dear a price, for it involved the sacrifice of high ideals, as is evident from the restless and joyless drudgery of the people.

III.

GREEK EDUCATION.

CHAPTER IX.

The Content of Greek Education.

1. The difference between the East and Greece is too striking to have escaped the Greek philosophers, and they have, indeed, described very clearly the contrast between the two civilizations. They prefer their own countrymen for all that pertains to the activities of the State and public life. For the Greek, so they contend, was by nature, by his inherent energy and the consciousness of his powers, well qualified to enjoy the boon of liberty, whereas the Orientals, lacking in political sagacity, had sunk into slavery.[1] Still they are broadminded enough to pay generous tribute to the knowledge and learning of the East, which, dating from the earliest times, continued to grow about a never-changing core, and was guarded as a sacred treasure and transmitted in an unbroken line to successive generations. Occasionally, the Greek philosophers even express the wish that their own people, alert and active though they were, might leave off from running after the novel and cling to some similar foundation of culture.[2]

Though a former age might, in its idolizing of the Greek spirit, have refused to admit Hamitic or Semitic influences in Greek education, we must at the present time, in the light of well-known facts, acknowledge that the East played a large rôle in the development of Greek learning and civilization. It is to-day an established fact that the glory of the Greek learning at Alexandria was the result, at least in part, of the treasures collected there by the Egyptians, and that the Egyptians had in still earlier times been the teachers of the Greeks in the mathematical and technical sciences. It is equally certain that forms of worship, myths, fables, tales, songs, and wise sayings, were

---

[1] Her., VII, 101-105 and elsewhere; Arist., *Pol.*, VII, 6, p. 1327; *Her.*, II, 4, 77, 79 ff.

[2] Plato, *Tim.*, p. 22 (see *supra* p. 89); I. *Alc.*, p. 121; *Legg.*, VII, pp. 798 ff.; Diod., II, 29 (see *supra* p. 104).

imported into Greece from the East, and that it was the Sem-
ites who in pre-Homeric times taught the art of writing to the
Greeks. Eduard Röth has collected the oriental influences of
the different periods and presents them as links of a chain; he
has demonstrated that Greek culture is based on oriental, and
particularly Egyptian, elements.[1] Otto Gruppe takes a similar
view in his great, if incomplete, work,[2] and adduces a wealth of
material to prove his contention, though his erratic conception
of the nature of religion makes many readers doubt some of his
conclusions. These researches have called attention to another
factor, already noted by Friedrich Creuzer,[3] but later lost sight
of, viz., pre-Homeric theology, which is unmistakably similar to
oriental beliefs, and which is a cultural element preserved by
the priests, and at the same time, because it cannot be entirely
drawn from foreign sources, native to Greek soil.

In this pre-Homeric theology we must look for the beginnings of Greek intellectual life and, therefore, also for the first
sources of Greek education. The Appolonian circle of beliefs,
to which the worship of the Muses belonged, and from which
the epic and the lyric sprang, represent one side of these priestly
teachings, while the mysteries, which are the source of the
occult ritual and the drama, are their other side.

The service of the Muses—which term later designated the
devotion to the arts and sciences—was originally a form of
religious worship practiced by priests. The Muses had bestowed
not only the arts of singing and music, but (as is apparent from
the names of some of them: Mnemosyne, Clio, Urania, Polymathia) the knowledge of early times, the remembrance of glorious deeds, the knowledge of the cosmic phenomena—the learning, in fact, of all kinds was recognized as the gift of the Muses.
Plato calls Calliope and Urania the eldest of the Muses, which
is the same as saying that the knowledge of the past and of the
heavens antedates all other sciences.[4] Orpheus was celebrated
not only for having brought to men the charm of song, but
also for having disclosed the secrets of nature and for having
taught men the art of healing. Musæus is said to have written

---

[1] E. Röth, *Geschichte unserer abendländischen Philosophie*, Mannheim, 1862,
particularly Vol. II, pp. 278 ff., III, 1 ff., 71 ff.

[2] O. Gruppe, *Die griechischen Kulte und Mythen in ihren Beziehungen zu
den orientalischen Religionen*, Vol. I, Leipzig, 1887.

[3] Fr. Creuzer, *Symbolik und Mythologie der alten Völker, besonders der
Griechen*, 2nd ed., I-IV, Leipzig, 1819.

[4] Plato, *Phæd.*, p. 259 d.

a book on astronomy, and Linos' poetry dealt with astronomy and natural history.[1] The hymns and prayers of these poet-priests were preserved even at a later day in shrines and temples, *e. g.*, in Delos. From these hymns and prayers the later poetry derived "the first notions concerning the structure of the world, the dominions of the Olympian gods and the Titans, the established epithets which are applied to the gods, without reference to the peculiar circumstances under which they appear, and which often disagree with the rest of the epic mythology."[2] But the ideas current among these Pierian bards assumed no sufficiently definite shape to prove the foundation of a priestly education; it was left to epic poetry to become the standard for all later time.

2. Among the epic poets Homer held undisputed sway, and the Greeks regarded him as the father of their whole intellectual life. Common opinion had it that he had, in union with Hesiod, "fixed the genealogical table of the gods, had given them their names, their character, and had determined the forms of worship."[3] Homer was the teacher of all poets that came after him: their works were but "crumbs from his sumptuous banquet."[4] He was for all writings "the model and the source, even as the ocean is the source for all streams and springs."[5] He was the eternal fountain-head of the national spirit, whence the Greeks could ever draw new strength for their struggle with the forces of barbarism.[6] His poetry was considered the inexhaustible source of ideas, of views of life and nature, and even of scientific knowledge and of philosophical principles:[7] "He is the source of all culture and all science that has entered

---

[1] Horace, *Ars Poet.*, 391; Diog. Laert., *Proœm.*, §§ 3 and 4.

[2] K. O. Müller and J. W. Donaldson, *History of the Literature of Ancient Greece*, London, 1858, p. 39.

[3] Her., II, 53.

[4] Plato, *Rep.*, X, p. 585; *Athen.*, VIII, 49, where Aeschylus calls his tragedy τεμάχη τῶν Ὁμήρου μεγάλων δείπνον.

[5] Quintilian, X, 1 in.

[6] Isocrates, *Paneg.*, 159.

[7] Though Plato is opposed to the Homeric worldview, he does not hesitate to quote quite freely from Homer's verses, which he calls ἔπη κατὰ θεὸν πως εἰρημένα καὶ κατὰ φύσιν (*Legg.*, III, p. 682). Alkidamas calls the *Odyssey* a beautiful mirror of human life: καλὸν ἀνθρωπίνου βίου κάθοπτρον (Arist., *Rhetor.*, III, 3). The Sophists were eager to prove Homer the father of their system (Plat., *Prot.*, p. 316). Krates of Mallos interprets all the learning of the Alexandrian age into the poet (Strab., III, p. 157).

into human life."[1] "He was the educator of Greece and laid
down the norms for the inner and outer forms of life."[2]

The canon, then, of Greek education is not the sacred texts
of priests, but the creations of poetic genius. At the bottom
of this poetry there was no set of teachings that would attach
the mind to a fixed content, but the pictures of the nation's
great achievements, which ennobled the young as well by the
easily understood meaning as by the perfection of form. To
behold this glorious panorama, to understand it, to enjoy it,
was not reserved to one privileged caste which would share
only in a small measure its knowledge with the masses. No,
it was granted to each and everyone of the Greeks to learn of
Achilles' wrath and the wanderings of Ulysses, to train his ear
with the hexameter's rythmic flow, to store his fancy with the
splendid pictures of the epic, and to enrich his mind and heart
with the wisdom of the father of poets. All poetic and artistic
activity of the Greeks followed in the wake of Homer, and, as
his poetry appealed to the whole people, it was a thing of beauty
that enriched in many ways the national and public life.

3. To make Homer's poetry accessible to all was one of the
chief objects of the liberal education (*musische Bildung*) of the
Greeks, for the latter tended to make the individual apprecia-
tive and receptive of the intellectual treasures belonging to the
whole nation. It comprised the teaching of reading and writing, the reading and memorizing of texts, and vocal and instrumental music. The elements of grammar were taught by the
γραμματιστής, who made use of various helps. One such help
was the grammar play written by Kallias, a writer of comedies of about 400 B.C., in which the 24 letters of the Ionic alphabet, which was then to be introduced, appeared on the
stage in due order. Combinations of the different letters were
spoken and sung. The play was written in verse, and followed
in all its details (prologue, chorus, etc.) the plan of the classical
tragedy.[3] In the Alexandrian age grammar was taught in connection with the elementary instruction. Three parts of speech
were recognized: noun, verb, and conjunction (ὀνόματα, ῥή-
ματα, συνδεσμοί). The pupils were taught the phonetic changes
(συστολαί, ἐκτάσεις, shortening and lengthening); accents, and
the categories of inflection (γένη, genera, πτώσεις, casus, ἀριθμοί,

---

[1] Dion. Hal., *ad Cn. Pomp.*, § 13.

[2] Plato, *Rep.*, X, p. 606: τὴν Ἑλλάδα πεπαίδευκεν οὗτος ὁ ποιητής κ. τ. λ.

[3] For the most detailed account see Grassberger, *Erziehung und Unterricht
im klassischen Altertum*, Part II, Würzburg, 1875, pp. 263 ff.

numeri, ἐγκλίσεις, modi).[1] The matter read, or memorized, as
well as the texts of songs differed in the different parts of Greece;
the Cretes memorized their laws set to music, the Arcadians
memorized hymns; and the Athenians, both laws and hymns.[2]
The fables of Aesop were read everywhere: it was proverbial to
say of an uneducated man, "he has not worn Aesop down on his
shoes."[3] Homer was likewise read in all schools, and it would
seem that anthologies were also in use; at least the model collection made by Plato (*Legg.*, VII, p. 810) seems to presuppose
an earlier collection of the kind. It was a common practice in
the golden age of Greek literature to interpret what had been
read, to declaim select passages, to repeat the contents, and so
forth   But in the Alexandrian age there was a distinction made
between the æsthetical appreciation and the interpretation of
the content. The æsthetical or rhetorical interpretation occasioned imitations of the style, the writings of chrias, sketches
of characters and of particular scenes.[4]

The popular view attached great educational value to music,
and the Pythagorean philosophy confirmed this opinion. Harmony and rhythm, we are told, enter into the soul, and, being
a civilizing influence, they give balance and symmetry to man's
nature. Furthermore, they render the soul sensitive to beauty
and justice, and this at an age when reasoning or formal instruction is out of the question. And, over and above these
considerations, music is called a most suitable occupation of
leisure hours, and the appreciation of musical masterpieces is
said to prove the source of refined pleasures.[5] The fine musical
sense of the Greeks attributed to each instrument, and even to
the different tones, a very definite character and a correspond-

[1] Ibid , p 259 and Ussing, *Darstellung des Erziehungs-und Unterrichtswesens
bei den Griechen und Romern*, Altona, 1870, p 107   The principal passages
in Dionys. Halic , *de compos verb* , 25 and *de admir vi dic in Dem* , 52

[2] Aelian Var , *hist* , II, 39, Polyb , IV, 20, Aristoph , *Nubb* , 967, Luc ,
Anach , 22

[3] Aristoph , *Av* , 471   Aesop's fables are still the most popular of all that
the Greeks introduced from the East into the schools of the West   The home
of these fables is undoubtedly the East, but some would trace them to Egypt
(Zundel, *Aesop in Aegypten*, Bonn, 1846); others to India (Otto Keller, *Unter-
suchungen uber die Geschichte der griechischen Fabel*, Leipzig, 1862), A Weber
(*History of Indian Literature*, London, 1878, p 211) inclines to the view that
the Greek beast-fable is a "Semitic growth," while Keller suggests an Assyrian
channel of communication

[4] Ussing, l. c , pp 123 ff

[5] Especially Plato, *Prot* , p. 326, *Rep* , III, p 398 ff , Arist , *Pol* , VIII,
5, pp 1339 ff

ing effect. The flute was said to awaken the passions. The tones of the seven-stringed lyre were thought to possess a certain fullness and to ennoble the listener. The Doric key was employed for voicing sentiments of masculine strength and consciousness of power; and some thought the Lydian, others the Phrygian, key expressive of tender feelings.

Gymnastics was considered the complement of liberal education, with which it was correlated by common aims and connecting links. The aim of gymnastics was to impart both strength and grace. Music and gymnastics were combined in the art of the dance and in the measured step, which kept time with, and followed the rythm of, music.[1] There was a complete system of gymnastic rules, which necessitated the theoretical instruction in the art. As physical culture, gymnastics was closely related to medical science, and in some regards overlapped it.[2]

The so-called *School of Douris* (c. 450 B. C.) is a good representation of the education of Greek boys.[3] In the middle of the picture we see a lad taking a bath. The four pictures surrounding this subject represent: a bearded teacher of the lyre with his pupil; the same teacher unfolding a roll to the lad before him, while the pedagogue with his walking-staff is seated in the rear; a young teacher of the flute with his pupil; and lastly the same teacher writing on a tablet with the pedagogue again near at hand.

After the period of formal schooling the course of liberal education was continued amid the splendid opportunities provided on all sides. The gymnasium and the palæstra invited the adults to their halls for athletic exercises and the pleasures of social intercourse. Concerts, public and private, kept alive the interest in music. The theatre did the same for Homer. Public orations and discussions stimulated the taste for oratory and style. Aristippus remarked that the least, but still appreciable, benefit of Greek schooling was that the youth would not sit like a stone on the theatre seats of stone.[4] With this co-operation between school and life, it was to be expected

---

[1] Plato (I, *Alc.*, p. 108) connects the ἐμβαίνειν ὀρθῶς with the μουσική; the dance and the measured step are, however, generally associated with gymnastics.

[2] Cf. Plato, *Rep.*, III, pp. 403 ff.

[3] Reproduced in *Cyclopedia of Education*, ed. by Paul Monroe, s. v. *Education in Ancient Greece*.

[4] Diog. Lært., VIII, § 72.

that the schools would readily add new subjects to their curriculum whenever a new interest entered into the life of the
people. "When the national wealth increased and with it the
leisure, when men were hungry for new deeds and achievements,
especially in the pride of their victory over the Medes, then
the people seized upon whatever was to be learned, intent less
upon selection than upon quantity."[1] Thus the study of drawing became popular about the middle of the fourth century
B C., through the influence of the painter Pamphilos of Sicyon.[2]
The Sophists had even earlier introduced the study of rhetoric
and the practice of public debates Mathematics and geography were introduced into the common schools only after
having been taught for a long time in the schools of the philosophers.

4. The aim of this liberal education was to refine the intellectual life so that it might accord with what was demanded
of the free-born Greek It made gentlemen, and it was originally concerned as little with religious training as with the
higher learning. The works of Homer, the basis of this liberal
education, were replete with cultural elements, but afforded
little incentive to science and research. Some enthusiastic admirers ignorantly hailed Homer as the father of science. But
they who saw the beginnings of scientific studies in the theological treatises of priests or in the wisdom brought from the
Orient, were much nearer the truth.[3] In historical times the
philosophers were the representatives of science. They were
not given to speculation exclusively, but commanded a wealth
of knowledge that may justly be described as real science:
Thales is the first Greek astronomer; Anaximander, the first
geographer; and Pythagoras, the first to cover the entire field
of the mathematical sciences. Their teachings, far from being
based on the national liberal education, are, for the most part,
opposed to it: "Philosophers and poets were ever at variance
with one another, and there are innumerable traces of their
ancient feud."[4] Chief among these traces are the attacks of
the philosophers on Homer. At times theological grounds are

---

[1] Arist., *Pol*, VIII, 6, p 1341

[2] Plin., *Nat. Hist*, 35, 10, 77: "Pamphili auctoritate effectum est Sicyone
primum, deinde in tota Græcia, ut pueri ingenui omnia ante graphicen, hoc
est picturam in buxo docerentur recipereturque ars ea in primum gradum
liberalium;" and Arist, I, I, c 3.

[3] Diog. Lært., *Procem*, §§ 1 ff

[4] Plato, *Rep*, X, p. 607.

at the bottom of the opposition to the poet, as in the case of Xenophanes and Plato, who censured Homer for making the gods into human beings. Plato, however, opposed the poet also on moral grounds, for idealizing the national character both in its strength and its weaknesses while failing to implant into the national consciousness any higher principles. At other times a contrary conception of the end and nature of education was responsible for the mutual opposition, as when Plato says that Homer can, like the conjurer, mimic all the human activities and arts, but is not at home in any single field, and thus deceives his readers with the shadow of things without introducing them into the matter and inner nature of the world.[1] Similar considerations seem to have induced Heraclitus, the uncompromising opponent of cyclopedic learning, to demand that Homer be driven from the stage and whipped.[2]

5. The most striking contrast between the scientific and the liberal education is furnished by the curricula of the Pythagorean schools, after which Plato modeled the plan of studies outlined in his *Republic*. Pythagoras examined every youth desiring admittance to his school concerning his early life, his tastes, and even his personal appearance. "The artist looks around for the right kind of wood when he desires to make a statue of Hermes," was a maxim of Pythagoras, which has become proverbial in the form, "*Non ex quovis ligno fit Mercurius*."[3] The time of schooling covered five years, and during this period the pupil might be dismissed at any time. The pupils were at first mere listeners (ἀκουσματικοί); they had to attend in silence, and were kept busy with memory work. The latter was highly esteemed by Pythagoras, who is the author of the familiar saying, "We know as much as we have in our memory." To assist the memory, the teaching content was couched in pithy, meaningful sentences, which were expressed in gnomic or catechetical form, *e. g.*, "Leave the highway, follow footpaths;" "Do not speak unless you have clear ideas;" "What is most wise? measure and number; and after these? the creator of language." The training in music was confined to religious melodies. Great importance was attached to the in-

---

[1] Ibid., X, pp. 598 ff.

[2] Diog. Laert., IX, § 1.

[3] "You cannot make a Mercury out of every log," *i. e.*, "Not every mind will answer equally well to be trained into a scholar." The proper wood for a statue of Mercury was boxwood - "vel quod hominis pulrorem præ se ferat, vel quod materies sit omnium maxime æterna" (Erasmus).

struction in music, for music was thought to possess the power of healing the diseases of the soul. In accordance with Appolonian theology, the words νόμος (law) and κόσμος expressed jointly the world of music and the order of morality. From the status of mere listeners the pupils advanced to that of the μαθηματικοί, *i. e.*, students. The studies (μάθημα) of these advanced pupils embraced the science of numbers and space, astronomy, and theory of music—all of which became known subsequently as the mathematical sciences It is more than probable, as Roth observes, that a due distinction was even then made between the elementary study of mathematics which dealt only with the memorizing and understanding of individual and isolated propositions, and the more advanced grade of work which studied the relations between the propositions. Theology, which dealt with the ἱερὸς λόγος, and with which the study of the esoteric sciences (cosmology, physics, symbolism of numbers) was connected, completed the course of education.[1] Plato describes education as a power of nursing and healing the soul[2] (παιδεία δύναμις θεραπευτικὴ ψυχῆς), and in so saying seems to refer to the practice of the Mysteries whose purpose was the nursing, purifying, and healing of the soul.

Plato would exclude from the teaching content all that was likely to lower the divine to the level of man, and hence he had to sacrifice all of Homer's poetry. He preferred lyrical and didactic poetry to the epic, and permitted only such music as had a solemn and dignified character. The environment of the child should mirror, so Plato contended, in form and rythm the elements of truth and beauty, so that he would become familiar with these as with the A B C of the moral order. Mathematics was to be studied only by the mature youth, and even then not systematically (χύδην); nor was it to be made obligatory Arithmetic was to be studied with a view to its training in mental work and in quickness of perception. Geometry was to open the pupil's eyes to the objects at rest in the midst of the changes in the universe. Astronomy was to lead to the discovery of the eternal laws governing the motions of the planets; and the theory of music, to the discovery of the eternal laws governing sound. Only youths of special ability should take up again, at a later period, the mathematical sciences,

---

[1] Roth, l. c., II, pp. 473-516 and pp 765 ff
[2] Plato, Ὅροι; p 416 The ὅροι belong, if not to Plato, at least to the Old Academy

which were then to be pursued systematically and in their relation to dialectics, *i. e.*, ideology, the science of the eternal.

Thus both Plato and Pythagoras assign to liberal education a merely preparatory function, and they regard mathematics as its complement and as the step leading to real science, *i. e.*, philosophy. Occasionally Plato refers to philosophy as being an art of the Muses,[1] but he is then harking back to the service of the Muses as practiced in the earliest times. Only in this sense can the following be rightly understood: "All men of education are servants of the Muses, especially the musicians, and they are likewise servants of Apollo, just as all who explain the sacred Mysteries are servants of Demeter."[2] It was Plato, too, who called the philosophers the true bacchanals and the truly consecrated.[3]

6. The keen mind of the Greeks could not fail to introduce some elements of the higher learning of the philosophers into their system of general education. The statement that Pythagoras introduced mathematics into the educational course of every free-born Greek,[4] or, as Ovid puts it, *"in medium discenda dabat,"*[5] has reference to a larger circle than that of his disciples. Even in the time of Plato we meet half-grown youths discussing questions of mathematical geography.[6] Pythagoras' method of writing music as well as his theory of music was introduced into the schools at an early date, and Speusippus systematized them for practical instruction.[7] Elementary instruction in mathematics was universal in the Alexandrian age. Higher ethico-religious views also became the popular opinions of the day, and the attempt was made to reconcile the latter with Homer's philosophy. Anaxagoras had interpreted Homer according to

[1] *Phædon*, p. 61: φιλοσοφία μεγίστη μουσική; Tim., p. 88: μουσική καὶ πᾶσα φιλοσοφία.

[2] Strab., X, 3, 10.

[3] Plato, *Phæd.*, p. 69d and *Phædr.*, p. 249d.

[4] Procl., *Comment. in Eucl.*, II, p. 19.

[5] Ov., *Met.*, 15, 66.

[6] In the dialogue *Amatores*, ascribed to Plato, there is a scene (p. 132) in which the youths dispute about different opinions of Anaxagoras and Oinopidas. They also draw circles and show with their hands their angles of inclination. In Aristophanes' *Clouds* (vv. 200 ff.) a young wiseacre is given to airing his knowledge of astronomy, geography, and geometry.

[7] This is probably the meaning of the ἐν τοῖς μαθήμασιν ἐθεάσατο τὸ κοινὸν καὶ συνῳκείωσεν ἀλλήλοις in Diog. Laërt., IV, § 2, because the speculative relationship of these disciplines had been established, if not by Pythagoras, then at the latest by Plato.

ethical principles, and he was followed in this work by the Stoics who gave special attention to this phase of the Homeric studies.[1]

While the higher learning, which drew upon the philosophy of the pre-Homeric age, was thus enlarging the content of liberal education, popular philosophy was active in the same direction. Though the popular philosophy of the Sophists affords evident proof that the learning and speculation had deteriorated and had not kept pace with the growth of the nation, yet their efforts had at least stimulated intellectual activity, and consequently the history of education may rate them a little higher than does the history of philosophy. The Sophists made utility the standard of all knowledge and skill, and their aim was to discover how the factors and forces of life could be made of the greatest possible benefit to the race and the individual. Gorgias recognized the art of speech as the art that would accomplish this, because, as he maintained, it embodied all other arts and superseded all knowledge. Other Sophists shrank from so extreme a view, and contended that a certain mass of knowledge must be mastered ere the gift of speech could appear at its best; and some Sophists, like Hippias of Elis, made researches in most diverse fields. By calling attention to the questions of the day the Sophists encouraged not only theoretical speculation, but also the practical application of knowledge, and thus politics, jurisprudence, political economy, and ethics began to be studied, even if the viewpoint was frankly utilitarian. Furthermore, once the interest in the spoken word was awakened, men did not rest satisfied with systematizing the methods employed in rendering language effective, but proceeded not only to trace the interrelations of thought, as exhibited in spoken and written language, but also to inquire into the nature of language as such. The debates of the Sophists gave birth to dialectics and logic. Their grammatical distinctions mark the beginning of the philosophy of language, and the latter has proved the source — a development quite different from that in the East—of the scientific study of grammar. Protagoras led the way in this field, for he was the first to distinguish between the different classes of sentences—which he called the "roots of language" ($\pi v \theta \mu \acute{\epsilon} v \epsilon s$ $\lambda \acute{o} \gamma \omega v$) — and he also discovered the genus of nouns and the relationship of agreement.[2]

---

[1] Diog Laert, II, § 11 and the commentaries on Horace, *Ep*, I, 21 ff.

[2] Diog Laert, IX, §53, Arist, *Rhetor*, III, 5, Soph *elench*, 14. Protagoras distinguishes at times four classes of sentences, then seven; either

Socrates examined into the same matters as the Sophists, but he opposed their frivolous tendency by taking a more serious view of life. He encouraged the serious pursuit of knowledge, for he declared knowledge to be not only the means for attaining virtue, but identical with it. The problems that he proposed, could not be solved by playful reasoning or dabbling in science, but only by deep and earnest study. The dialectic of the Sophists had been mainly controversial and frivolous, too, in its eagerness for a dispute, but Socrates changed it radically and put it to better use. By developing the analytic operations of the intellect, induction and definition, he laid the foundation for the structure of logic, which was later completed by Aristotle. The Socratic method is the happy union of the dialectic and didactic processes. The teaching process means the freeing of the mental powers; the knowledge is apparently presented to the pupil, yet he must find it himself, and his circle of thought becomes the birthplace of knowledge.

The honor of having continued and harmonized all that the Sophists and Socrates had begun belongs to Isocrates. Isocrates's school at Chios is said to have produced as many men of the finest type of culture as heroes issued forth from the Trojan Horse. He raised the art of oratory to a truly educational and cultural subject and made it subservient to a moral aim. He converted the egotistical polymathy of the Sophists into a many-sided receptiveness, after the example of the bee, which knows well how to extract what is wholesome from all flowers.[1] He popularized the view of Pythagoras and Plato, that the chief function of mathematics is to prepare for the study of philosophy.[2] Isocrates is also responsible for the blending of rhetoric and historiography, but this blending was not favorable to the development of history.[3]

7. It remained for the Alexandrian age to compress all the educational elements, introduced by the various philosophers, within the compass of the one system of the seven liberal arts, which was to be the standard in education for so many centuries. It was called ἐγκύκλιος παιδεία, ἐγκύκλια παιδεύματα,

---

wish, question, answer, command; or declaration, question, answer, command, message, request, and invocation.

[1] Ad Demon., §§ 52 ff.

[2] De permutatione, § 264 and § 256.

[3] Droysen, Grundriss der Historik, 2nd ed., Leipzig, 1875, p. 76.

ἐγκύκλια μαθήματα[1], *i. e.*, the common education or studies, with the connotation of a circle of education or studies. It comprised grammar, rhetoric, dialectic, arithmetic, geometry, astronomy, and music.

Grammar did not in this period lose its primitive philosophical character—the Stoics especially continued along this line—but it began at the same time to promote the scientific treatment of language by assisting in the emendation of texts and in interpretative criticism. Going back to the origins of education, it concerned itself mainly with Homer's poetry. It embraced the methodical or technical study of spoken and written language as well as the historical or exegetical study which dealt chiefly with the authors' texts[2] For the purpose of teaching the Greek language to young Romans, Dionysius Thrax reduced (c. 60 B. C.), the results of the grammatical researches to a system. His book was the first practical elementary Greek grammar, and it "became one of the principal channels through which the grammatical terminology, which had been carried from Athens to Alexandria, flowed back to Rome, to spread from thence over the whole civilized world."[3] Rhetoric examined the different species of oratory, treated of the invention and arrangement of thought, of style, memory, and elocution, gave directions for model compositions (chria), and classified the tropes and figures. Aristotle's *Rhetoric*, the Τέχνη ῥητορική of Dionysius of Halicarnassus, a contemporary of Dionysius Thrax, and the Προγυμνάσματα of Hermogenes, Aphthonius and other rhetoricians, or *technicians*, as they were called, of imperial Rome give us a good and succinct view of what was usually taught in the schools under the name of rhetoric.[4]

From the scant material extant in regard to the study of logic, we cannot say how much of this subject was studied in the schools There is no Greek textbook of elementary dialectic extant, and the Roman encyclopedias (see ch XII)—compilations of what was taught in the Greek schools—give

[1] For complete references see Wower, *De polymathia tractatio*, 1603, cap. XXIV, pp 208-213

[2] Concerning the different definitions and divisions of grammar cf Sext. Empir , *Adv Gram*, pp 224 ff Fabi Cf also Wower, l c , pp 51 ff

[3] Max Muller, *The Science of Language*, New York, 1891, I, pp 103 ff.

[4] Krause, *Geschichte der Erziehung bei den Griechen*, Halle, 1851, pp 179 ff. Cf R. C Jebb's translation of Aristotle's *Rhetoric* (ed by J E. Sandys, 1909) and his *Attic Orators*, 1876

more attention to oratorical training than to logical materials in what they quote under the head of dialectic from Aristotle and the Stoics.[1]

The *Elements* (στοιχεῖα) of the Platonist Euclid of Gela (c. 300 B. C.) were the basis of geometry and arithmetic. The *Elements*, however, were not the first systematic textbook, for the Pythagorean Hippocrates had written one 150 years earlier,[2] but the fame of Euclid's book eclipsed all former works. In Euclid's book plane geometry is treated in six books; arithmetic, in four; and solid geometry, in three. The presentation has been much admired, imitated even by philosophers, and is to-day still the standard for our textbooks: the definitions, postulates, and axioms head the list, and the teaching matter is contained in the theorems and problems. The structure of the whole reveals great art, yet allows no view into the relation of the mathematical truths, because the propositions are treated more as matter for memory and reflection than as members of a scientific organism. It would seem that only the first book— of which the theorem of Pythagoras is the last, and which was often edited and annotated—was in general use. From the Roman encyclopedias we can conclude that geographical matter was introduced into geometry, and that the encyclical arithmetic treated only the theory and symbolism of numbers and did not include the theory of the four operations.[3] From what Strabo requires of the readers of his work on geography we can infer how much astronomy was taught in the schools. He says that the reader "should be familiar with the shape of the earth and its circles (parallel, perpendicular, and oblique), and know the position of the tropic of Cancer and of the tropic of Capricorn, of the equator and the zodiac, as well as the paths of the sun which show the difference in the degrees of latitude and the winds; for he who is ignorant of the horizon and the Arctic and Antarctic Circles and of other elementary matters of mathematics, might well despair of grasping what is to be explained here."[4] Geography was naturally studied in connec-

---

[1] Prantl, *Geschichte der Logik*, I, pp. 528, 578 ff.

[2] Röth, l. c., II, p. 586. Cf. *The Thirteen Books of Euclid's Elements*, transl. with introduction and commentary by T. L. Heath, 3 vols., Cambridge, 1908; Allmann, *Greek Geometry from Thales to Euclid*, Dublin, 1889; on Euclid: Cantor, *Vorlesungen über Geschichte der Mathematik*, Leipzig, 1880, pp. 221 ff.

[3] Cf. Peacock's article *Arithmetic* in the *Encyclopedia Metropolitana*, which contains a detailed account of the Greek system.

[4] Strabo, I, pp. 12-13.

tion with elementary astronomy, and the form of the elementary
geographies of the Alexandrian age—they are written in verse
to assist the memory—leads us to believe that they were used
in the schools.[1] Music, as taught in the schools, embraced the
knowledge, first, of the instruments, next, of the height and
depth of the tones, and, finally, of their duration. Different
symbols were employed for writing vocal and instrumental
music, and the two styles were more difficult than our system,
as it took several months to teach the pupils to read music.[2]

In the golden age of Greek culture the course of liberal
education was kept up and perfected amid the multiform interests of a highly developed national life. But the encyclical
(enzyklisch) education of the Alexandrian age was rounded off
by literary work and higher studies. In the latter age the demand created a large supply of reading matter to take the place
of the public life and social intercourse of the earlier period.[3]
Didactic poetry formed part of this popular literature, and
though its artistic value is practically nil, it promoted the interests of education, for it made the elements of higher learning
the common property of the masses, and thus much of what
might otherwise have remained pure theory or inaccessible, was
made to serve the practical needs of the time. Astronomy,
geography (general and local), history, mythology, agriculture,
hunting, medicine, etc., were treated in didactic poems. The
term philology now came into use for designating the amateur
as well as the professional occupation with scientific matters.
Though this term had been employed formerly in the sense of
scientific or educational interests,[4] yet this use had been only
occasional, and it became general only after Eratosthenes had
first called himself a philologist. There is some relation in the
meaning of philology and polymathy, which latter term also
came into general use about the same time. But while philology implies primarily book learning, polymathy expresses
primarily the desire for many-sided knowledge.

8. Philology and polymathy were never considered the completion of education. They were regarded as merely extending

---

[1] Bernhardy, *Griechische Literaturgeschichte*, I, p 99
[2] Boeckh, *Enzyklopädie und Methodologie der philologischen Wissenschaften*,
ed by Bratuschek, Leipzig, 1877, pp 503 ff
[3] At this time ἀναγιγνώσκειν came to mean to read, to occupy oneself
with books; popular writers were called ἀναγνωστικοί Bernhardy, l. c , I, p 57,
Grassberger, l c , pp 283 ff
[4] φιλόλογος φιλῶν λόγους καὶ σπουδάζων περὶ παιδείας

the boundaries of knowledge and as leading up to the highest
field, to philosophy. In this sense Strabo assigns to the philologist Eratosthenes a middle place between him who devotes
himself to philosophy, *i. e.*, scientific research, and the other
who would not venture so far, yet is desirous of going beyond
the encyclical course of studies.[1] Philosophy had to maintain
its superiority the more as it had begun with Aristotle to embrace as its own department all that was proper to polymathy.
Aristotle, whom Dante calls "The master of those who know,"
the type of the man who combines the scrutinizing eye of the
research worker with the gift of universal knowledge, was fit-
tingly born in the beginning of the Alexandrian age, for he
well marks the change ushered in with that period. All philosophers agreed that their science is the completion and end
of education, and they differed only in their evaluation of the
encyclical studies. The Stoics refused to acknowledge that these
studies had a propædeutic function. However the Academy,
true to its founder, held the opposite view and looked particularly upon the mathematical sciences as the handmaids of
philosophy;[2] but to such as rested satisfied with this preparatory
work instead of taking up the higher studies, the words of Aristippus were applied: they resemble the suitors of Penelope, who,
when the mistress was refused them, were content with her
maids.[3]

How the deeper natures of the age sought to combine philosophy and polymathy, is seen in the beautiful allegory of
Nicholas of Damascus, contemporary and friend of Augustus.
The studies are compared to a journey: at one place the traveller makes a brief call, at another place he takes only a meal,
at other places he spends entire days. Some objects he scru-
tinizes carefully, at others he merely glances, but having returned home, he takes up his permanent abode in his own house.
The friend of studies will conduct himself in a similar way:
he will give much time to one subject, to another but little;
some sciences he will try to master, while he is satisfied with
the elements of others; and after he has tasted of all that seemed
inviting, he turns to philosophy to dwell permanently in her

[1] Strabo, I, p. 15.

[2] For Zeno's opinion see Diog. Laert., VII, § 32; Chrysippus expressed
himself more favorably, ib., § 129. When a youth who was ignorant of music,
geometry, and astronomy applied to Xenocrates for instruction, the philosopher
refused saying, πορεύου, λαβὰς γὰρ οὐκ ἔχεις φιλοσοφίας. Ib., IV, § 10.

[3] Ib., II, § 79; cf. Pseudoplut., *De lib. educ.*, 10.

company.[1] To have traced philosophy back to its theological elements, is the principal achievement of the Neo-Platonists and Neo-Pythagoreans. They tried to recreate the oldest wisdom and to convert philosophy into a theological science. In this way the formal disciplines of philosophy came to be considered as a preparation for theology, the latter remaining, as it were, the core of the former. Hence there are four steps in education conceived in the highest sense: liberal studies, mathematics, philosophy, and theology.

Greek education finds its completion, then, in that very element with which the schools had in the East, and, to some extent, even in Greece, begun. While the priestly learning of the East and of Greece in the Pelasgian age formed the foundation of all general education, the liberal education of Hellenic Greece was at first saturated with æsthetical materials. It was only later that the scientific research workers began to add scientific elements to the cultural subjects, and their solid contributions proved a basis of profane knowledge that was almost equal in strength to the religious beliefs that had been the foundation of primitive education. It has been frequently observed, and that justly, that Providence guided matters so that at the time when Christianity was to be introduced into the world, the culture of Greece had stamped itself upon the whole ancient civilization and was fast making its way into the most distant countries, with the result that national differences were rapidly disappearing. It may be added that the very development of the content of Greek education was also providential: the education of the Greeks was not, as with the Hindus, Egyptians, and Persians, a thing that was added to old and unchangeable beliefs. It was rather a union of loosely joined materials, and one that was seeking solidity and depth; and this was undoubtedly the happiest condition for giving welcome to the new theology and philosophy.

CHAPTER X.

The Ethos of Greek Education.

1. It is undeniable that there were vast differences among the ancient Greeks arising partly from the division of the people

---

[1] Suidas, s v. Νικόλαος, cf Pseudoplut., *De lib. educ.*, 10, and G. J. Vossius, *De ratione studiorum*, Ultraj, 1651, p 12.

into tribes and commonwealths, entirely distinct from one another, and, partly from the opposite tendencies, which at different times, or even at the same time, influenced Hellenic life.
In view of these differences it may well appear most difficult to
describe briefly and succinctly the ethos and character of Greek
education. The education of the Athenian differed *toto cœlo*
from the education of the Spartan. The Athenian could boast
"of his ability, skill, and grace displayed in many fields," and
could point to his own Athens as being "the school of whole
Greece."[1] The Spartan had to bear the reproach of his own
countryman that he was an ἄμουσος, one lacking a liberal
education. However, he was proudly conscious of his training
to self-reliant manhood: "Man differs but little from man,"
says Archidamus, "but he who has passed through the severest
training will prove most valiant in life's battle."[2] Similarly,
we have, on the one hand, the serious and deep views of education which the Pythagoreans expressed in their principles
concerning the proving of the mind and heart, and which they
embodied in their systematic grading of studies. But, on the
other hand, we have the shallow view of the Sophists, the lo-
quacious busybodies who dreamed that all could be learned and
all taught, as though nature or the gods had bestowed the same
gifts upon all alike.[3] And there is almost as great a difference
between the doctrinairism of Xenophanes and Heraclitus who
opposed the popular beliefs, and Aristotle's universality which
was born of historical studies. Nay, even the same philosopher
will give expression to views diametrically opposed to each
other: in his *Republic* Plato assigns to philosophy the highest
place; but in his *Laws*, where he appears to be convinced of the
need of an historical faith, he declares the worship of the gods
as practiced in early Greece to be the foundation of the inner
life.

Still, there are certain traits broadly characteristic of Greek
education, and the most prominent of these is the sharp distinction made between cultural or liberal education and voca-

---

[1] Pericles in Thuc., II, 41, 1: τῆς Ἑλλάδος παίδευσιν, cf. Diod., XIII, 27:
κοινὸν παιδευτήριον πᾶσιν ἀνθρώποις. Isocrates (*Pan.*, 50) says that Athens is so
superior to all other places, that the Athenian pupil is able to be the teacher of
others, and that they alone deserve to be called Hellenes who have been educated in Athens.

[2] Thuc. I, 84, 4.

[3] Steinthal has given a good sketch of this "philistinism" in the *Zeitschrift
für Völkerpsychologie*, IV, p. 470.

tional training. The freeman should receive only a liberal education; it alone deals with liberal arts and works (ἔργα, μαθήματα ἐλεύθερα), whereas the preparation for a trade qr profession smacks of manual labor, of working for gain, and even of slavery (βάναυσον, θητικόν, δουλικόν). Even in the liberal arts it is forbidden to aim at virtuosity (πρὸς τὸ ἐντελές). The purpose of the gymnasium is not the training of athletes, neither should the training in music produce the professional musician. Only such studies are worthy of the freeman as are pursued for the sake of the interest and pleasure found in them, or for the purpose of attaining virtue, or of occupying one's leisure; and they alone constitute a liberal education (παιδεία ἐλευθέριος καὶ καλή).[1] The Greeks refused to apply the test of profit, usefulness, or gain, to what was learned in the schools, and several anecdotes are related to illustrate how vile any such valuation appeared to the Greek mind One of the best-known is that told of Euclid. Some one who had begun to read geometry with Euclid, when he had learned the first theorem, asked, "But what shall I get by learning these things?" Euclid called his slave and said, "Give him three obols, since he must make gain out of what he learns." It was likewise contrary to the Greek sense of the fitness of things to let the teachers be paid for their services, and the Sophists, who were the first to demand financial remuneration for their instruction, were severely censured by the Athenians. Isocrates, who followed the example of the Sophists, seems to have set up his school just on this account in Chios instead of in Athens. The rhetoricians of a later age accepted compensation regularly, but it is significant that it was a universal complaint that not interest, but pecuniary gain was the sole incentive of study.[2]

2. In keeping with these views, education was not considered an instrument, an equipment, or a fitting out for one's lifework, but was prized as an ornament of man. Aristotle calls it so,[3] and Diogenes compared it to a gold crown that conferred highest honor upon the wearer [4] Demonax has a still happier comparison. as the cities are adorned with votive offerings (ἀναθή-μασι), so must the minds of men be adorned with the choice

---

[1] Arist, *Pol.*, VIII, 2 and 3 in , pp 1337 and 1338

[2] Diod , II, 29, Galen, *Method med*, I, 1　The Greek ἐργολαβία corresponds to our "bread-and-butter studies "

[3] Quoted by Diog Laert, V, § 19

[4] Joh Damasc , in the appendix to Gaisford, *Stob Ecl phys et eth*, Vol. II, No 92: καὶ γὰρ τιμὴν ἔχει καὶ πολυτέλειαν

gifts of education.[1] But this adornment is to be not a mere appendage, but to become part and parcel of the personality. Education, once acquired, is man's inalienable possession, and Stilpon's answer to the question as to what he had lost in the devastation of his native town, must be understood in this sense; for he replied, "I have lost nothing that belonged to me; I still possess my mind and my education; all the rest belongs to the conquerors no less than to me."[2] And the same is probably the meaning of this saying of Democritus, "Nature and teaching are much the same; for the teaching changes man and through this change gives him a second nature."[3] As an element of the personality, education strengthens and directs man's inner life; it makes his mental faculties keen and alert, and affords both joy and consolation. And thus the man without an education is described as lost amid the maze of things, like strangers wandering about the streets of a city. He is said to be dreaming away his life, while the educated man has in himself the source of perennial joy and undying hope, and a safe refuge from all distress.[4]

Being the most precious ornament of the freeman, education should not and can not be imparted by force: "The free and voluntary study of the arts and sciences is the only proper course, and the only one that will prove successful; all forced study is of evil and will defeat its own purpose."[5] Again, "No freeman should be forced to acquire any knowledge; the body is not debased by being forced to work, but knowledge forced upon the mind will never be rooted in the memory."[6] The joy of studying should be the strongest incentive, and after it the desire "to be the first in everything, and in all things to surpass all others."[7] The latter motive is that thirst after glory which was celebrated by Homer, which animated the wrestlers at the Olympic games, which called forth the emulation of poets and artists, and which was the mainspring of all ancient activity down to the last days of the ancient world, when the desire to excel came to be considered a harmful influ-

---

[1] Gaisford, l. c., No. 53.

[2] Ibid., No. 152: λόγος καὶ παιδεία.

[3] Mullach, *Democr. fragm.*, Berlin, 1843, p. 186 and p. 293: ἡ φύσις καὶ ἡ διδαχὴ παραπλήσιόν ἐστι, καὶ γὰρ ἡ διδαχὴ μεταρρυσμοῖ τὸν ἄνθρωπον, μεταρρυσμοῦσα δὲ φυσιωποιεῖ.

[4] Gaisford, l. c., Nos. 134, 131, 140; Diog. Lært., I, § 69.

[5] Aristoxenos in Gaisford, l. c., No. 119.

[6] Plato, *Rep.*, VII., p. 537.

[7] *Iliad*, VI, 208; XI, 783.

ence as interfering with man's inborn liberty. The teaching process was also to follow, as far as possible, the path of free and unhampered development. He was the best teacher who had a free and creative command of the entire field. The Greeks recognized three kinds of teaching and named them after the three first ages of Hesiod: the teachers who impart knowledge which they have received from no source other than themselves, are performing a golden work; the labor of those who impart only what they have themselves received, is of silver, and of brass if they withhold from others what they have received.[1] Here we have the Greek conception in opposition to the traditionalism of the East, but also the overvaluation of creative work

A further trait of Greek education is its fullness and many-sidedness Socrates compared it to a pageant or a great fair where the eye and ear are busy with seeing and hearing,[2] and to a fertile field which produces fruit and grain of many kinds[3] At the same time, however, he bids his countrymen heed the example of the fruit-grower who does not plant the fruit trees too near to one another, in order to allow them space enough for development.[4] This advice was sorely needed. The content of Greek education was so rich and the Greek mind so keen and receptive that there was great danger lest the very many-sidedness should, in the midst of all the wealth of material, render a unity of view impossible, and lest the mere appearance of things should be considered their nature and essence. The greatest men of the nation recognized this danger, and they never ceased warning their countrymen not to be busybodies and dabblers in all sciences. Homer caricatured the Jack-of-all-trades in his *Margites*, who "was conversant with many fields, but master of none"[5] Pindar says that "to sip of a thousand virtues would never satisfy man's heart." Heraclitus is convinced that "much learning does not give spirit;"[6] and Democritus demanded that one should strive not for a fullness of knowledge, but for a fullness of the mind.[7] Socrates and

---

[1] Gaisford, l c , No. 97
[2] Gaisford, l c , No 44· πανήγυρίς ἐστι ψυχῆς ἡ παιδεία, πολλὰ γάρ ἐστιν ἐν αὐτῇ ψυχῆς θεάματα καὶ ἀκούσματα
[3] Ibid , No. 103
[4] Ibid , No. 102.
[5] Πόλλ' ἠπίστατο ἔργα, κακῶς δ' ἠπίστατο πάντα
[6] Diog. Lært., IX, §§ 7 and ff.
[7] Mullach , l c , p. 187 Πολυνοίην οὐ πολιμαθίην ἀσκέειν χρή

Plato opposed the Sophists for dabbling in too many things: "Ignorance is not the greatest of evils; it is much more harmful to dabble in all things under the direction of a bad master."[1] Plato's command, "Let each one perform his own proper duty," is levelled at the multiplicity of occupations engaged in by the Greeks, and the same principle is the foundation of his ideal Republic. However, the Greeks continued to be dabblers in all kinds of knowledge. The science of the Alexandrian age struts about in patches of many hues. And in the Roman period the satirist made sport of "the diminutive and hungry Greek who is a master of all the arts and sciences, and who can, upon command, ascend even into heaven."[2]

3. This erroneous tendency is attacked at the very root by those philosophers who, in contrast to the purely æsthetical conception, stress the moral factors inherent in education. It would be unfair to the earlier thinkers to regard Socrates as the first to bring out these moral elements, as it is likewise contrary to fact to assert that he, by substituting moral speculation for the exclusively physical, called philosophy from heaven to earth. Yet it remains true that the efforts of Socrates were most effective in directing the minds of his contemporaries as well as the succeeding generations to the moral side of education. Consistently with his view that knowledge and virtue are identical, Socrates looked upon education as the most efficient, if not the sole, means for arriving at virtue, and hence intellectual growth involved a growth in virtue also. The philosphers who came after Socrates did not ignore the moral force of education, but were wise in not accepting his exaggerated views in this regard. Aristotle considers education one of the means for acquiring virtue, but he holds discipline and the acquiring of habits to be greater moral forces.[3] The Stoics regard all studies as means of discipline and as a medicine of the soul.

The moral and æsthetical aims of education pushed the religious end into the background. The religious end, however, was never entirely ignored. The entire system of liberal education had been named after the Muses. Apollo and Hermes were its personifications among the gods. The poets whose creations were the common property of the nation, were regarded, not merely as the favored servants and disciples of the

[1] Plato, *Legg.*, VII, p. 819.
[2] Juv., *Sat.*, III, 7.
[3] Arist., *Pol.*, VII, 13, p. 1332 and *Eth. Nic.*, X, 10, p. 1179.

Muses, but as the interpreters of the gods [1] "To educate oneself or other men," was considered "a sacred and divine work." [2] Education was itself worshipped as one of the gods, and its devotees were described as a religious brotherhood (θίασος). [3] Plato and Pythagoras declared the directing of the mind to sacred things to be the essence of education. Plato taught that man could not turn to the divine without having first undergone a complete change and without turning away his attention from the shadows of the material world, and thus education would be both a περιαγωγή and a μεταστροφή. He considered the process of instruction to involve the purification and quickening of that organ of the soul "that is more deserving of being preserved than a thousand eyes, since it is with it that we behold the truth, the divine." [4] Continuing along these lines, the Neo-Platonists found no difficulty in making theology the capstone of education All the philosophers mentioned have a socio-ethical conception of education, and consider the work of teaching and learning to be the process of transmitting to those coming after the inheritance of a former age [5] But this view was foreign to the general trend of the Greek mind In their efforts to perpetuate the gifts of culture the Greeks were actuated more by the desire to gain for themselves immortal fame than by that of handing down to future generations their knowledge and learning

4 Education and culture were ever live topics with the Greeks, and the questions dealing with them were often discussed Aristotle gives us a brief list of the main subjects under discussion: "Our age disputes a great deal about the ends and aims of education There are different opinions as to what is to be learned by the young, either to make them virtuous or happy for life. It is still an open question whether more attention should be given to the development of the intellect or to the training of the character. The education prevailing at the present time throws no light on the subject, nor does it decide whether the schools should fit the pupils to meet the needs of practical life, or train them to virtue, or introduce them to higher studies: each of these several views has found

[1] Plato, *Legg*, III, p 882
[2] Plato, *Theag*, p 122
[3] Grassberger, l c, I, p 192 and II, p. 30
[4] Plato, *Rep*, VII, pp 521 and 527
[5] Cf *supra*, p 22

its defenders."[1] The philosophers generally dealt with the subject of education in their socio-philosophical writings. Thus
Plato's *Republic* and *Laws* and Aristotle's *Politics* treat of the
science of education, and it is to be regretted that Aristotle has
not completed his treatise on the subject (see *supra* p. 23).
But the subject of the science of education was also treated
separately or in connection with pedagogical matters. Of such
works the treatise on the education of children, ascribed to
Plutarch, is the only book that has come down to us. But
Democritus, Antisthenes, Aristippus, Aristotle, Theophrastus,
and Clearchos also wrote on education (περὶ παιδείας). The
work of the last-named writer must have included materials
belonging to the history of education; at least he discussed
therein the relations between the wisdom of the Indian gymno-
sophists and the learning of the Magi.[2] The Stoic Zeno wrote
Of Greek Education, with references, no doubt, to the points of
difference between it and foreign educational systems.[3] The
same philosopher, as well as Chrysippus and Plutarch, wrote on
the study of poetry. We find directions for private study
intermingled with general rules in several treatises of Isocrates
(*e. g.*, in the writings addressed to Demonicus and Nicocles)
and in the numerous exhortations (λόγοι προτρεπτικοί) of later
philosophers.[4] Some quotations from the lost works are preserved in later compilations, especially in those made by Sto-
bæus and John of Damascene, the latter placing the sayings of
the philosophers and of the Doctors of the Church in parallel
columns.

CHAPTER XI.

The Greek School System.

1. The educational institutions of ancient Greece were, with
few exceptions, not systematized, and the schools were private
foundations with the most meagre appointments. The teachers
of reading and writing set up their schools in booths and huts,
frequently even in the streets and the market place, and loafers

---

[1] Arist., *Pol.*, VII, 2, p. 1337.
[2] Diog. Lært., *Prœm.*, §9.
[3] Ibid., VII, §4.
[4] Cf. the list of educational writings in Grassberger, l. c., II, pp. 10 ff.

could at any time, as Theophrastus describes it in his *Characters*, disturb them at their work. The profession of the grammar teacher was held in low repute, and it was proverbial to say of one who had disappeared, "He either died or is gone to be a schoolmaster." Freedmen and slaves often conducted schools. In the homes of the wealthy, slaves taught the elements, and slaves (the παιδαγωγοί) were generally appointed to watch over the school-boys and to assist them in their lessons If a slave was unfit for other work he was generally entrusted with this office: a slave fell from a tree while picking fruit and broke his leg, whereupon the master remarked, "He has now advanced to the office of a pedagogue "[1] The music schools were distinct from the elementary schools and were of higher rank, occasionally, statues of Apollo and Athene graced their halls. The State contented itself with passing a few general laws. Athens limited the number of boys who were permitted to be at school at one and the same time and appointed the opening hour for the schools.[2] Some laws were also passed concerning the teaching matter: at the time of the Archon Euclid the State introduced the Ionic alphabet; and the parents were obliged to have their children receive a certain amount of liberal and gymnastic training.[3] The legislation of Charondas is the only case on record where the State provided for elementary education. Charondas ordained that all sons of citizens be taught to write, and that the State employ and pay the teachers of the poor [4] All the schools of Sparta were controlled by the State, and the rigorous censorship of music exercised in that country by the ephors, which prevented the introduction of new melodies, naturally influenced the musical training in the schools

The municipalities provided-better than the State, not only for concerts, plays, and other public entertainments, but also for gymnastic training Each city had its own gymnasium, and Athens boasted several. These gymnasiums were furnished with the necessary apparatus for physical culture, and were surrounded by extensive parks and spacious halls Long, shady

[1] Gaisford, l c , No 121

[2] Aesch , *Timarch* , 9

[3] Plato, *Crit* , p 50

[4] Diod , XII, 12 Grafenhahn (*Geschichte der Philologie im Altertum*, I, p 67) and Ussing (l c) refuse to accept the statement of Diodorus, because it is the one solitary case on record But we must consider that it is not a question of a state system of schools, but merely a form of state aid to the poor

avenues ran through these parks, and both the latter and the halls were adorned with statues of gods and national heroes. Thus there was ample opportunity for social intercourse and recreation. The physical instruction and exercise of the adults were supervised by the directors, and these in turn were subject, with the whole of the gymnasium, to the Sophronists. The Gymnasiarchs, whose office was held in turn by the wealthiest citizens, arranged the athletic games and other celebrations. In Athens, the Solonic laws regulated the matters pertaining to the attendance and supervision of the gymnasiums. The halls of the gymnasiums were popular meeting-places for social and intellectual intercourse; it was here that the philosophers delivered their lectures, and to attend the latter was considered an elegant occupation of one's leisure (σχολή). Plato and his successors lectured in the Academy, which was sacred to Athene and which had been named after Academos, the hero of Attica. Plato's pupils placed a statue of their master in the temple dedicated to the Muses, which had been built in the plane grove adjoining the Academy. Aristotle and his successors lectured in the covered walks of the Lyceum, which was dedicated to Apollo. The Cynics frequented the gymnasium which was sacred to the memory of Hercules, and which had been named Cynosarges because it was originally intended for the use of such youth as could not claim the full rights of citizenship.[1] All these institutions were sometimes called palæstra, with the connotation that their service to the mind was similar to the effects of athletics on the body.[2]

2. The philosophy schools were generally free associations of youths who, eager for knowledge, would crowd about a master. It is probable that a certain amount of knowledge had to be mastered by the pupil before he was admitted—in the well-known inscription Plato refused to admit those not versed in mathematics[3]—but no compensation was asked for the instruction. The continuity of the school was preserved by the teaching and the regular succession of headmasters (scholarchs). Theophrastus and Epicurus willed some real estate to their successors,[4] and this marks the beginning of securing material assistance for the schools. Pythagoras' schools alone enjoyed

---

[1] Ussing, l. c., pp. 135 ff.

[2] Cf. Longinus, 4, 4: Ξενοφῶν καὶ Πλάτων ἐκ τῆς Σωκράτους ὄντες παλαίστρας.

[3] Μηδεὶς ἀγεωμέτρητος εἰσίτω μου τὴν στέγην. Tzetz. Chil., 8, 972, turned into verse by the reporter.

[4] Diog. Lært., V, § 52 and X, § 17.

a more systematic organization, and they have been justly
compared to the temple schools of Egypt   But they found no
favor with the people at large, their foreign character brought
them under suspicion, and Pythagoras lived to see his school
at Croton suppressed by the government. The hostility displayed by the State against Socrates also shows plainly that
the Greek governments were suspicious of any attempts made
by a teacher to produce more lasting results   As late as the
end of the fourth century there was a conflict in Athens between
the State and the philosophy schools. The demagogue Sophocles had a measure passed prohibiting the philosophers to open
a school without having previously obtained the permission of
the council and people, whereupon all the philosophers, the
successor of Aristotle, Theophrastus, included, left the city and
returned only after the measure had been repealed and its author
punished for his illegal attempt.[1]

A middle position between the philosophy schools and the
lower schools was occupied by the rhetoric and grammar schools,
which had become common since Isocrates. They were not
controlled by the State, but were pay schools. Rhetoric and
grammar could and should have been taught in one school,
but this was never done. After having learned to read and
write, the boys attended the grammar school, and before completing the grammar course they were frequently admitted to
the rhetoric school[2] The study of mathematics also was not
assigned to any particular age, neither did it require any preparatory work, so that the encyclopedic studies did not represent
a real system of schooling or of classes, but only a framework
for the teaching content.

There were no special provisions made for vocational training. Of the learned professions, the priesthood, indeed, necessitated some certain knowledge, but this was not imparted in
any regular school   The most important of the priestly offices
were hereditary and thus the family traditions sufficed to preserve and transmit all the knowledge required. The so-called
ἐξηγηταί, i. e., interpreters of sacred rites and customs, seem
also to have instructed the candidates for the priesthood.[3] The
associations or guilds of the various mechanical professions undoubtedly provided for the conservation of the traditions that

---

[1] Ibid , V, § 38

[2] Cf. Quint , II, 1, 12 ff , who approves of this combination of studies

[3] Christian Petersen, *Ursprung und Auslegung des heiligen Rechts bei den
Griechen, Philologus*, Suppl Bd l, 155-212

belonged to their respective trades.[1] It is mentioned as something most unusual that instruction in the different trades was offered in Syracuse, and that the "sciences of the slaves" were thus made the subject-matter of formal teaching.[2]

3. While education and scientific research thus refused, in the golden age of Greek history, to be bound, as it were, by hard and fast forms, they submitted to these in the Alexandrian age. In the latter period they were represented chiefly by the Museum of Alexandria, which was truly magnificent in its kind, and which, while devoted to research and teaching, was built upon the foundation of the oldest learning. It had been founded in 322 by Ptolemy Philadelphus, and in its spacious and splendid halls it harbored as many as one hundred savants. These savants were governed by the ἱερεύς, the priest of the Muses, whose office was somewhat like that of the chancellor of the modern university. The librarian was next in dignity, and the different schools of philosophy as well as the representatives of the various sciences had their own deans. The institution was richly endowed. The members received bed and board free and an annual salary besides from the State. The large and valuable library, which contained not only Greek but also oriental works, was placed at their service along with the astronomical and physical apparatus, the medical research laboratories, the botanical garden, the menagerie, etc. The State employed copyists for reproducing the works written by members of the Museum. To have on hand an ample supply of writing material, a royal order forbade the export of papyrus. Much care was given even to the format of the books published. It can not be ascertained whether the savants were obliged to be actively engaged in teaching, yet it is known that large numbers of pupils frequented the galleries of the courtyard where the savants delivered lectures. The free and unconventional methods of study are reminiscent of the Greek philosophy schools. But the collegiate life of the savants, their being divided into different colleges, the supreme control by a priest, and the internal organization of the institution, these features are copied from the temple schools of Egypt, whose influence in this regard was as strong as the influence in general of the literary treasures of Egypt upon the development of Alexandrian polymathy. The historical importance of the Museum can not be over-

---

[1] Bœckh, l. c., p. 397.

[2] Arist., *Pol.*, I, 7, p. 1255.

estimated It encouraged scientific research and formulated the content of the higher learning; and because it continued to flourish during the age of the Roman emperors, it proved the model for all similar foundations, though no other institution ever approached its magnificence.[1]

The savants whom the Attalids had assembled in Pergamum, rivalled those of Alexandria. It is not certain that the κύκλοι Περγαμηνοί were organized along the lines of the Museum of Alexandria, but we know that the savants received all possible aid. The library, founded by Eumenes II., was almost as large as that of Alexandria. To obtain sufficient writing-material, the manufacture of parchment—which has received its name from Pergamum—was introduced. Attalus III. added a botanical garden[2] The savants of Pergamum were instrumental, through their connection with the West, in importing the elements of Greek learning into Rome. The Seleucidæ who set up their capitals in the old centres of civilization, Nineveh and Babylon, also encouraged education. At the court of Antiochus in Antioch there existed a famous school of rhetoric and a large library, and many savants took up their residence there; elements of Greek culture were carried from here into Persia and India

But it was not only the capitals that were the seats of extensive and organized studies, as may be seen from the fame enjoyed by the city of Tarsus, of which Strabo writes: "The Tarsians display such a love of philosophy and other Greek studies as to surpass even Athens, Alexandria, and every other place where philosophers have ever taught. The only difference is that the students and teachers are all natives, foreigners rarely coming to the schools of Tarsus, while other places boast more foreigners than natives. witness Alexandria whose schools are filled with foreigners, while the Alexandrians go abroad to study "[3] It was in Tarsus that St. Paul received his Greek education Dionysius Longinus numbers him among the Greek orators, and the Apostle quotes Greek poets on several occasions.[4]

[1] Parthey, *Das alexandrinische Museum*, Berlin, 1838
[2] Grafenhahn, l c, I, pp 410 ff
[3] Strabo, XIV, p 673
[4] Tit I, 12 "One of them, a prophet of their own, said, *The Cretans are always liars, evil beasts, slothful bellies* " I Cor XV, 33· "Be not seduced· *Evil communications corrupt good manners* " Acts XVII, 28 "For in him we live, and move, and are, as some also of your own poets said *For we are also his offspring,*" quoted from Aratos' poem on astronomy

IV.

ROMAN EDUCATION.

CHAPTER XII.

The Content of Roman Education.

1. Roman education must be traced, like that of the Greeks, to priestly origins. The first teachers of the Romans were the older Etrurians, who had a priestly literature in the sacred Books of Tages; and as late as the fourth century B. C. the Roman youth received their higher education from Etrurian priests.[1] The Books of Tages contained the ceremonies practiced by the Roman augurs; and they were repeatedly annotated, e. g., by the Etrurian Tarquitius and the jurist Labeo, the contemporary of Augustus. They treated also of the worship of the gods, of natural history, and of the world-ages.[2] There is a slight similarity between the Books of Tages and the Vedic and Hermetic books. However, the Romans drew upon them only for their divinations, their haruspicy and ritual.[3] The practice of teaching the priestly sciences was never discontinued in Rome, and all men in public office were expected to be familiar with the *theologia civilis*, as distinct, according to the Greek division, from the *theologia fabulosa* of the poets, and the *theologia naturalis* of the philosophers.[4] Julius Cæsar wrote a book on the auguries, and the familiarity with haruspicy is mentioned among the attainments of an educated man of the period of the Empire.[5]

However, the educational element represented by the serious wisdom of the Etrurians had to give way before the flood of new ideas pouring in when Greek education was introduced. Greek education was engrafted upon Roman life, its sap entered

---

[1] Liv., IX, 36: "Habeo auctores, vulgo tum Romanos pueros, sicut nunc Græcis, ita Etruscis litteris erudiri solitos."

[2] Diod., V, 40: γράμματα δὲ καὶ φυσιολογίαν καὶ θεολογίαν ἐπὶ πλέον.

[3] On this subject cf. Fr. Creuzer, *Symbolik und Mythologie*, II, pp. 819 ff.; Bailey, *The Religion of Ancient Rome*, London, 1907; Del Mar, *The Worship of Augustus Cæsar*, New York, 1899.

[4] Bœckh, l. c., p. 290; August., *De Civitate Dei*, VI, 5.

[5] Krause, l. c., p. 368, footnote 3.

into Roman civilization, and produced a fruit of a mixed
character. Roman education is the fruit, not of the national
civilization, but of the assimilation of the latter with a foreign
and complete system of education. This is the first authenti-
cated case for the path of education to lead through a foreign
language and a foreign literature. It was therefore natural
that language and the art of language meant more to the Romans than to other nations, and hence it is not surprising that
they later declared grammar to be the mother and guide of all
arts and sciences.

Political and social conditions first urged the Romans to
study Greek, and only after the second Punic War did cultural
aims influence them in this regard   In teaching this language,
the Greek slaves at first employed the natural method of conversation and reading. The study of Greek grammar was introduced by Crates of Mallos, who had come to Rome in 159
B. C. as the ambassador of King Attalus III. and was, because
of an accident, detained there longer than he intended   While
the honor to have introduced Greek grammar to Rome thus
belongs to the grammar school of Pergamus, the best textbook
for the subject was written by a representative of the school of
Alexandria, Dionysius Thrax (see *supra* p. 130)   During the
period of the Republic the study of Greek remained confined to
the select circle of the literati, and only in the beginning of the
Empire, and even then for only a short time, was Greek studied
generally. At this time "the children of gentlemen learnt Greek
before they learnt Latin, and though Quintilian does not approve of a boy's learning nothing but Greek for any length of
time (as this would estrange his ear from the mother-tongue),
yet he, too, recommends that a boy should be taught Greek
first, and Latin afterwards."[1]

2 After the grammatical interest had been awakened and
grown strong with the study of a foreign language and a foreign
grammar, it turned necessarily to the mother-tongue. L. Aelius
Præconius, surnamed Stilo, "the Quill Driver," inaugurated
the scientific study of Latin by interpreting old Latin works
and instructing his friends, Cicero, Varro, and Lucilius. His
method of language-studies soon began to be adopted quite
generally in the schools. Two schoolmasters, Q. Remmius Palæmon and M. Valerius Flaccus, the two first *artis scriptores* or

---

[1] Quint , I, 1, 12 sq.; M. Muller, *Lectures on the Science of Language*, New
York, 1866, I, p 101.

artilatores, *i. e.*, authors of school grammars, were celebrated in the first period of the Empire. But grammar was far from being confined to the schoolmasters, for the most distinguished men busied themselves with questions of grammar. Varro, the greatest savant of his time, composed twenty-four books on the Latin language. C. Lucilius, the associate of the statesmen Lælius and Scipio, devoted the ninth book of his satires to the reform of spelling. And Cæsar, while "fighting the barbarians of Gaul and Germany, and watching from a distance the political complications at Rome, ready to grasp the sceptre of the world,"[1] was busy with the declensions of nouns and the conjugations of verbs, for then he wrote his *de analogia* (*i. e.*, on grammatical regularity as opposed to the anomalia, the exceptions and irregularities); he was the inventor of the term *ablative* in Latin. The Emperor Claudius attempted to add new characters to the alphabet (for the sounds of v and ps and the intermediate sound of i and u); but his innovations were rejected by later grammarians.[2] This zeal for grammatical reform was frequently born of mere vanity, and the purists made some egregious blunders in translating the categories and terminology of the Greek grammar into Latin.[3] Yet with many it was the love for their native tongue that encouraged them to discover in it order and regularity and to improve it so as to make it worthy of the greatness of the Empire. The Roman grammarians preserved for many centuries the purity of the Latin sounds, checked the inroads of Græcisms, and conserved the language in its native purity while it was being spoken by the barbarians of all races. To them are the peoples that inherited the culture of Rome indebted for the well-elaborated system of grammar, which is an invaluable instrument of mental discipline and a model for treating the native tongues.

The character of Roman education, derived as it was from the Greeks, gave an impulse to the study of rhetoric also, and among the Romans rhetoric was considered of the same im-

---

[1] M. Müller, l. c., p. 110.

[2] Bœckh, l. c., p. 740.

[3] The Latin "genitivus" is a mere blunder, for the Greek word γενική could never mean "genitivus." "Genitivus," if it is meant to express the case of origin or birth, would in Greek have been called γεννητική, not γενική. (M. Müller, l. c., p. 112.) In the same way the Latin "accusativus" for the fourth case (Varro has "casus accusandi") expresses an act of accusing that is foreign to the Greek αἰτιατική, *i. e.*, the case of cause or reason, and fails to bring out the basic relationship of the case; cf. Trendelenburg, *Act. soc. Gr. Lips.*, I, p. 119.

portance as grammar. Because of its practical importance for
public life, oratory had been esteemed even in early times, but
as an art it was cultivated only after the introduction of Greek
education, when the mastery of the word was prized not only
for its practical usefulness to the statesman and the jurist, but
also as a means for rounding off the intellectual life and for
developing one's personality The foreign language had again
to supply the materials for the new art. Cicero, Pompey,
Antony, and Augustus "declaimed" in Greek before they delivered orations in their mother-tongue, and the first rhetoric
schools in Rome were Greek. L. Plotius Gallus was the first to
open (c. 90 B C) a school for Roman oratory, but he was opposed not only by the Roman patriots, but also by the state-
orators, who recognized the value of a thorough training.[1] But
after Cicero had proved himself equal to the Greek orators,
the opposition to Roman oratory died out, even if Cicero did
not continue to enjoy undisputed sway, as the rhetoricians of
the period of Adrian and the Antonines regarded the earlier
Roman orators as their models.[2] The art of oratory was regarded as the capstone in the education of the young Roman,
and for this reason Quintilian incorporated his system of pedagogy into his textbook of oratory.

3. Though the educational value of grammar and rhetoric
was rated highly by the Romans, yet these disciplines were of
too formal a nature to serve as the basis of education. In the
early times this basis consisted in the songs of the national
heroes, which were learned by heart at school and which were
sung at the feasts by young and old.[3] Beside these songs, the
young had to memorize the Laws of the Twelve Tables, and this
practice still obtained in the boyhood days of Cicero. The
sayings of Pythagoras, as compiled in a poem by Claudius
Cæcus (c. 300), were the first attempt to use foreign materials
for the same purpose. But the *Odyssia*, written by Livius Andronicus, a freedman of Tarentum, who taught grammar in
Rome about 240 B C., must be considered the first real textbook. It was used in the schools till the time of Augustus,
though its antique style and form—it was written in the old
Saturnian verse—had rendered it obsolete long before. Fifty
years after Andronicus a rival arose in the person of the half-

[1] Suet , *de claris rhet* , I sq.
[2] Eckstein in Schmid, *Enzyklopädie*, s. v. *Lateinische Sprache*, 1st ed ,
XI, 498
[3] Üssing, l c , p 129, expresses a doubt about this.

Greek, Q. Ennius of Campania, who in his *Annals* treated the history of Rome in the manner and verse of Homer. Both these works were superseded in the schools by the poetry of Vergil, who began to be read in the schools even during his lifetime, chiefly through the efforts of the grammarian, Q. Cæcilius Epirota. Horace, too, was read in the schools at an early time. In the beginning of the Empire the poets strove to be read by the young; and Horace considers the education of the young to be the sublimest mission of the poet, for he says:

> "His lessons form the child's young lips, and wean
> The boyish ear from words and tales unclean;
> As years roll on, he moulds the ripening mind,
> And makes it just and generous, sweet and kind;
> He tells of worthy precedents, displays
> The example of the past to after days."[1]

Quintilian is likewise of the opinion that the modern poets ought to be read first, and that only the mature should take up the old poets. But in the second century after Christ the older writers again obtained the precedence, and for a time Vergil had to give way to Ennius, and Cicero to Cato.[2] Thus various attempts were made to supply the Roman world with what Homer was to the Greeks. However, even if Vergil continued, almost uninterruptedly, to enjoy canonical authority, yet he never held the place in Rome that Homer held in Greece, and, owing to the bilingual character of Roman education, Homer was generally considered just as important as he.

After the school-authors, the writers of comedies contributed most towards acquainting the Romans with the new education. The sayings of Plautus and Terence passed into proverbs; their plays gave faithful pictures of Greek life, and familiarized the Romans with the philosophy and mythology of the Greeks. Public orations and recitations were also a cultural factor, and the lawyer with a fine education could count, because of the high esteem in which the practice of law was ever held by the Romans, upon a powerful educational influence. But public recitations of poetry were never so popular among the Romans as among the Greeks. Current poetry was, indeed, recited among friends, at banquets, or at the baths, which custom had been introduced by the orator and critic, Asinius Pollio. But, though these recitations may have evinced the desire of the

---

[1] Hor., *Ep.*, II, 1, 126 ff. (Conington's translation).

[2] Eckstein, l. c., and Hertz, *Renaissance und Rokoko in der römischen Literatur*, Berlin, 1865.

educated Roman to devote his leisure to cultural pursuits, they were a far cry to the spirited conferences of the Greeks from which the artistic dialogues of Plato developed.[1]

4 And thus only grammar and rhetoric, of the encyclopedic studies of the Greeks, found full acceptance with the Romans, their practical turn of mind making them suspicious of the other branches. The didactic writings of Cato Censorius— "who made researches into the whole field of knowledge and who was considered a past master in the learning of the age"[2] — show what knowledge appeared most important to a Roman of the old school. Cato contends that one should look at Greek literature, but not learn it thoroughly,[3] and consistently he gave little attention to the full educational system of the Greeks Pythagorean writings were probably the chief source for the materials of his *Disticha de Moribus*, and his rhetoric, intended to serve the needs of the Roman forum, is based on Thucydides and Demosthenes. His *Origines*, which he wrote in large and clear letters to facilitate its reading by the young,[4] treats the history of Rome His other works deal with law, medicine, and the science of war. Cato does not even mention the mathematical sciences, and these were, in fact, relegated at the time to the elementary school, where much time was devoted to arithmetic. In his own day, Cicero found the Greeks who cultivated geometry and held all mathematicians in high esteem, vastly superior in this regard to his own countrymen, who studied these sciences "merely with an eye to the profit to be derived from geometry and arithmetic."[5] The theory of music received even less attention, as musical performances appeared unseemly to the Roman[6] Astronomy, however, appealed to him for its usefulness to the farmer and mariner and for being a storehouse of mythological lore. The astronomical poems of Aratos (*Phænomena* and *Diosemeia*) were frequently translated, for instance, by Cicero, and were read also in the schools.

The cultural value of the mathematical sciences was first recognized in M. Terentius Varro's *Libri IX Disciplinarum*, which embraced the entire system of the encyclopedic studies,

[1] Krause, l c , p 305

[2] Cicero, *de oratore*, III, 33, 135.

[3] Plin , *Hist. nat* , 29, 1, 14 "Bonum illorum litteras inspicere non perdiscere "

[4] Plut , *Cat Maj* , 20.

[5] *Tusc* , 1, 2, 5

[6] Nep , *Ep* , 1.

and which remained the source for all later encyclopedias. Varro went beyond the seven subjects of the Greeks by adding medicine and architecture, for which innovation the old Roman esteem for medicine and the new interest in architecture must be held responsible. Varro was a many-sided savant and the embodiment, so to speak, of the learning of the last days of the Republic. He treated agriculture and civil law in special works, and Roman history in his *De Vita Populi Romani* and in the *Antiquitates Rerum Humanarum et Divinarum*, which St. Augustine praises for their wealth of learning and depth of thought.[1] To encourage the study of mathematics, Varro calls attention to the fact that it cannot be duly appreciated by the tyro: "Either we do not at all take up the study of these matters, or we leave off before we understand the reasons for their real usefulness; the charm as well as the usefulness of these sciences is experienced only when we have gotten beyond the elements (*in postprincipiis*); only the mastery of these subjects can persuade us of their charm and usefulness, while the elements may appear dry and useless."[2] Quintilian is fully alive to the cultural value of mathematics, and (following Isocrates) he discovers many points in its favor: it occupies the mind, sharpens the intellect and makes it more alert; it is not only the mastery, as with other studies, that is advantageous, but every hour devoted to it is useful; it is especially useful to the orator in supplying him with models of good order and scientific conclusions, and in extending his field of knowledge.[3] Surveying was raised to a vocational study when Julius Cæsar committed the cadastral survey of the imperial territory to Egyptian surveyors. The literature of this science—Julius Frontinus (c. 74 A.D.) was the first gromatic[4]—subsequently assumed vast proportions and exercised a great influence on the schools of the Middle Ages.[5] Roman education assimilated, to a certain degree, this branch of mathematics, and the encyclopedias of the later Empire invariably treat of mathematical topics.

5. The compendiums which comprised within small compass whatever seemed most noteworthy, illustrate the tendency of Roman educators to serve practical needs and to economize time. In the beginning of the Empire, A. Cornelius Celsus

---

[1] *De civ. Dei*, VI, 2.
[2] Gell., *N. A.*, 16, 18.
[3] Quint., *Inst.*, I, 1, 34 sq.
[4] The term is probably a corruption of γνώμων.
[5] Cf. Werner, *Gerbert von Aurillac*, Vienna, 1878, p. 74.

wrote a compendium in which he treated oratory, ethics, jurisprudence, military science, agriculture, and medicine. His work
was probably entitled *Cesti*, from the Greek κεστός, stitched,
embroidered (used especially of the girdle of Venus), connoting,
therefore, that the book purported to be an attractive treatment
of various subjects   However, only eight books of the medical
section—*Celsus medicorum Cicero*—have come down to us.   In
the age of the Antonines, the Neoplatonist L. Apuleius, the
father of African Latinity, wrote compendiums of rhetoric, dialectic, and the mathematical sciences; but only the textbook
of dialectic, *De Dogmate Platonis*, has been preserved.[1] His
countryman, Marcianus Cappella, also a Neoplatonist, has
reaped high, though ill-merited, honors as the author (c. 410-
427) of the encyclopedia that was the most widely used textbook of the Middle Ages. The first two books of his *Satiricon
Libri IX* describe the marriage of Mercury and Philology,
upon which occasion Mercury introduces to his bride the seven
liberal arts as her maids, whereupon each of these describes the
content of her respective science or art. However, the execution
of the plan is spiritless and out of harmony with the brilliant
setting. Medicine and architecture are mentioned among the
maids of Philology, but are not introduced as speakers [2] St. Augustine had begun, while still a teacher of rhetoric, to write an
encyclopedia, but did not get beyond grammar and music, and
scarcely touched upon rhetoric, geometry, arithmetic, and philosophy.[3] Cassiodorus, the contemporary of Theodoric, covered
the entire field of education in his work, *De Artibus ac Disciplinis Liberalium Artium*, which he wrote for the training of
the clergy. Many other writers treated matters taken from
the different sciences without adhering, however, to the Greek
system of the seven liberal arts, while some followed no plan
whatsoever in their compilations. The *Natural History* of Pliny
the Elder contains, in its 37 books, extracts from more than
2,000 writers on astronomy, geography, anthropology, zoology,
botany, medicine, mineralogy, metallurgy, and history of art
This *History* is aptly described by Pliny the Younger as an
"opus diffusum, eruditum, nec minus varium quam ipsa na-
tura,"[4] and it will ever remain a monument to the industry of

[1] Jahn, *Ueber romische Enzyklopadien* in den *Ber d Konigl. sachs. Gesellschaft der Wissenschaften*, Phil.-hist Klasse, II, 1856, 263-287.
[2] Ebert, *Geschichte der christlichen Literatur*, Leipzig, 1874, I, p. 459
[3] August , *Retract*, I, 6.
[4] Plin., *Ep*, III, ς.

its author and an inexhaustible storehouse of anecdotes. A. Gellius, the author of the *Attic Nights*, which he wrote for the instruction and entertainment of his children, is a representative of those compilers who, while following no system in their work, yet succeeded in amassing a wealth of information as well as in making it accessible to others. The didactic purpose of many similar works appears from the introduction, wherein the work is dedicated to a friend or a son—a custom of Roman authors which was not borrowed from the Greeks, but which can be traced to Cato. Many textbooks were thus written for individual needs, and they form a special department of Roman literature.

6. The Romans inclined more to philology and polymathy than to philosophy, and they accomplished little for the advancement of philosophy. Pure speculation had little attraction for the practical Roman, the man of war and action, yet he availed himself of the services of philosophy for the purpose of increasing his knowledge and of developing his mental faculties. The statement of Ennius, "*Philosophari est mihi necesse, at paucis, nam omnino haud placet*,"[1] expresses the subjective and eclectic attitude of the educated Roman toward philosophy, for even if Cicero and Seneca did not content themselves with a smattering of the subject, still self-enjoyment was the principal motive of their speculation. Cicero was moreover ambitious to try the powers of his native tongue on the abstract materials, and though Varro had taught dialectic "to converse in Latin," it was Cicero who inaugurated the use of Latin philosophical terms, a fact that was to have far-reaching effects in after times.[2] The study of philosophy is also largely responsible for the high stage of development attained by Roman jurisprudence, for jurisprudence is indebted to philosophy, not only for its first principles, but also for its perfection of logical form, which rendered it fully equal as a work of intellectual art to the mathematics of the Greeks.[3] The founders of the Neopythagorean and the Neoplatonic systems also drew largely upon Roman philosophy, *e. g.*, the learned mystic Nigidius Figulus and the Sextii. Here the history of philosophy repeats itself:

[1] Cic., *Tusc.*, II, 1, 1; cf. *de or.*, II, 37, 156; *Rep.*, I, 18.
[2] Willmann, *Geschichte des Idealismus*, 2nd ed., Braunschweig, 1907, I, 41 ff; Eucken, *Geschichte der philosophischen Terminologie*, Leipzig, 1878, pp. 52 ff. However, Prantl, *Geschichte der Logik* (I, p. 512) takes a less favorable view of Cicero's terminology.
[3] Bœckh, l. c., p. 705.

as formerly in Greece so now in Rome philosophy returned to
theology, whence it had first proceeded. This circumstance
explains the interest which the Romans at that time took in
the mysteries. This interest certainly betokened more than a
mere hankering after the wonderful and the occult, or an affected air of mysteriousness "The shallow mind," says Fr.
Creuzer, "was satisfied with the glamor of the garish gods of
mythology, but the man of deeper mind sought an answer to
his anxious questions and rest for his weary heart in the sacred
mysteries. In the midst of a dark and dreary world these
mysteries appeared to the Roman as a place of refuge, as an
oasis in the desert, where he found rest and peace."[1]

Thus all the essential elements of Greek education find a
home in Roman education But the results of this assimilation
of foreign elements compare unfavorably with the development
of the original content of Greek culture In their education
the Romans lack the proper foundation: they possess no literary
work, created in the olden days, revered and esteemed as an
oracle by the nation at large, and interwoven with its very fibre.
Instead, we see the Greek schoolmaster attempting to supply
both the literature and the subject-matter of teaching. There
is, furthermore, no harmonious co-operation between poetry
and science in order to produce the art of language and its
theory Instead, theory develops prematurely at the expense of
art, and hence the mind is first taken up with form rather than
with content. Finally, Greek polymathy transferred to Roman
soil, gains rapidly in extent, but, lacking philosophy, it lacks
unity, and while the Roman philosophers were eclectics, the
system of education had to serve the purely practical and useful.
But with all these defects, the form that Rome gave to the
content of Greek education was best adapted for spreading as
well as for conserving Greek culture The Mediterranean and
Northern peoples could not be properly introduced to the culture of the ancients before this culture had assumed the form
of practical sciences instead of its original spiritualized fullness
The rules of Donatus' grammar were more useful in the process
of assimilation than the Stoics' philosophy of language or the
Homeric criticism of the Aristarchs of Alexandria Again, the
art of oratory, allied with jurisprudence, did better service in
this connection than the ethical rhetoric of Isocrates; and greater results were obtained by the practical and expert gromatists

---

[1] Creuzer, *Symbolik*, 2nd. ed., II, p. 996.

than with the logico-architectonic wisdom of Euclid. Though the content of Roman education appear inorganic and unassimilated, yet it entered deep into the consciousness of the Roman nation, and thus the great nation of warriors and conquerors could employ it as the instrument for the intellectual assimilation of the most diverse peoples, and, in point of fact, it proved one of the strongest elements in holding together the nations that came under the sway of the Romans.

CHAPTER XIII.

The Ethos of Roman Education.

1. Just as the content of Greek education was changed and modified by being transplanted to a foreign soil, so the ideals, too, of Roman educators were not entirely the same as the educational ideals of the Greeks. The Romans accepted the distinct difference established by the Greeks between liberal and vocational education; and the terms: *artes ingenuæ, liberales, studia ingenua, liberalia* are faithful renderings of the corresponding Greek terms. However, the *bonæ artes, i. e.,* the arts of the *vir bonus,* the patriot and man of honor, imply something specifically Roman. But in Rome, as in Greece, the liberal arts are regarded as an elegant occupation of one's leisure, as a joy and an ornament of life, and as something that enters deep into one's personality: "Other occupations are not suited to every time, nor to every age or place; but these studies are the food of youth, the delight of old age; the ornament of prosperity, the refuge and comfort of adversity; a delight at home, and no hindrance abroad; they are companions by night, and in travel, and in the country."[1] Still, the Roman thought it perfectly compatible with the liberal character of cultural studies, that they should fit a man for the performance of certain duties. He insists much more emphatically than the Greek, that the mastery of language be the net profit of these studies. *"Linguas edidicisse duas"* belongs to the *"ingenuas pectus coluisse per artes,"*[2] and the power of oral, secondarily of literary, expression was put down as the tangible aim of the varied learning and teaching. To be considered an educated man, it is not

---

[1] Cic., *Pro Arch.,* 7.
[2] Ovid, *De Arte Am.,* II, 121.

enough to have pursued certain studies, but it is necessary that
one be able to "speak and write intelligently and incisively and
with nicety on a subject."[1] Owing to the close relationship
between oratory and jurisprudence, the latter was also considered one of the practical aims of liberal studies. The true
jurisconsultus is, unlike the *legulejus* (the American "shyster"),
a man of culture and refinement, and the knowledge of law is,
on the other hand, also indispensable to the orator.[2] After the
Emperors, especially Adrian, had introduced the class of state
officials, the vocational tendency became even more marked in
education, and the demands made upon the government officials
controlled henceforward the work of the schools

Roman writers complain occasionally that the education of
the young and the methods followed in the schools were but ill
adapted to meet the demands of practical life and were, therefore, worthless However, we must be on our guard lest we
inject a meaning into their words that was foreign to the writers'
minds, because our modern conditions, to which their sayings
are often applied, are entirely different from those obtaining in
ancient Rome When Seneca pens his *"Non vitæ, sed scholæ
discimus!"*—which has become a household word with many
and the shibboleth of all "practical" educationists—he does not
wish to say that the young people are compelled to learn matters that would prove useless for life. But his contention is
that no studies can impart the wisdom that comes of the experiences gained in life, and that literary affectation is not
conducive to virtue[3] The bitter attack made by Petronius on
the rhetoric schools of his time is more truly reminiscent of the
present-day complaint of the divergency between school and
life. "I think," he says, "that the schools stupefy our boys,
for there they hear and see nothing of what is generally useful."

[1] Corn Nep in Suet, *De Illust Gramm*, 4 "Litterati—qui aliquid dili-
genter et acute scienterque possint aut dicere aut scribere " "Litteratus" is
the translation of γραμματικός, and its specific meaning is, interpreter of literary works "Litteratura" is the Latin for γραμματική, and the Latin equivalent for the Greek γραμματιστής is "litterator," elementary teacher
[2] Cic, *De Orat*, I, 55, 236, cf ibid, 46, 202 and *Brut*, 49, and Quint,
XII, 3
[3] Sen, *Ep*, 106 fin It might be well to quote the context of the much-
abused passage. "Non faciunt bonos ista"—the subject was dialectical subtleties—"sed doctos, apertior res est sapere, immo simplicior, paucis est ad
mentem bonam uti litteris sed nos ut cetera in supervacuum diffundimus,
ita philosophiam ipsam, quemadmodum omnium rerum, sic litterarum quoque
intemperantia laboramus non vitæ, sed scholæ discimus Vale "

And after giving some examples of vapid rhetorical exercises, he adds, "He who is fed on such foodstuffs can attain to the use of reason as little as he who lives in the kitchen can breathe sweet odors."[1] Just like Cato in his caustic witticism about the perennial learning how to speak, without, however, getting one inch nearer the goal of being actually able to speak, Petronius here refers to the insipid trash of counterfeit rhetoric. But in attacking the abuse, he does not suggest that rhetoric should be banished from the schools. The practical value of the *fari posse* and the interest in the art of language were too deeply impressed on the ancient mind to permit the critic to suggest so revolutionary a change in education. The Roman schools were in the essentials never out of touch with life, even if the foreign character of their education would not permit the complete harmony between theory and practice as had been the case in Greece at the time when Attic culture was at its best.

2. In keeping with the high value that the Romans attached to practical oratory, they recognized a distinction between practical ability (*Fertigkeit*) and theoretical knowledge (*Kenntnis*), which two factors the Greeks considered inseparably united in their παιδεία. *Eloquentia* was the element of practical ability, and *eruditio* that of theoretical knowledge. The Latin *eruditio* is not co-extensive with the Greek παιδεία. It fails to express the element of gymnastic training no less than the formal element of education, and stresses, instead, the acquiring of positive knowledge, in which regard it is opposed to eloquence as well as to philosophy.[2] It is significant that Roman education, based as it is on bookish lore, has no adequate equivalent for the Greek παιδεία, and that it does not, as we should expect, adopt the latter among its stock of words, whereas φιλολογία is taken over into the Latin language and must often serve, for want of a better term, for παιδεία.[3]

The tendency toward many-sidedness was not lacking in

---

[1] Petron., *Sat.*, in.

[2] Thus in Suet., *Cal.*, 53: "E disciplinis liberalibus minus eruditioni, plurimum eloquentiæ attendit." Cic., *Fin.*, I, 7, fin.: "Vellem equidem aut ipse (Epicurus) doctrinis fuisset instructior—est enim non satis politus iis artibus, quas qui tenent eruditi appellantur—aut ne deteruisset alios a studiis."

[3] Attejus Capito, who "multiplici variaque doctrina censebatur", was the first to call himself "Philologus" (Suet., *De Illustr. Gramm.*, 10). Homer is called "poetarum parens et philologiæ omnis dux," in Vitruv., *Proœm.*: Marc. Cappella personifies education under the name of "Philologia."

Roman education, and the Romans consistently understood it as demanding that the mastery of language should be based on a solid knowledge of facts and things. There was less need for insisting on the correct expression of knowledge than for demanding that the chief concern should ever be the mastery of the content, that the matter was more important than the form. It is in this sense that Cicero demands of the orator that he be a master of all arts and sciences. With the same end in view Quintilian formulates his plan of studies. Tacitus likewise describes true eloquence "as proceeding from many studies, from diverse abilities, and a comprehensive and general knowledge, as the orator is not confined, like other professions, to a narrow field; for only he who can discourse beautifully and gracefully, convincingly and appropriately on any subject whatsoever, is worthy of being called an orator."[1] But the Romans were as much alive as the Greeks to the dangers of many-sided studies, and their literature abounds in warnings not to strive for a diversity of knowledge at the expense of unity and harmony, not to miss the necessary because of the interesting. The saying of Pliny the Younger, "*Multum, non multa*,"[2] is still an axiom of the schools, and Seneca's attacks on the smatterers of universal knowledge are spicy commentaries on what Heraclitus and other Greeks had said against pseudo-polymathy.

3. The Romans attribute to education the effect of civilizing all who come under its influence, and the civilizing process constitutes the moral side of Roman education. The very word "*erudire*" (to free from rudeness) signifies the moral influence that the Romans attributed to education. The nation of soldiers and farmers who set out to conquer the world and to spread their civilization among barbarian tribes, were quick to realize that civilization is the proper function of education: "The learning of the fine arts softens the manners, and does not permit men to remain savages."[3] Cicero maintains that eloquence first collected the scattered savages of early times into communities and so converted them to the ways of civilized men.[4] But the higher and truly moral influence of education

---

[1] Tac., *Dial.*, 30.

[2] *Epist.*, 7, 9: "Ajunt multum legendum esse, non multa." Cf. Quintilian: "Et multa magis quam multorum lectione formanda mens" (*Inst.*, X, 1, 59).

[3] Ovid, *Pont.*, 2, 9, 47: "Didicisse fideliter artes emollit mores nec sinit esse feros."

[4] Cic., *D. Ora.*, I, 8, 33; *De Inv.*, I, 2; cf., however, Quint., III, 2, 4.

and its utter worthlessness when it cuts itself off from ethical aims, are stressed by Cato of the old Roman school as well as by the Stoic Seneca. The latter satirizes the "vain and unprofitable show of the fashionable learning and the world of books from which no good can come."[1] Because they attached a special importance to the educational side of the liberal studies, the Romans had to insist more than the Greeks on the reverence which the pupils owed to their teachers: "It is the will of the gods that the teacher occupy the father's place;"[2] "the teachers have engendered, not the body, but the soul, and the reverence towards them is most favorable to progress in studies."[3]

With their strongly developed socio-political sense the Romans perceived the socio-ethical principles underlying educational traditions: "The education of the young represents the greatest and most valuable service to the state" (Cicero); "for a man to rear children, to immortalize himself and his race, is no mean honor and of greater value than immense wealth" (Plautus). But here, as with the Greeks, the individual motive to immortalize oneself is connected with the desire to preserve the intellectual treasures of the race. Still the Roman was not content with transmitting these treasures to posterity, for he took a special pride in spreading them broadcast among his own contemporaries. He boasts that he imposed on the nations not only his yoke but also his language, and thus united them into one whole through the imperial language and the imperial educational system:[4] "The Athens of the Greeks now belongs to us and to the whole world; Gaul is so well versed in the languages as to educate lawyers for Britain; and in Thule they discuss the appointment of a rhetorician."[5] This cosmopolitan tendency of Roman education was a distinct advance beyond the Greek ideal, because the latter remained more closely allied with the nationality. The opposition between Hellenes and barbarians disappears, and the state of mind which embodied all the educational elements was named, not after one nation, but after the common humanity of the whole race. Originally, *humanitas* signified what is proper to man as a social being: the kind feelings, dispositions, and sympathies of man, and

---

[1] Sen., *Ep.*, 59.
[2] Juv., *Sat.*, 7, 209: "Di præceptorem sancti voluere parentis esse loco."
[3] Quint., *Inst.*, II, 2, 8; cf. Sen., *Ep.*, 73, *de benef.*, VI, 15, 2.
[4] Cf. Aug., *De Civ. Dei*, XIX, 7.
[5] Juv., *Sat.*, 15, 111 sq.; cf. Plin., *N. H.*, 3, 6, 39.

hence was similar in meaning to the Greek παιδεία. Later, however, it came to mean the refinement of the mind in keeping with man's high nature and sublime destiny: "They who have coined the Latin words as well as they who used these words correctly, wished *humanitas* to express what the Greeks have called παιδεία, the knowledge, namely, and the instruction in those matters which, when known, produce men in the full sense of the term; for of all living beings, man alone can strive for such a mental development and refinement, and therefore it is most proper that this education has been named the study of the humanities."[1] *Humanitas* is, then, the proper word of the Romans for education, and we find it used extensively in connection with the different phases of education: *humanitas* was connected with *doctrina*, *bonæ artes*, and even with *sermo*.[2] It retained, however, the original meaning of the sympathetically human and elegant refinement, and in its full meaning it expresses alike the cosmopolitan and the ethical tendencies of Roman education.

CHAPTER XIV.

The Roman School System.

1. The freedman Spurius Carvilius opened a pay school in Rome, about 250 B. C., and his name is generally associated with the beginnings of the Roman school system,[3] but upon what grounds is not certain. The reforms inaugurated by Spurius—he changed some characters of the alphabet, establishing especially the difference between C and G—may have attached special significance to his teaching; the novelty of asking compensation may also have rendered him noteworthy. But be that as it may, so much is certain that schools existed in Rome before the time of Spurius,[4] and even if we had no positive

---

[1] Gell., *N. A.*, 13, 16: "Qui verba Latina fecerunt, quique iis probe usi sunt . . . humanitatem appellaverunt id propemodum, quod Græci παιδείαν vocant, nos eruditionem institutionemque in bonas artes dicimus, quas qui sinceriter percipiunt (al. cupiunt) appetuntque, ii sunt vel maxime humanissimi. Hujus enim scientiæ cura ac disciplina ex universis animantibus uni homini data est, idcircoque humanitas appellata est." Cf. Cic., *Rep.*, I, 17.

[2] Cf. Cicero, *De Or.*, I, 16, 71: "In omni genere sermonis, in omni parte humanitatis dixerim oratorem perfectum esse debere."

[3] Plut., *Quæst. Rom.*, 59: ὀφὲ δ' ἤρξαντο μισθοῦ διδάσκειν καὶ πρῶτος ἀνέῳξε γραμματοδιδασκαλεῖον Σπόριος Καρβίλιος ἀπελεύθερος Καρβιλίου.

[4] Liv., III, 44, where he tells the story of Virginia, and V, 27, where he tells the . . . . . . schoolmaster of Falerii, who turned traitor.

proof for this, we might conclude it from the fact that the Romans had written laws 200 years before him, and had even long before been interested in the priestly learning of the neighboring nations. From the earlier name for school, *ludus*, we may infer with some probability that the first schools were connected with religious services. The *ludi* were the festive games connected with public worship, and it is much more probable that the schools were named after these games, than that learning was considered a sort of play or sport. Furthermore, if Spurius occasioned so much comment by asking pay for his teaching, the earlier schools may well have been connected with the religious services. Still, we have no direct proofs to substantiate this view.

In the period of the Republic, the Censors were entrusted with the supervision of education, but their authority was restricted, as in the matters also of immorality and celibacy, to passing a vote of disapproval. For the rest the individual was free to follow his own views in educating his children: "The Romans have seen fit not to pass such laws anent the training of the young as would establish a uniform system of education."[1] This liberal policy of the Romans was often censured by the Greeks; but it was only the revolutionary changes which threatened to result from the introduction of Greek education that induced the Romans to pass school regulations. The first step in this direction was taken in 161 B. C., when the Senate ordered the Greek philosophers to leave the country. In 93 B. C., the Censors Cn. Domitius Ahenobarbus and L. Licinius Crassus published an edict against the Latin rhetors, which, though it failed to produce the desired effect, is an interesting document for the history of education: "It has been brought to our knowledge that there are certain educational reformers and that the young people flock to their schools. These reformers call themselves rhetors, and they demand of the young that they sit in their schools day by day. But our forefathers have ordained what is to be taught in our schools to the young, and what schools they are to frequent. We can not approve of these new practices, opposed, as they are, to the manners and customs of our forefathers; it is for this reason that we would publicly state that we disapprove alike of the new teachers and of their pupils."[2]

[1] Cic., *Rep.*, VI, 2.
[2] Suet., *De Clar. Rhet.*, 1.

2. The new education, however, continued to win favor, despite the government opposition, and shortly after the publication of the edict Rome had no less than twenty schools, directed, in great part, by capable grammarians and rhetoricians. The Grecism *schola* now began to supplant the old Latin *ludus*, and the schools were also graded according to the Greek system. The *ludi magister*—known also as *litterator*, which name later gave way to *grammatistes*—taught the elements; his school building was modest and his pay equally so. His instruction was known as the *trivialis scientia*,[1] *i. e.*, the knowledge to be found in the streets; or perhaps, too, the circumstance that his school was generally located at crossroads (*in triviis*) gave rise to a term which was later used so extensively. Larger schools employed assistant teachers and special tutors for writing (*notarii*) and arithmetic (*calculatores*).

A more honorable position was held by the *litteratus* or *grammaticus*, who taught grammar, read and interpreted the poets, practiced recitations and disputations, and occasionally taught the elements of rhetoric. Suetonius has given us fine sketches of some Roman grammarians; they are splendid types and men of strong character. There is the learned, but irascible, Orbilius Pupillus, the teacher of Horace, who, at war with the rest of the world, wrote a book on the sufferings of the schoolmaster, and died poor, but received a monument in his native city, Beneventum. Another type is Valerius Flaccus, who introduced competitive drills and prizes among his pupils, and who was so much attached to his charges that when Augustus appointed him tutor of his grandchildren, he would not leave his school, so that the Emperor was forced to transfer the whole institution to the imperial palace. Another interesting figure is Remmius Palæmon, who, having been born in slavery, accompanied the son of his master to school and acquired so extensive a knowledge from merely listening there that he was much in demand as a teacher. In this way he amassed an immense fortune, but his pride—he maintained that learning had come to the earth at his birth and would leave again at his death— and licentiousness gave offence.

The rhetorician finished the education begun by the grammarian. Adults, and even distinguished men, frequented the first schools of the rhetoricians. The rhetorician was always assured of a large attendance whenever he or his pupils con-

---

[1] Q... I, 4, ...

ducted public exercises in oratory. The public exercises in a good school of oratory were always an event for Roman society; every new turn of expression, every witty allusion to the questions of the day, was applauded; and the performers would ever after remember their parts. Seneca, for instance, in his old age recorded long passages from speeches he had delivered as a boy.[1] The technical rules were many and covered the most minute details. Not only the plan of the oration and the ornaments of style, but also the euphony of words and the delivery, were the subject of serious study and much practice. Whether the sentence should begin with an anapest or a spondee, was a question of great moment. Every movement of the hand, the folds of the toga, the dropping and the throwing back of the toga—all was subject to rules. "The art of oratory required the full development of both body and mind;"[2] and in the school of oratory the young Roman acquired the good taste, the manners, and the pleasing address of the gentleman.

The young Romans were accustomed, even after their own country had established a complete system of schools, to go to foreign countries for their higher studies, especially for a course in philosophy. Though Alexandria was considered the home of scientific research, yet Athens and Rhodes were frequented more by the traveling students. The higher forms of Greek oratory were likewise studied in Greece; and in the period of the Empire, the Sophists, who represented the last flowering, as it were, of Greek rhetoric, attracted pupils from all parts of the world.

3. The number of the lower schools must have been very great. "It is a mistaken opinion," says Mommsen,[3] "that antiquity was materially inferior to our own times in the diffusion of elementary attainments. Even among the lower classes and slaves there was considerable knowledge of reading, writing, and arithmetic: in the case of a slave steward, for instance, Cato, following the example of Mago, takes for granted the ability to read and write." Among the lower classes the truly gifted could find opportunities enough to learn to read and write, and thus the way was open to them to acquire an extensive knowledge. The schools of the provinces, the lower as well as the higher, were no mean factor in the Romanizing

[1] Ussing, l. c., pp. 148 ff.
[2] Burckhardt, *Die Zeit Konstantins des Grossen*, 2nd ed., 1880, p. 380.
[3] *History of Rome*, transl. by W. P. Dickson, New York, 1894, II, p. 494.

process and fully as important in this regard as the garrisons
and courts. In Spain, Sertorius had established, about 80 B. C.,
a school at Osca, for the purpose of introducing Greco-Roman
culture, and, as early as the first century of the Christian era,
the Spanish schools could point to such graduates as M. An-
næus Seneca, the father of the philosopher, and the celebrated
rhetorician Quintilian. The African Province became in the
second century the literary centre of the Empire, and Utica,
Carthage, and Madaura were the seats of famous schools. In
Gaul the Roman schools spread so fast that Horace expressed
the hope that the "*potor Rhodani*" would read his poems,
and not a few cities of France and the border country of Germany can boast of having possessed schools at the time of the
Roman occupation. Among the Britains, Agricola gave the impetus to study Latin; and the Pannonians learned the imperial
language under Augustus.[1] The East was slower in accepting
the language and education of Rome, as it had assimilated the
Greek learning long before the Roman invasion; but Latin
schools seem to have flourished there also, as may be concluded
from the textbook that Dositheus wrote in Latin for Greek-
speaking pupils.[2]

With a view to making the treasures of Greco-Roman culture accessible to the vast Empire, the Cæsars organized a

[1] Cf. Eckstein in Schmid's *Enzylkopädie*, XI, p. 497.

[2] For the references see Eckstein, l. c., p. 509. The exercises are written
in Greek and Latin and are placed in parallel columns. They give a good
view of the teaching methods as well as of the daily life of the pupils, and
hence we may be pardoned for quoting extensively. "I go to school; I greet
the teacher, and he returns my greeting. Good morning, master; good morning, my fellow pupils. Let me go to my place. Give me my chair and stool.
Move up. Come here. I am seated; I am studying, and learning by heart.
I know my lesson and can recite it. Write. I am writing. I studied, then
recited, then I began to read a few verses. I can not write first; please, write
it for me as best you can. The wax is too hard; it should have been soft.
I write, then rub it off. The page, the stylus. I know my lesson. I asked
the teacher for leave to go home for my breakfast. He dismissed me; I took
my leave, and he returned my greeting. After I returned from breakfast, I
recited my lesson. Boy, let me see your tablet. The others took their turn
in reciting their lessons. I also know my lesson. I must take a bath. I
am coming; I have arranged for the fresh linen. Then I ran and came to the
bath." The quaint little book contains, besides such conversations, a Latin
grammar, a Greek-Latin dictionary, fables of Æsop, a brief account of the
Trojan War, the names of the gods, the constellations, tales from mythology,
court-decisions of the Emperor Adrian in the form of anecdotes, and extracts
from a compendium of law. And thus classical antiquity did not lack the
medley of the modern reader.

system of state schools that was well adapted to this purpose. It is unfair to accuse them of having, through their system and laws, stifled a free and natural growth, because it is only through a system and laws that education could at all be organized, a *conditio sine qua non* for all later cultural progress. The imperial schools were the predecessors of the universities; their methods were copied by the Middle Ages and the Renaissance, and the *Didactica* of the 17th century was patterned after Quintilian's textbook, the latter being the fruit of twenty years of teaching in a school endowed by a Roman emperor.

Julius Cæsar, the creator of the Empire, took the first steps towards giving state aid to the schools. He granted the privilege of citizenship to the teachers of the liberal arts, and planned the founding of a public library of Greek and Latin books, the librarianship of which he offered to Varro. Augustus was a generous patron of scholars and artists, and founded the Octavian and Palatine Libraries. Vespasian was the first to grant the higher teachers a salary, and Quintilian is mentioned as the first salaried professor. Trajan provided for the education of the children of the poor, and the *Ulpia*, a library founded by him, surpassed all similar institutions. Encouraged by his example, the provinces also began to provide better for education and to employ teachers. Adrian founded the Atheneum on the Capitoline Hill, and here orators and poets appeared in public, and Greek and Latin rhetoricians conducted classes. Owing to his efforts the Athenian schools flourished anew, and he added a palatial gymnasium and a large library to the existing institutions, and scattered schools all over the provinces, particularly his native province, Spain. He honorably retired on pensions those men who had grown old in the teaching service. His successor, Antoninus Pius, paid high honors and salaries to the higher teachers in all provinces; he made a privileged class of these by exempting philosophers, rhetoricians, and grammarians from taxes, military service, the quartering of soldiers, and other public duties. But the number of privileged positions was limited, so that small towns were entitled to six, larger towns to eleven, and the capitals to fifteen.[1] Marcus Aurelius endowed two professorships at each of the four Athenian schools of philosophy (Academic, Peripatetic, Stoic, and

[1] Ussing, l. c., p. 160. These figures do not fix the number of teachers to be employed in the respective places, but only the number of the privileged positions.

Epicurean) and, besides, two professorships of rhetoric. Alexander Severus founded at Rome new chairs of rhetoric, grammar, medicine, mathematics, mechanics, architecture, and haruspicy, and granted free scholarships to poor students. In 301 Diocletian made regulations to prohibit the teachers from demanding too high a compensation of their pupils: the master (*magister, institutor litterarum*) was to receive no more per month than 50 denarii; the teacher of arithmetic, 75; the teacher of shorthand, the same sum; the teacher of architecture was allowed 100 denarii; the teacher of Greek or Latin grammar, 200; and the teacher of geometry, the same amount; while the rhetorician or sophist was entitled to the highest compensation, 250 denarii.[1] Constantine confirmed all the privileges previously granted to teachers and added that of personal inviolability.

The rich endowment of the professorships made them desirable, and this brought it about that the candidates for them had to submit to competitive examinations. The Emperor Julian was the first to issue a decree to this effect, and his decree is the oldest document extant relative to the admittance of candidates to the teaching profession: "The teachers and masters of studies should be distinguished, first, for their exemplary conduct and, secondly, for their eloquence. But since it is impossible for me to be personally present in each community, I order that the candidate for the office of teacher should not be admitted in a careless, haphazard way, but only after the governing board (*ordo*) has declared him fit for the office, and after the chief men of the council (*curiales optimi*) have unanimously declared in his favor."[2] The enactments of Justinian are the oldest academic laws extant. According to his regulations, the students must, before being admitted to the schools of the Capital, produce before the board their naturalization papers, must next decide for a certain science, keep aloof from forbidden societies, and, in general, lead a good life, and complete their studies when twenty years of age. The graduation papers should report upon the morals of the student and his progress in studies, "so that," as the document states in the end, "We may obtain full knowledge of the scholar's good points and the studies pursued by each student, and may be able to decide whether and at what time We shall need his

[1] Th. Mommsen, *Ueber das Edikt Diokletians*, etc. in the *Ber. d. Königl. Sächs. Ges. d. Wissenschaften* 1851, pp. 1 ff.
[2] Cod. 1.

services."[1] The number of professors teaching in the larger institutions may be inferred from the regulations passed by Theodosius II. in 425, which ordained that Constantinople University, which was rivalling the imperial university at Rome, should have 31 professorships: three for Latin rhetoric, and five for Greek rhetoric; ten for Latin grammar, and the same number for Greek grammar; one for philosophy; and two for jurisprudence. Only the holders of these professorships were permitted to lecture in the halls of the Capitol; but the public professors were, on the other hand, forbidden to conduct private schools.

The political magistrates controlled all the schools and institutions of learning. It would seem as though a special official had been appointed for a time for this work; at least there was an office charged with the supervision of schools and libraries: ἐπὶ τῶν βιβλιοθηκῶν καὶ ἐπὶ παιδείας.[2]

[1] Ibid., XIV, 9.
[2] Grassberger, l. c., II, p. 3.

V.

CHRISTIAN EDUCATION ON ROMAN SOIL.

CHAPTER XV.

The Aims of Christian Education.

1. In the process of changing the face of the world the forces of Christianity were first engaged upon the races and peoples belonging to the Roman Empire, and this Christianizing of Greco-Roman education is of basic importance for all later systems of education. This is not saying that all the educational influences of Christianity were called into play in this first period, for the influences received by the ancient peoples which were then the representatives of education, were other than were received later by peoples just emerging upon the scene of civilization. And these later peoples, too, in their maturity, received peculiar, though again different, influences from the same source. In point of fact, each age has come under the creative influence of Christianity, but none has exhausted the fulness of its blessings. The Age of the Fathers built, indeed, the foundation for later developments in education as well as in other fields, but it did this only in so far as it was the first to receive the educational elements of the new teaching and the first to witness how these elements, added to a soil rich with the materials of a different civilization, showed their strength by producing fruit a hundredfold.

The Gospel brought along no system of education and, only in a limited measure, did it furnish the wherewithal for the making of one, and the materials embodied in Christian education were only born of the ideals that Christianity brought into the world. But these ideals are by their nature opposed to the ideals of the education of classical antiquity, and the ethos of Christian education is the reverse, in more than one regard, of Greco-Roman civilization. Though the religious element was not lacking in heathen civilization, yet it was considered of secondary importance. To the cultured Greek and Roman the religious sense appeared of no higher importance than other phases of the complete character. But the religious element was the core of Christian education, and it was proposed to men, not in an abstract or obscure formula, neither in the imagery of poetic thought, but in the figure of a concrete person, the model for all followers of Christianity: "Other foundation no man can lay, but that which is laid; which is Christ Jesus." (I. Cor., 3, 11.) As the glad tidings were not transmitted "in the learned words of human wisdom, but in the doctrine of the Spirit, comparing spiritual things with spitirual (ibid., 2, 13)," so no knowledge and no ability, if disjoined from Him, before Whom the wisdom of the world is foolishness, could be held of any worth. The Christian sense turned away as well from the Jewish knowledge of the Law as from the æsthetical and worldly culture of the Greek, and turned to what appeared to these as an abomination and a foolishness. To the Christian the learning of the Jew and the culture of the Greek was the fountainhead of pride and self-justification, and the very opposite not only of that poverty in the spirit to which the kingdom of heaven has been promised, but also of that childlike spirit which is the spirit of the children of God.

A second element that was also strange to the ancient world, was introduced with the Christian hope for an eternal life. The innermost feelings of the ancients were bound up in this world as being the scene of their labors, sorrows, and joys; and their contentment with the things of sense was not disturbed by any teachings of the philosophers, though the latter, perpetuating the traditions of the olden times, taught the immortality of the soul and the judgment of the gods. The Christian, however, did then and does still look forward to the next world as man's true home, "for we have not here a lasting city, but we seek one that is to come." (Heb., 13, 14.) Hence he must in all his doings distinguish between such actions as have but a temporal end and such as will extend in effect into eternity. Consequently, the Christian attached less weight than the Greek and the Roman to the distinction between liberal and illiberal arts; his Faith established other and higher standards for evaluating the things of the earth, and hence the distinction between liberal and illiberal arts became less marked. It is now considered the chief aim of education to direct the minds of the young to "what is modest and sublime."[1] The sublime belongs

---

[1] Clem. Rom., *Ad Cor.*, I, 1: μέτρια καὶ σεμνὰ νοεῖν.

to the supernatural order; for this life it is enough, if we attain to what is modest: that a man be a true Christian in belief and practice—that is the all-important consideration. Of infinitely less moment is it whether he be practicing, beside his holy Faith, a liberal art, or whether he be only a humble mechanic. Education fulfills its chief purpose if it assists "the man of God to be perfect, furnished to every good work." (II. Tim., 3, 17.) The educational ideal of the Greeks ignored social and vocational relations; but this haughty aloofness had to give way before the teaching of Christianity that special gifts and offices and their organic co-operation, are traceable to divine influences, and are the type of the communion of the Church (see *supra* pp. 2 and 39). The Christian peoples have developed a concept of education that is essentially different from that of the ancients, and the very term "vocation," which is derived from the *vocatio* (κλῆσις) of the New Testament, reveals the influence of the Christian religion.

2. Having thus established as the chief end of education something that was foreign to the ancients, Christianity had to abandon also the exclusive character of ancient education, by reason of which culture was granted to only a few and denied to the uneducated masses. The latter condition of affairs appeared irremediable to even the greatest and keenest of the Greeks and Romans. However, Plato's saying, "It is difficult to discover the Creator and Father of all, but to announce Him to all is impossible,"[1] has been proved untrue by the achievements of Christianity. Even the lowest is now free to ask with Philip, "Lord, show us the Father;"[2] and St. Chrysostom could truly say in praise of the Cross that it had made all peasants philosophers. It is certain that the Church gave and gives to each individual, irrespective of sex, of family, or position in life, an ideal seed of the inner life, of which ancient education could offer a counterpart, inadequate at that, only through long and weary studies. It may be said that Christianity directs all to the path that leads to the life of the spirit, and so enables all to lead a spiritual life. Ancient philosophy had conceived the spirit as νοῦς, *mens*, mind, or reason, the faculty of thinking and reasoning, and deemed this to be the faculty of the soul that is destined to rule the sensuous appetite, and which was therefore to be trained to fulfill its function. This

[1] Plat. *Tim.*, p. 28
[2] Joh. 4.

training of the mind was to be done systematically and was to be encouraged in every possible way; but such a task could be undertaken only by the fortunate few. Christianity, however, sees the governing principle of man in another field of his mysterious inner nature, not in his intellect, but in his pneumatic or spiritual faculty. In this sense the Christian religion speaks of the spirit ($\pi\nu\epsilon\hat{\upsilon}\mu\alpha$) in opposition to the flesh ($\sigma\acute{\alpha}\rho\xi$), and the latter includes, not only the sensuous appetite, but everything connected with the earth earthly. The spiritual in man, the spirit that quickeneth, must also be kindled by the word and strengthened by discipline; but, as it has its source in God, it allows little opportunity for human development and endeavor. Its proper element is the life of Faith, but all faculties of the inner man, the understanding included, may become its instruments. The value, then, of the understanding is not absolute, nor beyond that of a most helpful instrument. But though the spiritual life does not depend on its development, yet the understanding, by having the power to raise man above the sensuous, becomes a strong weapon in the fight against the flesh. Thus the tendency of ancient education toward the spiritualizing of man is realized in a higher sense than was dreamed of by the heathen. The exclusiveness of ancient education is no more, but its moral value and content are preserved in the new order, and the spiritual tendency furnishes new arguments, even if only indirectly, for cultivating and ennobling the understanding. "The Logos enters," as Clement of Alexandria puts it, "through the gate of the thoughts."[1]

The regeneration in spirit demanded by the Christian religion takes place in the innermost parts of man's nature, where no teachings can assume such plastic forms as were possible within the field which ancient education had apportioned off as its proper domain. It is not the aim of Christianity to make a work of art of the inward and outward man. Hence the Christian religion appears to be unfavorable to the æsthetic tendency of education. The Christian ideal insists more on the complete changing of the personality than on harmonious and general development. Its doctrines are intended for a leaven in the inner man, rather than for a means to assist in the artistic development of the faculties. Nevertheless, the æsthetical element had its due place in early Christian education, for not only did the Church invite the arts to assist

---

[1] Clem. Al., *Coh.*, I., fin.

in her divine worship, but the spirit of Christianity supplied a content for the æsthetical forms in keeping with its own high nature. Even if the forms did thus lose somewhat of their purity, they were more than compensated for this loss by the richness of the content they received. Christianity deepened and spiritualized all human activity; and for this reason the creations of the Christian and of the ancient world are so different in conception and execution, so that the works of classical antiquity often appear to be, despite their greatness and perfection of form, cold, unsympathetic, and even soulless. This general tendency of the Christian religion extended in time and with ever-growing strength to music and the arts of design no less than to poetry and the art of language, and through these to the entire field of education. In Christian education, however, the arts never gained the high position they had occupied in ancient civilization: the civilization of the Christian religion has introduced so deep and serious a view of life as not to permit the spirit of play to remain the governing principle of inner formation.

3. The many-sidedness of ancient education was, like its æsthetical tendency, a hindrance rather than an advantage to the growth of the Christian educational system. The home of the busybodies, where the "natives as well as the strangers employed themselves in nothing else than either in telling or hearing some new thing" (Acts, 17, 21), proved an infertile soil for the seed of the Gospel. Yet the universality of Christianity influenced the entire field of arts and sciences. The mind of the Christian was naturally ready to receive all truth, for the truth of science and of art is in the end but "an emanation from Him Who has said: I am the Truth;"[1] and hence the Apostle could say truthfully, "All things are yours . . . . whether it be the world of life or death or things present or things to come; all are yours." (I. Cor. 3, 22.) But the universality of Christianity tends more towards the whole than the multiplicity of the parts; its aim is the totality rather than the diversity of the parts. This tendency renders Christianity so important a factor for the natural growth of science and, therefore, also of education. To establish the character of science as being one harmonious organism, it was necessary that a harmonious system of philosophy and theology be first established, and that, furthermore, the leading rôle in the world

[1] Au...

of learning be assigned to theology. Certain writers have found fault with this leadership of theology, contending that it prevented the free and unhampered development of science. But in point of fact, this leadership has been most favorable to science, for it gave to the endless variety of scientific efforts a kind of unity and harmony, and this resulted in the intensive, instead of in the extensive, work of the individual scholars. The peace that ensued among the wrangling philosophers was the stillness of recollection and a blessing for science, for it meant that the world of scholarship was rapt, as it were, in deep Pythagorean silence. Of the individual sciences, historical research admittedly received its universal character when the Bible became the world-book, as assembling in one book what Orientals and Greeks and Romans had written on history. The Bible furnished the first principles for the history of the human race; the sermon preached by St. Paul at Athens and Augustine's "City of God" contain the beginnings of all philosophy of history.[1] Similarly, the science of language is indebted to the "loosening of the tongues," because the Church, when preaching the Gospel, was the first to lay all languages under tribute and so afforded the first opportunity for treating all languages from a common point of view.[2] And the natural sciences, too, received from Christianity not only the impetus to dig deep into the nature of things—that tendency to search for the last reasons and the nature of things, which was more apt to encourage the laborious work of the scientist than was the care-free and happy-go-lucky character of the heathen[3]— but also the concept of nature uninhabited by fauns and nymphs. And hence it was only after the Christian view of physical nature had taken root, that the scientist was able to conclude upon laws, uniform and universal, governing the visible creation. The unity and harmony of nature could not be established but upon the grounds of monotheism, teaching one Creator for the whole creation, and it was the monotheism of the Christians, and not the monotheism of the Jews, that first let this principle of the unity of nature bear fruit in scientific research.

[1] Cf. Rocholl, *Die Philosophie der Geschichte*, Göttingen, 1878, pp. 21 ff. and 391.

[2] "The science of the languages of mankind is a science which, without Christianity, would never have sprung into life," M. Müller, *Lectures on the Science of Language*, New York, 1866, I, p. 128; Cf. J. Grimm, *Deutsche Grammatik*, I: Widmung an Savigny.

[3] Dubois-Reymond, *Kulturgeschichte und Naturwissenschaft*, Leipzig, 1878, p. 30.

The false many-sidedness of the ancients, the tendency of ancient education to fritter away its strength on a multiplicity of matters, the dabbling in all fields, offered little attraction to early Christian educators, as they were alive to the errors to which the subjective mind is liable. They recognized that this smattering of all knowledge involved an abuse of God's gifts. The truths of Faith are the centre; they must be received absolutely; and their objective nature is such as to admit of no change in favor of any subjective opinion The glad tidings announcing the coming of the great King. among the children of men and the truths proclaimed by Christ, His apostles, and His Church, are a precious inheritance that must be faithfully conserved and transmitted to future generations The mind and feelings may and should dwell on this content, but no man may ever presume to apply to it any standard lower than itself[1] But in this way the subject-matter of teaching is again endowed with that objectivity by virtue of which it is, not merely the instrument of education, but its content as well; and the narrow view of the Sophist, which obtained, at least to some extent, among the Greeks, that man is the measure of all things, is abandoned Still, it cannot be denied that the Christian nations have occasionally, in the course of later developments, gone to the opposite extreme by teaching what was much akin to the view of early oriental theology, that man is only the vessel for holding and receiving a certain educational content. This erroneous doctrine has, at different times, led to the revival of the subjectivity of the ancients But the Christian view, rightly understood, combines properly both elements: first, the objectivity of the content and, secondly, the demand to make this objective matter a vital element of the inner life And it is this Christian view which has had to serve again and again as the corrective of the mistaken relationship of the two factors.

As Christianity emphasized, in contrast to the subjective and æsthetical trend of the ancients, the discipline of truth inherent in all teaching and learning, so it has also established the love and care of souls as the chief motive for conserving and transmitting knowledge Consequently, the ancient love of fame and glory was no longer the principal consideration;

[1] "Keep that which is committed to thy trust, avoiding the profane novelties of words, and oppositions of knowledge falsely so called " (I. Tim 6, 20) Faith is a "good thing committed in trust" (II Tim 1, 13 and 14), a "treasure" (II. Cor 4, 7).

and ambition, the prime force in ancient education, lost much of its power with Christian peoples.

CHAPTER XVI.

The Content of Early Christian Education.

1. The content of early Christian education was, to a large extent, taken over from the educational system of the Greeks and Romans, but was considerably modified by coming into contact with the ideals of the new religion. The process of developing and organizing this content resembles the educational development of those eastern peoples whose intellectual life sprang from the national religions. But in the latter case the flexibility of the myths and the mythological philosophy facilitated the educational development from the heathen religions. A further favorable circumstance was the fact that the national consciousness of these eastern peoples was the instrument as well as the end of their educational development. The growth, however, of Christian education lacked these favorable conditions; the Faith that was its foundation is not born of myths, nor of poetry, nor of a poetic philosophy; neither was it connected with any definite nationality or any one language. The spirit of Christianity was obliged first to assimilate from the civilization, in the midst of which it found itself, all the elements of which it stood in need, in order to create its own language, literature, science, art, and education; and to accomplish this gigantic task, a force was needed, infinitely more powerful than any that had been operative in the ancient civilizations of either the eastern or the western peoples.

Still it must be conceded that there were also certain favorable circumstances, yet these were of such a nature as again offered special difficulties; and consequently even the favorable circumstances tested the creative power of Christianity. The two world languages, Greek and Latin, were an obvious advantage: the Greek language prevailed in the East, and after several centuries of growth and development, it was now a well-nigh perfect medium for the expression of thought; the Latin language, the language of conciseness and strength, of exactness and precision, prevailed in the West. But these languages had

12

to be adapted to the new doctrines which had found first expression in a Semitic, and therefore essentially different, tongue; and the Christian coinage of Greek and Latin words deserves to be called a creative process. The flexibility of the Greek language was of invaluable advantage for expressing the new concepts: "The cultured Greek took a special delight in applying all the resources of his wondrous language, with all its niceties, to any concept that met his eager and searching mind, and it was natural that he would address his questions to the Christian religion, and thus elicit many a reply."[1] Yet the over-refinement and the dialectical subtleties of the Greek offered as many difficulties as advantages, and neither its brilliant rainbow hues, nor the penetrating light shed by the Latin language on all the objects of the earth, sufficed by themselves to illumine the depths that the new doctrines disclosed.

These advantages and disadvantages of Greek and Latin obviously affected those sciences that dealt with these languages: grammar, rhetoric, and dialectic. However, the formal character of these subjects facilitated their assimilation. In as far as they tended to make human speech pure, fluent, and effective, they performed as great a service to the preacher of the Gospel as to the secular orator. Still their close connection with a literature and a system of poetics whose content was foreign and even hostile to the ideals of Christianity, stamped the heathen character on the sciences themselves. They were Christianized first on Greek soil, whence they had sprung, and only much later on Roman soil, where a further difficulty presented itself in their being so closely related to the laws and the government of the State. It is surprising how long it took to adapt these sciences to a Christian content. It might seem that the Epistles of St Paul, distinguished, as they are, for fiery eloquence, brilliant figures, and cogent argumentation, could have proved the basis of a new system of rhetoric and dialectic. But technical systems have a most tenacious life, and it is by far easier to change the language and literature of a people than to supply a new organon for them. Nay, these sciences have up to the present successfully withstood all attempts at a thorough reformation, so that even to-day—though we have at our command comparative philology and other sciences sufficient to revise the laws governing language, style, and the operations of the mind—we are still bound to the for-

[1] J A Mohler, *Patrologie*, Ratisbon, 1840, I, p 37.

mulas of the ancients, just as though Aristotle and the Alexandrians had decided all these matters for good and all.

2. It was an easier matter to correlate the mathematical
sciences with the Christian content. Geometry and arithmetic
appeared almost indifferent to the great disputes of theology
and philosophy. Music, instrumental and theoretical, astronomy,
and the science of the calendar were readily adjusted to the
service of the Church. The text of Scripture, "Thou hast
ordered all things in measure and number and weight,"[1] became
the guiding star of these studies, and this was no departure from
the spirit in which they had been conducted by the ancients.
It was a particular advantage that the ancients had generally
assigned to the mathematical sciences a merely preparatory
function. They had regarded them as preparatory to philosophy, and Christianity now set up theology as their goal, which
step involved no material change, because even with the Greeks
the theological aim had been the final end of mathematical
studies.[2] The demands of ecclesiastical writers that arithmetic
occupy itself with the mysteries of numbers and with the figures
quoted in the Bible, that geometry should deal with Biblical
and ecclesiastical measurements, and that astronomy study epochs and the cycles of feasts—these demands might, at first
blush, appear foreign to the proper functions of these sciences;
but they will no longer appear so if we recall that, in the East,
mathematics was originally considered an auxiliary science of
theology and was taken up with just such subjects as those
mentioned,[3] and that, in the West, the Pythagoreans and Platonists preserved the tradition that priests were the founders
of mathematics.

Philology was studied by the early Christian less for its
cultural value than out of sheer necessity: it embraced the
history, the myths, and antiquities of heathenism, and its mastery was thus indispensable for any successful controversy with
the heathen. Equipped with a knowledge of philology, the
Christian apologist could, on the one hand, show the foolishness
and inconsistency of old and recent myths and, on the other
hand, establish the *consensus gentium* by pointing to the traces
found among all peoples of the primitive revelation. To the
industry of ecclesiastical writers who worked with these ends

---

[1] Wisdom, xi, 21.

[2] Cf. *supra*, ch. IX, 5.

[3] *Supra*, ch. IV, 3 and ch. V, 3.

in view, we are indebted for much of our knowledge of classical antiquity. For instance, the account given by Clement of Alexandria of Egyptian literature is the safest guide extant among all the discordant reports concerning this dark field;[1] and the picture of Varro, so unique a character in the universality of his researches, has been preserved by Augustine.[2] The introduction of such matters into the theological writings was also of educational value to the early Christians, for in this way they became acquainted with choice elements of ancient education.

The Christians were from the first deeply interested in history, for the "fullness of time" represented to them the downfall of many nations and the beginning of a new epoch in the history of the world. They were interested in the history of the East as well as of Greece and Rome: the first formed the background for the history of the Chosen People; and the latter, the background for the history of the Church. Thus the impulse was given to write Christian history. But the written histories were assisted by other forces in keeping alive the historical interest. The very content of the Christian religion suggests, like that of the Mosaic Law, the style of historical presentation, and this circumstance led St. Augustine to adopt his historico-genetic plan of studies, in which "the heart and the lips would never lose the thread of the narrative, because the latter would prove the string of gold for holding the pearls of the doctrines."[3] This historical character of the teaching content had to react favorably on the growth of the historical sense in general. The study of history was also encouraged by the efforts made to preserve the memory of the Martyrs, for the purpose of establishing a vital solidarity with these heroes. Even in the first centuries the Church began to commemorate her joys and sorrows, her victories and persecutions, for she considered all these inseparably connected with the glorious records of her martyred Saints. This veneration of the saints has, like the Greek cult of the national heroes, inspired the fine arts, and has deepened and ennobled the soul of the whole Christian world.

3. The assimilation of philosophy, the capstone of ancient culture, with Christian education was a most difficult process: heathen philosophy furnished the enemies of the Gospel with

---

[1] *Supra*, ch. V, 1.

[2] *Supra*, ch. XII, 4.

[3] *De catech. rudibus*, c. 6.

weapons and the heretics with arguments against the Faith. The other departments of knowledge resembled fields where the new plants, though frail and weak in the beginning, would eventually supplant the vegetation of an older and stronger growth. Heathen philosophy, however, was rather like a fortress which the Christians had to take by storm before they could think of assimilating its good elements. This assimilation implied not a mere taking over of new and foreign elements; nay, the whole system must needs be made over and re-created in its entirety. One circumstance favorable to the Christian apologist was the fact that the tenets held by the various schools of philosophy were frequently diametrically opposed to one another. Another favorable circumstance was, that there existed no one school of philosophy but taught some truths that were closely related to the doctrines of Christianity. The transcendental philosophy of the Platonists appeared, in the beginning, to come nearest to the supernatural doctrines of Christianity. But as the struggle continued and as the dogmatic and philosophic position of Christianity became more clearly defined, it was found that just the ancient philosophers of a predominantly ethical or religious turn were the most insidious foes of the Christian religion. They represented, indeed, the highest form of heathenism, yet withal its most dangerous form also; and thus Plato, the Attic-speaking Moses, Μωύσες ἀττικίζων, could later be decried as the father of all heresies. It is a noteworthy fact that expiring heathenism clung tenaciously to the most abstruse of the ancient philosophers, Plato and Pythagoras, and sought among their teachings for the remains of earlier and more simple beliefs. But Christian philosophy accepted the supernatural at the hands of Faith and chose as its guide in earthly matters the sober clearness and keenness of the far-seeing and matter-of-fact Aristotle.

It was no light labor, and one of not a few generations, to assimilate the content of heathen education. There were seasons when the champions of the Christian cause grew faint of heart; then again they were elated with sudden and unlooked for success. At times all their efforts seemed to be naught but much ado about nothing, while at other times they grew eloquent with the supreme importance of the struggle. Much of what the early Christian writers wrote goes to show the heat of the strife and the varying moods of the parties engaged. The literature of the early Church reveals such widely divergent opinions, that certain writers have found in it authorities in support of their view that the Church was soon reconciled to the ancient philosophies, while writers of another school have likewise drawn from it arguments in support of their claim that Christianity looked with suspicion and even scorn on all ancient learning.[1] But it is this very divergency of views which should have opened the eyes of the student of history to read the signs of the times, as indicating the shifting of opinions and as betokening an intellectual and spiritual crisis—the greatest crisis, in fact, in the history of education.

4. The Greek-speaking East showed, in general, more readiness than the West to assimilate ancient education with the new religion. The Greek theologians of the period received their secular education at the old and venerable seats of learning; their teachers were, in some cases, celebrated representatives of the heathen sciences; and the theologians themselves realized, that they could not meet the heathen and the heretic on their own ground unless they were masters of the secular learning. Consequently, they defend the view that the Christian can and should assimilate the culture of the heathen; and they entertain little doubt that the difficulty presented by its polytheistic element can easily be overcome. Clement of Alexandria (died 217), the famous head of the catechetical school of the same city, was the first to combine the Christian and heathen studies in one system. The liberal arts form the lowest class, the philosophical sciences occupy the middle place, and the studies dealing with Christian Doctrine are supreme in rank and importance. A graded course of study prepares for the last-named subject, and this preparatory course Clement compares with the propædeutics of the Pythagoreans.[2] The course embraces the controversies with heathenism, the refutation of heathen errors, the directions for Christian living, and the doctrines of Christianity joined with the purer teachings of the heathen. This system of propædeutics forms the substance of the three chief works of Clement: *Hortatory Discourse to the Greeks* (Λόγος προτρεπτικός), *The Tutor* (Παιδαγωγός), and *Miscellanies* (Στρωματεῖς). While Clement adopted the methods of the eclectic, Origen (died 254), his successor, allowed the ancient learning as a whole to serve as a system of propædeutics: he

---

[1] The first view is taken among others by C. Daniel, *Des etudes classiques dans la société Chrétienne* (1853); and the second, by Abbé Gaume, *Le ver rongeur des sociétés modernes* (1851) (tr. by R. Hill, *Paganism in Education*, Lond , .

[2] *Strom.*, VII, p. 845

conducted his pupils through dialectic, natural philosophy, mathematics, and astronomy to ethics; then he returned to the philosophers and poets, employing an artist's skill in unraveling the tangled skein to detect the subtle errors. Only after all this ground had been gone over, did he begin the explanation of Holy Writ, and here he distinguished carefully between the literal, moral, and mystical sense.[1]

Similar cases of the mastery of the diversified learning of the age were not rare. Instances in point are Dorotheus (about 300), presbyter at Antioch and a Hebrew scholar, and Anatolius, bishop of Laodicea, to whom the Alexandrians offered the rectorship of their Peripatetic school[2]. There are, however, other instances evidencing that ancient philosophy was a hindrance to the perfect development of Christian philosophy. Stephanus of Laodicea, for example, proved at the time of the persecution neither a staunch Christian nor a consistent philosopher;[3] and even the great Origen was charged with having compromised between Christian theology and heathen philosophy.

5. The much-quoted oration of St. Basil, *Address to Young Men on the Right Use of Greek Literature*, treats professedly of the attitude of Christian youth toward classical literature. Employing a comparison found in Plato, Basil describes pagan literature as the material on which the young men are to exercise the eyes of their mind. Pagan literature should prepare, like shadows and mirrors, the eye for beholding the truths of Scripture. Christian wisdom is the choice fruit of the soul, while secular learning (κοσμικὴ παιδεία, παιδεύματα τὰ ἔξωθεν) is the foliage that protects and gives a pleasant appearance to the fruit. Moses and Daniel frequented the schools respectively of Egyptian and Chaldean sages, and were, therefore, pupils of pagan philosophers. The works of the poets may well elevate our feelings and infuse into our souls the respect for all that is noble and righteous. One who is familiar with Homer claims that all his works are one hymn in praise of virtue, and the poets, historians, and other representatives of the θύραθεν σοφία have written in a kindred spirit. All these works should be used as the bee uses the flowers: the bee neither visits all flowers nor does it ever attempt to carry off a whole plant; it takes of the single flower only so much as it finds useful and leaves the

---

[1] Greg. Thaum., *Paneg. in Orig.*, c. 5 sq.
[2] Euseb., *Hist. eccl.*, VII, c. 32.
[3] Ibid., c. 33.

rest.[1] As we beware of the thorns when plucking a rose from the bush, so we should select from these works what is useful, but beware of anything that might prove harmful. We must from the very beginning examine all learning and try to harmonize it with our final aim, or as the Doric proverb says, "test each stone by the measuring line."[2]

The countryman and fellow-student of St. Basil, St. Gregory of Nazianzus, is more emphatic in insisting on the necessity of secular studies, as we may see from his funeral oration on his departed friend. Here we have exact information relative to the status of studies in that age. In the eleventh chapter we read: "I think that all wise men will agree that education is our most valuable gift, and this is true not only of the sublime education proper to us Christians—which can neglect the ornaments of style and attend solely to the salvation of men and the beauty of truth—but also of pagan education, though this is looked upon by most Christians as harmful and as leading away from God. We need not scorn heaven, earth, and air, and all that belongs to these elements, because men have been so foolish as to pay divine honors to these works of the Lord. On the contrary, we may use them for our needs and comfort, though we must avoid the while all that might bring harm to ourselves, and never sink so low as to prefer the creature to its Creator, but rather discover in the work the hand and the power of the Architect and surrender up our minds and wills to the willing obedience of Christ. Similarly, must we use the pagan learning which occupied itself with the study and investigation of things, though we must here, too, shun all that might lead to error or perdition. The pagan learning may be employed to the best of purposes. Of itself it is indifferent, just as fire and food and iron or any other things are not of themselves useful or harmful, but the use or abuse makes them so, as even worms, if mixed with a drug, may give it a medicinal power. By taking over the learning of the heathen our fear of the Lord has been much increased: by noting what was of minor value we have come to have an eye for what is of the greatest value, and the impotence of the heathen has supplied our Faith with a strong support. We may, therefore, not make light of education, though many are inclined so to do; the probable reason for their narrowness being their own dullness and igno-

---

[1] The comparison of the bees has been much used in Christian pedagogy and has given rise to the pun: "Si capis sis apis."

[2] τὸν ἰδιώτα τὸ μεγάλων τιμᾷ

rance which they would fain conceal before others by making all like themselves, so that their own illiteracy would pass unnoticed amid the universal ignorance." But this clear and unmistakable commendation of education presupposes that—as had been the case in Gregory's own youth—"the heart be strong and surrounded by a strong wall" in order that the Faith of the Christian remain sweet and pure, like the River Alpheus (whose water is said to remain sweet while flowing through the Ionian Sea), and reject all harmful foreign elements. (Ibid., c. 22.[1])

Led by the same reasons, St. John Chrysostom did not permit the mythological fables to be read during the first period of schooling, for this might result, as he says, in an admiration of such heroes as were not able to control their passions.[2] The instruction in the elements of Christian Doctrine had marked the beginning of his own education, but later his mother Anthusa, who directed his training, did not hesitate to commit the rhetorical training of the mature youth to the care of Libanius, the celebrated Sophist and defender of heathenism.

6. The difficulties attendant upon the assimilation of ancient education were still greater in the West than in the East. This was in the nature of the case, for Roman education, being at best but an exotic growth, was controlled even more than Greek education by rhetoric and polite literature. A further reason was that philosophy offered the Greeks a goal that was somewhat akin in its idealism to the noble spirituality of the Christian religion, while the end-all of Roman education was the profession of the advocate, which could not, in spite of its scientific basis (the result of the development of Roman law), prove a fountainhead for the ideals of the higher life. To understand the opposition of the Latin Fathers to literary affectation, we must remember that some pagan rulers were even more strongly opposed to it than they. For example, Licinius, at first the co-regent and then the enemy of Constantine, describes literary education as a poison and pestilence to the State.[3] The artificial and stilted taste of the *homines literati* could not appreciate the greatness and simplicity of the Scriptures, and these æsthetes were more apt than the cultured Greeks to scorn the inspired volume as barbarous. The phrases: *Ciceronianus—Christianus*,

---

[1] Cf. K. Weiss, *Die Erziehungslehre der drei Kappadozier*, Freiburg, 1903.

[2] *Homil. 21 in epist. ad Ephes.*

[3] Burckhardt, *Die Zeit Konstantins des Grossen*, 2nd ed., Leipzig, 1880, p. 327.

disertus—desertus cultura Dei, were thought to imply an irreconcilable opposition; and among the Christians even professed imitators of classical models—as St. Ambrose, whose *De officiis ministrorum* is patterned after Cicero's *De officiis*, and the brilliant stylist Lactantius—warned their co-religionists against a devotion to secular studies.[1]   Speaking of mythology, Minucius Felix says, "These fables we learn from our unlettered parents, nay, what is still worse, they are the material with which we are constantly occupied in our studies and in our schools, especially when reading the poets, whose great influence has been most instrumental in preventing the spread of truth.   Hence Plato justly banished Homer, though celebrated and much admired, from the State."[2]   St. Jerome vehemently opposed the cult of pagan authors, for to his mind there could be as little intercourse between them and the Faith of Christ as between Christ and Belial, and as between the chalice of the Lord and the cup of the demons.   He tried to purge his style of all ancient reminiscences, but had to confess that dire necessity, and not his free choice, forced him to tolerate them occasionally.[3]   The character of St. Jerome as well as certain circumstances of his life must be taken into account in judging his passionate onslaught on the classical studies.   The climax of his attacks on the classics is reached in the report he gives of a vision he had in the desert and during which the divine Judge hurled at his head the sentence, "Thou art Cicero's, and not Christ's."[4] But if we consider the time, the place, and the situation, we shall better understand this fierce antagonism: Jerome had retired to the desert for the purpose of solitary study and meditation; his mind craved continuous occupation, and he had taken along from Rome a goodly number of books, among them the writings of Cicero and Plautus; and seeking at once both occupation and peace of soul, the hermit would turn from the Roman classics to the Hebrew prophets, thus allowing his mind no rest whatever, and a crisis was inevitable.   The earlier exaggerated views of Jerome must be corrected in the light of his later utterances, wherein he openly admitted that the Christian writer must needs be familiar with ancient literature, and

---

[1] Gaume, *Paganism in Education*, London, 1852, p. 67.

[2] Minucius Felix, *Oct.*, 23.

[3] "*Si quando cogimur litterarum sæcularium recordari et aliqua ex his dicere: non nostræ sit voluntatis, sed, ut ita dicam, gravissimæ necessitatis.*" *Proleg. in Dan.* (Gaume, l. c., p. 74, note).

[4] *Ep. 22 ad Eustachium*, c. 30 (Vallarsi).

that he may freely quote pagan authors. In a letter to the Rhetorician Magnus, he enumerates all that the champions of Christ, St. Paul included, had borrowed from 'secular writers.'[1]

7. However, the most complete picture of the gigantic struggle between ancient education and the principles of the Christian religion may be witnessed in the case of the greatest Doctor of the early Church, St. Augustine.[2] Here the conflict extends over the Saint's entire life, which was so rich in years and labors. In his youth Augustine delighted in classical poetry; he followed the wanderings of Aeneas and wept over the death of Dido. Without a teacher he mastered the liberal arts, and soon taught them in his own school. Cicero's *Hortensius* set his soul aglow with an eager longing for immortal wisdom; and what first struck him in the sermons of St. Ambrose, was their perfection of form. But when the hour of his conversion had struck and when his soul, new-born, first saw the light of Faith, he turned on all that had hitherto filled his life and condemned the whole system of secular education: "Such madness, then, is looked upon as a more honorable and a more useful study than reading and writing."[3] Yet the wealth of learning and the polished form, acquired in his early years, stood the Saint in good need in the continuous controversy that was now to ensue. The philosophy of the Greeks encouraged him to go deep in his own reasonings and researches, and the familiarity with the Latin classics contributed not a little to make his language so splendid and incisive an element. The admirers of St. Augustine have justly noted in his works, over and above their sublime Christian content, some of the grandeur of ancient Rome, and this grandeur of his style and manner had a special charm for Charlemagne, just as it later led the first Humanists, Petrarch, Vives, and Erasmus, to regard his writings as bridging the gulf between Christianity and antiquity. Concerning the value of ancient education, he has given expression to contradictory views; and in trying to get at his true mind we must take into account the circumstances that called forth the respective book as well as its aim, for these factors will necessarily modify the views expressed. The clearest and most dispassionate treatment of the subject is found in the work *De Doctrina Christiana* (Book II, written about 396), where St. Augustine outlines, from the

---

[1] *Ep. 70 ad Magnum*, c. 3-5; cf. *Ecclesiastical Review*, LXI (1919), pp. 266-269.
[2] Cf. Fr. X. Eggersdorfer, *Der heilige Augustinus als Pädagoge*, Freiburg, 1907; Spalding, *The Influence of St. Augustine's Teaching*, New York, 1886.
[3] *Conf.*, I, 13.

viewpoint of Holy Writ, a system of secular studies that has exercised upon the succeeding ages a powerful influence.[1] The basic thought of the whole inquiry is that the honest and righteous man will gratefully receive any truth, no matter where it be found, as coming from the hands of God. An error connected, through the fault of man, with a truth should not prejudice us against the truth itself· we do not shrink from learning the alphabet, though the invention of the letters is ascribed to Mercury. The arts and sciences of the pagans are partly human inventions and partly imitations of realities, *i e.*, of works of God, which have been rightly traced back by the pagans themselves to the deity. The works of man are partly reprehensible, *e. g*, haruspicy, astrology, etc., and partly dispensable, as the mass of fables, of fictions, and meaningless pictures and statues; but partly they are necessary, as the entire apparatus of social life: weight, measure, money, written and spoken language, etc The studies that are concerned with realities deal partly with the concrete and partly with the abstract Of the sciences dealing with the concrete, history easily stands first, for though concerned with human activities, it is not a human invention, as all happenings are controlled by the Lord, who shapes the course of the world The descriptive sciences, natural history and astronomy, are closely related to history. The technico-empirical sciences, as medicine, agriculture, political economy, mechanics and gymnastics, are co-ordinate with the descriptive sciences A superficial acquaintance with these sciences will enable one to pass an opinion on them and to understand the passages of Sacred Scripture that deal with these matters. However, our vocation may necessitate a more exact knowledge of these sciences. Dialectic, rhetoric, and mathematics are the abstract sciences. Dialectic is not man's work, because he has not invented the rules and modes of reasoning, and the misapplication of them by the individual does not invalidate them. Rhetoric is dialectic applied to language; the rules for attracting, holding, and persuading an audience are likewise based on laws that do not date from men. These sciences can not dispense with common sense, which is the common foundation of all their minute rules. They are a source of exquisite and elevating pleasure, and train the mind, and are, therefore, useful so long as their pursuit does not degenerate (a common danger)

---

[1] "He (St. Augustine), no infallible teacher, has formed the intellect of Christian Europe " Newman, *Apologia*, 1908, p 265.

into affectation and vain display. The truths of mathematics have been discovered, but not invented, by man; they are of use in explaining the meaning of those passages of the Bible that deal with forms, tones, and mystical numbers. At the same time they lead the mind to study the relationship between the changeable and the unchangeable, and thus the soul—provided it traces this relationship to its ultimate end, the love of God—will be conducted to the spring of wisdom. The God-fearing youth, talented and thirsting for knowledge, should be very cautious in taking up the study of any secular science. He may give some attention to those institutions that are indispensable to social life; and the sciences most useful to him are the history of past and present-day events, dialectic, and mathematics. But in studying even these sciences he must be guided by the principle, "Ne quid nimis." Works like Eusebius' *Ecclesiastical History* and the explanation of the concrete matters of Scripture should be the basis of the empirical studies. St. Augustine does not decide whether the dialectical portions of Scripture are to receive special treatment, but inclines to the negative answer, "because the art of the *pro* and *con* extends, in the manner of nerves, through the entire body of Scripture;"[1] and he grants that dialectic may be studied in schools not under the control of the Church.[2] The truths found among the heathen philosophers, especially among the Platonists, are compared to the vessels of gold and silver that the Israelites took, upon God's command, from the heathen temples of Egypt, to devote them to the service of the Lord. In like manner, the Christian should withdraw from the worship of the demons and devote to the service of God all that has been dug, in the course of time, from the mine of truth.[3]

8. With the gradual growth of a distinctively Christian literature and the corresponding decline of heathen literature, Christian educational writers, feeling sure of a broad and homogeneous Christian foundation, saw less danger in what was taken over from heathen education. And thus a considerable portion of the content of ancient education was incorporated into the Christian system. The framework consisted of the seven liberal arts as described, not without some African flourishes, by Marcianus Capella, or in a plainer style and with

---

[1] *Conf.*, II, 40, 56.

[2] Ibid., 32. Concerning rhetoric, cf. IV, 2 sq.

[3] St. Gregory of Nyssa employs the same comparison for enjoining the same duty in his *De Vita Mosis* (*Opp.*, Par., 1638, I, p. 209).

references to Christian materials by Cassiodorus (died 562).
In the West philology assumed an encyclopedic character as
may be seen in the *Origines* or *Etymologiæ* of Isidore of Seville
(died 636), wherein the compiler has assembled, by covering
the ground of the liberal arts and by adding biblical and theological materials, all that was thought worth knowing. His
Sententiæ is a compilation of the essentials of Christian Doctrine, and by these works Isidore prepared the way for the
encyclopedias and compendiums of the Middle Ages.[1] Boethius
(died 525), the translator and commentator of Aristotle, exercised in the West the profoundest influence on the study of
philosophy. The selections from the ancient classics were largely
made at random. It was not the internal value of the work,
or the importance attached to it by the ancients, that determined the reading of a poem; but other, often entirely mistaken,
considerations prevailed. The works of Vergil were highly esteemed — the reason being, besides the traditional attitude, the
interpretation of his fourth eclogue as a prophecy of the Messias.
His poems were interpreted allegorically, and the *Aeneid* was
considered a picture of human life. St. Augustine states (*De
Civ. Dei*, I, 3) that the little ones read him in order that, after
having in their earliest childhood imbibed his wisdom, they
might never forget the greatest and best of poets. Statius, who
was believed to have been a secret follower of Christ, was esteemed most after Vergil. The traditional attitude towards
Horace and his wealth of quotable sentences are responsible
for his being read in the schools Sallust was preferred to Livy,
probably because the introductions in his *Lives* abound in moral
maxims; but the authors of historical summaries were esteemed
above both. Seneca ranked high among the philosophers because of his sententious style, the later tradition represents him
as a Christian and a martyr to the Christian cause. The Greeks
cultivated for a long time an eclectic study of the classics. Their
anthologies contained, in parallel columns, texts from Scripture

---

[1] The *Origines* treat the following subjects (the figures indicate the respective book) 1 grammar, 2 rhetoric and dialectic, 3 arithmetic, astronomy,
music, 4 medicine, 5 jurisprudence, 6 of books, writing, literature, spiritual
offices, 7 of God and holy men, 8 of the Church, 9 of languages, 10 ety-
mologies in alphabetical order, 11 of man, 12 of the animals, 13 and 14 of
the earth and its parts, 15 of cities, houses, and rural estates, 16 of metals,
stones, weights, and measures, 17 of agriculture, horticulture, and plants;
18 of armies and games, 19 of architecture, navigation, and dress; 20 of
food and household furniture

and the Church Fathers and quotations from the classics; and of all collections that made in the eighth century by St. John Damascene enjoyed the greatest favor. The ecclesiastical schools conducted in Constantinople at this time taught the liberal arts and the philosophical disciplines, and read and interpreted Homer, Hesiod, Demosthenes, and Plutarch.

CHAPTER XVII.

The Early Christian School System.

1. As the process of assimilating the content of ancient education was slow, so the schools also were slow in adapting themselves to the new conditions. The Christians were obliged as late as the sixth century to study grammar and rhetoric in schools that held sacred the ancient traditions and that were, only too frequently, hotbeds of paganism. It was just the middle schools that preserved their pagan character longest, while the elementary as well as the highest schools were Christianized much earlier.[1] It was not difficult to correlate the Christian instruction needed for the youngest pupils with the subject-matter of the elementary school. The first schools for reading, writing, and the singing of psalms were founded in Syria, where the need of having the Scriptures translated into the vernacular urged the Christians to be active both in education and in general literature. The Presbyter Protogenes is mentioned as having opened, in the second half of the second century, the first Christian school at Edessa. We lack the data to trace the growth of the early Christian schools conducted by the presbyters. However, in the fifth century these schools had spread at least over the whole of Italy, as appears from the decree of the Council of Vaison (Vasio), issued in 443, which ordained that all Gallic presbyters should follow the custom which was said to be of long standing in Italy: to take boys into their homes, be spiritual fathers to them, and teach them the reading of the Psalms and of Sacred Scripture; and, in general, to instruct them in the knowledge and fear of the Lord. The Synods of Orange and Valence on the Rhone (529) decree the opening of schools in connection with the different

[1] Cf. E. Magevney, *Christian Education in the First Centuries*, New York, 1900; A. T. Drane, *Christian Schools and Scholars*, New York, 1910.

parishes. The third Council of Constantinople (681) ordained
that the priests should conduct schools in all places (*per villas
et vicos*) within the parish limits   From the lives of many
saints we learn that the missionaries who preached the Gospel
taught the neophytes reading and writing also   It is related
that the pagan pupils of Cassian, the traveling bishop of Rhæ-
tia, being incensed at the severity of his discipline, killed their
master with their styles; and St Patrick is said to have written
as many primers as there are days in the year.

The monasteries also played an important rôle in laying
the foundation of the Christian school system. The rules of
the religious orders of the East prescribed that the novices
learn to read, and they contained minute regulations for the
education and instruction of the children entrusted to the care
of the monks. Such regulations are found in the rule of St.
Basil the Great as well as in the older rule of St. Pachomius
(died 348), so that Egypt, which was the scene of St Pachomius'
labors, is considered the cradle of the monastic schools.[1] Orphan
asylums began to be opened about the same time, first in Constantinople and Rome, and in the latter city song schools were
connected with the asylums.

2. The system of higher education developed out of the
catechumenate. The term $\kappa\alpha\tau\epsilon\chi\hat{\epsilon}\iota\nu$—meaning originally to teach
by word of mouth—was employed in the early Church for desig-
nating the instruction and the training then required as a preparation for the Sacrament of Baptism.[2] The need for giving
this instruction to whole classes of catechumens suggested the
organizing of regular catechetical courses, which were conducted
during Lent preparatory to the solemn administration of Baptism at Easter, and which were in charge either of the priests
themselves or of such as were especially engaged for this work
(doctores, $\delta\iota\delta\acute{\alpha}\sigma\kappa\alpha\lambda\omega$). These courses developed into regular
schools wherever the scientific spirit was strong enough to
prompt a deeper and broader study of the teachings of Christianity. The catechetical school of Alexandria, which traced
its origin back to the Evangelist St. Mark, was at first devoted
exclusively to the instruction and training of catechumens, but
later took up the scientific study of the Christian religion, for
the purpose not only of converting educated pagans to the

[1] Brother Azarias, *Essays Educational*, New York, 1896, pp 6 ff
[2] Ad G Weiss, *Die altchristliche Padagogik dargestellt in Katechumenat und
Katechese der ersten sechs Jahrhunderte*, Freiburg, 1869, p 40, cf McCormick,
History of Education, Washington, 1915, pp. 65 ff

truths of the Church, but also of training efficient catechists.[1]
Christian schools of the same type were located at Antioch,
Edessa, Nisibis, Gandisapora, and other Syrian cities. The
African Bishop Junilius relates that the school at Nisibis was
celebrated for its methodical and well-regulated (*ordine et
regulariter traditur*) course in the law of Christ, which was
given by public teachers after the manner of the public teachers
of grammar and rhetoric.[2] The West had fallen upon evil days,
and hence it was in vain that Cassiodorus tried to persuade
Pope Agapitus to introduce the methods of the eastern schools.[3]

3. In the West, the bishops' schools, modeled after St.
Augustine's school at Hippo, were the first homes of higher
learning. Possidius states, in his life of St. Augustine, that no
less than ten bishops, celebrated for their learning, had studied
in the school at Hippo; and they in turn were the founders of
similar schools in their own cathedral cities. The primary purpose of these schools was to provide for the training of the
diocesan clergy. But there is no doubt that such as had not
yet decided for the clerical state were also admitted, for we
read of an inner circle of students that gathered about the
bishop, in contrast to a class of pupils who were not so privileged. St. Peter Chrysologus, for instance, who received his
education in the first decades of the fifth century under the
direction of Cornelius, Bishop of Imola, was trained for the
priesthood only after he had advanced from an exoteric class
to an inner circle.[4] The development of the bishops' schools
was contemporaneous with that of the monastic schools. It
must be admitted that the rule of St. Benedict was not more
explicit on the subject of education than the earlier monastic
rules had been. To studies in general the Saint himself was
rather opposed than favorable; and Gregory the Great, the
glory of the Benedictine Order, avows that "it is an indignity

---

[1] That the school at Alexandria never lost sight of its original aim, is clear
from the two courses offered there at the time of Origen: one elementary for
beginners and the other a theological course for advanced students. (Eus.,
Hist. eccl., VI, 15.) It is noteworthy that the mission schools of the 19th
century bear evidence to the wisdom of combining heathen and Christian
studies, as was done at Alexandria. The Catholic schools in China, opened
since 1840, devote the first seven or eight years to the national studies required
for the state examinations, and only after this ground has been covered are
the pupils introduced to the distinctively Christian branches.

[2] Junilius, *De part. div. leg.* in Conring, *De antiq. academ.*, I, 29.

[3] Cassiodorus, *De divin. et hum. lect.*, Præf.

[4] Bardenhewer-Shahan, *Patrology*, New York, 1908, pp. 526 ff.

that the words of the oracle of heaven should be restrained by the rules of Donat,"[1] and that the same lips can not be expected to praise at once both Jove and Christ. But that statement of the Benedictine Rule which enjoins the monks to devote three hours daily to reading and to peruse entire books during Lent, contained the germ of the glorious educational history of the Order; and it was not long before the education of the *oblati*—the children who had been dedicated by their parents to the religious life—and the training of the monks for the duties of the priesthood assumed the form of systematic schooling. The full realization, however, of their educational mission came to the Benedictines only after they found themselves far removed from the centres of civilization and face to face with semi-barbarous races, whom they could gain permanently for Christ by no other means than by becoming their teachers and masters in the mechanical as well as the fine arts, in agriculture, in science and in cultural activity of all kinds The Benedictine school of the Middle Ages is only a part of the complex system of institutions that assisted in the work of civilization, and which were the outgrowth of missionary activity. The early form of the monastic school embraced the whole content of education· the elements, the liberal arts, the reading of the classics, theology, and gave some attention, besides, to the professional sciences, as, medicine and surveying To meet the twofold purpose of educating the young members of the Order and of providing the secular training for the man of the world, the *schola claustri* or *interior* for the young monks was separated from the *schola canonica* or *exterior*. The monks shirked no labor, they were tireless in improving their schools, and hence their institutions became the models for all the schools of the Middle Ages [2]

4. Between the early Christian schools and the schools of classical antiquity there are three striking differences First, the Christian schools were, by virtue of their pronounced religious and moral aim, institutions not only for cultural, but also educational, purposes, and of this fact their practice of com-

[1] Gregory expressed himself thus "*Non metacismi collisionem fugio, non barbarismi confusionem devito, situs motusque præpositionum, casusque servare contemno quia indignum vehementer existimo, ut verba cælestis oraculi restringam sub regulis Donati*" (*Præf Jobi*, I, p 6) We can not say that these words imply a declaration of war on grammar; they only state that we do not demand grammatical scrupulosity of the theologian.

[2] Cf J H. Newman, *Historical Sketches*, 1912, Vol. II, pp. 450 ff.

munity life, which was unknown in the Greek and Roman schools, bears external evidence.   Secondly, the Christian schools were obviously bent on making religion the core-subject about which all the various branches were grouped, so that one institution embraced the whole field of general education; whereas the ancient schools taught generally only one subject, wherefore the young Greeks and Romans could obtain a general education only by passing through the different schools of the grammarian, rhetorician, music teacher, etc.   Thirdly, the Christian schools were considered, because they were controlled by the Church, public institutions, while the school system of the ancients represented, at least at the time when the schools were at their best, only the loose union of private establishments. Of ancient institutions, the temple schools of Egypt, with their affiliated colleges and priest-teachers, might perhaps correspond, in some degree, to the school system of the early Church.   But the few points of similarity will appear insignificant, when we consider that the spirit as well as the end of the Christian schools differ essentially from all that inspired the schools of ancient Egypt. The latter were confined to an exclusively national subject-matter of teaching. The different castes were allowed only a graduated amount of instruction, and the educational content, thus hedged in on all sides, could not enjoy a proper development, but grew more rigid with its increasing age.   In contrast with this, we know the Christian school system to be the member of an organism that transcends beyond the limits of nationality, and which, instead of stressing any class distinctions, obliterates these differences by dealing with the individual and by giving him, through teaching the loyalty due to the Lord of the earth, the liberty of a child of God.   The Christian school system will never grow rigid, because it is controlled by the teaching office of the Church.   An eternal youth is its prerogative, for it is continuously renewed by drawing from the waters of the eternally new teachings of the Christian Church. The Christian nations are teaching nations; they have attained this distinction by virtue of the teaching office of the Christian Church; and in organizing the system of education they have far outstripped the ancients, because they were assisted by the plastic forces at work in the Church.

VI.

MEDIEVAL EDUCATION.

CHAPTER XVIII.

The School System of the Middle Ages.[1]

1. The Middle Ages is the term (first used in the 17th century) for designating the thousand years intervening between the fall of the Roman Empire and the revival of letters in the 16th century. But the designation is obviously inappropriate, because it is founded on what is of most external significance. These thousand years are, in reality, not a middle period at all; they are the dawn of a new era, for they cover the first stages in the cultural development of Christian Europe, and represent the youth of the modern nations. As improper as is the name given to these thousand years, so little ground is there for the various notions popularly associated with the "Dark Ages." Modern historical research has shown convincingly that the world was not buried for a thousand years in a sort of wintersleep, but that there was, in fact, during the Middle Ages a most vigorous and general activity, and that much of our modern progress would have been impossible had not the Middle Ages first broken the ground Looking broadly at some of the results accomplished by the Middle Ages, we must note the civilization of the barbarian races of the North and the amalgamation of divers races with individual peoples of settled and national character. Furthermore, we see Europe as a whole superseding the geographical unit constituted formerly by the countries bordering on the Mediterranean Sea Ancient history had ever known only one world-empire, but the wars of the Middle Ages brought about the establishment of several independent nations united by the ties of a common culture. But the medieval nations were disadvantaged in this, that they drew much less than the ancient Greeks and Romans upon what was their own, being obliged to turn to foreign peoples

---

[1] E Magevney, *Christian Education in the Dark Ages*, New York, 1900; P J. McCormick, *History of Education*, Washington, 1915, pp. 86-210; cf also *Catholic Encyclopedia*, New York, 1907-14.

for essential elements of their historical life. Still, this process of assimilation, once it was well under way, inaugurated the growth of a culture that was immeasurably richer than that of the ancients. "European civilization from the Middle Ages downwards is," as Gladstone says,[1] "the compound of two great factors, the Christian religion for the spirit of man, and the Greek, and in a secondary degree, the Roman, discipline for his mind and intellect;" and these foreign elements had to enter deep into the national life, before the native forces of the latter could be set free for the work of co-operation.

Thus the educational forces of the Middle Ages were primarily occupied with receiving, assimilating, and imitating the matter that was on hand; and the medieval school system is consequently not free from the cumbersomeness (*Schwerfälligkeit*) that characterizes all such beginnings. Ancient Greece and Rome had never in their educational efforts met with such difficulties as confronted the Middle Ages on all sides. The Middle Ages had to assimilate, not only the entirely new elements of the Christian religion, but also the elements of classical education, the precipitate of Roman education. To convert these latter elements, which represented an apparently dead matter, into a life-giving factor, was not a light task; and the difficulty was the greater as dry and uninviting compendiums were the sole guides in this work. The medium of expression was, moreover, the Latin language, not only a foreign tongue, but itself dying and containing, at its best, a subject-matter that was at variance with the intellectual content of the new nations. It is true that the Church proved the patron of the new education, lending it the influence of her own organization; but at the same time she subjected it to her authority and determined its scope accordingly. In some points the hard schooling of those centuries may often enough appear meagre and unproductive in its details; but considered as a whole, it was the best preparation for free movement and independent efforts. Yet it was more than a mere preparation for better things: medieval education advanced far beyond the stage of tutelage. It was far from being merely receptive; for it did not only take over the various forms of schools of the early Church: the monastic, episcopal, and parochial schools (whose scope of usefulness it enlarged), but founded institutions wholly unknown in any previous age: the system of chivalric education,

[1] *Cyclopedia of Education*, s. v. Gladstone.

the guild schools, and the teachers' corporations of the universities.

2. Among the monastic schools of the Middle Ages the Benedictine schools hold the first place.[1] The black monks had early recognized the principle that the welfare, glory, and stability of their Order depend on its schools;[2] and the events following upon the Barbarian Invasion bore out the truth of this view. The educational leaders of the period of the Carolingians and Ottos were either Benedictines or their pupils. The Venerable Bede[3] (died 735), the *scholasticus* of Jarrow and the Father of English History, is the first of the long line of distinguished Benedictine scholars. Tradition is at fault in making Alcuin or Albinus (born 735, died 804) the pupil of Bede, but in his spirit and methods of teaching he is a disciple of the master of Jarrow. Alcuin was a friend and councilor of Charlemagne and the first of the masters from whom rays of culture (as it were) issued in all directions; his monastic school at Tours is the first of the model schools and institutions for the training of teachers that were in those centuries the chief seats of learning in Europe. Paschasius Radbertus, his fellow-laborer, founded the monastic school at Corbie, and this in turn became the parent of the school at Corvey, in Saxony. Of his other fellow-laborers, Leidrad was the glory of the cathedral school at Lyons, and Arnulph, of the Salzburg school; and of his pupils, Rhabanus modeled the abbey school at Fulda after that of Tours. The same was done by Ludger at the cathedral school at Münster and by Haimin at the school at Arras—the last-named proving the pattern for the schools at St. Amand and Auxerre. The educational writings of Alcuin spread his influence far beyond the territory of the Franks.[4] The school at Fulda, organized by Rhabanus Maurus (born 775, died 856) served as the model for the reorganization of the schools of Saint Gall (Wernbert and Hartmut) and Reichenau (Walafried Strabo), and for the founding of schools at Weissenburg (Otfried), Hersfeld (Strabus), Hirschau (Hidulph and Ruthard), and Ferriere (Servatus Lupus). The influence of Rhabanus, the *praeceptor*

---

[1] Cf. Newman, *Historical Sketches*, New York, 1912, Vol. II, pp. 450 ff.

[2] Ziegelbauer, *Hist. Ord. S. B.*, I, p. 652: "*Veterum cœnobitarum frequens erat istud keleusma: Ex scholis omnis nostra salus, omnis felicitas, divitiæ omnes ac ordinis splendor constansque stabilitas.*"

[3] Cf. Rawnsley, *The Venerable Bede*, Sunderland, 1903; Lingard, *Anglo-Saxon Church*, London, 1845.

[4] West, *Alcuin and the Rise of Christian Schools*, New York, 1892.

Germaniae, extended, like that of Alcuin, through his educational and encyclopedic works, far beyond his school and country. A position similar to his was held in the period of the Ottos and the first kings of the Capetian dynasty by Gerbert, known in history as Pope Sylvester II. (died 1003), who, though not a Benedictine, had been educated in the Benedictine monastery at Aurillac. This school at Aurillac had begun to flourish under Odo of Clugny, who was a pupil of Remigius of Auxerre, the latter being, through his teacher Heiricus, connected with the circle of Alcuin. Gerbert was "so brilliant a teacher that every school became under his management a training school for teachers;" he taught in Rheims and Paris, and was instrumental in raising the schools of St. Germain aux Prés (Ingo), of Auxerre (John of Auxerre), of Leury (Abbo), Chartres (Fulbert), Mittelach (Nithard and Remigius), etc., to a high degree of efficiency. He introduced the learning of the Arabians into the West; and the interest taken in his schools in dialectic gave rise to Scholasticism.[1] The monastic school connected with the Benedictine Abbey of Bec, in Normandy, where Lanfranc was prior and his pupil Anselm of Canterbury (born 1035, died 1109) abbot, was the most famous school of dialectic in Christendom, and one of the first schools to take up the study of Scholasticism. The Archabbey of Monte Cassino flourished anew during this period, and teachers connected with its school invented the so-called *ars dictandi*, a branch of rhetoric. St. Thomas Aquinas, the greatest and most influential philosopher of the Middle Ages, studied at Monte Cassino.

3. Beginning with the tenth century, many new and independent orders branched off from the Benedictines, but continued to observe—though in a more or less modified form—the Rule of St. Benedict. Though these new orders did not directly influence the schools, their indirect influence was large, for they raised the tone of the religious life and thereby improved general Christian morals. The Cluniac rule declared the study of the heathen classics to be dangerous, and the Cistercians as well as the Premonstratensians did not attach the same importance to learning as the mother-order. But the monasteries of these orders founded in Brandenburg, Misnia, Silesia, and Poland exercised, in these countries, the same wholesome influence on studies as the Benedictine schools had done in the West. The mere number of the monasteries—in 1500

---

[1] McCormick, l. c., pp. 111 ff.; cf. *Opera*, Migne, *Pat. Lat.* CXXXIX.

there were no less than 37,000 monasteries belonging to the Benedictines and to branches of their Order — is sufficient evidence of the important public function of the religious orders; and even if we granted that only one twentieth of these 37,000 monasteries had regular schools, they would still constitute no small part of the school system of the time.

The two great orders of the Franciscans and Dominicans, which were founded in the age of the Crusades and which enjoyed a phenomenal growth, influenced the schools in a different way than the older orders had done. They gave most of their attention to preaching and to the religious instruction of the masses, and therefore considered the pursuit of higher learning as foreign to their primary aim. St. Francis of Assisi deposed the guardian of the monastery at Bologna for having opened a house of studies, and justified this step with the words, "The life of the brothers is to be their learning, and piety is to be their eloquence;" but the same Francis gathered up any scraps of writing he found in the street and put them aside in reverence, "because the writing contained the letters which combine to form the most holy Name of God."[1] With the further development of the two orders it became evident that no teaching could prove successful unless the friars cultivated habits of study and research. But their world-wide educational activity, which embraced university teaching as well as elementary instruction, dates from the year 1259 when both the Franciscans and the Dominicans were granted the right to a professorship at the University of Paris; St. Thomas Aquinas and St. Bonaventure were the first to fill these chairs. The Mendicants followed the example of the Benedictines in opening schools in connection with their friaries; but they taught, besides, in city schools, and went about in the rural districts preaching and catechizing. They are known also as the authors of textbooks and popular encyclopedias. The Franciscan Alexander of Villedieu is the author of the most popular Latin grammar of the Middle Ages, the *Doctrinale*, which was first published about 1200, and which was reprinted more than a hundred times

---

[1] "Once when it was pointed out to him, perhaps not without sarcastic intention, that the scrap of writing he had rescued was from some heathen author, he replied that it mattered not, since the words, whether of heathens or of other men, all came from the wisdom of God." I Celano, 82; Cuthbert, *Life of St. Francis*, London, 1912, p. 294.

before 1500.[1]   The Dominican Vincent of Beauvais is the author of a large encyclopedia (about 1300) in which he summarized the learning of the later Middle Ages (see *infra*, Ch. xix).

Other orders that had an organization similar to that of the purely religious communities, but which combined spiritual and secular elements, were also active along educational lines. There are several instances on record where the Knights of St. John (founded 1048) established and conducted schools; and the same is true of the Teutonic Knights (founded at Acre in 1190), whose grand-master Winrich of Kniprode (died 1382) was a patron of the schools in Prussia, where the first schools had been opened about 1228 by Pope Honorius III. Winrich of Kniprode is credited with the statement: "Our Order will ever be well supplied with wealth and other earthly goods, but not always with prudent and faithful members, so that we must found in Prussia not only a few, but many, schools." The Order of Calatrava, founded in the 13th century, cared not only for the poor and orphans, but also opened schools at some places. The Brethren of the Common Life, founded by Geert Grote (Gerhardus Magnus) of Deventer, opened their first house in 1384 at Deventer; a hundred years later their schools had spread over the whole territory between the Scheldt and the Vistula; the motherhouse at Deventer continued the centre of influence, and by being actively engaged in both elementary and higher schools, the Brethren popularized the study of Sacred Scripture and prepared the way for the Humanists' reform of studies.

4. The bishops' schools of the primitive Church developed in the Middle Ages into cathedral schools. St. Chrodegang of Metz (died 766) based his rule of the common life, which he introduced among the cathedral clergy, upon the Benedictine Rule, and charged the *scholasticus* (*scholaster*, *didascalus*, *magiscola*, *cancellarius*) with the education of the youths that were committed to the care of the priests.[2] In the period of the

---

[1] The Humanists attacked the *Doctrinale* as being the authority for barbarous Latin; but in our time the book has received kindlier treatment at the hands of Haase, Eckstein, and others. Many syntactical terms of the *Doctrinale* are in use in our present-day grammars. Cf. Eckstein's article *Lateinische Sprache* in Schmid's *Enzyklopädie*, IX, p. 512; cf. *infra*, ch. XIX, 7.

[2] St. Chrodegang is not, as is frequently stated, the founder of the cathedral schools, for in the oldest version of his rule (Migne, *Pat. Lat.*, t. 89, p. 1057) we find mention merely of the supervision of the *pueri parvi et adulescentes.* It is only the later versions that contain specific details concerning the education of the young.

greatest efficiency of the cathedral schools, the bishops themselves would often teach, though the *scholasticus* was the ordi-
nary teacher. Later, learned monks, especially Benedictines, or
laymen, were engaged as teachers. These schools were attended, not only by the candidates for the priesthood, but
also by the sons of nobles and even of princes. The cathedral
schools had, like the monastic schools (Ch. xvii, 3), two divisions:
the *inner* school, a boarding school, for clerical students, and
the *outer* school for the laity. Some cathedral schools, for
example, the Lateran school at Rome, the schools at Lyons,
Rheims, Liége, Paderborn, and Goslar, were as celebrated as
the monastic schools, but were, for all that, patterned after the
best of the latter. But when the canons discontinued the
common life in the 11th century and committed the schools to
hired and salaried teachers, the cathedral schools were doomed,
for they could not compete with the universities. The great
Pope Innocent III., who was bent on conserving and improving
all the elements of ecclesiastical power as well as of early Christian education, stayed the downfall of the cathedral schools: he
is responsible for the decree passed by the Lateran Council, in
1215, ordaining that teachers of grammar and professors of
theology be employed in the schools to be opened in connection
with all cathedrals; and when instituting a trial against any
bishop, he always made it a point to inquire whether the prelate
had provided for the Christian education of the young.

The bishops were expected not only to maintain the cathedral schools, but to supervise all the schools of the diocese,
especially those connected with the parishes. It is a fact sub-
stantiated as well by the decrees of councils and synods as by
direct testimonies, that the work of the medieval parish church
always included a certain amount of regular school work. The
pastor or his assistants (clerics, sextons, or other persons in his
employ) did the teaching. That the sexton's school was common in rural districts in the latter part of the 12th century,
would appear from the law passed in 1183 by the diocesan
synod of Saint-Omer: "As the schools are intended to train all
such as will in the future have the management of ecclesiastical
and secular matters in Church and State, we ordain that the
parish schools, if fallen into decay, be rebuilt in all cities and
villages of the diocese, or, if they be still in use, be given more
attention than heretofore. To this end, the pastors, magistrates, and prominent members of the community should provide for the support of the teachers, for which office the sextons

are generally employed in the rural districts. The school is to be opened in a building near the parish church, so that the teacher may the more easily be controlled by the pastor and other authorities, and the pupils, too, be introduced more easily to the practices of our holy Religion."[1] Even if these parish schools represent only elementary schools, we must not overlook the fact that the Middle Ages did not regard, as we do, the elements of reading, writing, religion, etc., as belonging to a special kind of school; no school was thought worthy of the name unless Latin was taught in it, and the study of Latin was taken up as soon as the pupils had gotten beyond the rudiments of religion. The instruction in the elements was considered to be supplementary to the cure of souls, and even the higher studies were never considered to be independent of the teaching office of the Church.

5. The laity was intimately connected with the ecclesiastical schools of the Middle Ages: young laymen frequented these schools, and laymen were permitted to teach in them; and these conditions account for the fact that no lay schools developed during this period in contrast to the schools of the clergy. The lay schools of the early Middle Ages kept up Roman traditions. Especially in Italy and the South of France, learned laymen taught the seven liberal arts, but the Church tolerated and controlled their work without positively encouraging the founding of lay schools. Roman law was taught in Italy by secular teachers till the universities made it one of their faculty subjects, and it would seem as though medicine also—though some monks had practiced medicine—had been taught by secular teachers till it was recognized as belonging exclusively to the universities.[2] The palace schools (*schola palatii* or *palatinæ*), which were first opened at the Franconian court, resemble in many points the schools of the Roman emperors. The Merovingians had opened a palace school, in imitation, most probably, of the *schola Gallica palatii* at Treves; but the institution flourished most under Charlemagne, when Alcuin and Peter of Pisa were in charge of the palace school. Charles the Bald transferred it to Paris, where its most celebrated teachers were the Greek Mannon (who brought some

---

[1] A. Stöckl, *Lehrbuch der Geschichte der Pädagogik*, Mayence, 1876, p. 118.
[2] In Rome there was a school of law in the 10th century, and the Roman judge received, amid much ceremony, the Justinian Code "to pass sentence on Rome, Trastevere, and the whole world according to its behests." Gregorovius, *Geschichte der Stadt Rom im Mittelalter*, III, 161 and 525 ff.

of the writings of Plato and Aristotle to the knowledge of the West), John Scotus (Eriugena), and Remigius of Auxerre. This palace school was finally merged in the cathedral school of Notre Dame. In the 10th century Bruno, subsequently Archbishop of Cologne, the brother of Emperor Otto I., founded the palace school of the Ottos.[1] The palace school did not differ essentially from the ecclesiastical institutions. It prepared its pupils for secular and clerical professions, and its teachers were taken almost exclusively from the ranks of the clergy; but being founded and controlled by the secular authorities, it stands in a class apart and is, in fact, the forerunner of the state universities founded under the Hohenstaufen.

A peculiar kind of education, lacking the hard and fast forms of regular schooling as well as the materials of the higher learning, developed in connection with medieval knighthood. The training to knighthood reveals the influence of national elements, and the latter can be traced back to the pre-Christian Germanic age. The description in the *Edda* of the training of the young nobleman contains many elements later incorporated in chivalric education: "Modir then brought forth a boy; in silk they wrapped him, with water sprinkled him, and named him Jarl. Light was his hair, bright his cheeks, his eyes piercing as a young serpent's. There at home Jarl grew up, learned the shield to shake, to fix the string, the bow to bend, arrows to shaft, javelins to hurl, spears to brandish, horses to ride, dogs to let slip, swords to draw, swimming to practice. Thither from the forest came Rig walking; runes he taught him, his own name gave him, and his own son declared him, whom he bade possess his alodial fields, his ancient dwellings."[2] Turning to chivalric education, we find the warlike practices of the olden days exchanged for the arts and accomplishments of the tournament. Instead of learning the runes, the boy must now learn the harp, must study languages, and read tales telling of the heroic deeds of the past. The virtue of the knight is designated *vrümecheit, i. e.,* ability; and *courtoisie* is mentioned as his special accomplishment. The training of the young knight was regulated, like that of the young cleric, in its minutest details, and even the grading of the seven liberal arts was applied to the course of chivalric education. The court of some distinguished nobleman was the school for the noble

---

[1] Brother Azarias, *The Palatine School,* in *Essays Educational,* pp. 39 ff.
[2] *The Elder Edda,* transl. by Benj. Thorpe, New York, 1906, pp. 81-82.

youth.   Though the father controlled the education as a whole, he committed the carrying out of his plans to strangers: personal service was looked upon as inseparable from learning, and a strange house was undoubtedly better suited to this purpose than the home.   The son of a knight was known as a page till he attained the age of fourteen, when he received at the altar the sword blessed by a priest, being thereafter known as a squire. He had to serve as squire for seven years, and at twenty-one he was dubbed knight, for which great honor—it marked his freedom from service—he had to qualify by deeds of chivalrous courage.   The night of watching in the church, the confession, the Holy Communion, the *Missa de Spiritu Sancto*, the sermon on the knightly life, preceded the most solemn ceremony of his life.   The principal part of a boy's education was carried on out of doors.   All kinds of exercises and games were practiced, such as wrestling, boxing, running, riding, tilting at the ring and quintain; and such amusements as bull and bear-baiting.   The squires who had charge of the pages or henchmen were required to "learne them to ryde clenely and surely, to draw them also to justes, to learne them wear their harness, to have all curtesy in wordes, dedes and degrees. . . . to learn them sondry languages and other lernings vertuous, to harping, to pipe, sing, dance . . . with corrections in their chambers."[1] The pages and squires were frequently dispensed from learning to write, but great importance was attached to learning foreign languages, especially French; Latin was frequently learned, but Greek only in rare instances.   The boys were imbued with the knightly spirit of the age by being steeped in the poems and tales that told of the chivalrous deeds of all times; for it was thought that these *aventiuren* were the embodiment of the ideals of knighthood, showing concretely what should be the goal of knightly ambition.   Classical antiquity furnished its quota of tales, for the stories of the Trojan War, of Aeneas' wanderings, and of the wars of Alexander had been treated by national poets and adapted to the national way of thinking. Though chivalric education was adapted to meet the needs of the nobility, a particular class, and though it was, therefore, vocational in aim, yet it was based on the broadest of human elements, for it included Christian, German, Latin, and roman-

---

[1] Furnivall, *Forewords*, E. E. T. S., 1867, quoted in Cornish, *Chivalry*, London, 1908, p. 64.

tic elements, and it was thus well calculated to develop the whole personality of the young nobleman.[1]

6. Despite the contrast between the life at court and that of the citizenry, the guild schools have much in common with chivalric education. The guild schools recognized as basic principles that serving and learning are inseparable, that the education of the young must be graded, and that the training for a mechanical vocation is, like the training for knighthood, concerned with the transmitting of specific arts, customs, concepts. However, the last-named elements are so closely inter-related with the universal consciousness and the ideas of the age that the training for the trades, though vocational in aim, may be considered a branch of general education. Besides the proximate aim of safeguarding the interests of their members, the guilds followed the higher aim of conserving and transmitting to posterity mechanical skill and the approved customs of the various trades. This higher aim gave rise to the *scholæ* of the guilds and brought it about that the full-fledged members were called *magistri*, masters. Only legitimate boys, who were "born in honorable wedlock, of father and mother according to the laws and regulations of Holy Church,"[2] could learn a trade; for the members of the guild must be pure and spotless. Neither could a boy begin to learn a trade before he was well grounded in the elements of Christian Doctrine, and after the establishment of writing schools in the 14th century he was expected to be familiar also with the elements of general knowledge. When receiving a boy as an apprentice, the master acted in the name of the whole guild: "I will engage this boy in the name of the whole guild." The master had to do more than teach the boy "how to use his hands," for he took upon himself, "during the time of apprenticeship, all parental obligations, educating him under the supervision of the guild."[3] The master was advised to allow his apprentice "a small sum for bathing;" and the apprentices are told to "use this money well, for every laborer, whatever be his age, must keep himself clean in body, which cleanliness also ministers to the soul's good."[4] They are, furthermore, enjoined to hear "every Sun-

---

[1] For further details, see *Chivalric Education* in the *Cyclopedia of Education*.

[2] So run the statutes of a glovers' guild of Danzig in 1412, quoted by W. Stahl, *Das deutsche Handwerk*, Giessen, 1874, I, p. 100.

[3] J. Janssen, *History of the German People*, transl. by M. A. Mitchell and A. M. Christie, London, 1896-1910, II, p. 11.

[4] Ibid., p. 34.

day and Holyday a mass and a sermon and to read good books. They must be industrious and seek not their own glory, but God's." [1] The apprentice was obliged to pay a certain fee, which, however, was returned to his parents, if he proved unfit for the trade; if he ran off because of ill-treatment received, the master was forbidden to take in a new apprentice, "because the apprentice-fee is still sitting on the chair." If he made good, he was advanced to the rank of a *companion*. Upon this occasion the master addressed him thus, "Thou hast till now been a boy and hast associated with boys, now thou art made a *companion* and wilt associate with *companions;* but if the Lord will give thee the grace to advance to the rank of a journeyman, thou mayst associate with honest journeymen." [2] An examination finally determined the fitness of the *companion* for the position of journeyman, and he was advanced to this rank amid much ceremony, though games and merrymaking also entered into the celebration. The journeyman was still bound to obey his master, whom, however, he was free to choose. He generally went on travels, to increase his knowledge and to improve his skill by serving different masters. This travelling of the journeymen was a common practice in the 14th century and became compulsory in the 15th. After having attained a certain degree of perfection in his trade, the journeyman might expect the mastership, which the guild eventually conferred on him—if the need for a new master arose—upon the ground of some skilled piece of work. These customs continued to prevail down to an age that could no longer realize their advantages, but only suffered from their rigid enforcement. But once these customs had been abolished, the system of apprenticeship training had also lost the mainstays of its stability, and neither the improved elementary school, nor the manual training school, nor the technical school can adequately supply what was lost. And hence our educationists and economists are still searching for a substitute for this medieval institution that was well adapted to the primitive conditions of the time, and which gave artisans and mechanics such a training as assured them of technical skill besides a class-consciousness based on religious and moral grounds.

It is obvious that the organized citizenry would not confine their educational influence to the guilds, and many city schools

---

[1] Ibid., p. 20.
[2] Stahl, l.c., p. 222.

were opened either by the city authorities (*scholæ senatoriæ*) or by private men. These schools, as a rule, were purely elementary, but occasionally they also offered advanced courses. The local clergy frequently frowned upon them as undesirable rivals of their own institutions; but the Church in general preserved a neutral attitude, and thus it is not surprising that members of both the regular and the secular clergy taught in the city schools.[1] Still, the teaching body of these schools was largely secular, and the need of safeguarding their common interests gave rise, towards the end of the Middle Ages, to the teachers' associations. The latter copied many features of the guilds: the teachers were engaged like the apprentices, and several years were spent in training for the mastership in the teaching profession. One feature, however, also copied from the guilds, could not but work harm among the teachers, *viz.*, the custom of wandering from place to place. The schoolmasters were themselves in the habit of going from place to place, and set up their schools in whatever town or village struck their fancy. It was not long ere this *Wanderlust* took hold of the pupils also, and led by the *scholares vagantes*, they travelled from place to place, looking for bread and schooling. This vagabondage of teachers and pupils represents the reaction of the age against the rigid forms of the medieval schools.

7. The highest educational achievement of the Middle Ages is represented by the universities, and they are the last word in the realization of the cultural ideals of the age. They are representative of the best elements of the spirit and customs of the period. They are united with the Church, for they recognize the Pope as their supreme head, and convert their faculties of theology into the homes of ecclesiastical learning. In contrast to knighthood, they represent the aristocracy of learning, and the graduates of the universities were considered socially the equals of the *nobiles*. The university corporations have many

---

1 In illustration of the liberal and generous policy pursued by the Popes in the controversies between the clergy and the city schools, we may quote Pope Alexander III., who in 1170 directed the Archbishop of Rheims to examine into the prohibition passed by the director of schools at Chalons on the Marne against an individual teacher. The Pope writes: "*Unde quoniam, cum donum Dei sit scientia litterarum, liberum esse debet cuique talentum gratiæ cui coluerit erogare, fraternitati tuæ per Apostolica scripta mandamus, quatenus tam Abbati quam Magistro scholarum præcipias, ne aliquem probum et litteratum virum regere scholas in civitate vel suburbiis, ubi voluerit, aliqua ratione prohibeant vel interdicere quolibet occasione præsumant.*" Cf. Schwarz, *Erziehungslehre*, 2nd ed., 1829, I, 2, p. 169.

points in common with the guilds of the citizenry, and the university degrees (scholastic, bachelor, master) mark a gradation of rank similar to that of the three kinds of members of the guilds (apprentice, journeyman, master). The universities countenanced the growing power of the State, and eventually proved the instrument for the latter to monopolize the schools. With their learned character they would seem to be out of sympathy with the broad interests of the people. Still, they were interdependent on all that concerned the masses; and what was said of Oxford may be said of other universities as well: "*Chronica si penses, cum pugnant Oxonienses, post paucos menses volat ira per Angligenenses.*" By assembling teachers and students from all countries and by conferring dignities that were recognized in all Christendom, the universities proved a clearing house for the exchange of intellectual values, and a mighty agency in providing the broadest possible field for any ideas—whether born of the Crusades, the Schoolmen, the Humanists, or the religious Reformers—to spread over Europe.

As varied as are the relations of the universities, so diverse are also their origins. Some universities grew out of older ecclesiastical institutions, either by enlarging and making independent the *schola externa*—for instance, the University of Cambridge;[1] or by uniting under one management several institutions that had been independent before—for instance, the University of Paris.[2] The *aulæ* built by Alfred the Great may be considered the beginning of Oxford University, and Alfred is rightly called the founder of this celebrated seat of learning.[3] The University of Naples, founded by the Emperor Frederick II., is the first university on the Continent founded by royalty. The

[1] "The town of Cambridge was raised into a seat of learning first by the monks of Croyland, a place about 30 miles to the north of it. Their Abbot Goisfred had studied at Orleans, and promoted their teaching (1109-1124) at a farm called Cottenham near Cambridge, and afterwards in a barn at Cambridge itself. The great press of students rapidly raised up schools; and though we have no direct proof of their continuing to exist for some time, these may probably have been the germ of the University." Huber, *The English Universities*, ed. by Francis W. Newman, London, 1843, I, pp. 61-62.

[2] The earlier palace school had been merged in the cathedral school of Notre Dame, and the latter was the nucleus of the University of Paris. The school of St. Victor, an Augustinian monastery founded by William of Champeaux, and the monastic school of St. Geneviève, and several other smaller secular schools were affiliated with the central school of Notre Dame. Cf. *Catholic Encyclopedia*, s. v. *University of Paris*.

[3] Huber, l.c., pp. 46 ff.

14

University of Bologna must be traced back to the studies of law pursued under the direction of the judges of the Imperial Court residing in the city The brilliant lectures of Irnerius, in the beginning of the 12th century, attracted large numbers of law students to Bologna The students gathering about Constantine of Carthage, a baptized Jew, inaugurated the medical school of Salerno. If older schools form the nucleus of the new institution, the teachers establish the *universitas;* but if the circles of students mark the beginning of a new university, as they did in Bologna and Salerno, the teachers depend on the scholars, and the latter form the corporation and appoint the rector and masters. But both these types of universities agree in this that they constitute corporate bodies possessing full autonomy. Originally, this autonomy was exercised in the conferring of the teacher's dignity (*magister, doctor*), while the chancellor enjoyed the exclusive privilege to confer the right to teach. The individual teacher was at first authorized to confer the bachelor's degree, but since 1250 this was reserved to the university as such, and this regulation marked the introduction of the regular university degrees [1] The privilege of being amenable only to the university court was, along with other privileges, a guarantee of the independence of the teaching corporations. The studies of the northern universities were originally the same as had been pursued in the monastic and cathedral schools, *i. e.*, theology and the liberal arts; the latter were taught also in the Italian law and medical schools. The system of the faculties (*ordines*) owes its origin to the separation of the theological studies from the arts course and to the later addition of medicine and Roman law. The maxim *universitatem esse fundatam in artibus*, originally expressed this historical development, but later connoted that a liberal education is the basis of professional studies. The idea, too, that the university was the home of all the sciences came into being at a comparatively late time Originally, the term *universitas* signified the union of the teachers and, in part, also of the students. *Studium generale*, another common term for university, implied that the diplomas of the universities were recognized the world over. But it is well known how these two terms subsequently changed their meaning, just as with the ancients ἐνκύκλιος eventually stood, not for the representatives of education (its original meaning), but for its content.[2]

---

[1] Huber, l c, pp 26 ff. [2] *Supra*, Introduction, I, 9, footnote; ch IX, 7.

8. The aim of the ecclesiastical schools was the moral and intellectual education of the pupil, and they were much assisted in their twofold object by having as nucleus the boarding school, which constituted the "inner school." The universities, however, having largely originated in the "outer schools," and being intended primarily to impart knowledge, lacked the helpful influences of institutional life and found it difficult to provide a proper substitute. The need of such a substitute was felt the more keenly, as the view prevailed in the Middle Ages that discipline is inseparable from instruction, and that education is unthinkable without sound discipline. This view was borne out by the conditions existing among the university students, many of whom were, indeed, of mature age and mind, yet a large percentage of them gave evident proof that they stood sorely in need of discipline. Furthermore, the heads of religious orders felt that when sending young religious to the university they were obliged to provide for them safeguards similar to those afforded by the cloister, and hence they frequently transferred the "inner school" to the university city. Students' inns, colleges, halls, dormitories took, to a certain extent, the place of the "inner school," for in these institutions the students received board and lodging, their morals and application were controlled by special officers (*provisores*), and provision was made for preparatory or supplementary instruction. The affiliation of these institutions with the universities offered little difficulty, as the universities themselves tended towards the college type of school. Paulsen describes them as "collegiate foundations, with a more elastic organization than that of the regular abbey schools, and concerned rather with instruction than with the inculcating of religious practices."[1] The colleges developed in the different universities along entirely different lines. The colleges came to be the most important feature of the Universities of Oxford and Cambridge, and there retarded the development of the university faculties. Some of the colleges of the University of Paris, *e. g.*, the Sorbonne (founded in 1255), were important centres of independent teaching, and in the middle of the 15th century the students of the various colleges were in the majority, though the regular courses of the University were still considered the most important. At the German universities, the students' halls never attained any such position, but were important in so far as at places (for

[1] Paulsen, *Geschichte des gelehrten Unterrichts*, 1885, p. 15.

example, in Cologne), they developed into preparatory schools, which became known in the 15th century as "gymnasia."[1]

As the *facultas artium* dealt with the liberal arts, which were the foundation of higher education, there was no need of special preparatory schools, and in this regard the medieval university fulfilled the function of both the modern university and college. But local conditions occasionally brought about the establishment of preparatory schools, either by branching off from the parent school several less advanced schools, or by affiliating with the university divers smaller schools. Thus the English Bishop Wykeham of Winchester founded not only a college at Oxford, New College (1386), but also opened a preparatory school for it in his cathedral city, Winchester College, whose capacity was limited to 70 students, in imitation of the number of Christ's disciples. King Henry VI. followed his example by founding, in 1441, for the same number of students King's College in Cambridge and a preparatory school, Eton College. The University of Paris controlled in the 13th century many Latin schools in and outside the city, and in the beginning of the 15th century the University of Prague was the centre of the whole secular school system of Bohemia.[2]

The universities of the Middle Ages show some defects. Their organization after the manner of the guilds impeded the free movements of the teachers; the teaching was confined to dry dictation and commenting on texts; and to us their disputations appear vacuous and unfruitful. But they are, nevertheless, landmarks in the history of education. They were the first autonomous corporations of teachers; they were social organisms, equipped with rights, self-perpetuating by co-opta-

---

[1] Wiese, *Das höhere Schulwesen in Preussen*, Berlin, 1864, I, p. 338. The term "gymnasium," generally spelled "gignasium" or "gingnasium," was used in the Middle Ages in its primary sense (*palæstra*) for monastery, and only occasionally for an educational institution. Ducange (s. v. *Gymnasium*) is authority for the statement made about an Abbot of Monte Cassino: "*Hoc sacrum gymnasium regere promeruit;*" and the term "*gymnasium monasteriale*" is illustrated by "*stadium vitæ præsentis agonizando percurrere;*" the famous monastic school of Bec is described as "*gymnasium Lanfranci;*" two men who were kin of soul are described thus: "*Ætsi essent in uno gingnasio educati.*" The circle of philosophers whom Pope Urban IV. befriended, are called a "*philosophiæ gymnasium.*" (Jourdain, *Geschichte der aristotelischen Schriften*, tr. by Stahr, 1831, p. 55.) Occasionally, the school director is called "*gignasiarcha,*" and the pupil, "*gignasista.*" But for a particular kind of school, the designation was as little used in the Middle Ages as in the Renaissance; cf. *infra*, ch. XVIII

[2] Tomek, *Geschichte der Prager Universität*, 1849, p. 41; cf. ibidem, pp. 187 ff.

tion, and devoted exclusively to the conservation and transmission of knowledge. They grew into real conservatories of higher learning, which they embraced in its entirety. Their union of the various faculties is the embodiment of the unity of science; and their grading of the different departments of knowledge embodied the truth that the science of divine things is superior to that of human matters, that philosophy, based on theology, is the connecting link between the various sciences, and that consequently the course of study should proceed from the general sciences to the special, and a general education precede professional training. Even if the freedom of teaching was somewhat restricted, there was no check whatsoever upon the freedom of learning, and the pursuit of knowledge was much facilitated by the uniformity of the universities, in organization, in didactic apparatus, and in the language used in the lecture halls. With such conditions obtaining quite generally, a French student would find little difficulty when taking up his studies at an English or Italian University.

CHAPTER XIX.

The Content of Medieval Education.

1. In keeping with the derived character of their culture, the peoples of the Middle Ages turned for the content of their education, first, to the ennobling elements that had come to them from outside sources, from Christianity and classical antiquity, and only secondly to what could be drawn from their own national traditions. Theology was the contribution of Christianity, and represented the highest knowledge; it was the end-all of higher studies and the centre about which all education revolved. Classical antiquity had contributed what was rightly considered a complete and perfect course of general education, the seven liberal arts,[1] and the latter were recognized, throughout the Middle Ages, as the standard system. A deep meaning was attached to the very number seven, as symbolizing the seven pillars of wisdom or the seven steps in the soul's approach to God. The seven arts were also compared to the seven planets, the seven virtues, etc. The minds of the age were

---

[1] For the following cf. Willmann's article, *Liberal Arts* in *The Catholic Encyclopedia*,

busy with the meaning of the individual arts and with their mutual relations. Their praises were sung in verse and prose; puns were made on them; and their content was expressed in mnemonic verses.[1] Though retaining the classical name, *artes liberales*, the age failed to recognize that the term implied a reference to the free man, and, following the fanciful method of Cassiodorus, *liberales* was derived from *liber*, the book; and thus the *artes* were conceived as the sciences contained in, and taught through, books. Another designation for the liberal arts, *sapientia Hybernica*, or *methodus Hybernica*, clearly shows the leading rôle played in the school system of the early Middle Ages by the Irish monks.

Grammar, dialectic, and rhetoric are called *trivium*, *artes triviales*, *artes sermocinales*, *artes rationales*, *logica*. Dialectic is studied in the schools after grammar and is considered to be second also in importance. The mathematical sciences, arithmetic, geometry, music, and astronomy, are called *quadrivium*.[2] The latter were also called *artes quadriviales*, *reales*, or *physica*, *mathematica*. Cassiodorus is responsible for the order in which they are generally enumerated.[3] The writings of Marcianus Capella, Cassiodorus, and Boethius were used as textbooks besides many compendiums of either all seven arts or of only one, or several, of them. In form, the schoolbooks were either

---

[1] For instance, in Alcuin, *De arte gramm.*, in.; *Epist.* 78; *Carmen de Pontif. et Sanct. Eccl. Ebor.*, 1431 sq.; see also Rhabanus Maurus, *De inst. cleric.*, c. 18 sq.; William of Conches, *De elem. philos.*, in the *Opp. Bedæ*, Basil., 1563, II, p. 313; Hugh of St. Victor, *Erud. did.*, III, 3. For a poetical description of the arts by Walter of Speyer, see Pez. *Thes. Anecd.*, II, 3, p. 27. Minnesingers and Meistersingers also treated the subject, as Henry d'Andely (see *infra*), Muscatblüt, Michael Behaim. Cf. Liliencron, *Ueber den Inhalt der allgemeinen Bildung zur Zeit der Scholastik*, Munich, 1876, p. 35. The liberal arts were often represented in pictures; Alcuin describes such a pictorial representation. Of the mnemonic verses, the following were most popular: *Lingua, tropus, ratio, numerus, tenor, angulus, astra;* and the barbaric distich: *Gram loquitur, Dia vera docet, Rhe verba colorat, Mus canit, Ar numerat, Geo ponderat, As colit astra.* Tzetzes, a Byzantine savant, enumerates the arts in political verses (Χιλιάδες, II, 525 sq.): Ὁ κύκλος καὶ συμπέρασμα πάντων τῶν μαθημάτων Γραμματικῆς, ῥητορικῆς, αὐτῆς φιλοσοφίας, Καὶ τῶν τεσσάρων τε τεχνῶν τῶν ὑπ' αὐτὴν κειμένων, Τῆς ἀριθμούσης, μουσικῆς καὶ τῆς γεωματρίας Καὶ τῆς οὐρανοβάμονος αὐτῆς ἀστρονομίας.

[2] Boethius used this expression, which originated from a mistaken notion of the meaning of trivium.

[3] Marcianus Capella, following Varro, enumerates the arts in the following order: 1. grammar, 2. dialectic, 3. rhetoric, 4. geometry, 5. arithmetic, 6. astronomy, 7. music. However, Cassiodorus enumerates them in this order: 1. grammar, 2. rhetoric, 3. dialectic, 4. arithmetic, 5. music, 6. geometry, 7. astronomy.

catechetical, or metrical, or contained only a digest, or at times only a tabular statement of the subject-matter of the respective science.[1]

Though the system of the seven liberal arts was held in high esteem, and though the several arts were regarded as parts of one organic whole, yet they were never regarded as of equal value, and the successive development of the single arts occasioned different evaluations of them. The Quadrivium was never so popular as the Trivium, and was generally considered as the domain of the specialist, especially after its subject-matter, which had been originally drawn only from older encyclopedias and grammarians (supra, ch. XII, 4), was increased by the materials taken from the writings of Euclid, which had been made accessible by the Arabians.[2] There was some speculation about the mysteries of space and number,[3] and also some appreciation of the aprioristic character of mathematics,[4] but this branch never became a vital element in medieval education. Only the applied sciences, music and astronomy, had a

[1] For the literature of the textbooks in grammar and rhetoric, see Eckstein's article, Lateinische Sprache in Schmid, Enzyklopädie, 1st ed., XI, pp. 507 ff. For interesting details on medieval grammar teaching, see Ch. Durot, Notices et extraits de divers manuscrits latins pour servir à l'histoire des doctrines grammaticales au moyenâge, 1868 (vol. XXII of the Not. et ext. des man. de la biblioth. impériale. Cf. Prantl, Geschichte der Logik, II (textbooks in dialectic); Cantor, Vorlesungen über Geschichte der Mathematik, I, Leipzig, 1880, pp. 703 ff. (textbooks in mathematics); see Lipowsky, Das Schulwesen Bayerns, 1836, for compendiums with tabular statements. The last famous schoolbook of the Middle Ages to include all the materials of the artes (it treats other matters besides) is the Margaritha philosophica of the Carthusian Gregory Reisch of the 15th century. It contains 12 books: 1. De rudimentis grammaticis; 2. De principiis logicis; 3. De partibus orationis, de memoria, de condendis epistolis; 4. Arithmetica; 5. De principiis musicæ, i.e., musicæ speculativæ et practicæ; 6. De elementis geometriæ, again, speculativæ et practicæ; 7. De principiis astronomiæ; 8. De principiis rerum naturalium; 9. De origine rerum naturalium; 10. De anima; 11. De potentiis animæ; 12. Principia philosophiæ moralis. The form of the dialogue is employed, and the Strassburg edition of 1512 is illustrated. The Appendix contains: Græcarum litterarum institutiones, Hebraicarum litterarum rudimenta, musicæ figuratæ institutiones, architecturæ rudimenta, compositio quadrantum, astrolabii, torqueti, polymetri, with many illustrations.

[2] Euclid was first translated from the Arabic by Alexander of Bath, the author of the translation known as The Text of Campanus; cf. Sprenger, Muhamed, Berlin, 1861, I, p. 111.

[3] Cf. the description, in the Eruditio didascalica, VI, 3, of the busy studies of Hugh of St. Victor, who studied these problems deep into the winter nights.

[4] For instance, in Rhabanus, De inst. cler., c. 22 sq. Of the Schoolmen, Roger Bacon gives most attention to mathematics, which he calls the "alphabetum philosophiæ." (Erdmann, Grundriss, I, § 212, 5.)

kinship with the ideals of the age: the study of church music
naturally led to a study of the musical relations and to improved
methods of musical notation; and the movable feasts of the
ecclesiastical year required the clergy to be familiar with the
calendar.[1] But even among the laity familiarity with the calendar and some knowledge of the solar system seem to have been
not infrequent.   Different features of the Ptolomaic system—
for example, that beyond the ether element there are certain
zones or heavens, each heaven containing an immense crystalline
spherical shell, the smallest inclosing the earth and its super-
incumbent elements, and the larger spheres inclosing the smaller
—such features suggested comparisons with Christian ideas, and
brought the universe much nearer to the mind, the fancy, and
poetry, than does our advanced astronomy.   The Hindu-Arabic
notation is the greatest gift of medieval mathematics to the
intellectual life of the race, but a long time time elapsed before
it became generally known.[2]

2. The branches of the Trivium were studied quite generally,
and represent, in a narrower sense, the cultural education of the
period.   However, with the growing ascendancy of Scholasticism,
in the beginning of the 12th century, there came a different
evaluation of the Trivium.   The pre-Scholastic period closely
followed what the Fathers had written about the various subjects; *e. g.*, Rhabanus Maurus, in his work on clerical training,
scarcely does more than reproduce the viewpoints of St. Augustine's *De Doctrina Christiana* (*supra*, ch. XVI, 7).   Grammar

[1] The science of the calendar was taught by means of the verses of the
Cisiojanus, which date from the 10th or 11th century and are truly charac-
teristic of medieval taste.   The following is a list of the Feasts of January:
Circumcisio Domini (Jan. 1st), Epiphania (6th), Octava Epiphaniæ (13th),
Felix (14th), Marcellus (16th), Antonius (17th), Prisca (18th), Fabianus (20th),
Agnes (21st), Vincentius (22nd), Conversio Pauli (25th), Polycarpus (26th),
Carolus M. (28th); and these Feasts are turned into the following mnemonic
verses: "Cisio Janus Epi sibi vindicat Oc Feli Mar An Prisca Fab Ag Vincenti
Pau Pol Car nobile lumen."   The number of the respective day of the month
is indicated by the position that the first syllable of the word abbreviated
occupies in the verse; thus E is the sixth syllable, Fe the fourteenth, etc.
[2] The medieval scholars had only an imperfect notion of the value of the
system.   Vincent of Beauvais writes of it rather coldly—it had then been
introduced only a short time before—in his *Speculum doctrinæ*, c. 16: "*Inventæ
sunt novem figuræ* (follow the numerals); *quælibet in primo loco ad dexteram
posita significat unitatem vel unitates, in secundo denarium vel denarios, in tertio
centenarium etc.; quælibet figura posita in secundo loco significat decies magis
quam in primo et sic in infinitum.   Inventa est igitur decima figura talis o nihil-
que repr*   *sunt ..... significare.*"

was considered the basis and mother of all arts, as teaching the correct use of language and the art of interpreting texts. It was also the organon of theology, because the latter had not yet been systematized and was still largely confined to explaining Sacred Scripture and the writings of the Fathers. Symbolical explanations were employed to demonstrate that there was no conflict between theology and classical studies; Vergil and Seneca were dubbed half-Christians; Horace was styled *ethicus*, teacher of morals, and from him Alcuin borrowed his surname "Flaccus," by which he was known in the cultured society that gathered at Charlemagne's court. In his schools, Gerbert read other authors also: Terence, Juvenal, Lucan, Cicero, Cæsar, Sallust, etc. Though the age did not appreciate the differences between classical Latin and low Latin, it strove to preserve the purity of the ancient idiom. The science of tropes and figures was applied to Sacred Scripture, and rhetoric was thus coordinated with theology. Yet it never recovered the high position it had occupied with the ancients, for the Middle Ages, though preserving the technique of rhetoric, had no deep and vital interest in the art of language. Pedagogical works insisted that the rhetoric study should not crowd out more necessary and higher things, and that its real usefulness lies only in allowing one to cover the ground more quickly than could be done by reading or hearing good orators.[1] Dialectic, finally—called by Cassiodorus *oratio concisa* — was valued partly because of its formal aid to all studies and partly because of its being a weapon against the sophisms of the heretics. The study of this subject was based, up to the middle of the 12th century, on the textbooks of Boethius, the *Isagoge* of Porphyrius, and two works of Aristotle known as the *Vetus logica*, *De categoriis* and *De interpretatione*.

But after the whole organon of Aristotle had become known to Europe, especially after the Schoolmen had converted it into a ready serviceable tool, it was inevitable that dialectic studies should flourish, and that the entire system of education should experience a corresponding change. When the Schoolmen revived the study of speculative theology and began to construct a complete system of theological sciences, it was natural that the studies preparatory to theology as well as to other studies should assume another form, and that the art of defining, distinguishing, reasoning, proving, debating, and systematizing,

[1] Rhabanus, I, 1, cap. 19.

should be held in higher esteem than before. Thus logic was materially increased with an apparatus of new formulas, and a familiarity with its terms and definitions became indispensable to the man of culture. The art of disputation became the university of all science and research; it seemed that no subject could be studied otherwise than by scrupulously examining the *pro* and *con*, the *if* and *but*, and the pupil had to travel, as early as possible, the rugged path of syllogistic studies. The public disputation took the place of the speeches and recitations of the Greek and Roman schools. Not only masters and scholars, but princes and prelates attended these intellectual tournaments: after attending a long disputation, Charles IV. remarked that he would not go to dinner after having enjoyed so intellectual a feast. And even the masses were seized with the spirit of the battle of the reasons for and against. With this new interest the grammar and literary studies lost in favor: the number of classical school authors decreased, and modern authors were read instead. The grammars were adapted to the prevailing usage and legitimated the barbarisms that had crept into the language. The application of dialectic to language gave rise to a new science, the science of the *modistæ*, so called from the titles of their works, *De modis significandi*, known also as *grammatica speculativa*.[1] Rhetoric received more practical value by being co-ordinated with the study of law, particularly with the study of the revived Roman law. Its new title has quite a musical ring: *Liberalium artium imperatrix et utriusque juris alumna*. A new department of rhetoric, the *ars dictandi*, dealt with the style to be used in letter writing and in business affairs.[2] The friends of classical literature were few, and fewer still were the schools devoted to it. However, Orleans remained a city of authors and grammar studies.[3] A group of scholars, among them William of Conches, Adelard of Bath, and John of Salisbury, gathered about Bernard of Chartres (born c. 1070) for the purpose of studying the classics both scientifically and æsthetically. It was an axiom of the Chartres (Carnotum)

[1] Eckstein, l. c., p. 513.

[2] The object of the *ars dictandi* is described as the *congrua et apposita litteralis editio de quolibet vel mente retenta vel sermone aut literis declarata*.

[3] Helinand, a Cistercian, who died 1227, in speaking of the chief studies pursued at the different universities, says: "*Ecce quærunt clerici Parisiis artes liberales, Aureliani auctores, Bononiæ codices* (the *corpus juris*), *Salerni pyxides, Toleti dæmones* (alchemy)." Thuror, l. c., p. 114, says, "*Aurelianis educat in cunis auctorum lacte tenellos.*"

school that the modern writers stood on the shoulders of the ancients, like dwarfs on the shoulders of giants.[1] In this school Plato was preferred to Aristotle; a deep interest was taken in mathematics, and it was Adelard of Bath who acquainted the West with Euclid's works. The Scholastics did not approve of such classicists, and the *Battle of the Seven Arts*, an allegorical poem written in the 13th century by the Trouvère Henry d'Andely, represents the struggle between Scholasticism and the movement that harked back to the glories of classical antiquity. The Orleanists and the Parisians are pitted against each other; the former fight under the banner of grammar and are defended by the ancient authors, while the latter fight under the banner of logic and are defended by theology, physics, surgery, mantic art, and the Quadrivium; the Parisians gain the victory, but the poet prophesies that the day shall come when the classical writers will be reinstated in their place of honor.

3. This prophecy was fulfilled when Humanism arose in the 15th century. Some of the Humanists were opposed to the Church, and they have brought the whole movement of Scholasticism under suspicion, so that it is difficult for many of our own day justly to appraise the work of the Schoolmen. But it is much easier to ridicule the caricatures of Scholasticism that appeared in the days of its decline, than to appreciate the brilliant work wrought in the period of its glory: "When kings are building, draymen have something to do." It is certainly not fair to overlook (because of the dialectical pedantry with which the age abounds, and which savors indeed of the work of draymen) the truly great and kingly structures reared by such intellectual giants as Albert the Great, Thomas Aquinas, and the Seraphic Doctor Bonaventure. Much of the schoolwork of the Middle Ages, especially in dialectic, resembles the scrolls of Gothic architecture. However, the eye must not be riveted on these, but must take in the vaulting height, flooded with light, and must dwell rather on the massive columns and the gorgeous

---

[1] The axiom, often quoted by Bernard as well as by Peter of Blois, reads: "*Nos esse quasi nannos gigantium humeris insidentes, ut possimus plura iis et remotiora videre, non utique proprii visus acumine aut eminentia corporis, sed quia in altum subvehimur et extollimur magnitudine gigantea;*" cf. Schaarschmidt, *Joh. Saresbriensis,* Leipzig, 1862, pp. 60 ff.

[2] The following are mentioned: Donatus, Priscian, Persius, Vergil, Horace, Juvenal, Statius, Lucan, Sedulius, Propertius, Prudentius, Aratus, Terence, Homer; but Plato, Aristotle, Porphyry, Boethius, etc., fight on the side of the Parisians. Cf. Liliencron, l. c., p. 47.

tints of the stained glass than on minutiose details. The cathedral of Scholastic science combined into one splendid harmony theology and philosophy, the teaching of the Fathers and the wisdom of Plato and Aristotle, mysticism and dialectic. Whole generations and whole nations joined hands in rearing the magnificent temple, but after all it was permeated by one spirit and destined to serve one and the same end. The great masters did not engage in quarrelsome dialectic; they revered and loved one another; and, though employing the form of the *quæstiones*, in which the *pro* and *con* were examined, they also treated their subjects both systematically and connectedly. St. Thomas' *Summa contra gentiles* is, with all its depth, a model of transparent clearness and genetic thought-movement.

As the Middle Ages were confronted with a culture ready-made, for whose assimilation a high form of mental training was required, they had to cultivate more than other periods in the history of education the formal sciences. Still, they were interested also in the sciences that deal with facts and realities; and of these sciences history was esteemed most. Though this subject had no definite place in the medieval curriculum, yet both learned and unlearned were interested in the records of the past. The historical portions of the documents of Faith, the reverence ever shown by the Church for her past, the conviction that the Holy Roman Empire was one with the empire of ancient Rome—all these factors were incentives to historical studies. The textbooks in history compiled in the early centuries of the Christian era by Jerome, Eusebius, and Sulpicius Severus were widely used, and of the ancient Roman histories enough was still extant to serve at once as a source and a model for the medieval historian. It can not be denied that what did pass current in the Middle Ages as history, abounded with myths and legends; and medieval histories fare poorly enough at the hands of present-day critics. Yet works such as the *Hanno-lied* and the *Kaiserchronik*, both dating from the end of the 12th century, evidence the desire of connecting the present with the past and of merging in one harmonious whole Biblical, Christian, and ancient elements. Some chronicles also show that serious efforts were made to separate fact from fiction, and to transmit to the young only such facts as could bear the light of searching criticism. For instance, the author of the *Kaiserchronik* says: "Certain writers invent lies and patch together their lies with deceiving words, but I fear lest their soul will suffer for this crime, since their work was not inspired by the love of God,

Theirs is but teaching lies and falsehoods to the children that will come after us. The latter will take for granted what is but a lie, and falsehoods they will believe to be true; but lies and conceit are harmful to all, and the wise man dislikes to hear of such doings." We smile at the town chroniclers who begin with the creation of the world and the fall of Adam and Eve and then proceed to give the history of the Jews, the Romans, and their own country, before they say one word referring to their local history. Still, their joining what is small to what is great and their connecting the present with what is remote in time and place—this reveals a sense of deep reverence for the records of the past; and Niebuhr did not hesitate to class the author of the Chronicle of Cologne, which was written in this manner, "with the brightest minds and truest hearts."[1]

4. The sense for natural history was less developed, and the following saying of St. Bernard of Clairvaux is typical of the general spirit of the age: "The whole earth is of less value than one single soul, for God has not done for the whole world what He has done for one immortal soul: think well on't and adore His holy will." Medieval science was based on books that were not favorable to the observation of nature, and the few writings of the ancients that continued to be popular—particularly Pliny's works—encouraged the collecting of curiosities instead of entering into the nature of things. The scientific study of nature was unknown except among the alchemists, who did not, as was formerly believed, toy with vain experiments, but were engaged in solving important and live problems.[2] However, their influence on general knowledge and the world-view was practically nil. Nature study occupied, nevertheless, an important place in the system of sciences. The Scholastics placed it in the middle of the field of intellectual vision, because it observes the intellectual in the sensuous, i. e., the law in the phenomena. The spirit of the Middle Ages was keenly alive to the beauties of nature, and could well commune with her every mood. The medieval poets possessed a deep and true understanding of nature's language; their fables reveal an intimate acquaintance with animal life; and Dante's comparisons are

---

[1] Joh. Janssen, *History of the German People*, London, 1896, I, pp. 293 ff.

[2] In his *Familiar Letters on Chemistry* (London, 1851, III. Letter, pp. 25 ff.), Liebig has shown the serious and scientific aim of alchemy. In the researches concerning the philosophers' stone he sees the beginnings of inorganic chemistry, and in those concerning the elixir of life, the beginnings of organic chemistry.

strongly realistic.   The knights and monks were not blind
to scenic beauties, and showed exquisite taste in selecting
sites for their castles and monasteries.   The same Bernard,
whom we just quoted as counselling introspection, did not
scorn the lessons taught by nature: "Much that thou canst not
find in books wilt thou find in the woods, and the tree and the
stone will teach thee many a thing that a master can not teach;"
and these words the realists of the 17th century, the disciples
of Francis Bacon, might well quote in defence of their policy.[1]
The so-called *Physiologi*, which were very popular and of which
copies are still extant in Latin and Old-German editions, reveal
a quaint union between the religious thought of the period and
the interest in nature: they are books of edification, purporting
to show how the qualities of animals symbolize Christ and
Satan as well as the virtues and vices of men.   But that natural
objects were not used merely for the purpose of comparison,
but were examined for the sake of gaining a knowledge of them,
can be seen from the respective parts of medieval encyclopedias.
Although these treatises on natural history are written in an
unscientific spirit and with scant knowledge of actual conditions,
yet these defects will be pardoned more readily when we remember that the popular encyclopedias of the 17th century
discuss dragons and basilisks with the same naïveté as the works
of the early Middle Ages.   Bartholemew, surnamed Anglicus of
Suffolk, a Friar Minor, compiled in the 14th century an encyclopedia of natural history, *De proprietatibus rerum libri XIX*,
and at least fifteen Latin editions of it, beside many French,
English, Dutch, and Spanish editions, were in circulation towards the end of the 15th century.[2]

5. The encyclopedias which contained information gleaned
from many fields, were of special importance for the intellectual
life of the Middle Ages.   In an age when books were few and
costly, these encyclopedias took the place of libraries.   They

---

[1] Comenius, *Did. magna*, 5, 8 and 18, 28.

[2] Liliencron, l. c., p. 27, and Gesner, *Isagoge in erud. univers.*, ed. Niclas,
1775, §25.   Bartholemew used Western as well as Arabian authors, and wished
only to collect what others had discovered; he says, "*Parum vel nihil de meo
apposui, sed simpliciter Sanctorum verba et philosophorum dicta pariter et commenta veritate prævia sum secutus.*"   He treats the following subjects in 19
books: 1. God; 2. the angels; 3. the soul; 4. the body; 5. the members of the
body; 6. the periods of life; 7. diseases; 8. the world and the heavenly bodies;
9. time and its division; 10. matter and form; 11. air; 12. birds; 13. water;
14. and 15. the earth and its parts; 16. gems; 17. plants; 18.animals; 19. of the
accidents color, smell, taste, fluidity, number, weight, measure, tone.

preserved the knowledge of such sciences as could not claim any popular interest, for instance, economics, archeology, and the like; by introducing details and by using illustrations, they made the dry materials more inviting; and by treating whatever was of interest to the men of the time, they connected the sciences with the present. Theological matters are invariably treated first, and the secular sciences are all treated from the viewpoint of theology. The authors, looking more to amassing a wealth of material, pay little heed to style or the order of arrangement; their compilations are frequently but centos; later writers copied entire pages and chapters from their predecessors; fables and errors were transmitted from one book to the next. It is these glaring defects that have brought all medieval encyclopedias into disrepute and have prevented many writers from properly estimating their importance for the history of education. Isidore of Seville heads the list of the medieval encyclopedists (see *supra*, ch. XVI, 8). Rhabanus Maurus' *De universo* [1] is the most important encyclopedia produced in the period of the Carolingians. The *Hortus deliciarum* is a compilation made in the 12th century by the learned Herrad of Landsberg, Abbess of Hohenburg in Alsatia, for her canonesses who followed the rule of St. Augustine; Latin poems, many set to music, are inserted in the text, which is richly illustrated with Biblical and other religious pictures. The illustrations, showing a remarkable skill of execution, have given the work a special interest for the art historian.[2] The *Eruditio didascalica* (or *Di-*

---

[1] In 22 books the following subjects are treated: 1. God and the angels; 2. the human race; 3. persons of the Old Testament; 4. persons of the New Testament; martyrs, clerics, monks; heretics; divine service; 5. sacred writings; canon of the Gospels and the Councils; the paschal cycle; canonical life, etc.; 6. man and his organs; 7. periods of life, degrees of relationship, marriage, death, etc.; 8. animals; 9. the world; elements, heaven, light, heavenly bodies, etc.; 10. time; moment, hour, day, week, month, year, century; the feasts; 11. water; ocean, sea, river, etc.; 12. the earth; paradise, parts of the earth, islands, etc.; 13. mountains, valleys, groves, shores, etc. (here also Erebus and Cocytus); 14. the city; streets, market, town hall, gymnasium, theatre, citadel, bath, prison, temple, graves, etc.; 15. of philosophy; the poets, sibyls, magicians, heathen; 16. of languages; names of nations, with derivation; terms pertaining to public life and military service; 17. mineralogy; 18. weights, measures, number, music, medicine; 19. agriculture and botany; 20. military and naval affairs; 21. trades; 22. daily life; meals, utensils, etc.

[2] Cf. Engelhard, *Herrad von Landsberg*, Stuttgart and Tübingen, 1818. The manuscript of the *Hortus deliciarum* was kept at Strassburg, but was destroyed by fire along with the city library during the siege of 1870; but fortunately a copy, made in Paris, is still extant. The pictures have been

dascalos, or *Didascalion*) by Hugh of St. Victor, an Augustinian
monk (born c. 1097, died 1141 in his monastery near Paris), is a
book on methods rather than an encyclopedia.   It is especially
important for its system of the sciences, which was adopted by
all subsequent encyclopedists.   Philosophy, according to this
work, includes all knowledge, and is defined as the *disciplina
omnium rerum humanarum atque divinarum rationes plane in-
vestigans* (I, 5); it is divided into *philosophia theoretica, practica,
mechanica, logica* (II, 2); theoretical philosophy is divided into
theology, mathematics (arithmetic, music, geometry), and physics; practical philosophy is divided into ethics, economics, politics, which treat of the individual, the family, and the State
(II, 20); the mechanical field embraces the seven mechanical arts
(called also *adulterinæ, mechanicus* being derived from *mœchus*):
of the weaver, the smith, the sailor, the farmer, the hunter, the
physician, and the actor.   Logic is called the *disciplina sermo-
cinalis*, because it treats of words; it is partly *grammatica*, partly
dissertiva, i. e., dialectic (III, 19). One bond unites all the sciences,

frequently reproduced.   Engelhard gives a summary of the contents of the
book.   The whole is based on the Bible narrative, and the pictures illustrate
texts from Scripture.   Cosmology is treated in connection with the creation;
Sol appears on the sun chariot.   The fall of Adam and Eve and the building
of the Tower of Babel introduce mythology and the profane arts.   Here a
picture represents the nine Muses and the seven liberal arts: in the centre is
philosophy, from whose headgear three heads issue, labelled *ethica, logica,* and
physica; below philosophy Socrates and Plato are seen writing.   The arts issue
from philosophy as streams, but the text is added, "*Spiritus Sanctus est inventor
septem liberalium artium.*"   Female figures represent the arts: Grammar appears with book and rod; Rhetoric with tablet and stylus; Dialectic with a
dog's head in her hands; Arithmetic with a knotted rope; Geometry with a
pair of compasses and a rule; Astronomy with bushel and stars.   Circles and
semicircles with appropriate texts surround the whole group.   Beneath it four
figures read and write, with black birds perched on their shoulders. In explanation the text is added, "*Isti immundis spiritibus inspirati scribunt artem
magicam et poeticam fabulosa commenta.*"   After the history of the Old Testament follows an account of general history to the reign of Tiberius; after this
follows the history of the New Testament, which is interspersed with many
digressions owing to the need of explaining the symbols.   Thus the Sirens
enticing Ulysses represent the temptations of the world; the picture of the ship
offers an occasion for further digressions anent the meaning underlying the
different names of ships and the names of their parts.   After this the subject
of the Church is treated: her organization, ministers, her mission, etc., are
treated in detail.   The work contains, besides, a list of the popes, a calendar,
martyrology, and the dates for the Easter-tide from 1175 to 1707.   A picture
of Herrad and her canonesses is the last of the book.   The Latin language is
used throughout the work, but of the more difficult words (about 1200) the
German equivalents are given

and if but one branch is missing, the rest will be unequal to the task of making one a philosopher (III, 5). Poetry and history are not included in the *orbis disciplinæ;* they are *appendices artium* and are of value only to such as have been graduated from the *artes.*[1]

6. The encyclopedias of the Dominican Vincent of Beauvais (Bellovacensis), surnamed *Speculator* (from the title, *Speculum,* of his works), and who died in 1264, are the most comprehensive of the Middle Ages. His works follow the order of Holy Writ. The first subject treated is the Creator and the Creation; the second, the fall of man and his restoration with the aid of science and moral discipline; and the third, the chronological sequence of events. The four *Mirrors* are arranged accordingly: the *Speculum naturale* treats of God, the angels, and nature, according to the order of the hexaëmeron; the *Speculum doctrinale* treats of the sciences, and is the encyclopedia proper;[2] the *Speculum morale* treats of virtues, the last things, and sin; the *Speculum historiale* gives, in its 32 books, the history from the Creation down to the time of the Emperor Frederick II. Only three parts of the whole were written by Vincent, the *Speculum morale* being added by another author, though not before the beginning of the 14th century. The text is, to a great extent, not original, but compiled from many sources: the Bible, the Fathers, the classics, Arabian writers, etc. With the methods of study Vincent deals partly in the first book of the *Mirror of Sciences* and partly in a separate treatise, *De eruditione filiorum regalium,* dedicated to Queen Margaret of France; chapters 3-22 treat of teaching, and here Hugh of St. Victor is the chief source.[3]

---

[1] In the Venetian edition of Hugh's works (1638) the *Eruditio didascalica* is printed as the beginning of the third part (pp. 1-17). It contains six books (the seventh, *de eruditione theologica,* may be considered an appendix). The following subjects are treated in the six books: 1. *de studio legendi* in general; 2. of the division of the sciences; 3. of the conditions of study, the aids to study, memory, etc.; 4. of sacred writings; 5. of the interpretation of texts; 6. of the study of Sacred Scripture.

[2] In its seventeen books the following subjects are treated: 1. introduction and vocabulary; 2. grammar; 3. logic, rhetoric, poetics; 4. of the science of practical life; 5. of good morals (ch. 48, *De pueri instructione,* is largely taken from St. Augustine); 6. economics; 7. politics; 8.-10. law matters; 11. of the mechanical arts: wool-dressing, architecture, military science; theatre, navigation, commerce, hunting, agriculture, alchemy; 12. practical medicine; 13. theoretical medicine (physiology); 14. diseases; 15. *Physica* or *naturalis philosophia:* metaphysics, natural history, and mythology; 16. mathematics, including some metaphysics; 17. theology, divided into: a) *theologia fabulosa, i. e.,* mythology, and b) Christian theology.

[3] Cf. McCormick, *History of Education,* pp. 118 ff.

All later compilers drew upon Vincent's work. The *Speculum* suggested Brunetto Latini's *Grand Tresor*, which is the first encyclopedia written in a modern language and calculated therefore to appeal to a larger reading public than the Latin encyclopedias. Latini was the teacher of Dante, and the universal tendency, so characteristic a trait of the poet, can be traced to his influence.[1] Present-day writers are wont to consider Dante the first of the Humanists, since he extolled the greatness of old Rome and popularized the ancient ideas. Yet in so doing the poet never leaves the medieval circle of thought, for all his thinking and imagining was so deeply rooted in it that he is its most brilliant representative. If anything of Dante may be called modern, it is, besides his language, his subjectivity, which does not (after the manner of the Middle Ages) render itself up to the treasure of knowledge and make itself the receptacle of ideas; rather he boldly introduces his own soul, its hopes and fears, its love and hate, into the picture of heaven and hell. We can not expect to exhaust the meaning of the *Divine Comedy* by showing its relation to the medieval encyclopedias, yet it is illuminating to look at the wonderful poem from this viewpoint also. The *Divine Comedy* is a picture of the universe; a commentary on it is an encyclopedia; and the Florentines did well in establishing a professorship for the interpretation of the work of their greatest townsman. The poet tells us that heaven and earth have worked on his poem,[2] and we may truthfully add that all sciences have joined hands in creating it: the philosophy of history and sociology supplied the basic ideas, astronomy and physics reared the framework of the gigantic structure, ancient history furnished the characters, especially for the first part; theology and Scholasticism, conceived in the spirit of the great Aquinas, furnished the thought-content of the two last parts, historical science was the guide through the places that have been the scenes of the good or bad deeds of men, and geography and natural history furnished the coloring for the pictures that are scattered with a profuse hand throughout the work. The *Divine Comedy* shows splendidly what can be accomplished by a union of science and poetry.

---

[1] Dante calls him the master who "taught him hourly how man makes himself eternal" (*Inferno*, 15, 85). The *Tesoro*, or *Tesoretto*, is an allegorical didactic poem in Italian; but the larger work, *Li Livre dou Tresor*, or *Grand Tresor*, Brunetto wrote in French, but a contemporary, Bono Giamboni, translated it into Italian.

[2] *Par.*, 25 in.

It was Dante's aim to concentrate the scattered efforts of his nation, to give to Italian poetry a worthy content, and to create a foundation for Italian culture; and this aim the *Divine Comedy* has realized in a way that almost surpasses the fondest dreams of the poet.

7. Dante and Brunetto stand alone in their efforts to treat scientific subjects in a modern language, for it was the general opinion of medieval scholars that Latin should be the medium of expression in science as well as in education. In that age Latin was not a dead language, nay, not even a purely literary idiom, as it was the language not only of the Church, but also of public life and diplomatic intercourse. It had never ceased to influence the languages of Southern Europe; it had accepted a new metrical principle by introducing the rime; and, being used so generally in the sciences, it was continuously readjusting itself to the current way of thinking. But, being a literary language, it was still learned through written grammar, and thus preserved its scientific character. A happy comparison has it that Latin is the queen of languages, Greek the teacher, and Hebrew the mother of tongues, while all three are in common the language of divine worship and of the glad tidings of Christianity.[1] Through the study of its logical side, language became connected with philosophy. The writings that treated this phase of the subject generally bore the title *De modis significandi*. One of these books, included now among the works of Duns Scotus, is praised by the philologist Haase as the "first complete system of a philosophy of grammar."[2] The study of Greek was never neglected entirely in the West, yet never became during the Middle Ages a real element in general education. During the centuries previous to the Eastern Schism there were reasons of Church and State that encouraged the study of this language; and the Benedictine monasteries in Italy had their *fratres Ellinici*. In the 7th century the learned Greek scholar, Theodore of Tharsus, was appointed the Primate of the Church in England, and it is said that even thirty years after Theodore's death one could meet men in England who were as much at home in both Latin and Greek as in their native tongue.[3] Charlemagne ordered that the Bishops of Osnabrück should have Greek taught in their cathedral school, in order to fit clerics

[1] Hugo von Trimberg in his *Renner*, 22, 278.
[2] Haase, *De medii ævi studiis philologicis*, Breslau, 1856.
[3] Cf. Cramer, *De Græcis medii ævi studiis*, 1848.

for the diplomatic service.[1]   At the court of Charles the Bald
it was customary to insert Greek words and phrases in Latin
poems.   An elementary Greek textbook, dating from the 9th
or 10th century, has been found in Laon.[2]   It is true that the
interest in philology decreased with the spread of Scholasticism;
still by accepting many of the teachings of Plato and Aristotle,
the Schoolmen encouraged the study of original Greek texts.
Robert Grossetête (died 1255) was the first to translate from
the original of the Greek philosophers, and Thomas Aquinas
heartily seconded these efforts: "Throughout the Middle Ages
there is a steady increase in the knowledge of the books and the
educational methods of classical antiquity."[3]   The conviction
that deeper scientific research is impossible without a knowledge
of Greek, is responsible for the custom of giving Greek titles to
books;[4] and occasionally the court poets represent their heroes
as being accomplished Greek scholars.[5]   It was not the Schoolmen, but the glossarists of Roman law at Bologna that coined
the phrase, *Græca sunt, non leguntur*.   The establishment of the
Latin Empire in Constantinople (1204) appeared to offer new
opportunities for intercommunication between the East and the
West; Pope Innocent III. called upon the University of Paris
to send Greek scholars to Constantinople, and Philip August
opened in Paris a *Collegium Constantinopolitanum* for young
Greeks.[6]   But it was only the efforts made in the 15th century,
towards the Reunion and the exodus of Greek scholars after the
Turkish invasion, that brought about in Europe, where the
Humanists had prepared the ground, a real familiarity with
Greek culture.   To understand and appreciate Greek art and
poetry was not given to the Middle Ages, but it is the undying glory of that period to have incorporated into its own
philosophy the leading ideas of the greatest of the Greek philosophers, Plato and Aristotle.   Greek philosophy is after all of
greater value than Greek philology, and it is to be regretted

---

[1] The order is quoted in Conring, *De antiquitatibus academicis*, 1739, pp.
73, 302.
[2] Eckstein, *Analekten zur Geschichte der Pädagogik*, Halle, 1861.
[3] Dilthey, *Einleitung in die Geisteswissenschaften*, 1884, p. 452.
[4] Thus Bernard of Chartres called his work *Megakosmus* and *Mikrokosmus*;
William of Conches, *Peri didaxeon*; John of Salisbury, *Policraticus*, or *Metalogicus*.
[5] The passages are quoted by A. Schultz, *Das höfische Leben im Mittelalter*,
Leipzig, 1879, I, pp. 120 ff.
[6] Jourdain, l. c., pp. 61 ff

that a later period studied this philology to the neglect of Greek thought.

Hebrew had even in the Patristic period been studied only by such as were extraordinarily industrious, and in the Middle Ages its study was rarer still. Lanfranc taught Hebrew in his school at Bec, and the subject is mentioned among the studies of the University of Paris, yet it appears that there was no unbroken line of teachers of Hebrew at the University. In 1312 the Council of Vienne had decreed that chairs of Hebrew be established in Paris, Oxford, Salamanca, and Bologna— Germany was not considered the home of higher learning— but this decree was never fully carried out.[1] Besides the difficulty of the subject itself, there was the strong antipathy against the Jews, who, indispensable as teachers of Hebrew, were the victims of a general race hatred. Moreover, the Vulgate of St. Jerome was deemed far and away superior to the original Hebrew text. Cardinal Ximenes, who was responsible for the Complutensian Polyglot, was of the opinion that the Vulgate stands midway between the original Hebrew and the Septuagint, like the Cross of Christ between the crosses of the robbers.

8. The Arabian language, being the key to a rich scientific literature, was widely studied in the Middle Ages, and, being the living tongue of a civilized people, it exercised an abiding influence on the languages of modern Europe. The learning and culture of the Mohammedans had developed phenomenally, and in mathematics and history the followers of the Prophet had soon outstripped the Christian schools. In the 7th century the Arabians had been the pupils of the Eastern Christians, but after the 10th century they were the teachers of the Western Christians. Mohammedan culture is, despite its opposition to Christian culture, still somewhat analogous to it: it was born of a religious principle; it assimilated pre-existing elements of culture; it drew into its circle different nations, and bound them together for the purpose of intercommunicating their influences. Mohammedan science is based on the deposit of faith, and a traditional saying has it that "the scholars are the heirs of the Prophet." Theology and the closely allied study of law developed from the study of the Koran. Among the non-Arabic peoples the study of law led to the study of language, and the latter, having been begun by the Arameans and Persians, was continued and more fully developed by the Arabians.

[1] L. Geiger, *Johann Reuchlin*, Leipzig, 18-1, p. 1-3.

Because of the instruction in the Koran the need for schools of reading and writing was felt early, and the elements of these branches were taught in the *Mekteb*, which were conducted either in connection with the mosques whose personnel was employed for teaching, or as private schools, opened near markets, wells, or burial places, etc. The new religion supplied much of the educational content; other elements grew from the contact with Greek education. Of the liberal arts, the Arabians cultivated logic and mathematics most, of rhetoric they took as much as seemed to improve their own art of language, while the polite literature of the Greeks exerted but little influence on them; but the study of the natural sciences and of medicine they pursued with remarkable success. Arabian philosophy early evinced a tendency towards polymathy, and many encyclopedias were written by Arabian philosophers, the principal ones being Alkendi's *Book of Science and of Its Division*, of the 9th century, and Ibn Sina's (Avicenna) *Well-Ordered Pearls*, of the 11th century.[1] Originally, the mosques were the seats of higher learning. Under the same roof the congregation worshipped, the scholar explained the law, another interpreted a poet, and a third recited his own verses.[2] Since the 11th century the State and liberal individuals founded higher schools (the *madrasas*), which spread from India as far west as Spain. Their organization was varied and allowed the greatest freedom in studies to both teachers and taught, the State interfering only when the orthodoxy of the religious instruction was endangered. Travelling teachers and pupils made possible the intellectual intercourse between schools far distant from one another.[3] The interest in

[1] The titles of the Moslem encyclopedias are varied enough. *The Supplies of the Sciences, The Spring of the Sciences, The Marrow of the S , The Advance Guard of the S , The Divine Tree, The Jewels of Knowledge*, and the like. In their arrangement the encyclopedias differ much, in several we find a scheme of fourteen sciences, for instance, in *Sojuthi* (1505) 1 fundamental doctrines of faith, 2 exegesis, 3 science of tradition, 4 fundamentals of law, 5 science of inheritance, 6 syntax, 7 grammar, 8 art of writing, 9 of the arrangement of thoughts, 10 figures of speech, 11 expression of thought, 12 anatomy, 13 therapeutics, 14 mysticism. Cf Hammer, *Enzyklopädie der Wissenschaft des Orients*, 1804, id in the *Denkschriften der Kaiserl Akademie der Wissenschaften*, 1856, pp 205 ff

[2] Haneberg. *Das Schul- und Lehrwesen der Mohammedaner im Mittelalter*, Munich, 1850, p 10

[3] Ibid, p 22 The Moslem fondness for educational travel has been well expressed by Ruckert in the following lines, which are modeled after Abu Seid "On travels I started, from home I departed, through many lands darted, deep learning my quest, and fleet steeds bestriding, through rivers now riding,

knowledge was not confined to the learned. A due distinction was made between the savant (*aalim*, plur. *ulema*), who specialized in one subject, and the educated man (*edib*, plur. *udeba*), who occupied himself with several sciences without specializing in any subject. He who was "content with the science of religion and with the rudiments of secular knowledge,"[1] was classed with those who had only a common education.

The Christian peoples of the West first learned mathematics and medicine from the Moslem and only through their translations did they become acquainted with the Greek sources: Ptolemy, Euclid, Galen, and Hippocrates. The many technical terms, particularly in chemistry and astronomy, that were borrowed from the Arabians, or formed after Arabic words, and of which many are still in general use, evidence the deep influence of Arabian learning.[2] Philosophy is indebted to the Arabians, not only for their commentaries on Aristotle, but also for certain works of this philosopher, especially for his treatises on metaphysics and physics. These new accessions were certainly responsible for much of the progress made in Scholastic philosophy—yes, the fondness of the Schoolmen for disputations may perhaps be traced to Semitic influences. The Arabic encyclo-

now oceans dividing, observing with zest; I took no account of desert or mount, but to drink at the fount, 'stead at streamlets to rest." — "Since childhood's amulets I first unbound, and round my head the manly turban wound, I longed for education; I sought it with firm determination, 'mong every people and every nation, that it might be to me adornment before the crowd, against the noon-day sun a shading cloud. So desirous was I to roam upon its pasture and to don its flowing vesture, that I asked of high and low, and asked of friend and foe, where its sweet traces I might find, where 'twould dispense its blessings kind, in drops or streams, to my mind."

[1] Hammer, *Denkschriften*, l. c., p. 215.

[2] Ptolemy's work on astronomy was known in the Middle Ages under the title of *Almagest*, from μεγίστη (sc. τέχνη) and the Arabic article. Arithmetic was called *Algorismus*, derived from the name of Alchwarismi, an Arabian mathematician of the 9th century, whose book *Al-jebr w'almuqâbalah, i. e.*, reduction and comparison (by equations), has given algebra its name. Cf. Cantor, *Vorlesungen über die Geschichte der Mathematik*, l, p. 611. Algebra was also called "rule of coss," or simply "coss," from the Italian term for algebra: *regola della cosa* (rule of the thing, the unknown quantity being called the *cosa*, or the thing). The name of alchemy reveals its Egyptian origin (chemi, Ham) and its having passed through Arabian hands. Our astronomy still employs the terms: zenith, nadir, azimut; and traces of Arabic words can be seen in many names of stars. In chemistry we have: alkali, alcohol, etc.; and commerce and navigation reveal a similar indebtedness: magazine, arsenal, admiral, calibre, beside many names of articles of trade. Neither was superstition denied its share: witness elixir, talisman, amulet, etc.

pedias were drawn upon by later encyclopedists; Avicenna's *Pearls* was translated in the 16th century and published under the title, *Liber de divisione scientiarum.*

A strange fate thus made Moslem education serve as the bond between the education of Greece and that of Western Christianity. A further function of Moslem education was to stimulate Christian science   But the germs for producing lasting and far-reaching creations were lacking in Mohammedanism[1]. Certain writers have extravagantly lauded Mohammedanism for allowing the various sciences to develop freely, whereas with the Christian religion the teachings of science may never conflict with theology   Nay, to judge from sayings ascribed to Mohammed, science ranked superior to faith "The ink flowing from the scholars' pens is more precious than the blood of martyrs shed in the service of God;" and again: "One hour's reflection is better than the piety of sixty years."[2] But this esteem of learning is hardly the fruit of an enlightened policy of toleration; it is the result rather of the meagre content of Mohammedan faith which, being unable to furnish sufficient material to the awakening mind, was forced to accept whatever was offered by the profane sciences. The theology and philosophy of the Koran, being based on a syncretism, were not apt to be deepened by the influences of ancient philosophy, and there was never any intimate relationship between the theological system of the Koran and the work of the thinkers and scholars, but pantheistic and sensualistic systems flourished alongside of the deism of the dominant religion. Such conditions, it is true, assured rapid progress and unrestricted liberty   Yet the principles of Christianity are possessed of greater power and a greater content, and hence their application to the sciences must eventually, even if after a longer time and more labor, result in correspondingly greater gains

9 The studies comprised in, and connected with, the system of the seven liberal arts were not the only educational elements available in the Middle Ages. The system of chivalrous education demonstrated that the national and modern elements were important enough to serve as the materials for a new form of mental culture   The Church, entrusted with the education of the new peoples, had to force into the background their national traditions so long as these abetted the errors of pagan-

[1] Erdmann, l c , I, 181
[2] Hammer, l. c , p 215 and p 211.

ism; but this danger past, the Church tolerated and even conserved the traditions. It was the priests who carried out the order of Charlemagne to collect the songs about the ancient heroes, and it was a bishop who had a copy made of the tales of the *Nibelungs*. In the monastic schools national tales and legends were occasionally assigned as themes of Latin compositions; and in the same schools the gospel was put into a popular form. In the legends Christian and national elements were blended. The tales of classical antiquity were introduced through the schools into the folklore of the nation. The East contributed the tales of wonder, fables, and moral stories from India. Here we have the source of that wealth of stories, tales, fables, legends, etc., that passed from mouth to mouth, from one country to another, from one generation to the next, and which represented a most valuable asset of society and rich mental food for those classes that did not enjoy the benefits of a higher education. From this source the chivalrous poetry of the age drew what was kindred to its ideals; to it the *Meistersinger* and the didactic poets of the later Middle Ages went for their materials; and much of it was still in circulation in the form of popular books in the 16th and 17th centuries. But precious little has been transmitted to our own day, and most of this had to be unearthed by scientific research; yet even this little constitutes what is best in our modern readers and books for the young. The great value of this epic and didactic literature for the Middle Ages was realized only in the 16th century, when it was seen that the store was becoming exhausted. "O how many are the fine tales and sayings," says Luther in his *Address to the City Council*, "that we are now in need of, and which, once current in all Germany, are now lost, because no one preserved them when written, or noted down what was not yet written." These "fine tales and sayings" were an intellectual treasure of the Middle Ages, though they are easily undervalued because they were not directly connected with the schools of the time. A later age has undertaken to replace them by creating, with the aid of schools and scholars, a popular literature. But this attempt, though praiseworthy, lacks the originality, the freshness, and fullness of medieval folklore.

CHAPTER XX.

The Ethos of Medieval Education.

1. Religion occupies the central place in the soul-life of the Middle Ages, and also determines the spirit and tendency of medieval education. Studies, science, knowledge, intellectual development, are not valued for their own sake, but as means for attaining Christian perfection. "All human activity must, to be deemed wise, aim to restore the primitive purity and perfection of our nature, or to alleviate some of the sufferings of our present life   The right teaching will restore what we have lost, and hence the pursuit of wisdom is apt to be the sweetest solace of life, he who finds wisdom, shall be called happy; and he that possesses wisdom, is blessed."[1] The work of learning is long and serious, and the precious years of early youth must therefore be spent in acquiring knowledge: "The days of man are few and short, but eternity is at stake; we are destined for great things, but surrounded by untold dangers; we are far from the goal, and our progress is slow· why should we not, then, start out in the morning of life on the road to paradise?"[2] The aim of our studies should be pure and sublime, and free from base motives. "Some study merely to know, which is contemptible curiosity; others study to become famous for their knowledge. they are vain and conceited, and to them may be applied the words of the satirist, 'Thy knowledge is nothing to thee if others do not know that thou knowest it' Others study to obtain by their knowledge wealth and high places, and this is miserly covetousness But there are some who study to edify their neighbor. and this is Christian charity; while they who study for their own edification, are truly wise. Only the last two classes of students do not abuse learning, for their studies tend to righteousness "[3] The conditions favorable to peace of soul also make for success in studies: i e , humility, spirit of research, quiet life, silent examination, poverty, living abroad [4]

---

[1] Hugo a Sto Victore, *Erud did* , I, 2

[2] Vinc Bell , *De erud fil reg* , cap 24

[3] Bern Claravall quoted in Vincent , I, 1, cap 13, cf Hugo, I, 1, III, 15 and J J Becher, *Methodus didactica*, Munich, 1668, preface

[4] Bernard of Chartres says *Mens humilis, studium quærendi, vita quieta, scrutinium tacitum, paupertas, terra aliena. hæc reserare solent multis obscura legendo.*

The right education and its application in later life are conceived as divine service. "Those pupils undoubtedly," says
Caesarius of Heisterbach, "that lead a pure life and are happy
in the pursuit of knowledge, bear witness to the Faith, and
their heavenly reward will be exceeding great, if they turn to
good account, in the service either of their fellowmen or, better
still, of their God, whatever they learned in the schools." The
ethico-religious purpose of learning forbids the student to attempt what is beyond his powers, or to waste his energies on a
variety of subjects. "There are men," says Hugh of St. Victor,
"who would read and know everything, but of the number of
books there is no end; therefore, be thou wise, and do not presume to cover what is infinite, for where there is no end there
is no rest and hence neither peace; and where there is no true
peace there God can not dwell, for God dwells in a house of
peace."[1] "The great number of things and the shortness of
human life," to quote St. Bernard, "will not allow us to encompass all; he who would command too large a field of knowledge, will go astray, he will make no progress, and will know
nothing thoroughly; for the mind, when attending to many
different subjects, can not fathom the details of any individual
matter."[2] These dangers, however, of a shiftless browsing among
the sciences did not blind these men to the obvious advantages
of general knowledge. Hugh of St. Victor says of his own
studies: "I can assure you that I have not slighted anything
pertaining to erudition (*quod ad eruditionem pertineret*), but have
often studied many subjects which appeared in the eyes of others
ridiculous and useless." And he lays down the rule, "Study all,
and thou shalt later see that nothing is superfluous; knowledge,
if narrowly confined, is not attractive (*coarctata scientia jucunda
non est*)."[3]

The religious attitude of the Middle Ages was one of deep
reverence for the content of Faith, and with the then importance
of religion it is not surprising that a kindred reverence was
shown to all learning and its representatives. "The pupil must
believe his teacher in all that pertains to the sciences, but must
follow especially them who are the pioneers in a science, or
who have treated it with the greatest knowledge or eloquence;
i. e., Priscian in grammar, Aristotle in logic, and Hippocrates
in medicine."[4] As each vocation had its own patron, so each

[1] Quoted in Vincent, I, 1, cap. 13.   [2] Quoted ibid.
[3] Hugo, *Erud. did.*, VI, 3.   [4] Vincent, *Sp. c. doct.*, I.

science, too, was assigned to an ancient sage as to a procurator.[1]
The instruction was controlled by the recognized textbooks, and
consisted chiefly in explaining the standard texts. But the
writings of the great masters, the first sources, were rarely used
as texts Instead, the textbooks quoted only extracts from
these sources, and the greatest authority, though unmerited,
was enjoyed by the schoolbooks written towards the end of the
Roman period. Cicero was declared the prince of orators, but
instead of reading his orations, the schools used Marcianus
Capella's *Rhetoric*, which was based on them The Middle Ages
professed to be disciples of Aristotle, but of his works they had
for a long time only extracts, garbled at that, from his *Organon*.
Attempts were made in the later Middle Ages to remedy these
defects, but the numberless compendia produced in consequence
—the *Sententiæ, Summæ, Catenæ aureæ*, and the like—rendered
the original sources more inaccessible than ever. Once a doctrine had been admitted to one textbook, it was certain to make
the rounds of all books written on the subject, and it was generally copied without any reference to author or source Hence
the naive plagiarisms which confront us on all sides in the textbooks of the Middle Ages, and also the gullibility with regard
to the wildest of fables and grossest of errors, though the latter
might readily have been detected by merely consulting the
current authorities of the ancients. These glaring defects the
Humanists later made the butts of their attacks on the period,
and pointed to them as proofs for the barbarity of the Middle
Ages.

Though teaching was in actual practice conceived as the
process primarily of imparting knowledge—the chief function of
learning being to receive this knowledge—yet this view was
corrected, at least in theory, by the teaching of the philosophers.
The Schoolmen treated pedagogy mostly in connection with
St Augustine's *De magistro*, where the Saint lays down the
principle that teaching in its full meaning can be ascribed to
God alone. St. Thomas takes up the subject in his *Quæstio de*

---

[1] The title-page of the Strassburg edition (1512) of the *Margaritha philosophica* presents the picture of a tower-like structure, in the first story of which
Donat and Priscian are teaching, while the following are looking from the
windows of the higher stories Aristotle, the representative of logic, Cicero,
of rhetoric and poetics, Boethius, of arithmetic, Pythagoras, of music, Euclid,
of geometry, Ptolemy, of astronomy, Seneca, of morals, Aristotle (the *philo-
sophus*), of physics The highest point is occupied by Peter the Lombard,
the representative of *Theologia seu Metaphysica* Cf McCormick, l. c., p. 128

magistro, the eleventh in his book *De veritate*, and arrives at the conclusion that man can teach by exerting an external influence on the mind, just as the physician cures the ill body by calling into play the forces of nature. St. Thomas observes that with both teacher and physician success depends on imitating the ways of nature. Thus the self-activity of the pupil is declared to be just as important as the teacher's work; and the imitation of nature, which was later demanded so insistently, was even then laid down as a law.[1]

2. As the content of teaching was an object of reverence, so the teacher also was held in personal esteem. It was the gratitude of his pupils that obtained for the learned Bede the surname *Venerabilis;* and Alcuin, Rhabanus, and others were regarded by their pupils with filial reverence. When Lanfranc called on Pope Alexander II., his sometime pupil, the Pope arose and greeted him saying, *Assurgo tibi tanquam magistro et deosculor tanquam pædagogum.* Most pleasant relations existed between Bernard of Chartres and his pupils, as may be seen from the *Metalogicus* in which John of Salisbury extols the *Senex Carnotensis.*

This attitude of the pupils towards their teachers was apt to render less arduous the work of the school and to soften somewhat the rigor of medieval discipline. The retaining of the ancient traditions amid totally different conditions rendered the work of learning doubly difficult. The Latin grammar, written originally for Roman·boys, but now strange to the pupil in both matter and form, had to be learned first. Each subject demanded a vast amount of memorizing. The subtleties of dialectic, which retained its traditional place among the elementary studies, were the mental food for the growing boy. The spirit of mortification and penance that inspired the teachers of the older monastic schools, prevented them from making proper allowances for the weakness of the young; and in the secular schools the teacher was never in a position to assist the individual pupil. It sounds desperate to hear Thomas Platter relate how he cowered in a corner of the schoolroom and said to himself, "Here must thou learn or die." This is, however, but one side of the picture, for there is sufficient evidence that the medieval schools did not lack their attractive features, and the rod was not in absolute power. *Læti tirones, læti magistri,*

---

[1] Cf. F. A. Pace, *St. Thomas' Theory of Education*, in *Catholic University Bulletin*, July, 1902.

lætissimus rector, was said of Rhabanus' school. In the 12th century Alexander of Neckam confesses that the happiest years of his life were spent in the monastic school of St. Albans.[1] Hugh of St Victor has left us a charming description of the joys he experienced in the solitude of his cell in following the tangled paths of learning.[2] The mnemonic verses, abounding in the textbooks of the Scholastic period, are a signal proof for the pains taken to lighten the pupils' tasks; and aids to the vizualization of different subjects were also employed: in his school at Paris the Cantor Peter illustrated the history of the Old Testament with genealogical trees.[3] Neither was a state of passivity general with the pupils: the Scholastic determination (*i. e.*, definition), disputation, and recitation surely necessitated a large amount of self-activity on the part of the pupil.[4] It is a well-known fact that the beautiful school feasts of the Middle Ages gave full scope to the joys and pleasures of the young.

3 There might seem to be but little kinship between the cumbersome education demanded of the savant and the pleasant course of training outlined for the aspirant to knighthood The savant's training has in it much that is reminiscent of the hard and fast rules of Eastern education, while chivalrous education conforms in many points to the *paideia* of the Greeks. The knightly *vrumecheit* has in it something akin to the Hellenic καλογαθία. the tournament supersedes the gymnastics of the Greeks; the harp, songs, and tales took the place of several elements of ancient liberal education, the heroes of Homer, the ideals of the Greek youth, have their counterpart in the heroes of chivalry and knight-errantry, whose deeds are celebrated in the medieval epics. The knight realizes many of the cultural ideals of the ancients: his is a manly consciousness of strength; his personality, versatile and finished, combines knowledge and skill in beautiful harmony; and his noble feats of strength and hardihood are a fit preparation for the trying duties of life. Yet upon closer view, it will be seen that the education of the knight was, nevertheless, wholly and fully medieval. For here, too, religion was the final aim: the page must become a warrior

---

[1] In the following verses. *Hic locus ætatis nostræ primordia novit Annos felices, lætitiæque dies! Hic locus ingenuis pueriles imbuit annos Artibus, et nostræ laudis origo fuit Hic artes didici docuique fideliter,* quoted in Hurter, *Leben des Papstes Innocenz III*, Vol III, p 574

[2] *De erud did*, VI, 3

[3] Hurter, l c, IV, p 552

[4] Huber, *The English Universities*, London, 1843, I, p 35.

of Christ; he is dubbed a knight "for God's and Mary's glory;" he is trained for the service, not only of his King, but also of Mother Church; and his fondest dreams are realized when he journeys to the Holy Land in company with his fellows in arms. There is one ancient institution that is really kin of nature to medieval knighthood: the warriors in Plato's *Republic*, appointed to defend the community, who watch over the welfare of the State, while the intellectual treasures are committed to the care of the governors, whose life is devoted to contemplating the eternal verities. The severity of chivalrous education is likewise more reminiscent of Plato's regulations than of the general education of Greece. The younker was not spared the bitterness of hard study; he was obliged, according to Gottfried's *Tristan und Isolde*, "to journey to foreign and distant lands to learn foreign tongues; of all learning he was to give chief attention to booklore, and many days and many nights must he devote to his books and travels." Chivalrous education, then, does not lack the seriousness of the Christian ideals, and if inferior, on its æsthetic side, to Greek culture, it is immeasurably superior in moral worth.

The charge has been brought against the Middle Ages that the attention to the things of the next world prevented the "humanization and the harmonious development of the things of this world," and that the "one-sided spiritualism" made it impossible to interpret the ancients, to commune with nature, and to estimate aright the human powers. But while conceding these charges to be, to some extent, not unfounded, we may not close our eyes to the obvious advantages accruing to the Middle Ages from their deep and strong faith in eternity and their pure and lofty spirituality of aim. While it may be questioned whether the above complaints be at all in place, the fair-minded student of history will acknowledge that they can be reduced to the lament over the limitations imposed on the soul-life of man. If men would cover new ground and assimilate new ideas, they must perforce render up much of what they had hitherto prized. How narrow and how confined is the ken allowed to the human eye: when we direct our gaze heavenward and contemplate its glories, we are apt to let the earth escape our attention, and thus an extension of the field of human interests, any gain in knowledge, is accompanied with loss; intensive application in one field implies a corresponding loss in other fields.

VII.

THE RENAISSANCE.

CHAPTER XXI.

General View of Renaissance Education

1. The intellectual life of the Middle Ages was never out of touch with antiquity: the philosophy of the Schoolmen was based on Aristotle; the encyclopedias, on Roman compilations; all schooling, on the system of the seven liberal arts and on the reading and interpretation of a limited number of the ancient classics; finally, Latin had remained the language of scholarship and the basis of all higher learning. Hence the revival of classical studies at the end of the Middle Ages does not imply the rediscovery of something that had been lost, for the Renaissance did not take up a new subject of study, but only assumed a new attitude towards what had been for centuries the content of education. The Middle Ages had looked upon the intellectual treasures handed down from the ancient world as a precious inheritance and as indispensable for serious mental work. But despite this high esteem for the rich legacy, they rightly made it serve the peculiar needs of the time. They considered the writings of the ancients the standards of secular learning, the repository of immense erudition, and the starting-point for any further advance in secular science, so that they regarded progress in profane learning as only a continuation of ancient literature, specifically of Roman literature Consequently, Roman literature was not regarded as a monument of a past age, just as the Latin language was not considered dead and the Roman Empire not of the past.

The Renaissance, however, abandoned this (one may say) naïve view, for it realized that the writings of the ancients—especially the poets, orators, and historians, whom the Middle Ages had conceived as mere adjuncts of the *artes*—that these voiced the splendid and peculiar humanity of a departed age. In the ancient classics the Renaissance discovered a world peopled with men of striking and sublime individuality. It there beheld a fabric, many-hued and diverse in texture, which was indeed to be an object of marvel and study, but which was finished, and which would consequently not admit of any additional weaving at the hands of after ages.   In the old books it heard the living speech coming from the lips of the men of a bygone age and addressed to living men of like feelings, thus making possible an ideal intercommunion between the present and the past.   The ancient world was thus viewed in the proper perspective as belonging historically to the past, but as exerting with its broad humanity an unbroken and universal influence on the living present; and the ancient languages were declared to be dead, but as being classical they were recognized as immortal.

The age that assumed this attitude towards the ancient world may well be designated as the Humanistic age; and its general tendency may be called the spirit of Humanism.   But in calling it the Humanistic age we do not imply that the Middle Ages had known naught of human nature, had not had a deep and comprehensive view of the human spirit, had not felt truly the impulses of the common nature of the race. What we will say is that in this new age men passed from books and through books to human nature, found food in books for human feelings and human interests, perceived and bridged over the gulf that separated the ancient world from the present, and learned to appreciate the clear and broad views and the noble and graceful forms of the humanity of classical antiquity.   But educational writers and historians of education have so much misused this term "Humanism" that it will no longer embrace the system of education that resulted from the general acceptance of the new world-view.   The term is, moreover, used for the chief educational principle that governed the culture of the 15th and 16th centuries in contrast to the realism of the 17th century, and as this usage refers rather to one pedagogical concept than to the broad field of education, "Humanism" can no longer designate (what must be considered here) the sum-total of historical influences at work during the period.   Hence we find it expedient to borrow from the history of art the term *Renaissance* which, though likewise open to some misinterpretation, is happily free from the misconception just noted.   We are justified in thus borrowing this term for our broad subject, for in general usage Renaissance is being used more and more for the broad field of intellectual life.   In art-history the Renaissance is the movement that owed its inception to the study of ancient

16

models, and which followed consistently the conceptions and
ideals of the ancients. It originated in Italy in the 15th century, attained its highest development in the 16th, and finally
died out in the 17th century, after degenerating into the corrupt
taste and style of the Rococo. The history of education also
needs a term to embrace the work of about three centuries,
when men were engaged in engrafting the ideals and the spirit
of ancient culture upon the schools of modern Europe. This
movement in education also proceeded from Italy, achieved its
greatest successes in the 16th century, but was still a power in
the polymathy of the 17th century   We must, however, note
that a revival in art as well as in education occurred only in a
limited degree. The arts had never died (witness the Roman-
esque and Gothic cathedrals which challenge comparison with
the world's most splendid creations); neither had science and
learning passed from the earth. they had found a sheltering
home in the medieval universities; and it is only the narrow
view of the transitional and revolutionary period that could
ignore the achievements of medieval scholarship. Yet there
was withal a revival, inasmuch as many elements which had till
then been active only in a restricted and an indirect way, were
now given full sway   A new principle was introduced into the
intellectual world, and this new principle determined the ideas
and the world-view of the period. There was a revival also in
education inasmuch as the schools were enriched by the introduction of tendencies, forms, and materials of ancient education,
and stimulated by the wholesome influences proceeding from
other fields fructified by the new principles   Still, we must
confess that this revival and the new intellectual life occasioned,
on the other hand, the death of many older tendencies, nay,
certain classes of men, overfond of the novel, broke away completely from all traditions   These evil results explain why
Græco-Roman antiquity is more familiar to us than the Christian Middle Ages, and why a second Renaissance was needed
in the 19th century to re-connect, for the purposes of historical
research, the bonds that had been cut in twain. The study of
antiquity had sharpened the historical sense and had widened
the historical horizon, and hence the modern historians could
discover the relationship between the new and the inherited.

2. The leaders of the Renaissance wished to engraft the
spirit of the ancient world on the culture of the 15th and 16th
centuries, but while antiquity in general engaged their attention,
the Roman concept of education remained the highest ideal of

the epoch. Greek had in the Middle Ages received but scant attention, even in higher education. Now, however, it was added to the curriculum, and in a few cases considered even more important than Latin. Yet the latter retained its place of honor as the foremost cultural subject, and the *Institutes* of Quintilian remained the textbook of Renaissance pedagogy. The ideal of the Renaissance was not Greek culture, based on the liberal arts and gymnastics and culminating in philosophy, but Roman eloquence, which, in its essence of a purely formal character, was supplemented by general erudition, without, however, being internally correlated to philosophy. Keeping this in mind, we shall better understand the frequently so one-sided view of Renaissance educators concerning the importance of the mastery of language, the *fari posse*, which was both the capstone and the touchstone of education: hence the drills in style, the cult of Cicero and rhetoric, and the feverish activity of the Latinists. To acquire a Latin style was considered more important than the acquisition of positive knowledge, and the content of the classics imported less than the ancients' art of language. At no period in the world's history did the art of language hold so high a place in education as in the Renaissance, and in the worship of form this period surpassed even the Romans, as the imitator will ever tend to overdo what was praiseworthy in his model. The Renaissance revived the taste, long dead, for the most spiritual of all instruments of art and the most sublime of all objects of the fine arts; and lest we judge too harshly the formal tendency of the Humanists, we should contrast it with the naturalism of the medieval scholars who used the Latin language as a medium of expression, without, however, any æsthetic appreciation of its power and without any attention to its artistic form. Though the reincarnation of Cicero and Vergil smacked of affectation, and though the virtuosity of the *poetæ laureati* could not conceal the inanity of their verses (so striking if compared with the natural virility of the singers of the Age of Chivalry), yet the study of the organism of a highly developed language and the striving to master the subtleties of its technique proved a disciplinary course in æsthetics and linguistics whose value for the cultural development of modern peoples can not be overestimated, because it trained the sense for language and form. Still it must not be overlooked that the cult of the ancient classics blinded men to the power of their mother-tongue and to the glories of their national literature, and that it resulted in the tendency, so strong in Renaissance Germany, to ape foreign conditions instead of gradually assimilating the Roman civilization, as the Middle Ages had done, and thereby converting it into an element that could be amalgamated with a culture that was national in its general composition.

The term "Latinity," or "eloquence," as employed by the Renaissance, was very comprehensive, embracing all that made for the æsthetic improvement of the mind besides much of what belonged properly to moral and religious education. Hence Erasmus boasted of his *Colloquia* that they had—though it is hardly credible — made boys *latiniores et meliores*, and John Sturmius asserted roundly that a *sapiens atque eloquens pietas* was the aim of his school instruction. The refinement of taste, resulting from the study of the classics, was expected to refine the whole man and thereby prove an important contribution to the *civilitas morum*. This correlation of culture with moral training revived an ideal of ancient Rome, when education was conceived as the process of unlearning rudeness (*erudire*). The harmony of noble speech was declared to be "understandable of the ear, to betoken the sweet harmony of the inner man, and to be more intelligible than the harmony of the spheres, which, though never heard of mortal ear, was the subject of a Pythagorean doctrine."[1] The harmony of beautiful language was further said to be the image of a beautiful humanity, and the sincere and persistent striving after literary excellence was alleged to make men morally better.

3. The Renaissance had borrowed from the Romans, not only the spirit of Humanism, but also their cosmopolitan tendency. The Renaissance was intent on assembling "all nations under the leadership of the Muses," and this dream is reminiscent of the world empire of ancient Rome. The proud spirit of old Rome rings from the triumphant cry of Laurentius Valla, a Roman by birth: "We have lost Rome, but by the splendid power of the Latin language we are still lords of a great part of the world, Italy is ours, Spain, Germany, Pannonia, Dalmatia, Illyria, and many other nations bow to our sway; for the might of Rome extends over the Latin-speaking world."[2]

---

[1] Joh. Sturmius, *Nobilitas literata* in *H. Grotii et aliorum dissertationes de studiis instituendis* (Amstel , 1645,) p 166. ' *Linguæ concinnitas, quæ cum auribus audientium repræsentatur, mentis suavissimum concentum indicat, qui magis intelligi a nobis potest quam cælestis machinæ nunquam audita tamen tradita olim a Pythagoricis* ἁρμονία "

[2] K. v. Raumer, *Geschichte der Pädagogik*, I, p 42

The European family of nations was at that time united by the bonds of a common Faith as well as by the ties of a common ancestry: Reuchlin styled the Greeks and Romans the *majores nostri*. The Renaissance witnessed the establishment of the "Republic of Letters," which represented the union of all the learned and cultured, irrespective of their nationality or social standing, whereas in the Middle Ages the clergy had constituted the centre of the learned world. But the period went farther still by admitting women to the circles of the learned;[1] and the elementary schools of Latin, being open to all comers, assured a steady influx to the same circles from the lower strata of society. To further and spread the new learning was considered the duty of the race, and almost equal in importance to the reform of the Church. Rudolph von Lange, provost of the Cathedral of Münster (died 1519), looked forward in his old age to the realization of a fond hope: "that the spirit of darkness might pass from the churches and schools, and that her pristine beauty be restored to the Church and its pristine purity to the Latin tongue."[2] The didactics of the 17th century finally declared the school to be the organ of education, whose supervision was a legitimate function of the government of the State.

Besides these socio-ethical motives there were other less altruistic principles at work, and the latter were traceable, like the former, to ancient influences. Chief among these was the ancient desire for fame, which the Renaissance revived after the higher ideals of Christianity had for centuries forced it into the background. This ambition is especially marked in the early Italian Humanists, witness their leader Petrarch;[3] but the entire Neo-Latin literature breathes the same spirit. On all sides we may witness the striving for immortal fame, the happiness in being praised, and the ill-suppressed jealousy of a successful rival. The schools likewise followed but too eagerly the advice of Quintilian to lead the youth through ambition to higher things. In his book on the method of study Joachim Fortius (died 1536) writes: "To be satisfied with mediocrity is, by the immortal gods, a sign of a low, cowardly, and even depraved soul; but how noble is the soul of him who conquers the

[1] Mary A. Cannon, *Education of Women during the Renaissance*, Washington, 1916.
[2] Raumer, l. c., I, p. 92: "*Ut tenebræ ex ecclesiis et scholis exstirpentur et redeat puritas in ecc.... t m...lit. I......*"
[3] G. Voigt, *D.. Wi..erbel..... ... Il...... . .   I. ..   ..3*, pp. 72, 403.

foe, who takes the citadel whence his glory shall be visible to
all the earth to the end of time, and whose fame shall be celebrated by so many thousands of men as are grains of sand on
the shore of the sea. Hence we call upon all whom the Muses
have endowed with their gifts to bestir themselves and to strive
for what has fired the souls of the bravest of men."[1] The
teachers were the readier to arouse the emulation of their pupils,
because they had abandoned the severity of the medieval schools
as a remnant of a barbaric age, and thus the system of school
offices and prizes came into being, which, while appearing in its
extreme form in Trotzendorf's school at Goldberg (Silesia), was
in vogue, though in a modified form, in the Jesuit schools also.[2]

An educational ideal that attached so much importance to
the skill of the virtuoso naturally encouraged the tendencies
always associated with virtuosity The consummate skill and
the artistic finish served only too often as a mere adornment of
the individual personality The period was vain of its charms
and graces, and there was little concentration; men flitted from
one subject to another, without ever deciding on a special occupation or attaining to a mastery of any science. Many entertained a sceptical view of human things, were Epicureans and
naturalists in philosophy, and worshipped a subjectivity that
was opposed to the moral and the historical order The age,
however, was not frivolous, and the religious controversies of
the time as well as the efforts towards harmonizing ecclesiastical
and public conditions checked the growth of the evil tendencies.
However, these tendencies served subsequently as links in the
chain that connected the Renaissance with the Enlightenment:
the *Encomium moriæ* of Erasmus prepared the way for Voltaire,
and Montaigne's *Essays* popularized the ideas that later proved
the foundation of Rousseau's pedagogy.

4. With the Renaissance devoted to the study of the ancient
classics and intent on re-instating ancient ideals, it is not surprising that many elements were introduced that were by their
nature antagonistic to Christian educational principles. Yet in
spite of this obvious danger, the period remained on the whole,
like the Middle Ages, faithful in its final aims to the Christian

---

[1] Joach Fortu, *De ratione studii liber* in *H Grotii et aliorum dissertationes
de studiis instituendis* (Amstel, 1645), p 252 The book was re-edited by
Comenius, and it is remarkable that this truly pious man took no offence at its
pagan spirit

[2] Cf R Schwickerath, S J , *Jesuit Education*, St Louis, 1903, pp. 511 ff

ideals.[1] The example of the Fathers of the Church, who had succeeded in reconciling the spirit of antiquity with the Christian doctrines, was a favorite argument to show that devotion to the Church was not incompatible with the appreciation of the classics. St. Basil's *Address to the Young Men on the Right Use of Greek Literature* was frequently re-edited, translated, and quoted, and St. Augustine appeared as a convincing proof that apparently contradictory elements can combine to produce one harmonious whole. The process of assimilation was much assisted by the attention of the period being taken up, in the main, with the form and the technique of the pagan writers; and while the mastery of the language remained the sole aim, little harm would seem to come from the pagan content of the classics. Still, the cult of the classics was not without danger, for the mind was never so entirely taken up with the style as not to be affected by the pagan spirit of the works that were read and studied and imitated; and this pagan atmosphere is known to have given rise to many a soul-struggle and to much heartburning. There were some men, particularly among the early Humanists, whose world-view was that of the ancient pagans. Others were at war with themselves; their heart was Christian, but their head was hopelessly pagan. Others, again, tried to compromise between the hostile forces. In the lives of many, Christianity was relegated almost out of sight, and their thoughts and guiding principles were of ancient Greece and Rome. Yet others were actuated by the motive of making the new interests assist them in their striving for Christian perfection. The more gifted of the Italian Humanists were mostly semi-pagans; but Guarino, Vittorino, Pico, Traversari, were one in spirit with the conservative older German Humanists, Agricola, Hegius, Wimpheling, and Tritemius. In the spirit of this latter class the Spaniard Luis Vives describes, in his work *De disciplinis* (1531),[2] the ethos of education thus: "Education is based on diverse matters, on native talent, power of judgment, memory, and study. Now, the first three of these are assuredly

[1] Boccaccio was the first to engage in a systematic defence of "poetry" against the attacks of Scholastic theologians. In books XIV. and XV. of his *Genealogia deorum*, written about 1370, he maintains that the ancient poets had also been *theologi*, though not *sacri*.

[2] On the educational side Lange has traced the permeating influence of Vives as of startling significance in later pedagogy. See Schmid, *Enzyklopädie des gesamten Erziehungs- und Unterrichtswesens*, Vol. IX, pp. 810 ff.: cf. McCormick, *History of Education*, pp. 195 f., and Watson, etc. "Education," New York, 1913.

the free gifts of God's bounty; and the scholar may thus boast, perhaps, only of his amount of study, which is the last, and indeed also the least, factor in his success, and even it depends, in a large measure, on the Lord, for it is only when God grants us bodily health that we can study well. . . . It is, therefore, meet that we beg Him, who is the Giver of all, to assist us in order that we may study chiefly for our own advancement, lest He make us an instrument for the benefit of others while we ourselves become castaways . . . like the candle which gives light to others while consuming itself. Let us pray before all our studies, as St Thomas Aquinas and other holy men have done, and let us pray that our mental work be wholesome, harmful to none, and full of blessings to all."[1]

5. The religious conflict of the 16th century brought the crisis in the assimilation of the Humanistic elements with the teachings of Christianity.[2] In the first stages of the conflict the interest in education was reduced to a minimum, all scholars being busy with theological problems. It was only when men turned from the religious struggle to the organizing of a new order that the Humanistic movement again commanded attention, but all its forces seemed now to be separated by a great divide, which had sprung up, as it were, over night: the two religious parties directed the stream to their respective domains and controlled it in accordance with their own principles. The Protestantism of the 16th century and neological Humanism have many important points in common: they were one in opposing the Middle Ages and Scholasticism Both declared it their intention to go back, skipping the intervening centuries, to the olden days, and hence Humanism revived the learning of classical antiquity, while Protestantism revived what it interpreted as the teachings and practices of primitive Christianity. Both stressed—the Humanists in æsthetics and the Protestants in theology—the subjective and personal consciousness of the individual in opposition to what had been handed down by tradition and was received and treasured in the collective consciousness. Luther realized how much the revival of the classical studies aided him in establishing his new principle of the Bible's being the sole rule of Faith, and he publicly avowed that "None knew why the Lord brought about this new study of

[1] Joh Lud Vives, *De disciplinis libri XII*, Neap , 1764, p 385
[2] Cf Baudrillart, *The Catholic Church, the Renaissance and Protestantism*, transl by Gibbs, New York, 1928

languages, until it is now seen that this was done for the sake of the Gospel, of which the Lord desired that it be thereafter revealed." Accordingly he favored the new learning, addressing his followers thus: "As dearly as you love the Gospel, so much care ought you to devote to the study of languages." It is impossible to establish a closer union between philology and theology than is implied by another saying of Luther, "Nihil aliud esse theologiam, nisi grammaticam in Spiritus sancti verbis occupatam." Guided by these principles, the many schoolmen who followed Melanchthon's leadership undertook to assimilate Humanistic and Christian ideas. Sturmius' "wise and eloquent piety" may well describe the educational aim of these educators. Comenius' aim in education was somewhat similar; but he emphasized the positive content of education, when saying that the teacher should strive to prepare his pupils for eternity by teaching them the service of the Lord, pure morals, and an erudition based on a knowledge of things and the power of expression.

6. Catholic educators interpreted the activity of the Humanists to be primarily only the continuation of the educational work of the Middle Ages, with this difference, that there was an increase in matter and an improvement in form. Consequently, they set about to adjust the new learning to the theology of the Church and the philosophy of the Scholastics. The principle of authority — formulated by Valla as *pro lege accipere, quidquid magnis auctoribus placuit*,[1] and which was at the bottom of the cult of the classics—could not fail to be acceptable to the Church: the authority of Aristotle in philosophy and that of Cicero in style and composition was now paralleled with the authority enjoyed by St. Thomas Aquinas in theology. The æsthetical culture afforded by the study of classical antiquity gave little cause for apprehension, especially since the statuary and paintings of the Renaissance evidenced, that the technique perfected through the familiarity with ancient models might admirably serve the needs of religion and the Church. The knowledge, too, of antiquity was considered of as great a value as ever for the interpretation of theological sources (Scripture, Fathers, Church history), but of particular value for furnishing the weapons to defeat the enemy on his own ground; and these were plainly reasons enough to encourage the new interest in history. It was also recognized that the language

---

1 Laur. Valla, *Elegantiæ*, II, præf.

studies would provide wholesome discipline for the pupils and at the same time promote a greater uniformity of the curricula.[1]

Yet, notwithstanding all these advantages, voices were heard occasionally, among Catholics as well as Protestants, charging the ancient classics with being a source of pagan sentiments, and the accusations of the Fathers against Græco-Roman literature were reiterated. The learned Jesuit Possevini demanded that only Christian authors be read in the schools,[2] and Comenius advocated—at least in his *Great Didactic*—a Latin course without the ancient classics.[3] But the prevailing view had it that the ancient classics were indispensable for training the mind and developing the language consciousness, and the Humanists contended that the teaching content of the Christian religion possessed vitality and strength enough to oppose effectively whatever the pagan writings contained of foreign and heterogeneous elements.

CHAPTER XXII.

The Content of Renaissance Education

1. Philology, a new and modern science, was the most important and the most comprehensive of the Renaissance studies. It had originated in Italy in the 14th century, less as a science than as an organon to meet a universal need, and in its original form it was intended to further the study of antiquity as well as to assist in reviving the art of language. The formal and æsthetical character which it acquired during the Italian period, could be developed only after its scientific basis had been firmly established. French scholars infused the scientific spirit into polite literature, and the endeavor to provide the *thesaurus eruditionis*, which was needed for a complete understanding of antiquity, complemented the narrow cult of form. But the age lacked the philosophical training, the prerequisite for a correct

---

[1] We have here considered the subject from the didactic viewpoint only; considered from the pedagogical point of view, further differences would have to be noted between Catholic and Protestant education, as may be seen from Willmann's article on *katholische Pädagogik* in Rein's *Enzykl Handb der Pädagogik*

[2] Gaume, *Paganism in Education*, transl by Hill, London, 1852, pp 77-79

[3] *Did. Magna*, cap. 25.

interpretation of antiquity, and Renaissance philology eventually tended, in keeping with the general trend of the 17th century, toward encyclopedic knowledge.

As a school subject, however, philology retained in general its formal character; eloquence was considered the chief subject to be taught in the schools, while the acquiring of erudition was reserved for maturer years. Erasmus avowed—and his educational views were held in high repute—that the acquiring of a knowledge of words and formal training must precede the acquiring of a knowledge of things, though the latter is in itself of greater importance. He warns his readers against hurrying "with unwashed feet" to the study of things.[1] The school regulations are either silent on the subject of studying the content and the antiquities, or they mention these things only incidentally; as in the *Ratio studiorum* of the Jesuits, where the term *eruditio* implies merely the occasional introduction of antiquarian matters and that for the sake of affording relaxation or of stimulating to greater interest, but this may never be done at the expense of the study of style.[2] The didacticians of the 17th century were the first to demand that continuous attention be given to the content as well as to the form. However, even the *Orbis pictus* is primarily only a Latin language book, with illustrations of things to facilitate the memorizing of the words, and it was neither calculated nor adapted to prepare for such a reading of the classics as aimed chiefly to get at the thought content of the text. The latter method of reading the classics did not appeal to that age, and this was owing as well to the general striving for the perfection of form as to the prevailing interest in encyclopedic knowledge.

Latin was regarded as far and away the most important study, and most educational works of the period, the writings of the didacticians included, treat only of the teaching of Latin. Of the authors, Cicero was read most. He was considered the

---

[1] Erasmus, *De ratione studii tract.*, in.: "*Principio duplex omnino videtur cognitio: rerum ac verborum; verborum prior, rerum potior. Sed nonnulli, dum ἀνίπτοις (ut ajunt) ποσὶν ad res discendas festinant, sermonis curam neglegunt et male affectato compendio, in maxima incidunt dispendia.*"

[2] In the *Ratio atque institutio stud. S.J.* the professor of Humanities is advised, "*Eruditio modice usurpetur, ut ingenia excitet interdum ac recreet, non ut linguæ observationem impediat;*" and the professor of Rhetoric is told to treat the following matters:"*Eruditio ex historia et moribus gentium, ex auctoritate scriptorum et ex omni doctrina, ut parcia ul cautior   ...   senda.*"
Cf. Schwickerath, l. c., pp. 447 ff. and 48: ff.

model of letter-writers—his letters, as selected by Sturmius, were the elementary Latin reader—as well as of orators and philosophical writers. It was a favorite practice to read of the historians the orations only, as Trotzendorf is known to have done in the case of Livy. Of the poets, Vergil, Ovid, and Horace were read most. The plays of Plautus and Terence were read in Protestant schools on account of their conversational Latin, and the fact that the immoral content of these plays did not prevent their being given into the hands of the young, is another proof of the scant attention given to the content of the classics.[1] Special importance was attached to the memorizing of gnomic sayings and quotations that were witty or otherwise noteworthy. Collections of such sayings, called *Adagia, Florilegia, Spicilegia*, etc., were in use in the schools, and the pupils were encouraged to make their own "commonplace books" by making extracts from their reading.[2] These quotations (those in the textbooks as well as those collected by the pupils) served the double purpose of being used as arguments or ornaments in compositions and of getting the young to think. The textbooks and teaching methods of the medieval schools were out of favor with the Renaissance, the *Doctrinale* of Alexander was labeled as barbaric, and the attempts of Despauterius (Jan van Pauteran, died 1526) to compose more artistic verses for the teaching of grammar and rhetoric met with little encouragement Didactic aids were discarded in grammar, and this subject was presented in an abstract form, and its material was enlarged considerably In 1614 Lubinus complained that the pupils were compelled to memorize no less than 180 technical terms and more than 70 rules of syntax with an equal number of exceptions, some of which were so obscure as to be unintelligible to even the mature student[3] These and similar abuses led to the opposite extreme of demanding that Latin be taught in the manner of the mother-tongue. Montaigne favored this method, and Ratke tried it out practically when adopting some

---

[1] A Wurttemberg school ordinance provides that the *Præceptores*. when meeting dangerous passages, "call the attention of their pupils to the fact, that the writers were pagans and knew nothing of God and His Gospel, resembling herein some degenerate modern Christians who are likewise ignorant of the same holy law, they are to quote an example and a text from Scripture to show how the Lord has visited these sins with His just punishment; they are in general to be on their guard, lest they scandalize the tender consciences of the young " Vormbaum, *Evangelische Schulordnungen*, I, p 83

[2] *Cyclopedia of Education*, s v *Commonplace Books*

[3] Raumer, *Geschichte der Padagogik*, III, p 83

of the practices of the early Rabbinical schools (see *supra*, ch. vii, 3). The mean between these two extremes we see in the language books of Comenius, and his *Vestibulum*, edition of 1648,[1] is in methodical arrangement the best textbook of the period.

2. Theoretically, Greek was evaluated as highly as Latin. Erasmus declares that all that is worth knowing has been written in these two languages, and that it is easier, because of their kinship, to teach them conjointly than separately; yet he does not ignore the peculiar difficulties of Greek, its *magni labyrinthi et vastissimi recessus*. Quintilian's demand to begin with Greek is frequently discussed, and Vittorino da Feltre (died 1446) probably taught Greek before Latin. Robert Etienne (died 1559) followed the same course in the education of his son Henry (died 1598), and Tanneguy Lefèbre (died 1672) also gave the preference to Greek in the education of his son as well as his daughter, the celebrated Madame Dacier;[2] Lefèbre followed Scaliger's example[3] in basing the study of Greek on Homer. The "Father of the Poets" found enthusiastic admirers in this period. Claude Belurger, who introduced Greek into the Collège de Navarre in Paris, took his Homer along to church, had statues made of the Homeric heroes, and finally undertook a journey to Troy; but the hardships of travel were his death, and thus his extensive commentary on Homer was lost.[4] When Martin Crusius lectured on Homer at Tübingen, the lecture-hall proved too small for the students eager to hear him; hence a wall was removed to provide more room, and the hall was ever after known as the *auditorium Homericum*.[5] Many programs of study (for instance, the *Ratio studiorum* of the Jesuits) state that Greek should be begun simultaneously with Latin, and give long lists of Greek authors, pagan and Christian, to be read; but these ideals were not generally realized. In the Protestant schools the New Testament and a few moral writings—as, Xenophon's *Memorabilia*, Kebes' *Pinax*, or the treatise on education ascribed to Plutarch—were read, while Æsop, Phokylides, and passages from St. John Chrysostom, etc., were

---

[1] *Opp. did.*, III, pp. 134-214.

[2] Morhof, *Polyhistor litterarius*, II, 9, §47. Lefèbre's views on the course of study are embodied in his *Méthode pour commencer les humanités Grecques et Latines* (1672).

[3] J. Bernays, *J. J. Scaliger*, Berlin, 1855, p. 35.

[4] Morhof, l. c., VII, 2, § 2.

[5] J. M. Gesner, *Isagoge in erud. univ.*, ed. Nic', 1 ˑ ;, I, § 124

read in the Catholic schools. Greek was allowed at best only half the number of the Latin class periods. Especially in the 17th century Greek seems to have been taught only for honor's sake, and the opinion was quite general that it was of value only to the specialist in theology or medicine and, therefore, on a par with Hebrew and Arabic;[1] nay, Descartes declared the study of Greek to be of as little value as the study of the "Jargon of Bretony."[2] The taste of the period regarded the *Æneid*, the tragedies of Seneca, and the poems of Horace as the classics of poetry Homer was regarded as childish and vulgar, and Sophocles and Pindar were considered stilted and obscure. The Latin nations, the leaders in the Renaissance, were conscious of their kinship with the spirit of ancient Rome, and consequently remained impervious to the deeper meaning of Greek literature. It was left to the Renaissance of 18th century German literature to establish a direct intercommunion with the soul of the Greeks.

The interest in Biblical research brought it about that Hebrew was considered an element of higher learning. In Germany, Reuchlin was the foremost teacher of Greek as well as of Hebrew, and the latter subject was generally taught in the higher Protestant schools. Michael Neander, rector of Ilefeld, who has deserved well of German education, grows eloquent in speaking of the educational value of Hebrew. "The *Hebræa Lingua* is of use not only to the *Theologis* but to all *Studiosis*, who should be desirous to be for their lifelong day familiar with this language, for it is the *alma mater omnium linguarum omnibus ætatibus omnium gentium.* All other languages have come from the Hebrew, and it imparts of its wealth to them all, but itself lays no other tongue under contribution. .. The *Lingua Hebraica* should, therefore, be a thing of joy It should be studied by every one having the opportunity, *propter collationem cum aliis linguis* and *propter utilem explicationem multarum rerum in omni vita* and also *propter Grammaticam Latinam*, in which at times there is a question *de declinatione nominum Hebræorum.*"[3]

---

[1] Comenius, *Didact magna*, 22, 1. Arabic was still considered important in the study of medicine, as may be seen from the fact that Avicenna's canon continued to enjoy so great an authority as to appear in more than a dozen Latin editions during the 15th and 16th centuries (Sprenger, *Mohammed*, Berlin, 1861, I, IV).

[2] *Oeuvres*, ed Cousin, XI, p 341 (from Schmid's *Enzykl* II, 1st ed, p. 911)

[3] Michaelis Neandri, *Bedenken, wie ein Knabe zu leiten und zu unterweisen*, etc (1582), published in Vormbaum, *Evang Schulordnungen*, Gutersloh, 1860, I, pp. 747-765.

3. Although the system of the seven liberal arts was of classical origin, and though it had been highly esteemed by the Romans also, yet the Renaissance, while extolling it in academic orations and essays, failed to adopt it in the schools. One reason was the aversion of the refined taste of the Renaissance to the form in which it had been handed down by late Latin writers, not to speak of the barbarous Latin of the medieval commentaries. A second reason was the great divergency of opinions in evaluating the different arts and sciences belonging to the system. Grammar and rhetoric were no longer regarded as merely propædeutic studies, but were deemed of prime importance and declared to be the real organon of education. Medieval dialectic was made the butt of the Humanists' attacks; but in a modified form it was universally taught under the name of *ars disserendi*, because needed for rhetoric. The interest of the age being centred in the expression of thought, it was to be expected that logic should be connected with rhetoric, and it was conceived as the art of giving intellectual strength to what was said or written. Thus all three arts of the Trivium are frequently correlated with language: grammar teaches the *sermo emendatus*; dialectic, the *sermo probabilis*; and rhetoric, the *sermo ornatus*.[1] Melanchthon defined dialectic as the *ars et via docendi, i. e.*, as the art of presentation, and thus dialectic embraced what was later treated in the science of didactics. The rules of logic were now drawn, not only from Aristotle, but also from the orators and the rhetoricians. Vives and Nizolius "do not hesitate to acknowledge that they are more indebted to Cicero than to Plato and Aristotle, because the latter separated philosophy from rhetoric."[2] Peter Ramus (died 1572) even asserted that the study of the methods employed by Cicero and other orators to persuade their hearers, was a better means to arrive at a knowledge of logic than the study of Aristotle's *Organon*. Ramus' reform of logic, which was at first fiercely opposed, is based on the idea that rhetoric and logic are only parts of a more general and more comprehensive science; and, though Ramus failed to draw all conclusions from this first principle, his movement represents one of the most noteworthy features of the Renaissance, and has

---

[1] These are the terms employed by Jacob Micyllus (Molzer), rector in Frankfort on the Main; cf. Helfenstein, *Die Entwicklung des Schulwesens in bezug auf Frankfurt*, 1858, p. 90.

[2] Erdmann, *Grundriss der Geschichte der Philosophie*, Berlin, 1869, I, p. 500.

determined, to some extent, the teaching of logic down to our own day.[1]

While the disciplines of the Trivium were thus granted a new lease on life, the mathematical sciences of the Quadrivium were neglected. We should expect the exact opposite of the age of Copernicus and Galilei, but the mathematical sciences were at that time breaking with the past, and their consequently unsettled condition rendered them unattractive to the masses who are eager for definite results, but are not interested in the researches of the laboratory or the observatory. The scholars of the period gave most attention to philology and encyclopedic knowledge;[2] and the few men who were interested in the physical sciences, could not understand the importance of mathematics. Comenius tried to incorporate mathematics with technical instruction,[3] but in his *Janua* and the *Orbis pictus* we find little enough of mathematical material. The few schools that did teach the Quadrivium adhered to the Ptolomaic system, and Comenius himself does not even mention the system of Copernicus [4]

Philosophy also lost its popular character. No poet of the Renaissance would have ventured to imitate Dante who, after the Scholastics had popularized philosophical topics, could treat, in his *Divine Comedy*, the most abstruse questions of metaphysics and ethics without becoming obscure to his readers.

---

[1] Ibid, p 501   Ramus is responsible for the distinction between natural and scientific logic and for the practice of treating the concept before the judgment   His shortsighted opposition to Aristotle—at his master's examination, in 1536, he defended the thesis "All that Aristotle has said is false"—prevented him from reaping the full fruit of his first principles

[2] Galilei complains in a letter to Kepler as follows "What will you say of the first teachers of the Padua gymnasium, who one and all declined my offer to show them the planets, the moon, and my telescope? This class of people looks upon philosophy as contained within the boards of a book, like the *Aeneid* or the *Odyssey*, and are firmly convinced that truth is to be found neither in the world nor in nature, but only in the collating of texts   How you would have laughed at the first teacher of the Pisa gymnasium, who attempted, in the presence of the Archduke, to disprove with his syllogisms the existence of the new planets, he tried with his syllogisms as the magic formulas to tear down the new planets from the heavens " (Quoted from Zöllner's *Wissenschaftl Abhandl*, II, p 941)

[3] *Did magna*, 30, 8

[4] The *Janua* (Amsterdam edition of 1662) §§ 31 ff, treats the sun and moon as planets, speaks of the epicycles of Mercury, etc, of the eighth sphere of the fixed stars, etc,—and all this was possible 119 years after the *De orbium cælestium revolutionibus libri VI* had appeared!

Only select circles were engaged in restoring the ancient philosophies, and the attempts, few as they were, to strike out into
new paths did not meet with general favor.	The schools con-
tinued to teach Aristotelian-Scholastic logic. Melanchthon had
done well in simplifying the methods of teaching this subject,
and the textbooks used in the Catholic schools likewise became
less unwieldy in form.	The terminology of present-day logic
dates back to the Renaissance, and many of the philosophical
terms coined in that period are still part of the common vocabulary of the cultured.

4. More importance was attached to empirico-historical
knowledge, for this was recognized as a necesasry adjunct to
eloquence.	Works purporting to comprise all that was worth
knowing were produced in great number.	The term "cyclo-
pedia," or "encyclopedia," first came into use in the 16th
century, but there was no dearth of other terms to express the
same kind of work: polymathy, polyhistory, panepistemony,
pansophy, pankosmy, anatomy of heads and sciences, theatre
of life (of wisdom, of the world), etc.—these are some of the
high-sounding titles promising the reader a world of wisdom
and knowledge.	However, in many cases the grandiloquent
title heralded forth the beggarly contents of a meagre compendium; for instance, Laurenberg's *Pansophia, sive Pædia phi-
losophica* (Rostock, 1633).	It was less frequent that a modest
title was chosen for the storehouse of valuable knowledge: the
Commentarii urbani of Raphael of Volaterra is an encyclopedia
that begins with local geography and history, then enlarges its
scope to introduce extensive biographies, to deal with popular
philosophy and divers other sciences, and finally concludes with
an analysis of Aristotelian philosophy.[1]	These works differ from
the similar compilations made in the Middle Ages chiefly in
that most of the Renaissance encyclopedias exclude theology,
but treat classical antiquities.	There were isolated attempts to
systematize the whole of human knowledge; witness the *Thea-
trum humanæ vitæ* of Theodor Zwinger (1586), which follows a
psychologico-ethical plan, and whose three stout folio volumes
must have cost the author labor like that expended on the
compilations of Vincent of Beauvais.	Vives' *De disciplinis* and
Bacon's *Instauratio magna* are examples of the few attempts

---

[1] Cf. Burckhardt, *The Civilization of the Renaissance in Italy*, transl. by
Middlemore, London, 1898, part III, where the work is discussed in showing
how deeply the ancient learning had affected all departments of knowledge.

17

made to establish methods of study instead of merely collecting
materials.   Vives followed the traditional system of the sciences,
but Bacon based his division of the sciences on a psychological
principle: history he derives from memory; poetry, from the
imagination; theology and philosophy, from the intellect.   The
period was particularly fond of tabulating the various materials.
John Thomas Freigius elaborated Ramus' presentation of the
seven liberal arts into *Tabulas perpetuas ceu στρώματα relatas*
(Bâle, 1576), and Comenius recommends the map as a model
for synoptic compilations or anthologies.[1]   In connection with
the latter view, it may be noted that geography in general,
which had grown into a very comprehensive science and whose
maps were an excellent aid to clear and general views, exerted
some influence on all the attempts at compilation: the fact
that the terrestrial globe had become better known, suggests to
Bacon that more attention should be given also to the *globus
intellectualis*.[2]

Amid the wealth of new knowledge, the need was naturally
felt of improved methods of study and instruction.   The Renaissance revived the ancient mnemotechnics and the medieval
Ars magna of Raymond Lully (Raymundus Lullus, born 1234,
died 1315), whose aim was to employ the association of ideas
for the purpose of finding thoughts   A kindred tendency gave
birth to the rational art of teaching, to didactics, rhadiomethy,
Obstetricia animorum, and so forth.[3]   Comenius especially shows
the intimate relation between pansophy and these new sciences,
while Morhof shows their connection with polymathy.[4]   Frei-

---

[1] *Did magna*, 31, 8

[2] *Novum Organon*, § 84

[3] Cf *supra, Introd*, II, 2; the "didacticians" are classed with the Lullians,
for instance, in Garzoni's *Piazza universale* (in the German Frankfort edition
of 1659, pp 208 ff, where a list of representatives of this school is given)

[4] The *Polyhistor* of the learned Daniel George Morhof is a work that has
not been appreciated as it deserves (1st ed, Lubeck, 1688; 4th ed, 1747)   It
is superior to other encyclopedias in that it does not only present the materials
of knowledge, but also treats the course of study and all the apparatus belonging thereto   The latter subjects are treated in the first part (4th ed), the
Polyhistor litterarius, on which the author spent most labor   The first book
of this part *(Polyhistor bibliothecarius)* treats of libraries, books, learned societies, cultured conversation, biographies of scholars, letter-writing, etc   The
second book (P *methodicus*) discusses the differences in talents, schools, aids
to study and memory, etc, methods, particularly of classical schools, the
general course of study, university studies, education of princes, etc   The
third book (P παρασκευαστικός) treats of the art of making extracts   The
fourth book (P *grammaticus*) treats of language, writing, grammar, especially

gius, rector in Altorf and later assistant rector in Bâle (died 1583), is the author of the *Pædagogus*, which is a good example of the efforts taken to remedy with multifarious learning the defects of purely formal training. The book contains little more than an incoherent mess of materials, and is a more convincing proof for a much-needed reform in methods of study than the most eloquent expositions of the didacticians.[1] The chief aim of Comenius—both in his *Janua linguarum reserata* (first ed. 1631) and in his *Orbis sensualium pictus* (first ed. 1658), the latter reproducing all the essential matters of the *Janua*—was to correlate more systematically the encyclopedic knowledge of things with the Latin instruction. Both works are "encyclopædiolæ," intended to serve at the same time as Latin readers,[2] and the great pansophical undertaking of Comenius is nothing else than the realization of a similar plan, though this latter

Latin grammar. Books V. to VII. are a sort of general history of literature. The second, and smaller, part of the work (*P. philosophicus*) contains a history of philosophy and matter pertaining to physics, mathematics, logic, and metaphysics. The third, and smallest, part (*P. practicus*) contains matter pertaining to ethics, politics, political economy, history, theology, jurisprudence, and medicine. Morhof treats didactics as a department of logic and defines it, somewhat reservedly, as "*aliqua doctrinæ de methodo propago.*" (*Pol. litt.*, II, 4, 12.) Cf. W. Eymer's valuable work *Morhof und sein Polyhistor*, ein Beitrag zur Lehre vom Bildungswesen, Budweis, 1893.

[1] The full title of the book, which was first published at Bâle in 1583, is: *J. Th. Freigii Pædagogus, hoc est libellus ostendens, qua ratione prima artium initia pueris quam facillime tradi possunt* (sic). The catechetical form is observed throughout. The *artes* are divided into *exotericæ* (grammar, rhetoric, poetics, logic) and *acroamaticæ* (mathematics, physics, and ethics — the last-named including history, jurisprudence, and theology). The different subjects are treated in the following order: *Grammatica Latina* (pp. 1-18); *Græca* (to p. 50); *Hebræa* (to p. 80); *dialogi in linguam Gallicam addiscendam* (to p. 124); *de rhetorica* (to p. 130); *de poetica* (to p. 132); *de logica* (to p. 143); *de arithmetica* (to p. 156); *de musica* (to p. 217); *de geometria* (to p. 224); *de asse* (to p. 247; under this head are treated coins, weights, and measures, those of the Bible included); *de architectura* (to p. 263; Caesar's bridge across the Rhine, *Bell. Gall.*, IV, is here discussed); *de mechanica* (to p. 268); *de physica* (to p. 286; astronomy and geography are treated under this head); *de ethica* (to p. 290: of virtues and human organizations); *de æconomia* (to p. 292; the eight duties of the housewife are here treated); *de politia* (to p. 295); *de apodemica* (to p. 297; of the art of traveling); *de antiquitatis studio religiosæ et profanæ* (of temples, games, edifices, and so forth); *de polemica* (to p. 310; of recruiting, camps, etc.); *de historia* (to p. 313; lists of historians and the division of history); *de jurisprudentia* and *rudimenta institutionum juris* (to p. 341); *de medicina* (to p. 366).

[2] F .... gus of
Freigii   ed. of

work, being addressed to the learned, emphasized less the linguistic purpose.[1]   It is of interest to learn that a man like Leibnitz also entertained plans for compiling an encyclopedia.   He would have followed the example of Comenius (whose undertaking he describes as a "*concilium præclarum*") in beginning with words, but unlike him, he would have proceeded from words to clear-cut definitions and full logical treatises.[2]

1669)   The motto of the book is taken from Gen ii, 20: "Adam called all the beasts by their names, and all the fowls of the air, and all the cattle of the field "   The introduction consists of a dialogue between a teacher and his pupil, the German translation being placed in parallel columns with the Latin text: "Teacher· Come, my boy, and learn to be prudent and wise   Pupil What does 'to be wise and prudent' mean?   T   To have a right understanding of all that is needful, to act rightly, to speak rightly   P · Who will teach me all this?   T . I will do so with the help of God   P · How will you do it?   T I will show you all things, and will give a name to every thing.   P . I am at your disposal, lead me on with the help of God "   This introduction is followed by the alphabet, each letter being assigned to a different animal, a picture of which is placed beside the respective letter   The next 150 lessons, each having at its head a woodcut, present the things of the world   Each page contains three columns the first is the Latin column, all short and simple sentences, but not all words are classical Latin; the second column is the German translation of the Latin column, and the third column contains the new words occurring in the lesson   Lessons 1-34 treat of God, the earth, heaven, the elements, and natural history (dragons, basilisks, and unicorns are duly included)   Lessons 35-43 treat anthropological matters· of man, periods of life, parts of the body, and the soul, the soul is represented by dots so arranged as to fill the whole outline of the human body   Lessons 44-96 treat of man's activities and of the products of his labor agriculture, stockraising, etc, the art of writing and books are treated last   Lessons 97-108 treat of schools, museums (study-rooms), rhetoric, music, philosophy, geometry, astronomy, and geography (the maps of the hemispheres and of Europe are found here) Lessons 109-117 enumerate the virtues   Lessons 118-121 treat of the family, the genealogical tree, of the nursery, and domestics   Lessons 122-136 treat of the city, courts, merchants (weights and measures), medicine, funerals, and amusements   Lessons 137-143 treat of government, the country, the kingdom, the most important German principalities, of the army, and of war   Lessons 144-148 treat of religion heathenism, Judaism, Christianity, and Mohammedanism   The last two lessons treat of Divine Providence and the Last Judgment   The parting advice of the teacher reads "Thus you have seen in a brief sketch all things that can be created, and you have learned the principal German and Latin words, see now that you continue in the good work and read good books so that you may grow in wisdom, learning, and piety.   Remember these my words, fear the Lord and implore His aid so that He may grant you the spirit of wisdom Farewell " An index of Latin and German words is appended, with references to the lessons where the respective word occurs.
   [1] Cf *Prodomus Pansophiæ* and *Pansophicorum conatuum dilucidatio* (*Opp. did*, 1, pp 404 ff)
   [2] Leibnitz defines the encyclopedia as "*systema omnium quousque licet*

Johann Joachim Becher (died 1685), the inimitable author of the *Methodus didactica* (Frankfort, 1685), has well described the common aim of all these writers: "The one aim of the Januists, Pansophists, Encyclopedists, and Polymathists is to teach the boy as quickly as possible the relation of things to the respective sciences as well as the relation between the things themselves." This aim appears to him like "sweet sugar for them who would have their children made into learned scholars by a quick process;" but he finds fault with such educators "for thus ignoring the necessary part of language." He himself arranges all words according to three points of view: *affinitate derivationis*, according to their derivation; *affinitate significationis*, the relationship of their meaning; and *affinitate prædicationis*, the relationship of the things signified. "The first renders language correct; the second, ornate; and the third, reasonable." In this distinction we recognize the respective functions of grammar, rhetoric, and logic. But Becher's efforts resulted withal in a mere thesaurus of words.[1]

5. The tendency toward many-sided erudition often developed into a direct opposition to the cult of Latin, and in the beginning of the 17th century the *reales* were opposed to the *verbales*. Fr. Taubmann, a Wittenberg philologist, complains that the *reales* call those who use proper and elegant language *verbales*, as though the former alone attended to things and realities and the latter regarded the form only.[2] Karl von Raumer defends the *verbales* against the charge of a finical attention to words, yet accuses them of going to books for all

propositionum verarum, utilium, hactenus cognitarum." An *encyclopædiola* should, according to him, contain the following three things: 1. "*Definitiones vocabulorum crebriorum et insigniorum et ex his deducta theoremata et problemata insignioris usus, eaque in moralibus adagio aliquo dictoque sapientum aut historia memorabili vestita aut potius explicata.* 2. *Experimenta naturæ vulgariora.* 3. *Compendium historiæ et geographiæ tum universalis, tum imprimis hodiernæ*" (letter to Hasenthaler in Feller, *Monumenta varia inedita*, Lps., 1714; quoted in *Monatsschrift der Gesellschaft des vaterländischen Museums in Böhmen*, 1828, II, 550).

[1] Pedagogy owes a debt to Becher, and his educational principles and methods should be treated in a monograph. His services to political economy are treated in Erdberg-Krczenciewski's *J. J. Becher, ein Beitrag zur Geschichte der Nationalökonomie*, Jena, 1896. In the history of chemistry he holds a high place as the precursor of Stahl and as the author of the phlogiston theory. His small book *Psychosophia oder Seelenweisheit* (Frankfort, 1683), to which is appended an outline sketch of a philosophical society, is important in the history of psychology.

[2] *Dissertatio de lingua Latina*, first ed., 1602.

knowledge of things, and hence calls their system a "verbal realism" in opposition to the "real realism" taught by Bacon and applied by the didacticians, Ratke, Comenius, and others, to education.[1] We no longer regard Bacon's realism as perfect, for it was not even in touch with the discoveries of Bacon's own age in the natural sciences Furthermore, Bacon failed to recognize the value of the experiment and, instead, attached too much importance to simple observation of nature: amid his generalizations, he neglected to formulate laws based on his own experiments The realism of the didacticians labors under a similar defect Though they would fathom the nature of things, yet with their attention taken up with so many diversified fields, they do not go below the surface and remain ignorant of the methods of studying a single concrete thing. They are also too much taken up with linguistic matters, evaluate too highly the mere names of things, and seek a "real" language whose words should have such sounds as would convey the nature of the things signified[2] Because of this view, it were perhaps more in place to style them the "real verbalists" in opposition to the "verbal realists" For the genuine realism of the Renaissance we must look elsewhere, i e., among the Humanists, for they received the fullest and purest influences of antiquity, and through their contact with ancient art they had developed the sense of individual objectivity and the power to look at a thing objectively and independently of subjective impressions These happy traits were proper not only to the great artists of the period, but also to masters of language, as, for instance, to Aeneas Sylvius, Pope Pius II, "the normal man of the early Renaissance"[3] However, in this regard the Humanists influenced education, particularly the methods of teaching, but little, and that only indirectly

6 Both the philological and the encyclopedic elements of education were scientific in character. But in contrast to these subjects there were other branches of study which were intended to meet the practical needs of the day, and which, not being connected with Latin, were held of less value. Yet they were important in daily life and consequently cannot be ignored here. The Middle Ages had possessed some of these popular studies, and had in the system of chivalrous education converted them

[1] Raumer, *Geschichte der Padagogik*, I, p 330
[2] Comenius in his *Methodus linguarum novissima* (*Opp. did*, II, pp 67 ff)
[3] Cf his characterization in Burckhardt, *The Civilization of the Renaissance in Italy*, transl by Middlemore, London, 1898, pp 303 ff

into one harmonious whole. But the class-literature of that period had outlived itself, and the first step towards the establishment of a national literature had been taken in the later Middle Ages when Dante's immortal work was given to the world. Owing to the influence of the Humanists, the later steps in this direction followed the beaten path of the ancient classics, and consequently the national literature of the Renaissance, though it assumed a place in the general culture of the respective nations—first in Italy and last in Germany—was not admitted into the schools. Before that took place, the schools felt the influence of the systematic and grammatical study of the national languages. Though Erasmus could yet boast his ignorance of all modern tongues, and though school ordinances prohibited the boys from speaking their mother-tongue, still men of more penetrating minds perceived that a general movement was afoot for popularizing the interest in language studies. Agricola described the mother-tongue as the natural body of all thought;[1] and Vives demanded that the pupils be trained in the correct and elegant use of the vernacular, and that the old idioms of the native tongues be preserved and an *ærarium linguæ* be compiled for that purpose.[2] Leading Humanists laid the foundation for the grammatical study of their respective mother-tongues; Antonius of Lebrija (1492) is the father of Castilian grammar; Pietro Bembo (1525), of Tuscan grammar; Robert Etienne (1557), of French; and Janus Pannonius (1465), of Hungarian. Practical needs soon gave rise to rules for spelling the modern languages, and these rules gradually crept into the Latin grammars, where they were at first regarded as necessary evils. To speak and write the vernacular with a certain degree of correctness, was considered in Latin Europe an essential accomplishment of the cultured, and this at a time when the macaronic style of Latin-German writing was in vogue in Germany, *i. e.*, in the 16th century. It is, however, the glory of the German didacticians, notably of Ratke, to have established German as the elementary subject for training the language sense, and following their initiative, Comenius made the mother-tongue the starting-point and the core of all grammar studies. German language exercises came into general use with the teaching of letter-writing, since the Rococo style of the 17th century necessitated elaborate prepa-

---

[1] Raumer, l. c., p. 87.
[2] *De discipl. trad.*, L. III in., pp. 268 ff.

ration for the writing of fashionable letters. The "science of titles" was concerned exclusively with the proper addresses and titles, and learned men wrote manuals of correspondence.[1]

Of modern languages, French came to be considered, especially in Germany, essential to a liberal education. Modern history and geography were studied because necessary for becoming acquainted with the modern world. A special class of books dealt with the educational value of traveling[2] These modern subjects received little attention in the schools, but among the cultured the distinction between scientific studies and the accomplishments of the gentleman was very marked. Even in the early Italian Renaissance the culture of the "Cortigiano" differed much from that of the "poet," though both aimed at virtuosity and regarded the ancient classics as the chief content of education.[3] Mere Latinity could never meet the requirements of the cavalier, and the intellectual content of modern culture was too rich and varied to be perfectly amalgamated with the classical studies.

Thus the Renaissance observed the divergency between the schools and life, and the need of educational reforms was even then recognized Though the subject of the delatinization of the higher schools was not yet broached, voices were beginning to make themselves heard that the cultural value of Latin was overestimated, and that true progress could be attained only by breaking away from the antiquated standards Scholars and thinkers frequently expressed the opinion that the ancients, who lacked the centuried experience of the moderns, were in reality young in wisdom, while the moderns were old in expe-

---

[1] Riehl, *Kulturstudien*, Stuttgart, 1859, pp 22 ff

[2] The art of traveling was known by the musical name, *ars apodemica*, and many books were written on the subject, cf *Traveling as Education* in *Cyclopedia of Education*. Even Justus Lipsius wrote an *Epistola de nobili et erudita peregrinatione.*

[3] Burckhardt (l c., p 389) sketches the ideal "Cortigiano" thus "He must be at home in all noble sports, among them running, leaping, swimming, and wrestling, he must, above all things, be a good dancer and, as a matter of course, an accomplished writer He must be master of several modern languages, at all events of Latin and Italian, he must be familiar with literature and have some knowledge of the fine arts In music a certain practical skill was expected of him, which he was bound, nevertheless, to keep as secret as possible All this is to be taken not too seriously, except what relates to the use of arms The mutual interaction of these gifts and accomplishments results in the perfect man, in whom no one quality usurps the place of the rest "

rience.[1] Among the æsthetes, Perrault was the first to raise the question, in his *Le paralèlle des anciens et des modernes* (4 vols., 1688-1696), whether the modern poets were not superior to the ancient; and the disputes that ensued reacted on the schools, although the latter were slow in readjusting their curricula to the new standards.

CHAPTER XXIII.

The Educational Institutions of the Renaissance.

1. The schools and educational institutions of the Renaissance were either of the traditional medieval type, or new creations. The circles and societies of the Humanists, whose aim was the furthering of the new learning, were the most important of the new departures in education. The circle of scholars— among them the learned Luigi Marsigli and the statesman Collucio Salutato—who met at the Augustinian Monastery San Spirito near Florence, belongs to the 14th century. Greater influence was exerted by the Court of the Muses of Cosimo de' Medici, who employed the tireless collector, Niccolo Niccoli, as his "literary minister." The next generation of Florentines founded, on the suggestion of the Greek Gemistos Plethon, the Platonic Academy (1474); and Marsiglio Ficino, Pico of Mirandola, and Angelo Poliziano made it famous throughout Europe. In Rome the Humanists gathered about Nicholas V., Pius II., and Leo X., and in 1498 Pomponius Lætus founded the "Academia Antiquaria." The "Sodalitas Rhenana" at Worms and the "Sodalitas Danubiana" at Vienna, both founded in 1490 by Conrad Celtes, were German imitations of the Italian Academies.

Societies for cultivating one or several educational subjects continued to be organized until the end of the period. The Italian Academies took up the study of the vernacular only towards the end of the 16th century, and their example was followed in the 17th century by several German orders and societies, who gave some attention to the schools also. Louis of

---

[1] Bacon, *Nov. org.*, § 84; Jord. Bruno, *Cena delle cen.*, p. 132 (Erdmann, l. c., I, p. 562). Descartes says: "*Non est quod antiquis multum tribuamus propter antiquitatem, sed nos potius iis antiquiores dicendi; jam enim senior est mundus quam tunc, majoremque habemus rerum experientiam.*" Baillet, *Vie de Descartes*, VIII, 10.)

Anhalt-Kothen, the founder of the Order of the Palm Tree, invited Ratke to open a model school in the capital of his country. A private literary club was the beginning of the French Academy, which Cardinal Richelieu converted in 1635 into a national institution, and which subsequently exerted so powerful an influence on the development of French letters. The Italian Academies were also the pioneers in the study of the natural sciences. The *Academia secretorum naturæ,* founded in 1560 in Naples, was the first to take up this subject, and the Royal Society of London, founded in 1645, was patterned after it. Vives defined the Academy as an institution encouraging the study of both young and old and as a *"conventus et consensus hominum doctorum pariter et bonorum."* [1] Comenius demanded a *"collegium didacticum,"* or *"schola scholarum,"* as the capstone of the whole school system; [2] and Bacon described the international co-operation of all the learned societies of Europe— whose work was to be patterned after that of the religious orders, especially the Jesuits—as one of his fondest dreams, though he admitted that it could not be realized in his own day. [3]

In his *Societas philadelphica,* one of his early works, Leibnitz also sketched a plan for a cosmopolitan society, of scholars to be patterned after the Society of Jesus [4] Later he modified his original design considerably, though its main features were preserved in the Academies he planned for Berlin, Dresden, Vienna, and St. Petersburg, but which he realized only in Berlin.

2. Of the older schools, the universities were the first to welcome the new learning. They adopted the policy suggested by Erasmus· "The study of polite literature should be introduced into the higher schools only gradually so as to cause as little stir as possible   The new learning should present itself

---

[1] *De trad dic*, II, p 250

[2] *Did magn*, 31, 15, see *supra*, Introduction, II, 8

[3] *De augm. scient.*, Lugd Bat, 1695, p 117· "*Sunt enim, uti videmus, multi ordines et sodalitia, quæ licet regnis et spatiis longinquius disjuncta sint, tamen societatem et tanquam fraternitatem inter se ineunt et colunt, adeo ut habeant præfectos, alios provinciales, alios generales, quibus omnes parent*"

[4] Biedermann, *Kulturgeschichte des 18 Jahrhunderts*, II, p 235 "It is obvious, and Leibnitz acknowledges it openly, that he had in mind the magnificent example of the Jesuits His dream was an order of the scholars of the entire world, who, being inspired by a deep love for science and learning, were to direct not only the scientific work, but all the affairs of the individual state as well as of the whole world The members of this order were to fill all important offices, were to control the trades and industries no less than the schools, to establish colonies, and so forth "

not as an enemy that tramples upon all that was previously taught in the schools; instead, it should come as a friendly caller, and then it will be urged to make a longer stay, until it, welcomed at first as a guest, is considered a member of the family." The Italian universities were the first homes of Humanism, and even the poorest and smallest, though they had only three professorships (of canon and civil law and physics), added a fourth, of rhetoric. Only in Rome the old and the new learning continued to be taught independently of each other till Leo X. reorganized the Sapienza and founded 88 professorships. Of the German universities, Heidelberg and Vienna were the first to receive the new studies, but they were soon followed by Erfurt and Leipzig. Many of the new universities, as Tübingen, Wittenberg, and the universities of the North, had no difficulties in throwing open their doors to the new learning, for they had no scholastic traditions in this regard. The University of Paris frowned upon the Humanistic movement, and hence Francis I. founded in 1529 the Collège de France for the study of the classics. By the second decade of the 16th century courses in the Greek and Roman classics were given in all the universities.

In Italy the Humanistic studies were first taken up by the private tutors of the nobility and only later were they introduced into the schools. The Carraras of Padua employed, since 1390, the services of Pier Paolo Vergerio; the Estes of Ferrara employed, since 1429, the services of Guarino the Elder; and the Gonzagas of Mantua had as tutor, since 1425, Vittorino Ramboldini, known as Da Feltre. Da Feltre's pupils were recruited from all classes, and his school, the *casa giojosa*, was during the twenty-two years of his mastership favorably known throughout Europe. In Germany, however, the schools, and not home education led the way in the new learning. The Brothers of the Common Life of Northwestern Germany were its first patrons: John Wessel (1489) reformed the school in Advert; and Alexander Hegius (died c. 1503), that in Deventer. Of the cathedral schools, the school in Münster, reorganized by Rudolf von Lange (died 1519), provost of the cathedral, and the school in Osnabrück, reorganized by Alexander of Meppen, followed the new movement. The city school of Schlettstadt (Alsatia), organized in 1450 by Ludwig of Dringenburg, was celebrated far and wide for the thoroughness of its course.

But the organization of the school system as a whole was undertaken in Germany and in other countries only after the

Reformation had divided the great body of Christians, for at that critical time the religious needs of the different denominations intensified all other incentives to learning. It was considered a sacred duty to provide primarily for the perpetuation of the religious beliefs among the young. But the latter could not give a reasonable account of the faith they professed unless they were at home in the secular learning of the day. In the Protestant countries the respective ruler or the municipal government generally founded Latin schools, and endowed them with the funds obtained in most cases from suppressed and confiscated monasteries. The organization of these Protestant schools presents a great variety, owing partly to local conditions and partly to the individuality of capable masters. Many of the 16th century masters had a gift for organizing schools, and the Evangelical school ordinances (*Evangelische Schulordnungen*, ed. by Vormbaum, Gutersloh, 1860, vol. I.) are conclusive evidence of the zeal and the ingenuity of the pioneers of the Protestant schools. The uniformity of educational methods was due to the common principles underlying the new foundations, as well as to the influence of certain educational institutions and leaders Wittenberg became the chief training school for the masters and teachers of the German Lutheran schools, and Melanchthon, to whom Protestant education owes much, was hailed by his partizans as the *Præceptor Germaniæ* [1] The Strassburg school of John Sturm was considered the model school of the West, and Trotzendorf's school at Goldberg enjoyed a similar prestige among the schools of the 'East. The University of Prague was the intellectual stronghold of the Utraquists of Bohemia.[2] All these schools fitted their students for the learned professions, especially the ministry. The preparation for the profession of theology was stressed among the Lutherans, while the Reformed Churches attended more to the fitting for public life. The history of the Protestant schools presents some interesting types of capable teachers, for instance, Neander, whose sprightly humor is reflected in his *libri schustricales,* and who wielded an influence in Northwestern Germany akin to that of the indefatigable Trotzendorf in the East.

---

[1] Cf Richard, J. W , *Philip Melanchthon, the Protestant Preceptor of Germany,* New York, 1898

[2] The organization of the schools of the Utraquists is described in the work, *Ordo studiorum docendi atque discendi litteras in scholis civitatum regni Boemiæ et Marchionatus Moraviæ constitutus ab Universitate Pragensi Pragæ,* Weleslavin, 1586

3. Compared with the Protestant schools, the Catholic school system of the Renaissance appears more uniform and less individualized. But with the teaching orders in charge of the Catholic schools, the genius of an individual teacher would never stand out so prominently in the history of education, as would be the case if he had been independent of a teaching community. The organization of the schools was based on programs of study that were intended for different countries in different parts of the world, and which were the outcome of long and serious deliberation; and it was natural that, once the curriculum had received ecclesiastical approbation, it would be strictly and tenaciously adhered to. Only after a period of thirty years' experimentation was the *Ratio atque institutio studiorum Societatis Jesu* formulated by a commission of Jesuits of different nationalities, sitting from 1584-1588, and was then sent out on approval to the various provinces of the Order. After having been thus tried out, it was made the subject of a general discussion at a General Chapter, revised again, and only then published in its final and definitive form. This *Ratio studiorum* was the basis for the whole Catholic school system of the period, not merely by reason of the large number of schools actually in the hands of the Jesuits, but also because the educational methods of the latter were copied quite generally, not only by the friends, but also by the enemies, of the Society.

The most important of the educational writings of the Jesuits have been published within the last decades, and from them we can get a good view of the inner working of the Jesuit schools.[1] Fr. Paulsen has given, in his history of higher education, an impartial account of the Jesuit schools, and has praised the Jesuits particularly for being the pioneers in the systematic training of teachers.[2] Some of the Jesuit educators were un-

---

[1] Pachtler, G. M., S.J., *Ratio studiorum et institutiones scholasticæ Societatis Jesu per Germaniam olim' vigentes*, Vols. II, V, IX, and XVI, of Kehrbach's *Monumenta Germaniæ Pædagogica* (Berlin, 1887 ff.); Schwickerath, R., S.J., *Jesuit Education, its History and Principles*, St. Louis, 1903; *Bibliothek der katholischen Pädagogik*, Vols. X and XI (Freiburg, 1889 and 1901); s. v. *Jesuits* in *Cyclopedia of Education*.

[2] *Geschichte des gelehrten Unterrichts*, 2nd ed., I, p. 388 (Leipzig, 1886-1887): "The colleges are, then, in a certain sense, the first normal schools for gymnasium teachers: the teaching of methods was an important duty of the prefect of studies. This practice is probably responsible for the excellence of the Jesuit schools. In the Protestant countries the necessity of training the teachers was recognized only in the 18th century, when the pedagogical seminars were established for this purpose."

doubtedly of marked individuality Francesco Sacchini was born
1570 in Paciano, in Umbria, and began his studies with the
boldness of a self-taught man, who would "swim without a
life-preserver;" but experience soon taught him that "reading
is for the mind what food is for the body." Antonio Possevini,[1]
born 1534 in Mantua, was equally successful as a founder of
schools and as a diplomat; his *Bibliotheca selecta, qua agitur de
ratione studiorum in historia, disciplinis et salute omnia pro-
curanda* (Rome, 1593) proves him an eminent polyhistorian.

A considerable number of schools were in the hands of other
religious orders, and the secular clergy as well as laymen controlled many schools   Some of the old Benedictine schools
witnessed a revival in the 16th century, as, Monte Cassino,
Kremsmunster, Maria Einsiedeln, and others.   The French seminaries of the Maurists were celebrated seats of learning   The
Franciscans organized the school system of the New World.
The Theatines,[2] founded in 1524, and the Barnabites, founded
in 1535, labored in Latin Europe, while the Hieronymites,
known as *Fratres Scholastici*, conducted schools in Germany
till late in the 16th century   The Piarists, founded in 1617,
gained a firm foothold in Italy, Spain, Poland, and Austria.
The French colleges of the Oratorians, first opened in 1611,
were well attended.   The older universities and their affiliated
schools—for instance, the colleges of the University of Paris,
which were of the same rank as the Latin schools—remained
under the control of the secular authorities.

4. The Latin school of the Renaissance differed from the
present-day German gymnasium in that its scope was not determined exactly, the work of the elementary school was not
adjusted to that of the Latin school, nor was the curriculum
of the latter adjusted to the graduate schools of the university. The *Gymnasia academica*, or *illustria*, known also as
Lycea, or *Athenaea*, were very numerous in the 17th century in Germany, Holland, and other countries, and frequently
offered regular courses of university lectures   The several professors were, as in the universities, eligible to the rectorship;
and these schools could confer the baccalaureate, but not
the doctorate   Many gymnasiums developed into universities.

---

[1] Cf *supra*, p 250

[2] Bateus, an Irish Theatine monk, was the first to suggest a *Janua Linguæ*
to aid the missionaries in educating the heathen children; his idea was carried
out by the Jesuits of Salamanca College, and finally led up to the *Mercurius*
of Schoppe and the *Orbis pictus* of Comenius

the Nuremberg Gymnasium was converted, in 1575, into the Altorf University; the Gandersheim Gymnasium, in 1576, into the University of Helmstedt; and the school of Sturm was known after 1621 as the Strassburg Academy. The colleges of the Jesuits likewise introduced university studies; the so-called *collegium supremum* was in reality a *studium generale, i. e.,* a university with four faculties, whose chairs in the schools of law and medicine could, however, be occupied by laymen. The *collegium medium* comprised the five *scholæ inferiores (studia inferiora)* and *philosophiæ cursus triennales (studia superiora),* while the *collegium infimum* confined itself to the *studia inferiora.* The latter was a preparatory school for the course in philosophy, and was of the same rank as the Latin school. Thus the medieval view of the arts' course being preparatory to the study of philosophy was still upheld in the Jesuit system of education. The schools of the religious orders always had at least five classes. In the Jesuit schools these classes were known by the following names: *rudimentum* or *grammatica infima, grammatica media, grammatica suprema, humanitas,* and *rhetorica;* a sixth class was organized by distributing the work of the lowest class over two years.

The Latin school of five or six classes was the prevailing type in the Protestant countries also, though there were many exceptions to the general rule: Sturm's school had ten classes; and many city schools, only four or three. These incomplete Latin schools were also called *pædagogia,* "trivial schools," or "particular schools." The term "gymnasium," as used in the Renaissance, did not denote a special kind of school, but rather designated any higher school. The primitive meaning of gymnasium—an institution for intellectual gymnastics—was at that time more in evidence than in the present German use of the term.[1]

[1] In a comedy by Bebel, written in 1501 and treating of the best methods of instruction, a farmer takes his boy to a *gymnasium universale, ut dici solet.* Wimpheling makes a distinction, in his treatise *De proba institutione puerorum* (1514), between the *gymnasia trivilia* for boys and the *gymnasia universalia* for youths. The *Ratio atque inst. stud. S. J.* (Prov. 3) says: "*Quod si ob gymnasii amplitudinem ac varietatem per unum studiorum præfectum non videatur scholarum omnium rationibus satis esse consultum, alterum constituat, qui ex generalis præfecti præscripto inferioribus studiis moderetur;*" consequently, the *gymnasium* included both the *studia superiora* and the *studia inferiora.* The Roman University Sapienza was also known as an *archigymnasium.* Luther had in mind the form of a school of gymnastics for the Christian mind, when he wrot · · *masii christia·*

We have seen above that the scope of the Latin schools often overlapped with that of the universities, and, similarly, many elementary schools in the cities encroached upon the curriculum of the middle schools by teaching the rudiments of Latin. The elementary school of the Renaissance resembled the elementary school of the Middle Ages (see *supra*, ch. xviii, 4) in that it lacked a definite aim and scope. Primary instruction was regarded also in Protestant countries as part of the cure of souls, and was generally entrusted to the sexton. In fact, most of the rural schools of the 16th and 17th centuries were, as had been the case in the Middle Ages, sexton's schools. Popular education was benefited only indirectly by the efforts of the Humanists. Yet the case of the Duke Ulric's closing, in 1546, the German schools of Wurttemberg to prevent them from interfering with the activity of the Latin schools, stands alone, and is not indicative of general conditions, for the interest in the new learning promoted the cause of popular education in many, even if only indirect, ways. It is known that elementary schools were opened when the funds that had been collected did not suffice for establishing a higher school, and it was considered a matter of simple prudence to aid the rural schools so as to insure a large attendance at the Latin schools in the cities. The Humanists had inaugurated the grammatical study of modern languages, and after the grammar of the mother-tongue had been added to the curriculum of the elementary school, the view gained ground that the mother-tongue was the distinguishing feature of the elementary school just as Latin characterized the higher school, and that, furthermore, the *schola vernacula* must, though lower in rank, be recognized beside the *schola Latina*—a view that we find upheld by Comenius. The religious upheaval likewise brought about new elementary school methods. The catechism, treating the doctrines of Faith in the form of questions and answers, dates from the 16th century [1] The following catechisms were used most widely in the schools: the smaller catechism of Luther (1529), the Heidelberg catechism, and the *Catechismus parvus* of P. Canisius (1563). The Bible was read in the Protestant schools; its popularity encouraged the masses to learn to read and write, and the familiarity with the sacred text improved and enriched the common

---

[1] In the Middle Ages catechism denoted only religious instruction irrespective of its form For the history of the chief catechisms see Gatterer-Krus, *The Theory and Practice of the Catechism*, transl. by Culemans, New York, 1914, pp. 49 ff

speech of the people. But it is not true that the Protestant translations of the Bible are responsible for popular education: in Scotland the new religion carried book and pen into every hut, but in England it destroyed the old parochial schools, without supplying a substitute for them.

5. There is a tendency throughout the entire history of Renaissance education to push to the foreground a factor that had remained in the Middle Ages in the background—the State. The schools themselves prepared the way for the State-control of education, for the Roman law schools of the universities, the *ordines legistarum* had never ceased to teach the doctrine of the all-powerful State. The religious conflicts hastened the day of the State-control of the schools, and in the 16th century different governments issued school ordinances, which policy was the beginning of the secularization of the schools. Protestant governments considered the control of the church and the church schools as wholly within their province: Luther himself gave the initiative when he requested his sovereign to take over the schools of the country,[1] and his collaborators regarded themselves as state officials. The Saxon school ordinances, written by Melanchthon, were the first to be published (1528); they were followed in the same year by Bugenhagen's ordinances for Brunswick, and a year later by the Hamburg ordinances. The Württemberg ordinances of 1559, which were more detailed than those just mentioned, proved of great importance for after times, and were the basis of the Saxon ordinances of 1580. The Latin city schools of Denmark were subjected to government control in 1537, and those of Sweden, in 1571; the English schools alone remained independent of the State.

In the Catholic countries, the schools remained, for the most part, under the control of the Church. The cathedral schools were changed, in accordance with the decrees of the Council of Trent, into training schools for the candidates to the priesthood (Tridentine seminaries). The old monastic schools became train-

---

[1] Luther wrote, May 20, 1530, to the Elector John of Saxony: "The youth of your country is, indeed, a veritable paradise such as is found in no other country of the earth, and the good Lord has, in proof of His grace and bounty, committed this smiling paradise to your care, as though He would say, 'Herewith I commend to thee, my dear Duke John, my dearest treasure, and thou art to prove a loving father to it. It is to thy care and protection that I commend my paradise, and it shall be an honor to thee to be its gardener'". Baur in Schmid's *Enzyklopädie*, V, p. 769.

ing schools for the young members of the religious orders. The teaching orders controlled most of the universities and colleges as well as schools for girls (Ursulines) and poor boys (Piarists), while the bishops and synods provided parochial elementary schools.[1] However, the Church required and welcomed State aid for her schools, because the storms of the Reformation had impoverished her in many places and had also weakened her influence: hence the school ordinances issued by some Catholic governments, for example, those of Duke Albert for Upper and Lower Bavaria (1564) The doctrine of the secularization of the schools was first taught in France, where the government had even in the Middle Ages exerted through the University considerable influence on education. This doctrine found ready acceptance among a people bent on enlarging the scope of the Gallican liberties: France was quite eager to deny the Pope the *regimen scholarum*, and the political economists had only to recall the conditions in ancient Rome to find further arguments for extending the power of the secular rulers. "The King," says Servin, "is the first and chief founder of all schools, the University is beholden to him for its dignity, and he possesses full power to regulate its studies This is the principal prerogative of his royal power. In all that pertains to the studies, the rector is but the representative of the King, for the King, as the *Imperator*, has all imperial rights. He is, as Constantine the Great styled himself, the *episcopus exteriorum*."[2] The universities, however, retained their corporate rights until the Revolution.

CHAPTER XXIV.

The Renaissance in the Different Countries

1. The Middle Ages had united the Christian peoples of Europe in a confederacy of culture, and this circumstance accounts for the fact that the influence of the new learning was not confined to one country, but was felt throughout Europe. The culture of knighthood and the learning of the Scholastics had also been common property, and the national variations of them were but slight, although the several peoples had not contributed to them to the same extent. In contrast to this,

[1] Stöckl, *Geschichte der Pädagogik*, 1876, pp. 231 ff

[2] L Hahn, *Das Unterrichtswesen in Frankreich*, Breslau, 1848, pp. 70 ff

Humanistic education appears both general and nationally differentiated. The Renaissance was undoubtedly broadly European in character, still it gave free scope to national motives; yes, through its deep influence it has developed that national consciousness of the different peoples which prompts the peoples of modern Europe to regard one another as individual members of a higher order. The Humanistic studies produced different results in Italy, in France, in England, and in Germany.

Italy could point to the most glorious remains of the greatness of ancient Rome, and throughout the Middle Ages the ancient traditions had here shown more vitality than elsewhere. The names of public offices were those of ancient Rome; Roman law was practised in the courts; and Roman folklore was still the inspiration of the poet. While spinning, the Florentine mother related "stories of the Trojans, of Fiesole, and Rome."[1] The Italians had regarded the great men of Roman history as their ancestors long before the Humanists represented them as the teachers of the modern world. When the Italian poet struck the lyre, he seemed to make music in the familiar strains of ancient Rome, for the same spirit breathes from the old and the new song (Burckhardt). The Italian Humanists are reminiscent both in language and personality of the literati and grammarians of the ancients. There is an unmistakable resemblance between Rhemmius Palaemon and Filelfo, between Vittorino and Verrius Flaccus. The wandering orators and minstrels carry one's thoughts back to the Sophists of the Empire, and the immigrant Greeks of the 15th century recall the Greek grammarians who settled in Rome in the period of the Gracchi. All that was brought to light of the ancient world was regarded as common property and was, in some measure, appreciated and assimilated by the entire nation. Even if the Humanists—and the Italian Humanists stand alone in this— formed a class apart and kept aloof from the masses, yet their interests were shared by all the people. Everybody seemed to be ransacking libraries and out-of-the-way places for literary treasures, and thousands were employed in transcribing manuscripts. The courtier recited Latin verses, and in many instances they were of his own composition. On one day both peasants and townspeople would attend the (even if but half-understood) oration of the learned orator, and on the next day they would lustily applaud the mythological figures in the

---

[1] Dante, *Par.*, 15, 124.

pageant   The inhabitants of Arpino were proud of their towns-man Cicero, and when Pope Pius II. discovered some Arpinites among his prisoners of war, he set them free in honor of the great orator.   Every town connected the new interests with its memories and its hopes.   Florence could justly claim the honor of having formulated the new educational principle and of having made accessible the treasures of Roman as well as of Greek culture.   Hence Poliziano could exclaim, in the first of his lectures on Homer: "Ye men of Florence may be proud of your city, for here the whole of Greek culture, which had died long ago in Greece, has been recalled to a new and vigorous life . . . so that it may well seem as though Athens had not died and had not been pillaged by the barbarians, but had only been transplanted, according to her desires, along with her art and literature, to Florence, for with this city has she now been assimilated."   And, indeed, there is a kinship between ancient Athens, the school of Greece, and the new Etruria, the teacher of Italy; between the joyous greatness of the age of Pericles and the creative and gladsome genius of the Medici period. Florence appears democratic enough in its literary circles, but at Venice the Humanists were aristocrats in their oligarchic aloofness,[1] and in Rome they adapted themselves to the hier-archic traditions and thus secured the patronage of the Curia.

"The School of Athens," Raphael's famous painting in the Stanza della Segnatura in the Vatican (done between 1508 and 1511), illustrates the assimilation of ancient and modern ele-ments   The ancient sages are grouped about Plato and Aris-totle, but among their number we recognize the familiar faces of the Renaissance. One youth has the features of Maria della Rovere, Duke of Urbino, and another, the features of Frederick II of Mantua; Archimedes has the features of Bramantes, the great architect, and Perugino, Raphael's teacher, and the painter himself are in the scene.   The paintings of the whole hall are designed to represent the sum-total of the arts and sciences of the period.   The paintings on the ceiling represent theology (*divinarum rerum notitia*), poetry (*numine afflatur*), philosophy (*causarum cognitio*), and justice (*jus suum cuique tribuens*). The corresponding paintings on the walls are: the Disputa, the assembly of the Doctors and Theologians of the Church; the Parnassus, the poets and musicians of ancient and modern times; the School of Athens; and scenes from the history of

---

[1] G Voigt, *Die Wiederbelebung des klassischen Altertums*, Berlin, 1859, p 207.

law.   As Dante in the Middle Ages presented in his poetry all that occupied the minds of his contemporaries and fired their ambitions, so the painter now sought to express, in keeping with the spirit of the changed world, all that was the inspiration of his time.   The men of a later day could not appreciate the naïveté with which the pagan elements were intermingled with the Christian, and therefore interpreted the School of Athens as "Paul Preaching to the Athenians."

Italian Humanism began to decline after the first decade of the 16th century; the sometime celebrated poets and philologists passed under a cloud, and though they still held sway in matters of language and style, their company was no longer sought. Printed editions of the classics, of handbooks, and reference works dispensed to some extent with the personal teaching of the Humanists, and the latter were moreover suspected of being Epicureans and infidels.[1]   The Church had to take measures against the new paganism, which was the more dangerous as the ancient ideas had entered deep into life.   The Humanists subsequently confined their activities to the study and the school.   However, the whole nation had benefited by the movement: it learned to appreciate its glorious past, acquired an interest in art, a pure taste, refined manners, which happy gifts are still possessed by the Italians and mark them even to-day the richest heirs of the ancient world.   It is the glory of the Italian people to have transmitted their ancient inheritance imbued with the spirit of their own country to the rest of the civilized world.   "The conquest of the Western World was accomplished, indeed, by the Renaissance, but by the Renaissance as inspired by Italian ideals" (Burckhardt).

2. In France, too, there was much to connect the present with the ancient greatness.   "The might and power of Rome had built the roads, the aqueducts, the castles, and cities of France; the remains of Julian's Baths could still be seen in Paris.   The very language of France established an affinity with ancient Rome, and the Church told in her legends of the French martyrs of the early Roman Church.   French literature was, likewise, cast in the mould of ancient Rome: satires, comedies, idylls, odes, and the apotheosis of the king were as popular in France as they had ever been at Rome."[2]   The schools of

[1] See the masterly presentation of the history of the Humanistic movement in Burckhardt, *The Civilization of the Renaissance in Italy*, transl. by Middlemore, London, 1898, part III.

[2] K. Rosenkranz, *Diderots Leben und Werke*, Leipzig, 1866, I. p. 2.

Chartres and Orleans had during the Scholastic period remained centres of classical learning. Yet France had been at the same time a prime force in all medieval movements In France knighthood was most fully developed; here the universities received their definitive form, and in this country the Scholastics had their most frequented schools. Italy was the seat of the Holy See, and Germany of the Emperor, but France could boast the greatest seats of learning. Because the nation was thus permeated with the spirit of the Middle Ages, it never truckled to the Humanistic ideas. French Humanism differed from the Italian in that it did not appear as a vital element, but appealed to the learned only. The French kings patronized and popularized the new learning in the hope of aggrandizing their power, both in intellectual and political matters, by making their people familiar with the authority enjoyed by the Roman emperors. The influence of the classical studies on the French language was slow in asserting itself, but deep and abiding. The literary language of France is a product of the Renaissance, and the peculiar style of the French, logical, indeed, but rhetorical withal, bears evident traces of the influence of the Humanistic studies. The French classics combine in a masterly way the ancient motifs with the new national ideals. The individualism of the ancients, their striving for artistic expression, and the skeptical joyousness of their life have become vital elements with the French more than with any other people. The real fruits of the new spirit were enjoyed in the salons—witness Hotel Rambouillet—where the fashionable world had met even during the Renaissance period Still, the whole nation shared the good results. The vivacity and versatility of the French, their refined taste and courtly manners—all bear the impress of Renaissance influence The native love of the French for honor and glory was encouraged by the kindred ambition of the ancients, and the French schools used the prize system most extensively.

3. Latin schools had been opened in England in the 15th century, and several English works on Humanistic education were published in the 16th century [1] But among the English powerful influences were at work to check the enthusiasm with which Latin Europe had received the new learning The English High Church looked on it with no kindly eye and the Puritans were opposed to the cultivation of the fine arts Add to this the

---

[1] Cf McCormick, *History of Education*, pp 204 ff

narrow utilitarian standard applied, as a result of Bacon's teaching, to knowledge and learning, and we shall understand why a sympathetic study of antiquity was impossible in England. The pride of the Englishman would not permit him to enter fully into the beauty and spirit of ancient poetry. Shakespeare is very free in adapting the ancient materials to modern settings, and resembles, in this regard, more the medieval minstrels than the poets of the Renaissance. Yet in one point the English were more akin to the ancients than the other peoples. Of all modern peoples, England alone possessed a truly public political life; she alone offered opportunities to the orator and his living voice; and she alone had a class of men destined to wield political power and that had, therefore, to be trained for the political profession. The education of the sons of the gentry, "our noble and our gentle youth," presented problems similar to those of the education of the free-born citizens of Greece and Rome. A general education was required, not a narrow vocational training; the personality had to be developed; and—this was of the greatest moment—the youth had to acquire the mastery of language. It was thus advisable to use in England the same means as had proved successful with the ancients— the study of language in all its phases, not for the purpose of scientific research, neither, at least not directly, for the purpose of æsthetic appreciation, but, instead, as a formal element that would train the mind and bring out and perfect the pupil's individuality. Humanistic studies came to be considered, then, the ideal education of the English gentleman, because they seemed to be best adapted to develop and train the public character; and in this regard England remained more closely related to the ancients than the other modern peoples. She valued the Humanistic studies as a national asset, and held her Latin school in high esteem as being the training school of her gentlemen, her members of Parliament, and her statesmen.[1] This accounts for the fact that England, though slower than the other peoples in receiving the Renaissance culture, has tenaciously retained down to our own day the early Humanistic school system. The present-day Latin schools of England are faithfully preserving the traditions of more than three centuries. They still regard Religion, Latin, and Greek as the quintessence of a liberal education; they revere the headmaster, as did the first Humanists, as the head and heart of his school;

[1] L. Stein, *Vorlesungen über* Vol. V, pp. 27 ff.

and retain even so much of the old school customs as to assemble the scholars of all the classes in one large hall, where the headmaster reigns supreme, and where the greatest men of English history have sat in their boyhood days and have left their names in rude carvings on the old school desks.

4. Germany seemed to offer few opportunities to the Humanists. There was no kinship between the Germans and the ancients, there were no rulers eager to resuscitate the power of the Caesars; neither did an education to statesmanship along Roman lines appeal to the Germans. The Humanists were consequently obliged to strike the hard rock till the water would issue forth, and the schoolmen had to be at weary pains to dig the channels for its distribution among the people. Herder describes the Latin poets of the German Renaissance as being satisfied with reciting their lessons before their ancient masters. The German polyhistorians of the same period appear to be helpless beneath the mass and weight of their learning; and neither the poets nor the scholars of the German Renaissance can be compared to the French and Italian Humanists, for the latter had not only received the learning of the ancients, but had also imbibed their spirit The German Renaissance was undoubtedly rich in labors, but poor in creative power; eager for knowledge, but slow in assimilation, abounding in erudition, but wanting in culture. Still the labor was not in vain. Its fruits appeared, even if late, and Germany need not blush for the results. It was only in the 18th century that the spirit of the ancients had entered deeply and fully into the intellectual life of the people, and the names of Winckelmann, Herder, and Goethe prove, not only that the Germans had far outstripped the other peoples by penetrating beyond the culture of Rome to that of Greece, but that they had of all moderns appreciated most perfectly the real specific content of Humanism, that broad cosmopolitan view of the world and of men and of things which is so characteristic a trait of the ancients But even the drudgery of the 16th and 17th centuries was not in vain, for this drudgery was needed to adjust the Humanistic studies to the educative process This drudgery laid the foundation for the German school system, which seems to strike the happy mean between the French centralization of education and the sovereign independence of the English schools. The German school system has proved a reservoir (as it were) of German culture. From it the whole nation derives food and refreshment

of the spirit, while it itself remains open on all sides in order to receive, from every available source, an increase of its original supply. The German Humanists and savants did not explore the new fields of the ancient world. Instead, they minted and brought into circulation the gold that other peoples had thence brought home. Their aim was neither æsthetical, nor archeological, but pedagogical. The Germans have produced a goodly share of the many educational works of the Renaissance, and the conception of didactics as the science of education and the art of teaching is an achievement of the German polymathists of the 17th century.

VIII.

THE ENLIGHTENMENT.

CHAPTER XXV.

The Character of the Enlightenment

1. Education in general lights up the intellectual horizon, deals the deathblow to foolish and unfounded traditions, and insures independence of judgment Every new educational principle is a source of light, and its rays dispel the clouds and the darkness connected with a principle that has outlived itself Thus Christianity had taught the world to walk in light, and hence demonism, the foundation of heathenism, had to disappear along with all the darkness of superstitions and vague notions that were bound up with the curious mixture of cults and mythologies of latter antiquity: *Vetustatem novitas, umbram fugat veritas, noctem lux eliminat.*[1] Similarly, Humanism meant the deathblow to many superstitions current in the learning and the daily life of the Middle Ages: Petrarch considered the war upon astrologers and quacks no mean part of his lifework, and the greatest men of the period were engaged in correcting the misinterpretations of certain teachings of the ancients

All these effects of education are, though valuable, yet purely negative, and cannot compare in importance with the positive results accruing from a system of education that is rich in content and that rests on a solid foundation In the latter case the mind will turn to the full light itself, will find a sweet joy in its contemplation, and will not forego this joy for the pleasure of lighting up with torches some dark corner in the distance. But when clever minds are denied an education that is satisfying in content, they will be more interested in the enlightenment than in the light itself. This was the case at the time of the Greek Sophists, when the ethos of ancient Attica was fast losing its influence, and when philosophy had not yet developed sufficiently to serve as the basis of faith, knowledge, and human striving. The Sophists, and even Socrates and the

---

[1] Thomas Aquinas, *Lauda Sion*

282

one-sided Socratics, were apostles of enlightenment. Their aim
was, not to foster a certain content of knowledge, but to bring
light into things and into the heads, to remove prejudices, to
train to self-reliance, whether of the virtuoso, the δεινός, or of
the self-satisfied wise man.[1]   The same tendency may be observed in other philosophical systems at the time of their decline. The *Nil admirari* of the Epicureans (Horace, *Ep.*, I, 6, 1)
is the maxim of the ancient *Voltairien*, who scorns the prejudices
of the wonder-loving rabble as well as all "philosophical marvelling," the θαυμασμὸς φιλόσοφος.[2] The *sapere aude* (ibid.,
2, 40) is the motto of all such as consider the rejecting of the
opinions of others a proof of courage.   Though the Stoics respected the objectivity of human reason, yet they, too, sat in
judgment on the manners and customs of the past; their individual opinions were their standard of judgment, and the *ratione componi* was their rule of life.[3]

The tendency toward enlightenment did not in any of the
above instances extend beyond the field of education. However,
in the so-called Age of Enlightenment this tendency was more
than a principle of knowledge and learning; it was the leading
idea in all the movements of the period.

2. The 18th century has styled itself the *siècle éclairé*, the
Enlightened Age, or the Philosophical Age, and has tried to
formulate philosophically its own tendencies. We have quite a
number of these definitions and explanations of the dominating
idea of the period. However, all these explanations give too
broad a meaning to the term Enlightenment, attach too much
weight to its content, and judge the tendencies of the world of
the 18th century to be the tendencies of all men of all times.
Still, such mistakes were to be expected of an attempt to express
in a fixed and settled form what is still subject to change, or
to embody, while in the midst of a movement, its ends and
aims in a pithy and epigrammatic form.[4] *Aufklärung* (enlighten-

---

[1] The Greek language has a drastic simile for this activity: ratiocination
is described as the highest and most perfect of purgatives; Plato, *Soph.*, p.230:
τὸν ἔλεγχον λεκτέων ὡς ἄρα μεγίστη καὶ κυριωτάτη τῶν καθάρσεών ἐστιν.

[2] See *supra*, Introduction, II, 1.

[3] Seneca, *Ep.*, 123: "*Inter causas malorum nostrorum est, quod vivimus ad
exempla nec ratione componimur, sed consuetudine abducimur.*" Id., *De vita
beata*: "*Nulla res majoribus malis nos implicat, quam quod ad rumorem componimur, optima rati ea, quæ magno assensu recepta sunt quorumque exempla
multa sunt.*"

[4] Kant defines enlightenment as the "... ge to
which he had been reduced through his own ... onats-

ment) means literally the breaking up of the clouds, the clearing
of the sky; and figuratively, in the matter of education, the
human mind is the sky, that is clouded with prejudices, and the
latter include all views and beliefs that have been transmitted
from the past and that cannot be recognized by the minds of
the present generation as logically sound and objectively true.
These prejudices must be dispelled by the human reason, and
the critical faculties of the individual must pass sentence on
everything, especially on such matters as pertain to the well-
being of the individual. This independent reasoning is expected
to produce, not only intellectual results, but also to reform the
morals of the people; for by applying his mind to these problems, man will outgrow the nonage to which he has been reduced
through his blind obedience to the traditions of the past. Man
cannot be happy until he repudiates all these traditions, and
after the individual has done so, he must co-operate in spreading this enlightenment so as to make, as far as possible, the
whole human race supremely happy and good

With regard to religion, the individual was granted full liberty to decide for himself what he would believe   The human
reason sat in judgment on the truths of religion, and thus it
was inevitable that either revelation was discarded entirely
or that at least much of its content was thrown overboard
(Rationalism). Inconsistently, certain truths of Christianity
were retained—as the existence of God (Deism) and the immortality of the soul—while others were rejected. Christianity

schrift, 1784, quoted in *Werke in chron Reihenfolge* herausgegeben von Hartenstein, IV, pp 161 ff) M Mendelssohn, dealing with the same subject and
in the same *Monatsschrift*, arrives at the conclusion that enlightenment united
with civilization constitutes a nation's culture, while enlightenment as such is
"rational thinking and reasoning on the matters of human life, according to
their relative importance for man and their influence on his actions " See
Lazarus, *Ideale Fragen*, Berlin, 1878, pp 271 ff, for a criticism of the definitions of Kant and Mendelssohn Nicolai (*Beschreibung einer Reise durch Deutsch-
land*, 781) makes a distinction between "Kultur," "Politur," and *Aufklarung*,
and defines the last-named as the "understanding of all mattes of human life,
which are to be judged according to their bearing on the welfare of the individual and the community " For definitions of older political economists see
L Stein, *Verwaltungslehre*, V, p 34 C. F Bahrdt, the cynic among the
philosophers of the Enlightenment, considered it typical of the enlightened
man that "he followed in all things his own judgment " Of recent thinkers,
Erdmann gives a good analysis of the German Enlightenment, in his *Grundriss
der Geschichte der Philosophie*, II, §293, where he arrives at this definition·
"The Enlightenment (of the 18th century) strove to give to man, as to an
individual endowed with reason, the command over all things "

had ever maintained the intimate relationship existing between the *Lex orandi* and the *Lex agendi*, between belief and practice; but now faith was declared a matter of choice, and man was held responsible for his moral conduct only (Moralism). The Church was regarded, irrespective of her supernatural origin and her historical character, as an association of similarly-minded worshippers, and her teachings and laws were scorned as relics of the religious despotism of the Middle Ages. The State and Society were likewise reminded that the individual possessed certain inalienable birthrights; the relations between the government and its subjects were traced back to the social compact entered into in time immemorial. Yet this exalted sense of man's native rights did not prevent the 18th century from making the largest concessions to every State that placed its government machinery at the disposal of the philosophers of the Enlightenment. All social differences and distinctions were condemned as being opposed to the dogma: all men are born equal. That all class distinctions and all social relations be abolished—or, if that prove impossible, be much weakened, (Social Atomism)—was adjudged indispensable to the happiness of the race. Men no longer considered themselves citizens of one nation, but citizens of the world; and the day when the civilized peoples of Europe would be classed, no longer according to their respective nationalities, but according to their vocations, was hailed as the dawn of the era of universal blessedness (Cosmopolitanism). The historical development of certain conditions were, like the social relations, ignored: Ovid's line, "*Quæ non fecimus ipsi, vix ea nostra voco,*"[1] describes the attitude of the Enlightenment toward the historical foundations of human life. The period blindly applied the standard of the present to all the past. What appeared on the surface to be akin to the present, was taken over unconditionally and praised extravagantly; but no mercy was shown to any past movement that was out of harmony with the spirit of the 18th century. No historical period was so much misunderstood as the Middle Ages, the "Dark Ages," the "period of Roman obscurantism and Gothic grimaces;" and little wonder, for the spirit of the Ages of Faith is diametrically opposed to that of the skeptical and rationalistic Enlightenment. In keeping with the tendency to ignore all socio-historical ties, the end and aim of life was determined without regard to any higher relationship, but solely

[1] *Metam.,* 13, 140.

from the viewpoint of the needs of the individual (Individualism). Ethics confined itself to the study of the virtues; there were no longer any objective moral boons; and what was useful or merely pleasant, was often declared moral. Because the enlightening of the understanding was held to be mainly responsible for the morality and happiness of man, the feelings and the will were neglected, and most attention was given to the reasoning faculty. What entered into consciousness was of importance; the feelings, the moods, which remained subconscious, were of no importance (Intellectualism), and this trend accounts for the soulless and heartless spirit of the age. Logically the next step was to seek the foundations of psychical life, not in the broader circle of intellectual activity, but in the sense-impressions (Sensualism).

In all these fields the Enlightenment clarified only what was on the surface. It perceived, indeed, the superficial difficulties, but was at the same time wofully purblind to what was beneath the surface; and it is the depths, the deep truths, that have been muddied in this age Though the Enlightenment gloried in its opposition to all forms of barbarism, yet it was itself barbarous in its contempt for, and even destruction of, venerable monuments of the past.

3. The Renaissance had successively brought all the civilized nations of Europe under its influence, and the Enlightenment, following in its wake, assumed, despite its cosmopolitan tendency, a different character among the different nations. The Enlightenment, unlike the Renaissance, set out from England, where the religious conflict had raged longest and fiercest, bringing about at first the extremes of religious fanaticism, but eventually giving way to a reaction that led men to doubt the very objectivity of religious truth. The English Enlightenment attacked in particular the doctrines of the Church, and being thus confined almost exclusively to theological questions, it exerted, on the whole, but little influence outside the pale of scholars and philosophers. The French Enlightenment was neither so unwieldy nor so serious as the English; but with pleasant and engaging manners, it addressed itself first to the highest classes of society to whom it offered in the *Encyclopédie* much knowledge with little labor, next to the political leaders, and thus prepared the way for the great upheaval that devastated France before the end of the century. The German Enlightenment was deeply influenced by the form which the movement had taken first in England and then in France. It is,

like the English, theological and serious, but differs from it in that it spread, like the French, the new philosophy among the masses. It was, however, shorn of some of its baleful effects by the German Renaissance and the consequent revival of German patriotism.

Many considerations urged the leaders of the Enlightenment to take up the matter of education, and thus the "Philosophical Age" came to be known also as the "Pedagogical Age." The preceding ages had handed down educational materials enough to tempt the critical propensities of the Enlightenment. The higher schools were still conducted along Renaissance lines, and their teaching methods had been modified but little by the many improvements suggested by the didacticians. The elementary school, satisfied with catechism and primer, could not fit its pupils to take up the greatly augmented work of the trades and industries. Industrial and technical schools there were none. Moreover, for establishing a new basis of life—the dream of the Enlightenment—there could be no easier and smoother process than the instilling of the new principles into the young; for after the young generation had come to taste the new happiness, it would take only a short time until all the civilized world would be one in the enjoyment of the new boons. The principles of Christianity had been abandoned by society, and hence education must also be grounded on other principles than those of Christ. This reform of education did not appear difficult, because all socio-ethical and historical considerations had been cast aside, and consequently it was considered sufficient to adjust education to the needs only of the individual child. No more was required than that the school should make its pupils virtuous and happy, useful and healthy in mind and body. Because of its overestimation of intellectual work the age attached too much importance to instruction; and expected the improved teaching methods to produce far-reaching results.

CHAPTER XXVI.

The Content of the Education of the Enlightenment.

1. Theology had been the centre of early Christian education; Scholasticism, of medieval education; and philology, of the Renaissance schools. But the education of the Enlightenment lacks such a centre. Though the period vaunted itself as being

the philosophical age, yet philosophy was assuredly not its centre, for the philosophy of the time was not concerned with building up a connected system of views and principles, but collected only the elements for such a system. The natural sciences, which were now, for the first time in history, treated as a cultural subject, were prevented by their very nature from being the centre of general education. The basic principle of the Enlightenment expressed no content; it implied only the formal directions, that the reasoning powers are to be developed and that useful knowledge is to be acquired. These precepts did, indeed, suggest the modification of the educational content of the past, but not the creation of a new content; and, in fact, the Enlightenment did little more than adopt the encyclopedic tendency (adjusted to its own critical attitude) of the Renaissance

The theology of the older education was wholly discarded by only the most radical representatives of French Enlightenment. Diderot, a Theist in his exoteric writings, was a pronounced atheist in his esoteric works; and Rousseau preserved only a shadow of theology in his educational system, for he would have the child instructed in a purely natural religion. Among the Protestants there were too many intermediate stages between the spirit of the age and the orthodox teaching to allow the extremists to banish religion from the schools. Even the rationalistic school of Wolff was mildly interested in theology, although the content of Faith was at the mercy of their subjective criticism. And Pietism also, though intended originally to supply a real need of religion, was in its later development subversive of the authority of dogma and bore the brunt of the attacks made on Christianity. The Pietists had found their only guarantee for the truth of dogma in their own conviction of the need of justification, and hence they were ready to receive the doctrine of the rationalist who made the subjective mind the criterion of all truth [1] Still, the Pietists served, to a certain extent, as a breastwork for the defence of Christianity. They were most zealous in the service of the Lord, and could therefore not be induced to accept the ultimate conclusion from their first principle—the denial of objective truth. The German Enlightenment did away with dogma, sacrificed all that was characteristic of pure Christianity, united under the cloak of the fashionable Deism the different denominations, and permitted canting

[1] Erdmann, *Grundriss der Geschichte der Philosophie*, II, §293, 2

and unctuous devotions to crowd out the Sacred Scriptures and the time-honored hymns that had breathed a virile Faith. The religious instruction in Basedow's Philanthropinum in Dessau was based on the principle that "we owe the All-Father the service of righteous conduct;" it respected the religious beliefs of Christians, Jews, and Mohammedans, though opposing the "irreligionist;" and thus it may be considered typical of what the German Enlightenment accomplished in its attack on the theological element of education.

2. It is difficult to analyze the attitude of the 18th century toward the ancient classics, for while certain phases of the ancient world appealed strongly to the Enlightenment, there still remained a wide gulf between the two periods. However, the teachings of the wise men of Greece and Rome seemed to offer what the new age was striving for—a purely rational and natural religion that had no need of revelation or theology. Thus Seneca was esteemed for his praise of virtue, and Socrates was celebrated as the master of reasoning. The old republics were idealized, and fostered the enthusiasm for liberty. The cosmopolitanism of the ancients encouraged kindred sentiments in the moderns. It was recognized that the ancients offered the broad and liberal humanity that was lost when the coming of Christ divided the race into the two classes of Christians and unbelievers. Men were impatient to break away from the bondage of the past and to return to the breast of mother earth, and looked upon the works of Homer as picturing such ideal conditions as haunted them in their dreams. Hence Homer gave a new meaning to poetry. Similar points of contact were discovered between the Enlightenment and neo-classical Humanism. The latter had begun and the former now continued the war against the Middle Ages and their traditions. The criticism of Valla, the satire of Erasmus, the worldly-wise skepticism of Montaigne, all these were revived during the Enlightenment to assist in the universal reconstruction. Yet, notwithstanding all this kinship of spirit, the Enlightenment never entered into so close a relationship with the ancients as the Renaissance. Men were too proudly conscious of their own glorious achievements to devote themselves as unreservedly to the study of the classics as the Humanists had done. The opinion prevailed that the Enlightenment was superior in every regard to antiquity, and that only a limited study of the classics was at all desirable. Diderot loved the classics and could grow

10

enthusiastic over Seneca, yet in his *Plan of a University*[1] he made scant provision for the classical studies. D'Alembert, also a deep student of the classics, makes sport of the classical studies, which, as he observes, teach *"parler sans rien dire,"*[2] and he considers the time given to the writing of Latin as so much time lost for the real improvement of the mind.[3] Rousseau admits that he admires Plutarch, but drops the classics from his pedagogical airship as so much ballast Kant, it is true, concedes that the study of the classics "promotes the union of the sciences, and assists in giving man the character of humanity: polished manners, ready speech, and a pleasant address;" yet he says, "It is absurd to deem the ancient writers superior to the moderns, as though the world were decadent and all modern things, therefore, inferior to the ancient."[4] The German educators of the Enlightenment scorned the classical studies as being naught else than unprofitable drudgery. Trapp exclaims, "Would to God that the teacher had to master only his mother-tongue; but even if we could make education perfect, we should still expect in vain to have Latin and French banished from Germany "[5] Basedow did not hesitate to admit that Latin was taught in his Philanthropinum merely out of respect for the wishes of the parents of his pupils. The utilitarian trend of the period found little connection between ancient literature and the practical needs of the day, and the tendency to develop as early as possible the reasoning faculties blinded the educators to the importance of developing the language consciousness. The latter point marks a direct contrast between the Enlightenment and the Renaissance The language studies held supreme sway in the Renaissance, and the *fari posse* was regarded as the crowning achievement of a liberal education But the Enlightenment was so taken up with the things of sense and with the purely abstract thought as almost to overlook the field of language, which is intermediate between the two, belonging as it does to both the senses and the mind. Only in the light of this general tendency can it be explained how Kant, when analyzing the perceptive faculty,

[1] Rosenkranz, *Diderots Leben und Werke*, Leipzig, 1866, II, pp. 335 ff
[2] *Encyclopédie*, s v *Collège*
[3] *Discours préliminaire* of the *Encyclopédie*
[4] *Werke in chron Reihenfolge* herausgegeben von Hartenstein, VIII, p 46, and VII, p 262; cf. Willmann's edition of Kant's *Pädagogik*, Leipzig, 1873, p 7.
[5] *Versuch einer Pädagogik*, 1780, § 102.

could ignore the natural guide in any such inquiry—the language consciousness.

The situation in the schools, however, remained practically unchanged, and their Humanistic traditions suffered but little from the theorizing of the Enlightenment. Rollin in France and Gesner and Ernesti in Germany were able defenders of the old education. Yet withal they knew how to meet the new demand: "Things instead of words." Rollin's statement: "*Ce qui doit dominer dans les classes, c'est l'explication,*" and Gesner's rule: "*Verborum disciplina a rerum cognitione nunquam separanda,*" are expressive of the realism of the Humanists, which held the day against the realism of the Philanthropinists. The Philanthropinists tried to exclude the classics from the schools, for nothing was to be taught but what was of the present and, therefore, directly useful. Their efforts, however, were thwarted, because the new German classicism introduced an idealistic conception of education and thus defeated all their plans. The creations of the German classicists demonstrated that the ancient classics were not a heap of learned rubbish, but still a very vital element and one that offered such educational and cultural opportunities as the age stood sorely in need of. Lessing reinstated Aristotle's *Poetics*, and Herder showed how the classical studies ennoble man's heart and feelings. Schiller appealed to the enemies of the classical studies with this argument: "You call the languages of Greece and Rome dead languages, but all that lives in your mother-tongue has come from Greek and Latin." The poetry of Schiller and Goethe, which dealt so extensively with antique subjects, popularized the ideas and the mythology of the ancients and rendered them more familiar to the masses than they had been even in the Renaissance period. By being introduced into the schools, this poetry was a telling factor in favor of the classical studies. German literature—much more than English literature or the literature of any of the Latin peoples—is a sealed book to any one unacquainted with the ancient classics. Thus the German higher schools suffered no harm from the attacks of the Philanthropinists. On the contrary, they gained by adding Greek, which had been the chief inspiration of the German neo-classicists. But with the encyclopedic tendencies of the period many modern subjects had also to be added to the course of study, and the ancient classics never regained the absolute sway that they had exercised in the old Latin schools. The studies of the Protestant gymnasium, as organized under the influence of the educational reforms of the 18th century, represent a compromise between the curricula of Melanchthon and Basedow.[1]

3. The encyclopedic tendency of the 18th century was originally closely allied with that of the preceding period. Johann Matthias Gesner, the celebrated Gottingen professor and trainer of teachers, tried seriously in his Latin lectures to preserve the traditions of the latter Renaissance and to meet, besides, the new demands of his own time. He confessed that the chief defect of the old schools was the neglect of the mother-tongue, and this he would remedy by adding the study of modern languages, especially of the mother-tongue, to the classical studies. He also demanded that geography and history be studied beside literature. Geography he describes as *"historiæ omnis diverso respectu prima pars, atrium, fundus, lux;"* and history, he says, can teach practical wisdom most effectively by entering into details. He also insisted that mathematics be studied, for "he who slights mathematics, deprives himself of one eye." Gesner was in favor of beginning the course with Greek and Homer's poems, but saw a practical difficulty in the *"rationes scholarum, quibus quodammodo ratio ecclesiæ innititur."*[2] A somewhat similar union of old and new elements is presented in Pierre Bayle's widely-read *Dictionnaire historique et critique* (1696). Bayle is reminiscent of the old school in that he "passes his life within the walls and the shadows of libraries, in the company of learned journals and correspondence," and "regards the

---

[1] K L v Roth quoted by Lubker in Schmid, *Enzyklopadie*, s v *Gelehrtenschulwesen*, II, p 682

[2] Gesner's *Primæ lineæ isagoges in eruditionem universalem*, ed by Niclas, 1774 and 1786, 2 vols, contain in the "proœmium" a "brevis recensus dicendorum," a résumé of the older encyclopedias, and "præcepta discendi generalia" The first part treats "de linguis seu philologia" the mother-tongue, Latin, Greek, modern languages (§ 9 sq); of poetry (§222 sq), of music and painting (§277 sq), of oratory (§418 sq) The second part deals with history, geography is treated in §418 sq , chronology (§450 sq); universal history (§481 sq), the φιλοσοφίας μητρόπολις, which is divided into "historia civilis, ecclesiastica, litteraria, miscella" The third part deals with philosophy first, its history (§662 sq), next, psychology, ontology, natural theology, logic, and ethics (§823-1536) The work proves Gesner a man of vast erudition, and if he has the interest of an earlier age in literary curiosities, he never lets it interfere with his practical purpose Unlike Morhof (see *supra*, ch XXII), he observes due moderation in the selection of his materials, and a certain gentlemanly refinement saves him from the disorderly arrangement of the earlier polyhistorians Herder's criticism of the book (printed in his *Sophron*) was unfair on many points The *Isagoge* was, in matter of fact, the divide between two periods of classicism.

world as raw material for books." But he is at the same time the "Father of the Age of Criticism," for he was the first to subject all traditions to the withering test of the skeptic's doubts and to examine everything in the white light of cold reason. His work is noteworthy as being the first of the encyclopedic dictionaries in which all subjects were treated in alphabetic order. This method was now universally adopted and rendered the new encyclopedias more serviceable and more popular than the old, which had invariably been arranged according to some preconceived system. This change in form is significant. The unwieldy, though scholarly, arrangement of the earlier day had to give way to practical usefulness; the content had to be made easily accessible; and the labyrinth of the old school, the *orbis doctrinæ* is done away with, and in its stead came the hundreds and thousands of externally unconnected articles, which offered, we may say, so many pathways to the information desired.

The greatest of the new encyclopedias is the *Encyclopédie ou dictionnaire raisonné des sciences, des arts et des métiers*, edited by Diderot and d'Alembert. It was begun in 1751 and completed in 1772 in 17 volumes folio of text and 11 volumes of illustrations, and by 1774 it was translated into four languages. The gigantic undertaking owed its inception to the modest plan of making Ephraim Chambers' *Cyclopedia* (2 vols., Dublin, 1728) accessible to French readers, but in its final form it represents the combined efforts of the leaders of the French Enlightenment. On the one hand, it purported to present in an accessible form all the arts, sciences, and achievements of the race; but on the other hand, it was intended to steep the whole content of the circle of thought in the philosophy of the Enlightenment. The *Encyclopédie* was at once a storehouse of modern learning and a battery of guns levelled at the "last remains of the Middle Ages." It was thus a monument to the industry and the refined taste of the French, as well as the mouthpiece of the "*sainte confédération contre le fanatisme et la tyrannie*," as Cabanis called the circle of the Encyclopedists. The plan of the work, as outlined in Diderot's prospectus and in d'Alembert's *Discours préliminaire*, is based on Bacon's division of the faculties of the soul. The principle of history is in the memory, for history records past events; the principle of the fine arts is in the imagination, for they present sensuous images; and the principle of philosophy is in the human reason, for its function is to judge everything. It is significant that the principle of the division was based on man, who made the division, which is merely the division had been based on the distinctions suggested by the matter that was treated. The reason for this change is not far to seek. The Enlightenment being out and out nominalistic, recognized no content as being valuable in itself. Again, in dealing with a science one must connect the criticism of it with the history of the respective science, for in its changes and developments a science is, one may say, criticizing itself. Due attention is given not only to the fine arts, but also to the trades and industries; inventors are declared the benefactors of the race, although historians have only too often failed to acknowledge this indebtedness, while extolling the victorious general, whose glorious deeds are often no more than the butchering of his fellowmen ' The *Encyclopédie* was intended to develop the true principles of things, to describe their relations, and promote knowledge and learning by increasing the number of scholars, artists, and lovers of science It was to be like a landscape that is unlimited in extent and that contains hills, cliffs, rivers, forests, etc., all of which receive the light from the same heavens above, but some more and others less, because some are in the foreground, others in the middle of the scene, while still others disappear in the distance. The *Encyclopédie* was to be for the educated man a library of all the arts and sciences, and for the specialist a library of all learning outside his own special subject.

While the plan of the *Encyclopédie* assured some unity in the treatment of the diversified content, and while the scholarship of its contributors guaranteed its solid character, the popular encyclopedists, particularly in Germany, produced only disjointed compilations of commonplace materials Their favorite occupation was the making of children's encyclopedias containing useful and entertaining information. As the *Orbis pictus* embodied in an elementary form much of the pansophy of the 17th century, so the *Elementary Book* ("Elementarwerk") of Basedow was the textbook to be used, to the age of 15 years, for teaching the polymathy of the Enlightenment. It is avowedly an imitation of the *Orbis pictus*, but written in an entirely different spirit, as it substitutes for the Christian views of Comenius the Deism of the period and also discards Comenius' basic relationship to language instruction In form the *Elementary Book* is likewise inferior to the *Orbis pictus*. Where Comenius was concise, Basedow is diffuse and wordy; and the illustrations, too, are hardly an improvement over Comenius' work. In their treatment of the different subjects they follow no system whatever, and in presenting the non-sensuous in pictures they are more ingeniously vulgar than even the illustrated *Janua*.[1]

4. The tendency of the 18th century to make knowledge a common property of the masses showed itself not only in the publication of encyclopedias, but also in the popular treatment of individual sciences. The gulf that had hitherto existed between the books for the learned and those for the general public, was bridged over, and the writers appealed less to the select circle of the learned and more to the educated public in general, and regarded less the objective value of a book than its appeal to the multitude. This change cannot be explained solely on the ground of the prevailing tendency toward the enlightenment of the masses, but is the result, at least in part, of the development of the national literatures, for these now employed prose (after having begun with poetry in the Renaissance) for both artistic and scientific purposes. As long as Latin was the language of science, the scholar rested satisfied with seeing his books in the hands of the learned few. But now that the sciences had come to speak English, French, and German, the representatives of higher learning strove to catch the ear of the populace, both by offering matter of present-day interest and by writing in a style suited to the taste of the man in the street. This nationalizing and popularizing of the sciences had, however, some obvious disadvantages. The solidarity of scientific research, established in the Middle Ages and fostered by the culture of the Renaissance, was now destroyed, and certain departments of learning were, in consequence, isolated from the rest—German philosophy has ever since developed independ-

---

[1] The cost of publication of the *Elementary Book* was defrayed by popular subscription. Money poured in from all sides—from Germany, Switzerland, the northern countries, from high and low—and the work appeared in 1774 and 1785 with illustrations by Chodowiecki. The nine books (3 vols.) of the 1785 edition treat the following subjects: B. I, "Only for older friends of children": pedagogical rules, sketch of the schools of Alethinia (*i. e.*, land of truth, a pedagogical Utopia), etc.; B. II, "Of sundry matters, especially of man and the soul"; here is the much-abused sexual instruction for children; B. III, "Generally useful logic"; B. IV, of religion, a popular treatise on "natural religion" and a sketch of the historical religions; B. V. ethics: proverbs, stories, fables, precepts of virtue; B. VI, of the occupations and classes of men; B. VII, the elements of history: a) first principles of government, illustrated, in part, by stories; b) and c) geography; d) and e) matters from universal history in chronological arrangement; f) mythology and fables; g) heraldic lore; h) meaning and connection of the historical sciences; B. VIII, and IX, natural sciences. A supplementary volume, the fourth, containing B. X, ... essentials of grammar and rhetoric.   96 plates by Chodowiecki ...... B. ... II-IX.

ently of Anglo-French thought. Further effects are the striving for the popularity of the hour, and sham education which is the inevitable result of sham science. Fichte denounced, in his attack on Fr. Nicolai, the dangers inherent in popular science: "Men were proud that they had at last learned to write German, and were anxious to have everybody understand what they wrote, and so they wrote on every conceivable subject in such a manner that a knowledge of German did, indeed, suffice to understand their books. The style was the sum and substance of a book, and the content must needs adapt itself to the expression. If something could not be expressed so as to be perfectly intelligible to the lady half-asleep at her dressing table, it was not worth saying; and as all that was learned was learned merely for the purpose of saying it, it was not learned at all; so that eventually all abstruse and difficult questions were scorned as hair-splitting and over-refinement. In brief, to popularize all science became the order of the day, and henceforth popularity was the criterion of the true, the useful, and of all that was worth knowing." Still, it were unfair to consider only the dark side of this popularizing tendency. There were some real advantages connected with this passing of the sciences from the narrow confinement of the schools. That the sciences were thus brought into intimate relationship with the life and spirit of the people, and that, consequently, scientific research and the practical and public life of the world began to influence each other—these facts could not fail to improve modern education

Popular philosophy assumed the leading rôle in this movement. Locke is the father of English Sensualism, and his philosophy addressed itself less to scholars and thinkers than to those who found pleasure in reasoning out simple problems Many French writers followed his example and proclaimed themselves "philosophers for the world;" the society of Paris and its æsthetes constituted their audience, and without these they could not have existed In Germany philosophy proceeds from the schools and finally also returns to them, but during the intervening period it exerted an influence far beyond the schools, and even when apparently confined to the schoolroom, it continued to influence the national life indirectly Wolff's system prevailed in the lecture halls during the first half of the century, and the eclecticism of Mendelssohn, Garve, Engel, and others is based on it To some extent, the philosophy of Kant leads back to the school reform, but at the same time it stimulated and even aroused whole classes of the nation. Philosophy in general exerted a deep influence on the education of the period: it supplied some of the content of education and also outlined some of the educational methods. This was to be expected of the philosophy of a period that claimed the right to inquire how the individual might, through enlightenment and the fullest development of his own personality, obtain happiness, or, as Kant would have it, the autonomous fulfillment of duty. Such a philosophy did more than promote the development of pedagogy, for it had itself a pedagogical tendency which, though confined to the education of the individual, still fostered a lively interest in education as such.

5. Owing to the influence of popular philosophy, three groups of sciences received a new form and were thus added to the list of cultural studies: the historico-political sciences, polite literature, and the natural sciences. Though the world-view of the Enlightenment lacked all historical basis, and though the period did not think it necessary to look in the past for the causes of present conditions, still the universal tendency of the time to throw light on each and everything under the sun could not ignore the claims of history. The Enlightenment undertook a complete revision of the traditional conception and treatment of history; a deeper influence on life was assigned to natural conditions and environment; the development of intelligence was asserted to be the main factor of historical progress, and the wise men of the race, the inventors and discoverers, received as large a treatment as kings, statesmen, and generals. The so-called "history of civilization" (*Kulturgeschichte*) is an invention of the 18th century. The term "philosophy of history" dates also from the same period, but denotes, not a new field of speculation, but only that the human reason is to deal with the facts of history, and that the theological considerations of earlier times are, therefore, out of place in the interpretation of the past. Voltaire's *Essai sur les moeurs et l'esprit des nations* is the first work written in the new spirit, and set the fashion for all similar undertakings. Former historians had never given much attention to customs and morals, and on this head contented themselves with giving a few anecdotes for the curious. Now, however, this department of history was correlated with the present, and was made the occasion for general observations and reflections, some of a high order, but many, too, just plain palaver and lip wisdom. Imitating Voltaire, the salons looked with admiring eyes upon the civilization of China, had

only a smile of contempt for the superstition, the misery, and
the crimes of the "Dark Ages," and glowed with enthusiasm
for their own progress in the industries and arts of peace. After
Rousseau had pointed to the primitive forest as being the starting-point in history, the philosophers made the primitive races
the subject of intensive studies, for here they hoped to find the
beginnings of civilization, and the ladies of the salons grew
enthusiastic over the Patagonians and South Sea Islanders.

Montesquieu, hailed by Madame Pompadour as the "Law-
giver of Europe," is responsible for the popularizing of the
political sciences. Of his *Esprit des lois* 20 editions appeared in
18 months, and of its influence on the nation a contemporary
writes: "It has revolutionized the spirit of the nation, all men of
talent are now discussing political matters, and politics has become a department of philosophy "[1] The higher classes studied
the English constitution, the rights of parliaments, and also
questions of political economy as well as the opposition between
the physiocrats and the mercantilists; and thus political writers
had a large reading public. Rousseau introduced a fantastic
and radical tendency into the discussion of the problems of the
State and society He also dragged in the large subject of education, and declared it to be the best means for correcting the
abuses of civilization. The French, however, soon abandoned
the discussion of educational problems in favor of politico-social
questions. But the Germans studied the subject of education
the more: a special literature of education was the result, and
poets and philosophers, scholars and statesmen, wrote upon
education.

6. Polite literature, even if held in high repute in the Renaissance, remained restricted to the higher schools until the
Enlightenment set it free. The classics of both ancient and
modern literatures were now interpreted according to the canons
of a refined and cultured taste The new criticism complemented poetics and rhetoric by controlling the literary output
of the day, but too often it went beyond the mere control and
directed—and not always aright—the course of literature. In
the field of criticism the need of fixed principles gave birth to
the new science of æsthetics,[2] whose first principles were taken

[1] Grimm in the *Litterarische Korrespondenz*, I, 2, p 74, quoted by H Hett-
ner, *Literaturgeschichte des 18. Jahrhunderts*, Brunswick, 1865, II, p 260
[2] The word was first used for the science of the beautiful by Baumgarten,
a disciple of Wolff, in his *Æsthetica* (1750) to designate the science of sensuous
knowledge, the goal of which is beauty, in contrast with logic whose goal is

from the philosophy then taught in the schools—Batteux followed the teachings of Aristotle; and Baumgarten, those of Aristotle and Christian Wolff. The German classicists had soon left these beginnings behind, and created their own organon of appreciation and interpretation. They possessed both the power of poetic creation and the delicate and discriminating sense of interpreting their own works, and consequently their writings have proved a national school, not only for the enjoyment of beauty, but also for its artistic interpretation. The ancients, as well as the writers of the Renaissance, had confined themselves in æsthetical criticism to poetry and oratory. But in the period of the Enlightenment the works of the arts of design were also examined critically and studied æsthetically, and thus the history of art began to be cultivated extensively. Winckelmann led the way in organizing the archeological materials, and unearthed the wonderland of ancient art. Lessing was the pioneer in the comparative study of art. Herder and Goethe demonstrated the universal character of poetry and art. Schiller, basing his first principles on Kant, tried to outline the moral aims of art, and thus connected æsthetics with practical philosophy, while the others made it a department of the history of civilization. All these efforts are controlled by the subjectivism of the period. The beautiful is not considered as a good which the human mind strives to create and which is itself a reflection of higher and greater things; instead, it is regarded merely as an instrument for perfecting the faculties of the individual. Winckelmann stands alone in upholding the former and deeper view, first propounded by Plato; and the fine historical sense distinguishing his history of art proves him superior to all his contemporaries.

Philosophical, æsthetical, and practical considerations prompted the educators of the period to add the natural sciences to the course of general education. The materialists declared the study of nature to be the basis of the science of man and the foundation of their world-view, and, to meet their objections, their opponents had likewise to study the natural sciences. The salons showed a deep interest in the observatories

truth. "Kant objected to this use of the term, and used transcendental æsthetic to denote the *a priori* principle of sensible experience, namely time and space. Hegel (1820-1830) elaborated a science of the fine arts which he called with some protest *Æsthetik*, and won so much approval for his work that since his time the word in its widest application to all fine art has . . . W . . . *International Dictionary* . . . . "

and laboratories, for of them they expected a solution of the
most difficult problems. The spirited and graceful style of the
French naturalists was an important factor in popularizing the
natural sciences Buffon was the first to attempt what then
might well have seemed impossible, to treat a science (hitherto
regarded as dry and as Greek to every one except the savant)
in a manner interesting and intelligible to the general reader.
Yet he succeeded in his ambitious project, for his natural history
is French literature; and his success illustrates the truth of his
contention that a writer's immortality is based, not on his
wealth of knowledge, nor on the mass of astounding facts he
has recorded, nor the discoveries he has made—because these
things are external to the man himself—but that his fame rests
on what is most truly himself—his style. At the same time the
Encyclopédie also spread broadcast much valuable knowledge of
the applied sciences, and prepared men to accept Bacon's view
of the end of man: to conquer nature by learning its secrets.
Educators began to recognize that the natural sciences had
grown to be a power which had to be reckoned with in practical
life, and the leaders of the Enlightenment perceived the need of
establishing a proper relationship between the mechanical arts
(which had been much advanced by the discoveries made in the
natural sciences) and general education

CHAPTER XXVII

The School Reform of the 18th Century

1 The very principle of the Enlightenment prompted a
reform of the school system. And a reform was actually needed:
the forms of government, the administration of justice, economic
relations, were being reconstructed all over Europe, and hence
the system of education had also to be reorganized in order to
correspond to the changed conditions. Some changes, though
not to the same extent, were made in the school systems of all
the European countries. Some nations remained faithful to the
educational traditions of the past, and allowed the educational
reformers only so much range as was compatible with them.
But other countries broke away from their educational traditions, and tried out novel and revolutionary experiments A
third class of nations enjoyed the advantage of a connecting

bond between the old and the new, so that the continuity and solidarity with the past was not destroyed; and in these countries the reforms introduced did not interfere with the uniform and steady development of the schools.

It is remarkable that the schools of England, though that country was the first home of the Enlightenment and of the new ideas in education, were only slightly influenced by the reform movement. Locke had recommended that the schools for the sons of the gentry should attend more to what was practically useful than to the study of the classics.[1] But he found as few sympathizers with this view as with the other, to substitute private education for the public schools; for the Latin schools continued in universal favor, and David Williams' plan of reform, based on Locke, found more interest among the Philanthropinists of Germany than among his own countrymen.[2] Adam Smith, the father of English political economy, favored the education of the masses as increasing the wealth of the nation, but met with little encouragement when he suggested a system of national education. His followers fared no better than he. The English people were too jealous of the power of the State to grant the monopoly of education or the control of the individual to such an extent as to enforce attendance at the public schools. The education of the lower classes was left to the initiative of private organizations, and the poor schools were not considered as a part of the state system of education, but as belonging to the charitable activity of individual societies.[3] "The Society for Promoting Christian Knowledge," founded in 1698, opened free schools for the poor; the Sunday schools, existing since 1761, were much assisted and increased in number by the "Society for the Support and Encouragement of Sunday Schools," founded in 1785 by Robert Raikes. Both kinds of schools did not go beyond the scope of the early Christian elementary school, but in organization they were hardly equal to the parochial and sexton schools of the Continent.

---

[1] Cf. J. H. Newman, *Idea of a University*, New York, 1902, pp. 158-160.

[2] *A Treatise on Education, in which the general Method pursued in the public Institutions of Europe; and particularly in those of England; that of Milton, Locke, Rousseau, and Helvetius are considered, and a more practicable and useful one proposed.* By David Williams, London, Payne, 1774. A German translation, by Trapp, was published in 1781, and was reviewed in the *Allgemeine deutsche Bibliothek*, Bd. 51, I. Hälfte. The English original was reviewed in the *Monthly Review or Literary Journal*, Vol. II, London, 1774, pp. 254-260.

[3] Stein, *Verwaltungslehre*, V, p. 93.

2. The reform of the French schools was not yet complete when the Revolution set in. The new tendencies and ideas had found favor with the higher classes of French society, and were fully developed in the salons—the *bureaux d'esprit* as they were humorously called. The wits of society were interested not only in political events, the latest books, and the new works of art, but also in the deep problems of the sciences. "Philosophical inquiry was the centre of interest in the salons, and all that met there, wished to arrive, by means of public and many-sided discussion, at clear views Moral and æsthetical questions were always popular, but in the early fifties philosophy commanded the greatest interest, and in the sixties this gave way to political economy, and in the seventies, to questions of government."[1] The Enlightenment of the salons consisted in being at home in the questions of the day and in the world-view that had done away with all traditions. This Enlightenment was of such a character as forbade its being introduced into the schools of the young, even the most advanced thinkers could not seriously entertain the plan of making the young as frivolous and as critical in art and religion as were the *mesdames* and the *messieurs* of the salons. Thus the representatives of the most advanced thought had no direct interest in the schools, and left these to the hands of the statesmen to do with them as best suited their own plans. The expulsion of the Jesuits, the "Revolution of 1762," was made the occasion for inaugurating a series of radical reforms. All education was to be secularized, though the unity of the school system as handed down from the past was to be retained; but the control was to be taken from the clergy and to be committed to a "secular hierarchy" which derived all its authority from the State.[2] The plan of President Rolland, submitted to Parliament in 1768, adopted, with regard to the subject-matter of teaching, the principles of Rollin and the Jansenistic traditions of Port-Royal. Four grades of school are mentioned: the village school; the preparatory college (*demi-colléges*) with two or three classes and instruction in religion, ethics, the mother-tongue, and the elements of Greek and Latin; the full college (*colléges de plein exercice*); and the university. The teachers are to be seculars

---

[1] Rosenkranz, *Diderot*, II, p 83

[2] H Compayré, *Histoire critique des doctrines de l'éducation en France*, Paris, 1879, II, pp 239 sq. and 273; "Les parlamentaires empruntaient aux Jésuites ce que l'institut des Jésuites avait d'excellent: l'unité et la suite dans les méthodes, la discipline et la hiérarchie "

exclusively and to be trained in an *école normale des professeurs;* the capital of the country is to be the governing centre of the school system; and the *bureau de correspondance*, the centre of administration. La Chalotais' plan for a national system of education[1] is even more closely correlated with the tendencies of the period. He regards the greatest possible public benefit as the aim of public education. The national principle should hold in religious instruction also. The system of morality and its teachings are to be secularized. Nature is to be the guiding star in instruction, and all schooling should begin with the training of the senses. The ancient languages offer nothing of permanent and solid worth, and chief attention should be given to the study of modern languages. Of history, too, the modern periods are the most useful; the children should learn reading, writing, and reasoning from a collection of stories to be written by philosophers. La Chalotais is opposed to the education of the masses, because it would estrange the laboring classes from their proper vocation; and he attacks the Brothers of the Christian Schools for teaching the children of the poor to read and write instead of how to use the plane and file. He considers the carrying out of his ideas as fraught with no difficulties, the only requirement being a supply of teachers and books, but particularly of the latter, which are to be compiled (*compiler*) by men of thought; the King would only have to approve his plans, and in two years all schools would be in working order. In reality, however, it took almost two decades before the reforms were carried out, and even then the movement was impeded by the stormy times and wasted its energy on fruitless efforts; and it was only at the beginning of the 19th century that the new ideas could finally be realized.

3. Each new phase of the Revolution gave birth to some new plan for the national educational system which was to be tried out first in France and later in all other countries. All these plans—shortlived they all were—are now again of some interest, since the present educational policy of the French is reviving some of these earlier projects. The views of Mirabeau, as expressed in his posthumous work, *Travail sur l'instruction publique*, are surprisingly moderate. He demands liberty of instruction for the secular teachers, but would grant the same

---

[1] *Essai d'éducation nationale ou plan d'étude pour la jeunesse* par Messire Louis René de Caradeux de la Chalotais, Procureur-général du Roi au Parlement de Bretagne, Genève, 1763.

to the religious teachers also; the State can not make instruction compulsory, because it can not impose greater burdens than are necessary for the liberty and security of all. He attaches little importance to the unity of the educational system. All higher schools are to be patterned after a national lyceum The secondary schools are to devote two years to the ancient languages, two to the study of oratory, and two to the study of philosophy and the exact sciences. The Constituent Assembly commissioned Talleyrand to outline a system of education to correspond to the direction laid down by the Constitution of Sept. 3, 1791. "Il sera créé et organisé une Instruction publique, commune à tous les citoyens, gratuite à l'égard des parties d'enseignement indispensables pour tous les hommes et dont les établissements seront distribués graduellement dans un rapport combiné avec la division du royaume." Talleyrand proposed a system of four grades of schools: the primary, or canton, schools are to teach all that is necessary for each and everyone; the secondary, or district, schools should develop more fully the mental faculties, the department schools are to fit their students for the four learned professions, and the "Institut" is to be the capstone of the whole system All schools must adopt the *Catechism of the Rights of Man*, and the higher schools must teach mathematics, the art of thinking, the history of free peoples, and philosophical ethics. The schools are open to all, and every citizen has the right to open a school that is not contrary to law The Memoir was read Sept 10th and 11th, and on the 30th of the same month the Assembly was dissolved. It was succeeded by the Legislative Assembly, which formulated the problem thus: "L'instruction est le besoin de tous, la société doit favoriser de tout son pouvoir le progrès de la raison publique et mettre l'instruction à la portée de tous les citoyens." The Legislative Assembly entrusted Condorcet with the making of a new plan, and his plan was submitted April 20, 1792 It is inspired by the "principles of philosophy which are free from the bonds of tradition and, therefore, enlighten the present age, but promise for the future even greater light, thereby assuring to future generations the necessary progress of the human race." The education of the whole country is apportioned among five classes of schools. Every village of 100 inhabitants is to have a primary school, and every city of 4,000 or more inhabitants, a secondary school. In the secondary schools the following subjects are to be taught: orthography; history of France and the neighboring countries; the elements of the mechanical arts, of commercial science, and drawing; ethics; sociology; applied mathematics; and natural history. Institutes, to the number of 110, are to teach the useful sciences, particularly mathematics and physics, but of Latin only so much as is needed for reading Latin books, and, in the opinion of Condorcet, a smattering of Latin will suffice for that. Nine lyceums are to take the place of the universities, and the national society of the arts and sciences is the capstone of the educational system. All instruction is founded on the virtues of the citizen, and, consequently, belongs to the State; but education is still left to the individual. The National Convention abolished even the latter limitation, and so made the State omnipotent in matters educational. Lepelletier submitted, on July 13, 1793, a plan for a nation-wide compulsory system of education modelled after the Spartan system. Of this plan Robespierre said that it was inspired by the genius of humanity.

Not one of these projects, which posthaste succeeded one another, was ever carried out. However, the universities, colleges, and the parochial elementary schools were suppressed by the National Convention. Of the educational foundations of the Revolution, only two have continued in existence: the *Ecole normale* in Paris and the *Ecole polytechnique*. After order had been restored, it was found necessary to build up a system of schools from the very foundation. From the ruins of the French school system arose the Napoleonic Université which embraced all the educational institutions of the country, and which was, in a way, a magnificent creation, since it contained some of the best elements of the past: the co-operation of the clergy, the classical studies, the system of faculties, and represented at the same time a centralized state system of education comprising the elementary school and the university.[1]

4. The French Enlightenment gave the impulse to the reform of the schools of Latin Europe as well as of Poland and Russia. There was an interchange of educational ideas between

---

[1] The educational schemes of the Revolution have been the subject of the most varied and even contradictory criticism: Théry (*Histoire de l'éducation en France*, Paris, 1861, II, p. 188) does not think them deserving of being looked into: "On n'étudie pas le vide, on n'analyse pas le néant." Compayré treats them at great length (*Histoire critique des doctrines de l'éducation en France*, Paris, 1879, II, p. 281 sq.); but in his extravagant praise he goes to the opposite extreme. Much information is contained in Guillaume's article *Convention* in Buisson's *Dictionnaire de pédagogie*, and in Dreyfus-Brisac's article in the *Revue internationale de l'enseignement*, 1881, N. . .

France and Sardinia: the reforms of Charles Emmanuel (1730-1773) were suggested by the centralizing tendencies of the French kings, and the University of Turin, founded by the Sardinian king in 1771, led Napoleon to establish in France a similar educational corporation.[1] In Naples, Genovesi and Filangieri promoted a centralized system of secular schools; the former was actuated more by reasons of national economy, and the latter, by his view of state rights. But both were one in pointing to the ancients as models in this regard. Genovesi, following Plato (*Polit*, p. 261), considers the art of government as analogous to the keeping of herds (ἀγελαιοτροφία) and would introduce the athletic games and the police surveillance of the ancients. Filangieri's plan is largely based on Spartan models.[2] These two writers exerted a deep influence on the reforms of Tanucci. In Portugal, Pombal was most violent in reforming educational conditions. In 1759 he expelled the Jesuits from their 24 colleges and 17 residences. Their place was to be filled by 27 schools of philosophy, 21 chairs of rhetoric, history, and literature, 8 Greek schools, and 250 elementary Latin schools. A bureau of education, under the presidency of the Rector of Coimbra University, was to control all schools; and a special tax, "subsidio litterario," was levied to defray the expenses of the schools.[3] In Spain, Aranda and Campomanes worked in the same spirit, though with somewhat less violence, for they did not disturb the universities, nor the teaching orders of the Church, except the Jesuits with whom the revolutionary spirit of the age could never be at peace. Poland and Russia accepted the French educational ideas unconditionally, and the leaders of the Enlightenment hoped to realize their dreams in these two countries. J. J. Rousseau outlined plans for reforming the government as well as the schools of Poland: the young are to be taught patriotism and the proper use of liberty, foreigners as well as priests are to be excluded from the teaching profession; the teaching office is to be made a stepping-stone to higher things, and not a life work, because the "homme publique" has no vocation for life except to be a "citoyen"; every school should have a ground for public drills; certain educational institutions are to be faithful reproductions, on a small scale, of

---

[1] Hahn, *Das Unterrichtswesen in Frankreich*, Breslau, 1848, I, p 132
[2] Genovesi, *Lez di commercio*, 1765 (new ed, Milan, 1824), part I, ch. 6, §§ 1 and 9, Filangieri, *Scienza della legislazione*, Naples, 1780-1785, book IV
[3] Le Roy in Schmid's *Enzyklopädie*, VI, p. 123.

the organization of the State.[1] These pedagogical views of Rousseau are diametrically opposed to the educational principles laid down in *Emile*, but Rousseau's rhetoric did not fight shy of such considerations. Diderot sketched a plan for the reorganization of the schools of Russia, and, though he paid little heed to the peculiar needs of that country, he was very moderate in his views: the German schools and universities are to be imitated in Russia, but the faculty of philosophy is to be first in rank, and most attention should be given to the natural and the technical sciences.[2] French adventurers have not deserved well of Russia for foisting upon the country the educational theories of the Enlightenment. For a short time these theories attracted the eyes of all Europe, but eventually proved a hollow show. A real beginning was made only after 1780, when Russia followed the example of the Austrian school reform, imported Felbinger's teaching devices from Vienna, and opened training schools for teachers in several large cities.[3]

5. In Germany several factors conspired in shaping the form of the school system, and as these factors operated as mutual aids and also, at times, as mutual correctives, the Enlightenment produced more lasting results here than elsewhere. These factors were Philanthropinism, the state control of schools, the rivalry between the smaller states, and the traditions of the older pedagogy.

The Philanthropinists derived their first principles from Locke and Rousseau, and dreamed of new foundations which should wield a far-reaching influence. Basedow planned a large publishing house and a training school for teachers to be connected with "an immense school for the race and humanity." He began to realize his ambitious projects with the publication of his *Elementary Book*. School cabinets, teaching devices, and an elementary institute were also considered as means to assist in improving the schools. The elementary institute was no other than the school at Dessau, which, however, was far below the expectations raised by Basedow's announcement of an institute in which "children as well as teachers were to be trained

[1] *Considérations sur le gouvernement de Pologne et sur sa réformation projetée*, 1772, chap. 4. This state pedagogy of Rousseau is complementary in more than one point to *Emile*, and a critical comparison of the two educational theories would be illuminating.
[2] *Plan d'une université pour le gouvernement de Russie ou d'une éducation publique dans toutes les sciences*, 1774.
[3] Helfert, *Die österreichische Volksschule*, Prague, 1860, I, p. 9.

for reforming the schools."[1] Basedow hoped to enlist the aid
of the State for his plans, and repeatedly petitioned the
government to establish a "bureau of morals or of education"
to control the education of the young by means of a "moral
State examination."[2] He was at the same time eager to improve the condition of the people, especially of the middle
classes. In fact, the Philanthropinists in general addressed their
educational writings to the people at large, and thus their efforts, instead of remaining pure theory, assumed a certain
solidity It is not the least achievement of these men—particularly of Campe and Salzmann—that they secured the interest of the middle classes for educational matters, and thereby
bridged in Germany the gulf that still separated in other countries the active leaders from the apathetic masses. While the
German educationists may appear, in comparison with the
French, poor in ideas and pedantic in manner, still they are
superior to the latter in their honest effort to share all they
acquired with a class of the people to whom even a small number of new ideas meant a great gain. This social gain was the
real and, perhaps, the only tangible benefit accruing from the
work of the Philanthropinists. Even their contemporaries recognized the untenableness of their didactic principles. Of modern writers, Trendelenburg has summarized the objections
against these principles in the following criticism. "They (the
Philanthropinists) ignored the fact that the intellect cannot be
developed except by dealing with solid matter, and that the
will cannot be strengthened by purely intellectual training. It
is unthinkable that there could be real education without mathematics and the classics. It was ridiculous to expect a purely
natural religion, a collection of intellectual abstractions, to impress the heart of a child and even to supersede the deep and
soulful truths of historical Christianity."[3]

6. The Philanthropinums were intended to prove the centres of a new kind of educational institutions. This, however,
they failed to do, for they were short-lived, and only one, Salzmann's school at Schnepfenthal, has survived beyond the 18th
century down to the present time. Still, they gave the governments an opportunity to inaugurate a state reform of the school.
Among the German states, Austria and Prussia set the example

[1] Schlosser, *Geschichte des 18 Jahrhunderts*, II, p 631
[2] *Methodenbuch fur Vater und Mutter der Familien und Volker*, 1770, part IX
[3] *Kleine Schriften*, Leipzig, 1871, I, p 147; in the oration on Frederick the
Great and Zedlitz, his prime minister

in this reform, and their being military states disproves the old saying that the Muses are silent in the midst of arms. The increase of the military forces necessitated a corresponding increase of the taxes, and the latter called for improved trades and industries for which practical knowledge and technical skill were indispensable. These countries, then, began to reform the national schools because of economic and political needs. But the egoism of the State was not the sole reason for the contemplated reforms, but was softened by the humanitarian tendency of the Enlightenment: the perfecting of the human faculties was expected to make man happy, and the improved schools were regarded as sources of general welfare. The terms *landesväterlichen*, or *landesmütterlichen Fürsorge*,[1] which occur so frequently in the royal decrees of the period, were in many instances inspired by the ruler's kindly interest in the welfare of his people. This kindly attitude atones considerably for some of the violent measures taken by the different governments. Still, the policy of allowing scarcely any opportunity for private initiative does not accord with the general tendency of the age toward independent thought and action. The founders of the German state school system undervalued the historical elements of education and overvalued the powers of the State, believing that a royal decree could create what can actually develop only from the slow growth of many years, and in this regard they were akin of soul to Pombal and Tanucci. However, a certain reverence for existing institutions and a certain practical turn of mind preserved the German reformers from the revolutionary measures of the Portuguese and Neapolitans.

The educational reform was less difficult in Prussia because of the schools established there in the beginning of the century by August Herman Francke. He, the father of Pietistic pedagogy, had largely carried out what had in the case of Basedow never gotten beyond the stage of promise and project. Francke's institutions had become the motherhouses of many other schools; they supplied the German Lutherans with public school teachers, private tutors, and textbooks; and demonstrated how the higher schools could correlate technical and industrial training with the traditional subjects. Frederick William I. recognized the valuable services of Francke's schools; witness his *Principia regulativa* of 1736 and his statement, "If I build up and improve the country, but do not make Christians of my subjects, all my

---

[1] A sovereign' father's, or most ...

work shall be in vain." Frederick II. also entrusted a follower of the Halle movement, John Julius Hecker, with the organization of the national school system. Hecker is the author of the school ordinances of 1763, whose purpose was "to banish from the country the ignorance which is so harmful in its effects and so great an obstacle to the spread of Christian ideas; and we trust that by improving the schools our subjects will be made morally better and industrially more efficient." He is likewise the founder of the Berlin *Realschule*, which was, in principle and organization, an imitation of the Halle institutions. That this *Realschule* was not content with the flat realism of the Philanthropinists, may be seen from the declaration of J Fr. Hahn, Hecker's collaborator: "True realism must be sought in the things that promote a quiet and peaceful conscience "[1] The educational principles of the Enlightenment were championed by Zedlitz, the patron of Basedow and Trapp. Zedlitz, however, was alive to some of the dangers of their theories, for he confessed, "One cannot be wary enough about the metaphysical education of the peasants", and he feared lest the schoolmasters, unless they be under the guidance of a man like Rochow, "should come to grief and develop into *raisson-neurs* " Zedlitz prepared the ground for the establishment of a central bureau of education, but his plan was carried out only in 1787. The "Oberschulkollegium," however, continued to be true to what he had stated as its aim, "to exercise a general control over the whole school system." When the new King, Frederick William II , entrusted the formation of his cabinet to Wollner, a conservative churchman, a radical change in the school system seemed to be impending, but the schools continued the same policy of centralizing all education, and the Prussian Statute-Book of 1794 defines schools and universities as "institutions of the State, whose aim is to instruct the young in useful knowledge and the sciences " The doctrine of the state rights in education came to be universally accepted in the schools, as appears from the following statement of Eilers, who voices the common sentiments of the teachers of his time and country: "I regarded my office of teacher as a small part of the King's office, for I considered the authority of the King of Prussia to be a power for the moral good of the whole country,

---

[1] Program of the Berlin *Realschule* (1753), quoted by Biedermann, *Altes und Neues von Schulsachen*, 1752-1755, Vol VIII

and I conceived the education and training of the young to be the most sacred function of this moral power."[1]

In Austria, the educational reform was confronted with more difficulties than in Prussia, and this for various reasons: the territory of Austria was three times as large as that of Prussia; its population was made up of alien races, some of them of a low stage of civilization; lastly, because of the suppression of the Jesuits, the higher schools had also to be reorganized. The success of the reform hung in the balance between the doctrinairism of a Pergen, who considered as most important the secularization of all education, and the conservatives, whom Maria Theresa favored. The reforms inaugurated by the Empress were moderate, practical, and not hostile to the traditions of the past. She once remarked, "The school system is and must ever remain a *politicum*," and this principle of the state school governed her whole educational policy. Some of her reform measures for instance, the "drilling" of the teachers and the standardizing of instruction according to the normal method —savour of the military. But the organizing of the school system was entrusted to the clergy, and Maria Theresa was fortunate in securing the services of capable men, interested and versed in matters educational. The memorial of Count Firmian, Prince-Bishop of Passau, which was entitled *Of the Usefulness Accruing to the State and to Religion from Good Schools* (1769), occasioned the first measures of reform; the *General School Ordinances* (1774) of Abbot Felbiger outlined the methods of the reform; Dean Kindermann was active in co-ordinating industrial training with the elementary school, and thus enlarged the scope of the new institutions. After the Jesuits were suppressed, the Piarists took over their colleges, and thereby preserved the continuity of higher learning. In this way the new school system gained sufficient strength to survive the experimentations of Joseph II. This ruler was guided by the best of intentions and really improved the elementary schools, yet on the whole he abandoned the wise course pursued by his mother.

7. All the German princes promoted the educational reform in their respective countries, and the rivalry between the different governments spurred them on to the greatest possible efforts. Most of the Protestant states followed in their reform measures the example of the Philanthropinists, although they

[1] Eilers' *Wan* .... II. ;

did not accede to their extreme demands. The Catholic countries
followed the lead of the Austrian reform. Among the organizers
of the various school systems, we find not only professional
educators, but also eminent scholars—as Gesner in Hannover
and Ernesti in the electorate of Saxony; writers of the first
rank—as Herder, who founded the normal school in Weimar;
and cultured churchmen—as Franz von Furstenberg, the father
of the Munster school system. The greatest minds of the age
were occupied with the problems of education. Not only newspapers and magazines, but savants, poets, and philosophers—all
joined in the educational discussion; all were eager to introduce
the new educational motives and materials into the schools and
thereby make them a vital force for the future.

The elementary school reaped the first fruits of these efforts.
The elementary school system—if understood "as the elementary instruction which the State regards as necessary, and which
it furnishes in public institutions of the State (the State being
here conceived in the broadest sense),"[1]—is a creation of the
18th century, and may be said to have originated in Germany,
inasmuch as it was here that it first developed along natural
and uniform lines. The elementary school system is based
upon the state control of schools, and implies that the individual
communities must build and support the school. The vocational
training of teachers and the fixing of their duties and rights are
further prerequisites of an elementary school system. These
features were common to the school systems of the different
countries, but local needs called for many variations. Compulsory school attendance (i e , laws compelling the parents who
cannot provide for the home instruction of their children to
send them to school until certain elements of knowledge have
been acquired) was not introduced everywhere, but remained
confined to Prussia and several smaller Protestant states. The
Catholic governments only encouraged the parents to send their
children to school, but did not compel them to do so. The
State began to take cognizance also of private schools, and made
them comply with certain government regulations. In Austria
the government prescribed the teaching methods as well as the
textbooks, but not all governments issued such formal regulations. The same diversity obtained with regard to the subject-

---

[1] Stein, *Verwaltungslehre*, V, p ˉ₃, for more definite distinctions see *infra*,
Ch XXX

matter of teaching, some countries allowing more scope than others to industrial training and the natural sciences.

After elementary instruction the training for the trades and the mechanical arts profited most. The origins of almost all training schools for the mechanical arts can be traced back to the 18th century: commercial and business schools, schools of agriculture, forestry, engineering, architecture, technology, etc., were established during the period of the Enlightenment.[1] The *Realschule*,[2] as founded by John Julius Hecker in Berlin in 1747, was a Latin school with elective courses in commercial and technical sciences. Hecker's successors, Silberschlag and Andrew Hecker, organized three distinct courses: first, a *pædagogium* for higher learning; second, a school of art with courses in commerce, architecture, engineering, the fine arts, military science, etc.; third, a German, or industrial, school. It was only in the 19th century that the *Realschule* united into one organic whole the rudiments of general cultural studies and the elements of industrial training. The *Realschule* developed not only from those schools which taught from the beginning only modern subjects, but also from those Latin schools that gradually added modern subjects in order to meet the needs of the lower classes. To this latter class belong the *Bürgerschulen*[3] (municipal schools) of northern Germany, the *Hauptschulen* (high schools) of Austria, the girls' schools and female academies, and all delatinized town schools, which now began to occupy the middle field between the elementary school and the gymnasia and universities.

The state reform of education was, on the whole, not favorable to the institutions of higher learning. The Enlightenment could not appreciate the autonomy enjoyed by the universities in matters educational. The Revolution robbed France, the land of universities, of its seats of higher learning, and gave in exchange a paltry substitute—the state faculties of the Napoleonic system. The Austrian universities were deprived of their

---

[1] The first commercial school of Hamburg was opened in 1767; the commercial school of Vienna, founded in 1770, was later changed into a *Realschule*; the *Georgicon* of Count Festetics in Kessthely is the oldest school of agriculture; the agricultural school of Schwarzenberg in Krumau and Thaer's agricultural school in Oderbruch were opened in 1799. A school of mining was opened in Schemnitz in 1760; the Berlin school of engineering was opened in 1799; the oldest of the technological schools is the Ecole polytechnique in Paris, founded by Monge in 1794.

[2] Monroe, *Cyclopedia of Education* [...]

[3] Monroe, *Cyclopedia of Education* [...]

autonomy both in teaching and in the administration of their finances. Joseph II. went so far as to turn some of the Austrian universities into lyceums, and obliged the teachers to confine their lectures to the matter contained in the prescribed text-books. In these radical measures he followed his avowed principle, "the essential studies of the universities are intended for the training of state officials, and not for the training only of scholars." Frederick II. did no more than issue the order that "the heads of the students are not to be crammed with meaningless and useless subtleties, but are to be enlightened and prepared, especially by the study of philosophy, to acquire and apply truly useful knowledge." The founding of new state universities affected the older universities, and Gottingen particularly was regarded as the model in reorganizing the older institutions in the interest of a state centralization of the schools. Several new departments were added to the universities: the fiscal sciences were introduced into the faculty of law; laboratory methods were introduced into the school of medicine; semi-popular lectures on æsthetics, pedagogy, ethics, encyclopedias, etc., became a feature of the school of philosophy, which was further augmented by the introduction of the historical sciences.

IX.

MODERN EDUCATION.

CHAPTER XXVIII.

The Character of Modern Education.

1. The tendencies of 19th century education and its organization might well seem to be inspired by the ideals of the Enlightenment. However, the term Enlightenment is no longer a catchword; the criticisms of the Romanticists and of the representatives of the Historical School have broken its charm, and it is now generally associated with a cold, unsympathetic, and soulless movement. Nevertheless, the shibboleths of to-day, "knowledge is power," "to know is to be free," still voice the sentiments and the tendencies of the Enlightenment: to make the individual free, to make him his own master, to cast off the trammels of tradition and thereby obtain human perfection and happiness. It is to-day preached from the house-tops that the progress in every field of human endeavor together with the development and liberation of the mind should be the goal of man, and this gospel does not differ essentially from that of the Enlightenment. The tendencies are the same. The men of the 20th century believe, as did the men of the 18th, that an age of unparalleled happiness and perfection is dawning upon the human race, and that we shall attain ultimate perfection, not by following the past in appraising things and actions according to their bearing on eternity, but rather by believing that happiness will come to us through the application of our individual powers of mind and body. The schools of to-day are still pursuing the aim of the encyclopedists of the Enlightenment: to adjust the various branches of the course of study to the practical needs of the present; and the modern curriculum is, in consequence, overcrowded. The realism, too, of the Enlightenment, which applied the standards of immediate usefulness to all studies, is still abroad and very active in the world of to-day. Our age is striving to carry out on a large scale the design which was first conceived by the Enlightenment: to spread useful and diversified knowledge among the masses. Our age has striven for the

schools, elementary and secondary, to all comers, and has supplied the millions with such educational instruments as were
formerly available to the savant only. This has been made
possible by the wonderful inventions and discoveries that anni-
hilate space and that facilitate the reproduction of books and
works of art The press in its various forms—periodicals, magazines, newspapers—spreads knowledge and useful information.
Much as the State had accomplished in the 18th century in
organizing the schools, it dwindles into insignificance when compared with the educational activities of the modern State. The
theories of the economists of the Enlightenment have likewise
expanded into the broader conception of the economists of the
early 19th century, who fostered the theory of the omnipotent
State. The pedagogy of the Enlightenment is still exerting
much influence upon the pedagogy and didactics of to-day.
Pestalozzi's system is patterned all too closely after the intellectualism and the worship of method so characteristic of the
Enlightenment Dinter and Diesterweg championed a modified
Philanthropinism and converted many schoolmen to it. The
individualistic conception of Locke and Rousseau enters even
into philosophical pedagogy. English educational thought is following a sensualistic or materialistic utilitarianism, and looks
kindly on Trapp's suggestion to make pedagogy a department
of medicine.

   2 Notwithstanding these points of contact, there are many
points of divergence between the educational system of the 18th
century and that of the 19th. In the very first years of the
19th century the views and tendencies of men changed to what
was diametrically opposed to the ideals of the Enlightenment.
This change was connected with the agitation of mind produced
by the horrors of the French Revolution and the subsequent
phenomenal growth of Napoleon's power. The French Revolution had destroyed the historical foundations of society, and
Napoleon's successes had unbalanced the political status of
Europe and was threatening to crush the national spirit of the
subjugated peoples The fear was general lest the destruction
of all existing institutions and of all that had till then been held
most sacred was impending, and in their despair men seized
upon everything that promised help in the mad struggle for
existence The best men of the time demanded less enlightenment of the intellect and more strengthening of the will. They
were not bent on throwing off the "shackles" of tradition.
Instead, they were anxious to hold fast to all of the past that

gave any hope of proving an anchor in the tempest; they turned to the great deeds of their forbears to fill their souls with the spirit of high courage. They recognized that the vaunted individualizing of the Enlightenment tended ultimately to tear away the individual from the mainstays of his strength, *viz.*, the inspiration of the past and the cheering and invigorating influence of his fellowmen. The individualizing tendency appeared in its true light as the selfishness, the social egoism and moral atomism that had destroyed all order and which were responsible for the moral horrors lately perpetrated in Europe. The Cosmopolitanism of the Enlightenment was likewise condemned as being fraught with the same dangers, for, on the one hand, it would eliminate all national differences and substitute an abstraction in their stead, and, on the other hand, it would substitute for the historical religions a colorless and undenominational religion of natural humanity. The early 19th century realized that the national spirit is a priceless inheritance and that the Church is the foundation stone for the reconstruction of society. Thus the Enlightenment appeared as robbing the race of its most valued treasures, as undermining the foundations of order, and as destroying the true boons of life. Hence the leaders of the new age went beyond the Enlightenment and finally arrived at that period which had been most maligned by the Enlightenment, the Middle Ages, in which era Christian idealism and the Germanic spirit had achieved their greatest triumphs.

The new age was a renaissance of historical, national, and Christian elements, occurring at a time when the inner life was intensified by the pressure from without. Like all violent movements making for a change in ideals, this renaissance had its dark sides. Many of its principles and ideas were obscure and not clearly defined; much was done without due deliberation; there was also some unfairness to certain parties; and the evil effects may be seen in the aberrations of the Romanticists, in the Teutomania, and in the politics of the Restoration. Still, the results were, on the whole, favorable, and education gained in depth, clearness, and consolidation. The renaissance of the 19th century did away with the vague Cosmopolitanism of the Enlightenment, counterbalanced the one-sided systems of politics, and prepared the way for the historical conception of education.

It would be incorrect to describe the 18th century as simply cosmopolitan and the 19th century as the century of national tendencies, because the former nationalized many elements of education by popularizing them, and the 19th century promoted the intercommunication between different nations and opened up world-perspectives.   But the ideal of the 18th century was cosmopolitan That century considered it a duty to foster European patriotism, to raise men to a height where they would lose sight of the fragments of humanity (as the national distinctions were then regarded), and where they would be conscious of only the one common race of man   The 19th century, however, encouraged certain national instincts, which restrict the assimilation of different peoples, and which prompt the intensive cultivation of national characteristics.   It must be conceded that these national tendencies produced some undesirable results The consciousness of a general humanity, a commendable feature of the Enlightenment, has not been cultivated sufficiently; the countries whose population is made up of alien races note with alarm the growing national consciousness among their unassimilated inhabitants, a kind of hero worship has been encouraged, in which success is the sole criterion, and which pardons even the most serious moral crimes in view of the liberties allowed to genius.   Yet the reintroduction of national elements into life and education has meant real progress.   It is well that Rousseau's suggestion to expunge the words citizen and fatherland from the lexicon has never been acted upon, and that they still hold a prominent place in our dictionaries.   It is an obvious gain that the view holding all peculiarities to be an evil and all ties an obstacle to man's liberty, is gradually giving way, though as yet only in the domain of nationality, to the appreciation of the importance of social and ethical relations. To have a solid foundation, humanity must assimilate those elements of general humanity that are embodied in the various nationalities, and to which the individual is indebted for the very first gifts received from the race The plastic forces of nationality are not to co-operate merely unconsciously and secretly with the intellectual development, but should introduce it, accompany it, and complete it.   Higher learning, freighted as it is with goods from many lands, may never grow oblivious of the home-port whence it first sailed and whither it is to return. National education is not to aim solely at educating "intelligent and useful men," but also at impressing the members of all classes with the consciousness of their solidarity as parts of one national organism; and it is only the consciousness of this solidarity which will ensure to each individual member his proper share of the treasures handed down from the past and which are now the common property of the whole nation. This heritage is of the soul, the heart, and the memory, and is, therefore, a heritage of ideals, a priceless asset to any and every nation. These ideals are most real in their influence upon the new generation; and particularly in our own day, when the corroding influences of materialism are at work, is a national idealism a most important factor for the well-being of a nation.

3. As the 19th century rejected the false Cosmopolitanism of the 18th century, so the present-day world is gradually abandoning the position taken by the Enlightenment in political science when it conceded to the State an almost unlimited power, so that the latter was regarded as the only agency for directing the collective activities of the race and as the macrocosm of man. This doctrine dates from the political theories of the ancients, was accepted by the medieval students of Roman law and by the economists of the Renaissance, and found practical expression in the police-governed State. It still influences the conception of the modern State, yet it has been losing ground ever since the historical and organic method of study has been applied to its basic principles. No statesman of deeper views to-day regards a nation from the viewpoint solely of its numerical strength, nor considers its trades and industries merely as filling the State's coffers, nor looks upon the Church as a government institution that furnishes the opportunities for public worship. Though the development of the public school system may still be following the lines drawn by political economy when it was conceived as the science of the police system, yet we have gotten beyond the State pedagogy, which was the foundation of the false views. It is true that the State must control the educational apparatus, and that the educative process requires certain legal forms authorized by the State; but apparatus and form are not the thing itself. The main educational forces exist independently of, and prior to, any State interference, and the State must base all its regulations on the forces at work among the people. The State cannot produce a national civilization and culture; it is at best only the administrator of the educational and cultural materials belonging to the people. But little of this material is at all accessible to the State, for most of it is bound up with institutions and manners and customs that are beyond the control of the State. There is evident need of a science treating of the transmission of the educational and cultural treasures, i. e., a science of intellectual economy; and though the full development of this science is

still a thing of the future, yet it is a distinct achievement of the present day to have recognized the need of it.

This change to the historical point of view has been a great gain to the sciences and has thus benefited the content of education also. The moral sciences as well as the natural sciences now recognize the value of historical research. Instruction indirectly and the concept of education directly have been benefited by this appreciation; and that education must be based upon a historical foundation, is a truism among thinking educators of the present day. Antiquities are studied in our schools less for the sake of their training the æsthetic or formal sense, than for the reason that they let us understand and appreciate our culture by showing the roots from which it has sprung. The same consideration, namely, the discovery of the source of our present possessions, has led to the study of the early forms of the mother-tongue. The teacher of religion is also at pains to bring home to his pupils, how important an element Christianity is in the historical development of modern civilization and culture. The present-day teacher of history, too, must do more than summarize wars and battles and the deeds of kings: he must both present and interpret pictures of the different periods; must lead his pupils to understand their color and spirit, and thus train them to observe the historical background of the infinite variety of modern life The idea of a genetic method which permits an object of study to be developed before, and in, the mind of the pupil in accordance with the historical development of that object, is a result of the historical method introduced into the curricula, and constitutes the truly modern problem of methodology[1] We cannot approve of all the applications made of the historical principle and the historical method, its importance has been exaggerated and it has also been wrongly applied. There is a historicism no less than a naturalism, and both join hands in the modern science of evolution, which places the beast-man on the threshold of history. It is a wrong application of the historical principle to be so taken up with the successive changes as to overlook the forces that remain permanently at work; or in the process of evolution to miss that which is evolved; or amid the material successes to lose sight of the end and aim of man The application of the historical principle to the educative process will be wrong, if we do not understand aright the nature of the mind and the end of

---

[1] Cf *supra*, pp 54 ff and Vol II , Ch. XLII.

man, for education must be shaped in accordance with these; also, if we are satisfied with looking at the mere facts and neglect to correlate them with the vital and moral consciousness of the subject; thirdly, if we—to use the illustration of Schleiermacher—forget that history is the picture-book of ethics, and ethics, the rule-book of history. Thus classical and national antiquity, and especially Christianity, would be treated unfairly if considered solely as keys to the historical understanding of the present. Nor shall we reap the full fruits from the study of history if we treat it merely as the record of the progress of civilization; nor is the historical study of any science sufficient even for only cultural purposes. But the mistakes made in the application of the historical principle cannot detract from its obvious benefits to education, especially with regard to consolidating the educative process. The historical principle has prompted the jealous safeguarding of all educational elements, whether transmitted from the past or produced in the present. It preserves the world from the barbarism of the Enlightenment, which was ready to destroy all that did not appeal to the corrupt taste of the time. Our education owes much to the intellectual movements of the present, but it is likewise a fruit of the past; and the roots imbedded in the past are still supplying nourishment to what has grown for ages and has laid on with the different periods successive concentric layers. Let educationists uphold this truth, and they will be able to oppose effectively any attack of utilitarianism or Americanism and thereby postpone the fulfillment of the prophecy that natural history, hygiene, technology, etc., will occupy the first place in our curricula.

4. The elements and impulses dating from the renaissance of the early 19th century have preserved modern education from being deprived of some of its richest elements, as the principle of the Enlightenment had threatened to do. Still, it would be too optimistic to assume that modern education is consequently both rich and deep. Modern education lacks the strength to coordinate the wealth of its content and its multitudinous viewpoints with a governing and organizing principle. This is the chief defect of modern education, and we cannot find in it, as in the education of other periods, one prevailing view and tendency. The historical principle is a powerful factor at present, as is the national principle also. But these principles are mere factors. They are not core principles. Our age scorns none of the educational ideals of earlier periods and would take them

21

over in their totality: it is alive to the beauty of Greek culture, to the enthusiasm of the Renaissance, to the varied erudition of the early polymathists, and would fain admire, too, the Christian ideals that reared the great cathedrals of Europe and that lent wings to the genius of Dante. We are not content with transplanting into our gardens all that is great and beautiful and choice in every age of the world's history; nay, we would derive the greatest possible benefit from each of these exotic plants and would let all the masses enjoy their fruits. We would reduce all that is choice and rare to a handy literary form, would compress it all into the textbooks used in the schools, and thus make it the subject-matter of the curricula   The eclectisism of other ages was light and frivolous, but the eclecticism of the present time is thorough and pedantic. Polymathy was formerly the favorite browsing-field of the amateur, but it is made a matter of duty in the schools of to-day.

The division of labor, as practiced in modern scientific research, is diametrically opposed to the polymathy of the schools. It was possible in former times, because the curricula were not so comprehensive as to-day, to continue in later life all the educational work of the schools. But present-day schools build, indeed, a broad and comprehensive foundation, but the superstructure, raised on this broad foundation, soon tapers to a slender point   In our scientific research we adopt the principle of the factory, that one workman can make perfectly only one thing But in teaching we follow the principle of polytechnics, the very opposite of specialized factory work. General education and vocational training are now regarded as diametrically opposed to each other. The former is built upon the broadest lines, and the latter restricts the student to one special point. There is a second disproportion between general education and vocational training   Although genuine education, whether general or vocational, should stress the elements of knowledge no less than that of practical skill, yet our general education stresses knowledge, but neglects almost entirely practical skill; and our vocational training, on the other hand, stresses practical skill at the expense of knowledge   The schools impart knowledge well enough, but neglect the practical training, and this while the world is clamoring for practical skill and voting as worse than useless most of the theoretical knowledge acquired in the schools. Our educational system is the very antipode of the system of the seven liberal arts. Our skill is professional, and our liberal education is knowledge. In matters intellectual we speak of instruction only, and not of schooling, which is committed to the illiberal field. The work of instruction is performed by teachers, who have dropped the honorable name of schoolmaster for that of school-teacher (which implies less); and that not without reason, for they have abandoned the work of the schoolmaster who fitted his pupils for active life.

To discover the ultimate causes of these two defects of our system of education (the ill-advised eclecticism and the opposition between life and school), would lead us too far afield, since it would necessitate an analysis of the whole modern spirit. But without leaving the domain of education, we may note two causes of these defects. Goethe remarks that a harmonious development is impossible if "because of the progress in culture not all the parts of human activity, in which education shows itself, can develop in the same degree, and thus more scope is granted to some few, thereby occasioning jealousy among the members of the great family that has so many various branches."[1] This is true of modern education, for here the preponderance of certain forces never permitted the development of harmonious family relations. The attention given in the Middle Ages to dialectic involved some loss of symmetry. Still more was lost when philology usurped, in the early Renaissance, the first place in the curriculum. But this science was, in turn, antagonized by the dialectic of the Enlightenment. The dialectic of the 18th century reduced the State, society, and education to individual and isolated atoms, and substituted for the ideals of the earlier periods the rational sciences, which naturally won favor with isolated individuals. The renaissance of the 19th century reinstated some of the elements of the earlier periods and made a strong defence against the inroads of utilitarianism, though it never vanquished this insidious foe. Modern education may be said to have fallen heir to the battlefield where all educational principles join in the fray, and it is making an honest effort to establish peace, to be fair to all, and to exchange the narrowness of older periods for the broad and varied culture of the present. Modern education is a compromise between Humanism, Realism, and Romanticism; it combines the Renaissance style, the Rococo style, and the Gothic style, and injects this variety into the inner life no less than into the style of our public buildings and churches.

---

[1] *Werke in der Ausgabe letzter Hand,* Vol. XXXVII, p. . Wooster).

But the mere joining of these cultural elements does not produce the desired family relationship. Cohabitation does not imply harmony, and mere juxtaposition is no fusion. This suggests also the second cause of the defects of modern education. We assume that mere addition, a mere joining of educational elements, produces real education. We are concerned only for what can be called the body of education, and are persuaded that, once the body is present, the vivification of the inert mass will take place of itself. This mechanistic conception is the basis of the eclecticism of general education as well as of the specializing tendency of modern science. General education would create something living by combining atoms, and the specialist would discover the vital elements by breaking a living whole into atoms. Wise men have, indeed, called attention to the organic nature of education and have recognized it as a postulate for the educative process; but it remains a postulate and is no guiding principle. Though we have in theory proved the untenableness of the mechanistic position, and though we strive to abandon it also in practice, still we cannot break away from it; it is in the air, we breathe it, and are influenced by it.

Modern education thus presents contradictions on all sides, but it would be unfair to conclude that it is therefore only a battleground of conflicting elements. The past ages may well have presented similar scenes, though we, intent as we are on discovering the permanent forms of education, fail to note the discord; or even if we should discover in the past some opposition between the educational elements, we should still not realize it so much as the conflicts of the present, which, being so close to us, force themselves alike upon the mind and the feelings.

CHAPTER XXIX

The Content of Modern Education.

1. The forte of modern education is the diversity of its content. Not only have the school subjects grown in number, but the contributions of the individual sciences to education have been augmented, and new elements of educational value have been unearthed. Sometime professional sciences have become school subjects, and sometime school subjects have developed into professional sciences, without, however, abandon-

ing their educational function. The last is true primarily of
the science that we have inherited from the Renaissance and
which fortunately survived the onslaughts of the Enlightenment—philology. The older philology was essentially a school
subject, and its position in the *universitas litterarum*, was purely
propædeutic. It was, indeed, the basic discipline, the vital element of higher education, but was prevented by this very fact
from developing into a professional science. With its general
and elastic character it never became clear whether its object
was merely language and the art of language, or whether it was
to embrace all erudition and eventually be co-extensive with
polyhistory. It was likewise not clear whether philology should
be restricted to the language and literature of classical antiquity,
or whether it was to embrace the higher study of all languages
and literatures. Only in our time was its scope definitely fixed
by marking off the borderland between philology and the related
sciences. The proper function of philology is, according to the
modern conception, the ideal reconstruction of the total activity
of a people. Friedrich August Wolf, the first modern to call
himself a philologist, defines the subject compactly, but broadly,
as the biography of a people. The purpose of it is to reconstruct all the life of a past period that can be recovered from
records. August Bœckh defined it (*Enzyklopädie*, p. 16) as "the
putting together again in its entirety of all that the human
spirit has fashioned."[1] Modern philology is one of the historical sciences, taking these in their broadest conception. But
while the history of an individual field of human activity "follows only one line of development, philology collects all these
lines into one group and lays them before the student as so
many radii issuing from the common centre, the spirit of the
respective people."[2] Both philology and history deal with historical facts, but they join them into different units. Political
history deals with political events and changes. The history of
art is concerned with the works of art of the different periods
and peoples. The history of philosophy records the speculative
work of the human mind, irrespective of territorial distinctions.
Philology has also to deal with the State, with art, with philosophy, etc., but only inasmuch as these represent important

---

[1] *Cyclopedia of Education*, s. v. *Philology*.
[2] Reichardt, *Die Gliederung der Philologie*, Tübingen, 1846, p. 69; Bœckh,
Enzyklopädie und Methodologie der philologischen Wissenschaften, edited by
Bratuschek, Leipzig, ... T: S... Ph.l.l... ... u...d Psy-
chologie, Berlin, 1864.

phases of a certain national life. Classical philology deals with the totality of the life of Greece and Rome; Sanskrit philology, with the life of India in all its phases, and Germanic philology, with the historical life of the Germanic peoples. Because the spirit of a people manifests itself most in its language and literature, greater attention must be given to these. Philology follows the example of history in regarding the language of a people as a key, and its written records as sources, but considers them, moreover, as objects of research, because the interpretation of them is of basic importance for all its findings. To conjure up the spirit of the past life of a people, philology must address this spirit thus, "Speak, so that I may see thee."

F. A. Wolf was the first to advance this conception of philology, and Bœckh clarified it and developed it methodologically. In this sense philology is a field for special scientific research, and offers, at the same time, new possibilities as a school subject. It is neither narrowed down to mere linguistics, nor so broadened as to be co-extensive with polymathy. The modern conception of the science of language encourages the philology of the schools to introduce scientific method into language instruction and the reading of authors, nay, even to reproduce, to some extent, the past life of the respective people. The classical teacher of the present time selects the school authors with more regard to their content than was ever done before. Anthologies, containing only language materials, have been almost entirely discarded in the higher and middle classes, and many educators object with good reason to the short and disconnected sentences of elementary exercise books. We now have school editions of classical authors whose text, notes, illustrations, maps, etc., are well adapted to reconstruct the particular phase of the ancient world represented by the writer. We recognize and follow the rule laid down by the old didacticians. the student must be interested in the content as well as in the style. The new methodology of classical instruction demands, in accordance with modern hermeneutics, that we evolve the thought content from the linguistic form. And to this end we must attend to the niceties of expression, without, however, attaching too much weight to individual phrases, as this would not permit us to grasp the meaning of the whole. Even if this high ideal is not realized in actual instruction, it is still a great gain to have given expression to the problem that was unknown to the older methodology, which rested content either with the appreciation of the literary form, or with the mere understanding of the content.

2. Classical schools had formerly given much more attention to Latin than to Greek, but the early 19th century adjusted the study of the two ancient languages more properly. Even in the halcyon days of the Renaissance, Greek was not studied so extensively, for so long a period of the school course, and in so well-graded a course as to-day. Latin is to-day of less practical value than formerly, when it was the language of all the sciences, and the modern world has also recognized that the originality and harmony of Greek culture are lacking in the culture of Rome. Hence modern educators have, at different times, declared themselves in favor of the plan advocated by some of the early Humanists, who assigned the first place in importance and in the order of studies to Greek in preference to Latin; and the modern conception of antiquity has furnished new arguments for this view. The German patriots of the Wars of Liberation, such as Fichte, Fr. Passow, Fr. Koch, recalled the internal relationship existing between the Greek and the German spirit. Others, among them Herbart, Dissen, Fr. Thiersch, stressed the kinship between the young mind and the poetical and historical creations of the Greeks, and advised that the course of study begin with Homer and then present in turn (by drawing upon Greek classics) lifelike pictures of the successive periods. Others, again, championed the same view because of the genetic element in a method that was so well adapted to conduct the student along strictly historical lines, whereas the traditional practice of the schools kept the most impressionable years of the boy busy with what was but a derived culture, and introduced him to its source, Greek literature, only after his most receptive period was over. But the schools have, nevertheless, not abandoned their traditional practice, believing that an elementary course of instruction, if based on Latin, develops better the language consciousness; and they still uphold the maxim, "From the Latin workshop to the halls of the Greeks." Yet the reform movement in favor of Greek has improved the methods of Greek teaching, has shown the need of correlating the classics with history, and has brought out the educational value of unified and co-ordinated materials.[1]

[1] These and other principles and undertakings of modern pedagogy will be treated ... y mentioned as feat...

Profiting by the results of linguistic researches, the teaching of modern languages has been much improved over the time when merely practical needs dictated the methods of language studies.   However, elementary instruction in the mother-tongue is still dominated, especially in Germany, by the formalism of Pestalozzi, which uses the language classes for mental training and neglects the body of language proper no less than the technics of linguistics.   Comparative philology has but begun to affect the teaching of languages, and after having proceeded from phonetics and etymology, it is now entering upon the field of syntax, but success will be attained only after the logical element of language has been duly emphasized[1]   The desire, which has been often expressed, for a parallel grammar of all the languages taught in the schools has not yet been realized, nor can it be realized before the categories of grammar and logic have been revised; and to do this, logic and philology will have to join hands

In view of all the impulses and influences emanating from modern philology, it might well seem as though we had reason to congratulate ourselves upon the splendid condition of language teaching.   Yet, existing conditions do not warrant too optimistic a view, because it is especially in language teaching that we see the baneful effects of the modern one-sidedness of imparting knowledge at the expense of practical skill   Pupils of the elementary school cannot write their mother-tongue with any degree of correctness. College graduates cannot write readable essays   Educated men cannot express their thoughts clearly and elegantly   A writer, who is exceptionally well qualified to speak upon the ancients and the Renaissance, says that our age is "neglectful of the first rules of correct speech and correct writing, and scarcely one out of a hundred educated men has the faintest idea of the art of periodic construction." He regrets that we have abandoned the "rhetoric of the ancients which was an essential complement of the general beauty and liberty of their lives," and that consequently "-we have not discrimination enough to note the incongruity of placing the vulgar beside what is refined; while our rush and hurry prevent us from noting our bad taste."[2]   We can certainly not be accused, as was the Renaissance, of attaching too much weight to verbal expression, and we look with contempt upon an age which wasted

---

[1] Vol II , Ch XLIII 2 and 3
[2] Birkha rdt, *Das Leben Constantins*, 2nd ed , p 379

its time with the building of fine periods; and if this attitude
indicates an advance along one line, our utter neglect of form
is fraught with obvious losses along other lines. It would be
unfair to make the school alone responsible for our disregard
of literary form.   The literary pabulum of the vast majority of
present-day readers consists exclusively of newspapers and popular magazines, and the notoriously slovenly style of these organs
of the press is assuredly more responsible for the prevalent lack
of literary taste than are the schools, although the latter might,
it is true, with improved methods of teaching, stem the tide of
weak and flabby language with which we are at present drifting.
A further factor that militates against beauty of language, is
the practical aim of most of our present-day writers, and though
this circumstance may produce a certain terseness and clearness, yet it means a loss in purity and neatness of style.

   3. While the scientific development of philology has been a
direct gain to the schools, by transforming and infusing a new
spirit into an old school subject, the benefit accruing from the
new development of philosophy was purely indirect and did not
affect materially the instruction in philosophy.   The systems
that established a close relationship between Kantianism and
the pantheism of the latter Renaissance, could not long remain
in control of the schools, but they have nevertheless exerted a
favorable influence on scientific research work as well as on
some of the school subjects.   Schelling's philosophy influenced
the natural sciences most, and Hegel's, the historical sciences.
Some scholars underrate the services of Schelling and Hegel,
whereas many of the principles that are of supreme importance
for scientific research have been established by these two philosophers.   The teachings of these philosophers were strong
forces in Ritter's reform of geography, in Bœckh's systematizing of philology, furthermore, in establishing æsthetics as a new
and separate science, and in applying the historical method to
the various departments of learning.   They furthered, to some
extent, even the restoration of Christian philosophy, for they
co-operated with the latter in opposing the philosophy of the
Enlightenment. They furnished some motives also for the science
of education,[1] though fewer in number than were supplied by
the speculative realism of Herbart, which was based on Leibnitz.[2]   But none of these schools of thought supplied higher

[1] Cf. supra, p. 44 and p. 69
[2] Supra, p. 28.

education with anything equal to what the older schools had
possessed in the elementary philosophy based on Aristotle. Hegel,
and especially Herbart, gave some thought to this matter, but
neither did anything positive; and Herbart changed his views on
this point so often that his real opinion cannot be stated with
certainty. Many circumstances conspired to let the instruction
in philosophy appear inadvisable. The popular philosophy which
had prevailed towards the end of the 18th century so largely in
the schools, had to give way, when the theological and philological elements reasserted themselves, and men were apt to
regard these latter subjects along with mathematics as more
useful than the formal study of philosophy, assuming that the
improved methods of these sciences would develop the mental
powers more effectually than any training to theorize about the
laws of reasoning. Moreover, the development of speculative
thought affected those philosophical disciplines that had formerly been regarded as impervious to change, and as offering,
therefore, a neutral ground between the conflicting systems,
which fact had fitted them admirably to serve as propædeutic
branches. Kant, however, joined logic, as a transcendental
science, with the theory of knowledge, and Hegel made it an
objective science, a criticism of the understanding practically
identical with metaphysics. Empirical psychology, which Kant
had treated in the form of anthropology, valuing it as a school
subject, had lost in favor because of the many divergent opinions concerning the speculative basis of the science of the soul
Ethics, too, being almost wholly neglected, could not be condensed into an elementary form Hence the study of philosophy has either disappeared entirely from the schools, or is
treated as a mere appendage of other branches. As taught in
the universities, philosophy is confined, owing to the encroachments of professional studies, to so narrow a field as to be of
scarcely any educational value. There is a tendency at present
to divide philosophy into many new sciences, so that the very
science that should represent, amid the modern division of
scientific research, unity and universality, is in danger of falling
a prey to specialization Just as earlier thinkers hoped that an
application of the "geometrical method" to philosophy would
lead to the establishment of universally recognized principles,
so some modern thinkers try to attain the same end by bringing
about a closer union between philosophy and the natural sciences. However, better results will be obtained from the historical treatment of philosophy, for this treatment familiarizes

the student with the best philosophic thought of the ages. We must, undoubtedly, turn also to the history of philosophy to ascertain which elements are best adapted to serve as the foundation of an elementary course in philosophy. Trendelenburg acted on this principle when he made the *Elementa logices Aristotelicæ* the textbook in philosophy.[1]

4. The spirit of the present time is as unfavorable to the theological element of education as to the philosophical. The naturalist refuses to recognize theology as a science; the so-called "higher critic" scorns it as an explanation of myths; and the indifferentist is apathetically tolerant of what has been handed down from the past under the name of theology. However, the historical view has led to a truer conception of the value, especially the educational value, of theology; for the historian must confess that Christianity has been for nineteen hundred years a creative force in the civilization of the world, and that, consequently, our whole life and being are interwoven with the ideas and ideals of Christianity, and that it is, therefore, the duty of the school to interpret and transmit to future generations this Christian heritage. Without a deep knowledge of Christianity, the modern man is, in fact, unintelligible to himself. From this point of view, the study of Christianity must be pursued alongside of the study of antiquity, because classical antiquity is likewise, though not in the same degree as Christianity, a creative force in our historical development;[2] and thus we witness the spectacle of the two mighty powers, which had for centuries struggled for the supremacy of the world, now meeting peacefully on historical ground and cooperating with each other in order to let the modern youth understand himself and his environment. But as the study of classical antiquity not only supplies the historical basis of modern education, but also gives it an æsthetical and broadly human character, so the Christian element also meets, over and above its historical value, the transcendental aims and tendencies of human nature. And, again, as the study of the ancient classics makes the educative process plastic, so the Christian element preserves the connection with those moral and religious aims that are essential to serious and contented work.

[1] Cf. Vol. II., Ch. XXIV, and Ch. XLV.

[2] "European civilization," says Gladstone, "from the Middle Ages downwards is the compound of two great factors, the Christian religion for the spirit of man, and the Greek, and in a lesser degree the Roman, discipline for his mind and intellect." *Cyclopædia of Education*

Reasoning such as this, which approaches the subject of religious instruction from without, is appreciated by the modern man. But in his worship of the real and the material, the modern man does not feel, not even in that part of his soul which is not yet consumed with materialism and subjectivism, the need of—or what one may call the homesickness for—the ideal and the spiritual. The irreligiousness of so many of our contemporaries differs essentially from the irreligiousness of the 18th century: the latter was anxious to retain certain doctrines of Christianity, and, while discarding much of the deposit of Faith, presumed to revise the teachings of the Church; but our age has a certain sense of the individuality and even the organic unity of Faith, and is hence preserved at least from the pathetic fallacy of fancying that irreligiousness is better qualified to adjudge what pertains to Faith than Faith itself. For this reason, if for no other, our age will never follow the example of Basedow, Bahrdt, etc, in substituting for the subject-matter of theological science the philosophy of the Enlightenment. Even the indifferentism of the present day would shrink from diluting Faith in so unnatural a way, for it is at least realistic enough to demand that each and everything be judged in accordance with its own nature.

Theology, having grown strong in its internal organization, contributed its goodly share toward the truer conception just mentioned. It has, moreover, been a deep influence in the defining of the general scope of education. Theological pedagogy in the form in which it began to develop in the early 19th century, is an important factor in our system of education. The writings of Dursch, Dupanloup, Palmer, Gustav Baur, etc, have demonstrated that theological pedagogy is not "a collection of pious phrases, nor a pedagogical sermon, but enters, on the one hand, unabashed into all the details and circumstances of daily life, and, on the other hand, utilizes all that pedagogical thought, or science, or the experience of the classroom has disclosed."[1] Theological pedagogy has been an eminent factor in combating the older individualistic conception and has fostered the social and ethical view of education; it has proved a defence against the encroachments of subjectivism, which tried to degrade the educational content to a mere tool, it has given the impetus to writing the history of education; has co-operated with the philosophy of education; has thrown the pedagogy of the secondary

---

[1] Palmer, *Evangelische Padagogik*, 1852, preface to the first edition

school into a higher perspective; has furnished the curriculum of the elementary school with a rich content; and has given rise to pedagogical collections which exercise a wide influence on educational studies. The whole development of theological pedagogy demonstrates that Christianity is still a powerful force, and that the oldest of the sciences is not at all in its dotage, but is vigorous enough to maintain its place in the midst of the new growth of branches of knowledge.

5. The historical sciences represent an element of modern education that has many ramifications. The higher schools have introduced a systematic and well-graded study of history. Pictures, maps, charts, and other illustrative helps supplement the written records. Modern methodology requires the students to consult, as far as possible, the original sources, and to trace the historical development of every branch of the curriculum. The elementary school has taken up the study of local and national history, and thus meets, at least in part, the demand for historical object lessons. The general reader has access to a rich historical literature, beginning with the historical classics down to the historical novel which is born of the union of history and literature. The arts assist the instruction in history with historical paintings, statues, and historical representations of all kinds; and even music transfers us in its historical productions to the past. Special societies are founded to encourage the study of local or national history and to preserve historically important sites; and every traveller's guide-book records not only the sights, but also the memorable deeds connected therewith. Still, this whole apparatus has not made what may be called historical education a common possession, for all the historical interest amounts frequently to only a listless reading of a few pages of history. Yet these agencies have, nevertheless, an important function. Even though historical polymathy does not unearth the entire educative content of history, still it renders one or the other element of it available; at least, it counterbalances the materialistic tendency, prevents absorption in the interests of the day, and teaches men to look at the world and human events with other eyes than those of the egoist. After all it is as yet too early to pass judgment upon the educational and cultural value of a subject that has been but lately introduced into the schools, and we must bide a longer time before appraising the results of a study that may yet prove an essential factor in deepening and otherwise promoting the educative process.

The modern science of geography is based on the sciences of
nature and the sciences of man, especially the history of man;
and the latter fact is stressed most in geography as a school
subject.   The educational value of geography was clearly recognized in the 18th century.   Kant considered geography as a
"physical, ethical, and political science," which "spreads before
us a large map of the human race."   He valued it highly because it "prevents the immature pupil from reasoning before he
possesses sufficient historical knowledge, the latter being the
only substitute for a boy's lack of experience"[1]   Rousseau and
the Philanthropinists cultivated successfully the illustrative side
of geography and also restored the vitalizing connection between
the pupil's environment and the world at large.   Karl Ritter's
reform of geography was first suggested by Gutsmuths' instruction in his school at Schnepfenthal, and was realized when
Ritter adopted Pestalozzi's principle that the function of the
educator is to assist the natural development so as to secure
natural, symmetrical, and harmonious progress[2]   Ritter's reform made geography a science by establishing it as the connecting link between the sciences of nature and the sciences of
man.   He proved that history must be co-ordinated with geography.   He made all the ramifications of geographical science
meet in one point, i e., all the phases of nature were to be studied
in their relation to man: the shape of the earth, topography,
climate, fauna, and flora—all were studied from the viewpoint
of their influence on the life of man.   The idealism which this
teleological conception of Ritter introduced into the science has
given a higher interest to geographical studies than would ever
be possible from the viewpoint of sordid utilitarianism—a common enough viewpoint in geography—and has connected it
with the highest interests of the race.   The natural sciences
have combined with history and graphic art to furnish geography with a splendid apparatus; modern inventions have anni-
hilated space and distance, and have made geography as needful
a science for travel and commerce-as it is a pleasant occupation.
The schools have thus gained a new subject which, however,
may lead, in the case of poor teaching methods, to distraction
or excessive memory work.   Still the wise teacher will welcome
geography as an excellent means for correlating such knowledge

[1] Kant, *Ueber Padagogik*, edited by Willmann, p. 11, *Complete Works*,
edited by Hartenstein, II, p 320.
[2] Cf *supra*, p 68

as might otherwise remain unco-ordinated, particularly history and the natural sciences.

6. The old education treated nature from its formal side only, and an elementary knowledge of mathematics was considered sufficient for all practical needs. Modern education, however, has enlarged the scope of both the mathematical and the natural sciences. The natural sciences are to-day no less important in general education than in the everyday life of the people. Their importance for the trades and industries renders them indispensable in vocational training. Formerly the traditions, as handed down from father to son, sufficed in many trades in which at the present time—owing to the improved methods introduced by technology and the applied sciences—a systematic education is required. The farmer and the manufacturer must take note of the findings of such sciences as natural history and chemistry. The superintendent of a large industrial establishment stands in need of technological training. Medicine, military science, engineering—all have been revolutionized by the progress made in the natural sciences. All professional schools, whether of secondary or more advanced grade, rightly demand of the general cultural schools that they familiarize their students with the elements of the natural sciences. But over and above this demand, no school of general culture may ignore an element that plays so important a rôle in the daily life of all of us. The educated man may not be a stranger in the new world discovered by the natural sciences, but must, to say the least, have the key that will unlock for him the intellectual work that is embodied in the scientific and technical achievements of the modern world, and must be able to discuss intelligently the train of thought that has made the dreams of the inventive genius a reality.

As a school subject, the natural sciences are still in their infancy, and they are still being studied from the narrow utilitarian point of view. We must, however, take a different viewpoint to discover the educative content of these sciences. The educational function of the natural sciences is to lead the student to study nature and her objects by himself, to train his powers of independent observation and investigation, and to let his knowledge of nature grow from continual communing with her. But the subject-matter taught at present is out of all proportion to, and not properly co-ordinated with, the vast and varied fields of research. Nothing has yet been done to correlate these modern studies with what must ever remain the core

of general education, the ancient classics. Educationists have
not yet accepted the Herbartian view which solves the problem
by proceeding from the end of man and then makes the vital
and unified fields in which man labors to shape and control
nature, the basis of all studies. We have not even established
anything approaching a close union between mathematics and
the natural sciences; but it is only after these two subjects
have been closely co-ordinated that we can expect to reap their
best educational benefits.

Mathematics, though not correlated as formerly, has remained in form essentially the same. It is owing to Pestalozzi's
suggestions, that object lessons and mental arithmetic now precede the study of mathematics. This subject should also profit
by the practical subjects that are now a part of the curriculum.
But our school mathematics is still based in its essentials on
Euclid; nor has it been correlated with the preparatory or the
parallel subjects. While modern thinkers do not deny that the
demonstrative method is a masterpiece of logical thinking, still
they maintain that it cannot serve as an adequate form for the
content of the science of magnitudes. Nevertheless, our instruction in mathematics is still following the methods of a
system whose acme of development is represented by the five
regular solids, the object of the mathematical cult of the Pythagoreans. Thus this branch also appears to be incomplete, not
as though it were, like the natural sciences, a new subject, but
because its new and old elements are not correlated with each
other

Defective correlation is, in fact, quite general in our course
of study. Our course of study has been augmented, not by
growth, but by accretion, and modern educators, while striving
to preserve the framework of the course, have often torn asunder
what should have remained one undivided whole They have
given too much consideration to the individual elements of the
course, and have thus lost sight of the one whole field of education. Instead of first providing a solid and fixed centre of
well-digested knowledge and the means for acquiring practical
skill, they have scattered their energies and have made our
course of study too rich and diversified, by introducing encyclopedic knowledge (which is a valuable adjunct if kept on the
outer circle of education) into the innermost department of
education

With regard to the number, the spread, and the practical
arrangement of the elements of encyclopedic knowledge, our age

is far superior to any previous period. Encyclopedias, both popular and scientific, and works of reference of all varieties are at hand to furnish in a moment any information desired; newspapers and magazines without number furnish knowledge and information; museums are open to all comers desiring object lessons in the various fields of knowledge and art; international expositions, marvellous encyclopedias, so to speak, of the arts and industries, display to the world, to specialist and layman, the latest achievements in every field of human endeavor. The hurry and bustle of modern life is ever giving new impulses to the varied interests; is ever discovering new sources of culture. But there is also danger lest our modern life spend itself on a thousand different subjects, and lest education, while madly rushing after the novel, forfeit its solid foundation and its inherited wealth.

CHAPTER XXX.

The Modern School System.

1. The three great fields of instruction with their historical centres: the elementary school, the Latin school, and the university, were considerably enlarged in the 19th century and were also brought into certain definite relations with one another.

There are at present several different systems for organizing the elementary schools of a country. But the highest esteem is justly accorded to the elementary school system of the Germanic countries, including Germany, Austria, Switzerland, Denmark, and Scandinavia. This system presupposes in the first place that the intellectual needs of society are relatively identical, and this will not be the case until the relations between the different classes of the people be such as to permit the elementary schools of the higher classes to be amalgamated with the elementary schools of the lower classes. Wherever this agreement has not been reached, the elementary schools of the higher classes are private schools, while the elementary schools of the lower classes are charitable institutions. This is the case in England where the sons of the gentry are educated at home or in private schools, while the children of the working classes are provided for in the schools conducted by charitable societies

22

(see *supra*, Ch. xxvii.), and only since the passing of the Elementary Education Act of 1870 are the poor schools supported and controlled by the State. A further presupposition for a national elementary school system is the co-operation between the State and the Church, and though this co-operation may be regulated according to different points of view, it must at all events allow the Church so large a share in the education of the young as will not oblige her to organize her own elementary school system in order to safeguard her children's rights of conscience.

Inasmuch as the modern elementary school system retains the religious teachings of Christianity, it is preserving the noble traditions of the past that have ever been the foundation of the elementary school system in Christian countries. But, while thus duly conservative, it has also incorporated certain features of modern educational development. The modern elementary school system delimits its subject-matter of teaching from that of the higher schools, and establishes it as a didactic unit. Acting on the suggestion of Pestalozzi, it makes the elementary school branches elements of formal training by converting grammar, arithmetic, and form study into somewhat of an equivalent of philology and mathematics. Imitating the example of the patriotic Pestalozzians, it introduces the national element, such as local and national history, singing of patriotic hymns, and gymnastics, into the curriculum. And acting on the principles of the Philanthropinists, it adds as many as possible of the modern and directly useful subjects

The elementary school system includes primarily the elementary school, which is either a city school or a rural school, and either public or private. The function of the elementary school is to lay the foundation, to teach the rudiments (upon which a higher course of study may thereafter be based), and at the same time to fit its pupils for their life work because the vast majority of them will never attend a higher school. Some institutions, such as the kindergarten, prepare for the primary school, while others, such as continuation schools, night schools, summer schools, folk high schools (in Sweden and Denmark), continue the work of the elementary school. The function of a third class of institutions is the elementary education of special classes of children: orphanages, reform schools, schools for the blind, deaf-mutes, feeble-minded, etc. The last category of schools originated in the 18th century (Francke, Oberlin, Hauy,

L'Epée, Heinicke, and others), but developed only in the 19th century (Fellenberg, Wehrli, Falk, Chr. H. Zeller, Wichern, etc.).

Training schools for elementary school teachers—normal schools, teachers' seminaries, teachers' colleges—are an integral part of the common school system. The growth and development of these training schools depend not only on the demand of the government for a certain degree of knowledge and skill in the teachers, but also on spontaneous movements among the teaching body. The teaching profession of Germany and the German normal schools are deeply indebted to the pedagogy of the elementary school, as developed since Pestalozzi. When L. v. Stein observes that the German elementary school system is based on science, the French, on administrative organization, and the English, on the individual-power of single persons and societies,[1] he seems to anticipate that the pedagogics of the elementary school will develop into a science. This is, of course, desirable; yet the pedagogy of the elementary school cannot be recognized as an independent science, but only as a part of the whole science of education.

Lest we overestimate the results obtained by and through the elementary school system, we must bear in mind the many demands made upon the elementary school and the inadequate means at hand to meet these demands. The elementary school must provide the working classes with all the knowledge they need or find helpful, must broaden and develop their minds; but may at the same time not forget that the children will be left to their own resources, once they are thrown upon a hard and cruel world, where their attainments will only bring them to grief unless they have within them, in their conscience, the mainstay to support them against the attacks of passion and egoism. The mere addition of new branches to the curriculum does not imply an increase in useful knowledge, much less a growth in practical skill, but tends rather to destroy harmony and to prevent the unified efforts possible in former times, when the course of study was less comprehensive. And this danger is all the more approximate since modern methodology is concerned more with the methods of individual subjects than with the concentric and harmonious development of the educational content as a whole. The training of the teacher offers the same difficulties. His future field of labor is very limited, and demands that he devote himself whole-souled to his humble

---

[1] *Verwaltungslehre*, V, p. 80.

work rather than that he should possess extensive knowledge and have wide and varied interests; and yet the normal school must do more than merely fit him for the branches he is to teach—it must prepare him to meet the intellectual requirements made of the modern teaching profession. Different attempts have been made to reconcile these clashing interests. For instance, Diesterweg demands that the teacher "be in his own circle the centre and master of learning and culture, and second to none in many-sidedness," and devote himself particularly to the study of the natural sciences. These are the principles underlying the program of studies that Diesterweg outlined for normal schools. The Prussian school regulations of 1854 described as the aim of the teachers' seminaries "to fit the students to grasp and master in all its bearings the subject-matter of elementary school instruction" They substituted the so-called *Schulkunde* for pedagogy and didactics and abolished universal history and literature, but increased the amount of memory work to be done in Christian doctrine. This system of too narrow a concentration was out of harmony with the best educational thought since the time of Harnisch, Zeller, and Pestalozzi, but it has now given way to the opposite extreme, and voices are again heard complaining that the elementary school teachers are superficially educated and that they waste their energy on subjects foreign to their profession. We have here a problem that is extremely difficult to solve, and it remains for the future to outline such a course of study for the normal school as will possess unity by meeting in all its parts the basic aims of the elementary school, but as will, at the same time, meet also the demands of a broader culture. This problem could be solved if the pedagogics of the elementary school developed systematically and continuously, however, at present it is concerned with so many details as to hold out no hope of reaching in the near future any definite and practical conclusion to govern the educative process as a whole. Still, the newly awakened historical interest may be expected to correct many mistakes

2. The Latin school has developed into the *gymnasium* of to-day, while the *Realschule* and the commercial and industrial schools have branched off from the Latin school and fit youths for other than the learned professions.

The scope of the modern *gymnasium*[1] has been definitely

---

[1] The term *gymnasium* is employed only in Germany and Austria, the corresponding schools are known in Italy as Ginnasi and Licei, in France as

delimited from the field of the elementary school as well as from the work of the university. No student can matriculate at the university before passing the "Reifeprüfung",[1] which is the examination at the end of the full course of the *gymnasium*. The *gymnasium* has a double function: on the one hand, to prepare for the work of the university, and on the other, to give the student a world-view that is broad because based on historical grounds. As preparing for the university, the *gymnasium* is the elementary school of science, but as imparting a world-view, it may be considered the final stage of a general education. The old Latin school had a similar double function, but in its case the function was fulfilled by stressing one and the same subject, Latinity, which was both the A B C of the sciences and the accomplishment universally expected of the gentleman. But modern conditions have changed this, and the double function can no longer be fulfilled by the classics alone. The *gymnasium* had to introduce the modern subjects in order to hold its own as an institution of general education; for to retain this distinction, it had to admit the studies that play so important a rôle in modern life. In view of its relation to the university, the *gymnasium* may not depart from its traditional policy of making its course of study a unified whole and one that is well adapted to serve as a preparation for the special studies of the university. The *gymnasium* represents, on the other hand, the culmination also of secondary training, and society and the State (at least in Germany) attach certain privileges to graduation from it. The modern *gymnasium* must not only deal with a considerably increased curriculum, but must also satisfy the wants of a very diversified student body, some of whom will later be engaged in fields of work that have little connection with science or classical antiquity. The demands of the modern studies as well as of the practically-minded students are at once

Lycées or Collèges, in Belgium as Athénées, in Switzerland as Collèges or Canton Schools, in the United States as High Schools and Colleges, in England as Colleges and Grammar Schools, and in Sweden as Lärowerk.

[1] The "Reifeprüfung" of the German *gymnasium* is unknown in the Latin school of England, as the English universities require matriculation examinations. In Scotland, Holland, and, to a great extent, in the United States also, some of the propædeutic studies are pursued at the university. Latin is still taught in some of the Scotch parochial schools, so that it is no unusual thing there to have "a barefooted girl translate a chapter from Caesar, or a boy called from his work to the ...." Eckstein in Schmid, *Encyklopädie*, VI, p. ....

a burden and a danger to the *gymnasium*, and threaten to estrange it from its distinctive function of the past. Still, these very demands demonstrate the power wielded by the *gymnasium*, and the latter may upon no condition abandon its task of spreading among large numbers of the population the influence of a broadly cultural training.

The secondary school systems of the different countries do not take the same position in regard to these modern problems confronting the college and the *gymnasium*. England has as yet made no attempt to organize and articulate its system of higher and lower schools. The grammar schools have preserved the type of Latin school of the 16th century, and the conservative Englishmen point to them as the links connecting their present schools with the past and as the checks against the inroads of modern cosmopolitan tendencies. The aim of the grammar schools is to train gentlemen by means of the liberal studies of Latin, Greek, and literature; the course of study is a strict unit, and the modern subjects are not strongly represented. There are many private secondary schools, of more recent foundation, but they lack systematic organization. The English scorn the practice of the Germans to attach special privileges to the graduation from any school, and consider all that pertains to education a private affair.

The Catholic secondary schools in countries having freedom of education, such as Belgium, Holland, Switzerland, the United States, etc, represent a still older type of educational institutions. The six classes of the Latin school constitute the substructure, and two additional classes, with philosophy as the core subject, are the capstone of secondary education. In the higher classes Latin is, to some extent, the language of the classroom; nature study, geography, and history are begun in the lower classes, but the natural sciences are taken up in the two last years only. The *Ratio Studiorum Societatis Jesu* of 1832 describes in full this type of secondary school;[1] Pachtler's and Schwickerath's works have been written in defence of the system.[2]

The Prussian *gymnasium* was seriously affected by the various educational movements of the last century, and the other German states have mostly followed the lead of Prussia. The

---

[1] *Catholic Encyclopedia*, s v *Ratio Studiorum.*
[2] Pachtler, *Die Reform unserer Gymnasien*, Paderborn, 1883; Schwickerath, *Jesuit Education*, St Louis, 1903

Unterrichtsverfassung of 1816, framed with the assistance of F. A. Wolf and W. v. Humboldt, stated that the *gymnasium* should aim "not only to impart to its students that amount of classical and scientific knowledge that is necessary to understand and utilize the systematic lectures of the university, but also to imbue them with the spirit of a refined humanity." The branches of study were selected with the view of allowing "each student not only to develop his own powers, both scientific and artistic, but also to study and practice, as much as possible, the special sciences." To combine the classical tendency with the encyclopedic, was obviously the aim of these regulations. The ministerial order of 1837, the so-called *Blue Book*, occasioned by Lorinser's pamphlet, *For the Protection of Health in the Schools* (Berlin, 1836), follows in the main the regulations of the *Unterrichtsverfassung*, and neither did the program of studies of 1856 make any material change. But the school regulations of 1882 made undue allowances to the encyclopedic tendency at the expense of the classics. The *Realgymnasium* with the nine years' course of the regular *gymnasium*, but without Greek, was established; and the *gymnasium* suffered also in that the number of class periods for religious instruction and the classics was decreased to allow for a proportionate increase for the modern subjects. Finally, in 1892, the Latin composition in the final examination of the *gymnasium* was done away with. It is only fair to demand that a third class of *gymnasium* be now established, *i. e.*, one that would do full justice to the basic subjects; for neither the *gymnasium* with its heterogeneous content of classics and modern studies, nor the polymathic *Realgymnasium* does that. Certain university subjects—such as theology, study of antiquity (*Altertumskunde*), philology, history, and philosophy—require an unabridged classical course in the preparatory school. But the tendency is rather in the opposite direction, the curtailing of the classics. Yet there is real need for an institution that is in close union with the traditions of the past and thus serves as a countercheck to the trend of the age. It is to be regretted that old and venerable seats of learning which kept alive the noble traditions of the classical studies, like the *Joachimsthal Gymnasium* and the *graue Kloster* (both in Berlin), sank to the level of the amorphous *gymnasium* of 1882 and 1892, when they might have proved the representatives of a special class of schools that would meet the higher needs of mental life. It is likewise to be regretted that the princely schools of Saxony and the splendid Lyceums of Württemberg have unwisely modified their courses of study in imitation of the modernized Prussian *gymnasium*.

In its external form the Prussian *gymnasium* has preserved the old type of Latin school of six classes, though the work is now extended over a nine years' course. There are three grades of classes: lower, middle, and higher, but the scope of these grades is not strictly delimited. The schools are denominational, but the State claims exclusive control of the course of study, and hence the free development of a system of study based on a religious foundation is not to be thought of.

3. Of German secondary schools, the Bavarian *gymnasium* comes nearest to the educational ideal of the German Renaissance   The philhellenism of Louis I, which inspired the King to adorn Munich with Greek edifices, is likewise expressed in the Bavarian *gymnasium* whose core subject is the study of the ancient classics.   The school regulations of 1830 are based on the course of study outlined by Frederick Thiersch, the disciple of G. Hermann and Herbart. "The ancient classics are the centre of the whole course of instruction, German, history, and philosophy are closely co-ordinated with the classics, and even religious instruction and mathematics are correlated as closely as possible with them.   The so-called problem of concentration, which has engaged the attention of all gymnasial reformers since 1830, has here found the best solution.   Its internal unity, simplicity, and correlation make the curriculum of the Bavarian *gymnasium* perfect in its kind."[1]   The Latin school, the substructure of the *gymnasium*, deals with the formal and technical elements of language. The *gymnasium* proper, the superstructure, acquaints the students with the writings of the ancients and stresses the philosophical side. Propædeutic studies in philosophy are also provided for.   It is to be regretted that Thiersch failed, despite his good intentions, to discover a bond that would have joined organically the new and the old. Nevertheless, his work represents one of the most important of modern educational institutions, and Bavaria has preserved a secondary school that has both character and individuality.

Up to the middle of the 19th century, the Austrian *gymnasium* remained faithful to the traditions of the older schools of the religious orders, but after the educational reform of Bonitz and Exner, in 1849, it adopted some of the features of the Prussian *gymnasium*, without, however, breaking entirely with the

---

[1] Fr Paulsen, *Geschichte des gelehrten Unterrichts*, Leipzig, 1885, p 659

past. The course of eight classes combines, according to the "plan of organization," the four grammar classes of old with two classes in the humanities and two years of philosophy. The four lower classes, forming the lower *gymnasium* (*Untergymnasium*), are distinct in gradation from the upper *gymnasium* (*Obergymnasium*) and offer a relatively complete course in the classics, while also treating, but only in a popular way, history, mathematics, and natural history. All these subjects are again taken up in the upper *gymnasium*, *i. e.*, the four higher classes, where they are to be taught "from a more scientific viewpoint." But the subject-matter of mathematics is in both the lower and the upper *gymnasium* treated hurriedly and without the proper exercises. The aim of the whole *gymnasium* is "to offer a higher general education by means principally of the study of the ancient classic languages and their literatures, and thus to prepare at the same time for the studies of the university." Less importance is attached to the classics than to the "mutual influence that the different subjects have upon one another." The modern subjects are accorded a liberal space in the curriculum. The writing of Latin is no longer the aim of the Latin teacher; and more weight is attached to literary and historical matters than to pure linguistics. Philosophy is taught in the upper classes as a propædeutic subject. The curriculum is obligatory, and the minutest details are regulated by law. But the subject-matter is too extensive for the number of class periods assigned, and the work should be distributed over nine years instead of eight. Most of the Austrian *gymnasiums* are state institutions. Schools under the control of municipalities or of the religious orders can not be recognized as public schools, unless they conform in all details to the institutions of the State. The concessions made to the tendencies of the age in the beginning of the reform have had at least this one good effect that they protected the Austrian *gymnasium* from further losses and assured it a natural development.

There are three divisions in the French *Lycée*: (1) the *Division élémentaire*, embracing the two lowest classes; (2) the *Division de Grammaire*, so called because the object of its three classes is the mastery of French, Latin, and Greek grammar; (3) the *Division supérieure* of the three highest classes, whose work is distributed over a four-years' course and which prepares for the *Baccalauréat ès lettres* as well as for the *Baccalauréat ès sciences*. Fourtoul introduced, in 1852, the bifurcation-system, which divides the highest division into two sections, one for classical and the other for science studies. This system was formally abolished by Duruy in 1863, but actually it is still in vogue in the French secondary schools. The *Lycées* are connected with boarding schools; they form a part of the *Université* of the State, and are noted for strict uniformity in studies and methods of teaching. The professors are trained in the *Ecole normale supérieure* in Paris, whose course includes, besides the school subjects and faculty lectures, a certain amount of practice teaching The municipalities support the *Collèges communaux* which are subject to the control of the *Université*, but not uniform in organization, and in grade frequently no higher than trade schools. The *Petits séminaires* were originally training schools for the priesthood, but later they were much frequented by students who wished to prepare for higher secular studies. But now that the government has deprived them of all rights, they may be doomed to extinction.

4. While the *gymnasium*, though readjusting its course to meet more general educational demands, still preserves the character of a preparatory school for the learned professions, the *Realschule*, a new type of school, has branched off from the *gymnasium* to devote itself exclusively to fit the student for such mechanical professions as require a certain amount of scientific knowledge besides an appreciation of the international character of work, and call for a broader point of view. The *Realschule* may be traced back to the schools established by Semler at Halle (1706) and by Hecker in Berlin (1847, now the Friedrich Wilhelms *Realschule*), but received its permanent organization only after the higher technological schools for which it was to prepare, had become firmly established. The State was slow in recognizing the new departure, and even to-day the *Realschule* has neither a pronounced character nor a fixed place in the national educational system The patrons of the *Realschule* strove from the beginning to secure for the new institution a scientific foundation like that of the *gymnasium*. But they could not agree on what should constitute this foundation. Some educators desired that the mathematical and natural sciences should serve as a foundation, so that the *Realschule* might complement the *gymnasium* based on the historical sciences (Spilleke, Kochly, and others). Others wished the study of modern languages and literatures to be the basis of the *Realschule*, so that the latter would be based on modern philology, while the *gymnasium* is based on classical philology (K. Mager). Others, again, wished to see the closest possible union between

the *gymnasium* and the *Realschule*, contending that both should have a common substructure. Particularly during the stormy years of 1848 and 1849 did men expect that a combination of the two schools would bring about a closer union between the education of the citizenry and that of the state officials, and thus result ultimately in a rapprochement between the higher and the lower classes. There are some educators who still expect great things of the *Realgymnasium*. But, as a matter of fact, not even the meaning of this term has as yet been agreed upon. Some schoolmen use the term *Realgymnasium* to designate the substructure common to the *Realschule* and the *gymnasium*, as in the experiments made in Austria in 1863. Others use it to designate the superstructure, *i. e.*, the courses in modern subjects, as in the debates during the convention of the Prussian rural school teachers in 1848. Finally, a third class use it to denote a *gymnasium* with the regular classical course, Greek alone being excluded, as in the Prussian school regulations of 1882.

Prussia preserved some historical connection between the *gymnasium* and the *Realschule*, for the latter tried by retaining Latin (up to 1882) to realize the aim of the middle classes of the *gymnasium;* and this still remains the policy of the *Realgymnasium*, while the *Realschule* is based on the study of modern languages. The Austrian *Realschulen* were first organized as a part of the elementary school system, and their independent organization dates from the time when they began to be regarded as preparatory to the technological schools. The statute of 1851 treats them as vocational schools, and a humanistic element in the form of modern language studies was introduced only within recent years. France has no organized system of *real* schools; the respective education is obtained partly in the *Instruction secondaire* and partly in vocational schools.

Modern educational needs have given rise to a great variety of schools that occupy a middle place between the elementary school and the university. Being so different in their aims and objects, they cannot be grouped under one head. The following may be described broadly as vocational schools: commercial schools, trade schools, industrial schools, agricultural schools, military academies, etc. Present-day female academies are amorphous institutions, and their educational organization offers unusual difficulties, owing partly to the vagueness of their aim, *viz.*, general culture, and partly to the ... known in former times, but prevalent in our ... assimi-

late a potpourri of educational titbits, but are too weak to take
a course of study seriously.

5. It was formerly the prerogative of the university to foster
the mutual interrelations between science on the one hand and
general intellectual life and the work of the learned professions
on the other. Modern conditions have very much increased
the points of contact between science and professional work,
and to-day we demand scientific training where practical training was formerly considered sufficient. The present-day artist
cannot be adequately trained in a master's studio, for he must
be at home in the history of his respective art, in æsthetics, and
anatomy. If the youth would be an engineer, he must frequent
not only the workshop; if a merchant, not only the counting-
house; and if a military officer, not only the military camp; for
the technological, commercial, and military sciences are important factors in these respective vocations. Technological schools
and special schools of many kinds offer the scientific training
necessary to-day in many mechanical professions, and these
schools strive to be equal in rank to the universities. But
though the university aims, like these special schools, to establish a connection between professional work and science, still it
has also another and higher function: to cultivate scientific
research and learning for their own sake and thus prove the
home of truly liberal culture   The discovery of new knowledge
is as essential a part of the duty of the university professor as
the imparting of what he already knows. Equally important is
another factor of the university, the stimulus to original research on the part of its students; so that professor and students
are conceived as co-partners in the great business of truth-
seeking. Despite the specialistic tendency of modern scientific
research, the four faculties of the university are still united by
a common bond, and notwithstanding the opposition of the
modern world to special privileges, the freedom of teaching and
learning is still maintained by the universities as the guarantee
for the ideal evaluation of science, and as the connecting link
between the present and the past of the institutions of higher
learning.

What has been said above, is true especially of the universities in the Germanic countries   The German universities have
preserved in the main the characteristic organization of the old
university, but have introduced some new features—seminars,
obligatory attendance at certain lectures, etc.,—to meet practical demands   England, however, has not abandoned any of

the old traditions, and has reserved the general science courses
to the university and the university colleges, while the vocational training can be obtained only in the shops and homes of
professional work. In trying to unify all the parts of the national
system of education, France sacrificed the unity of the university, and has, moreover, divided the faculty of philosophy into
the *Faculté des lettres* and the *Faculté des sciences*; the *Collège
de France* alone bears a semblance of the German university.
The Catholic universities, founded within the last decades,
have undertaken to revive the glorious traditions of the old
French universities. The many special institutions for scientific
research, more numerous in France than in any other country
(*Ecole des langues orientales, Ecole des chartes, Muséum d'histoire
naturelle, Bureau des longitudes, Conservatoire des arts et de métiers*, etc.), cannot take the place of the old French university
with which the noblest traditions of the nation are connected.

6. The modern system of education as a whole, especially as
organized with the elementary school as foundation and the
university as capstone, may be likened to a national system of
canals, which extend in many different directions, and which,
after receiving their water-supply from centrally located reser-
voirs, carry large streams of water over a vast territory. In
the modern State the work of education is supported by public
law, maintained by the general interest, and made a regulated
function of the social body by the system of education. The
modern system of education is an efficient factor in the intellectual assimilation of men, and is ever engaged in raising the
intellectual tone of all classes. The course of study embraces
the most diversified subjects, and because of this many-sidedness it appeals to the different dispositions, and offers many
opportunities for developing the abilities of the individual for
the benefit of the race. A complex system of examinations
compels the individual pupil to acquire the knowledge that is
imparted in his respective school, and thus the higher schools
and the professions are preserved from the influx of unsatis-
factory elements. Intellectual forces of all sorts are at work to
organize, to direct, to improve, and to perfect the organism
that has so many members.

In spite of all these favorable conditions, our age has not
only not outgrown, but has not even utilized all that was of
educational value in the past. It has been the tendency of the
modern world to organize the whole, to attend to the grand total.
This tendency has led us to reject much of the past that ap-

parently did not fit into the modern system of education, and
hence we discarded it instead of modifying it to meet present
conditions. This is to be regretted the more since we have as
yet found no adequate substitute for what was cast aside. The
smaller German universities can no longer keep pace with the
larger and better equipped institutions. But their suppression
would be a serious loss, as they represent unique and important
sources of German culture   The variety that obtained formerly
in the organization of the German, particularly the rural, *gymnasiums* was likewise an advantage to plastic adjustment, for
the schools could adapt themselves to meet local needs. In
this respect the old Latin schools of England—each of them is
an individual and, one might say, a character—are superior to
the German *gymnasiums* which are but specimens of a class.[1]
And even if the elementary school alone must conform in all
particulars to the national type of elementary education, there
is a loss of those valuable educational factors that result from
local conditions and historical development.

The modern school system has built educational highways,
and, though this saves the labor of seeking the right path, it
has likewise made it more difficult for the educator to take any
except the broad and beaten road. Home instruction was formerly recognized as an important element of the system of
education. The majority of educationists from Locke to Herbart
based their views on what they had observed in home instruction, and though this circumstance narrowed their field of study,
still it allowed them to see the results that can be achieved by
giving more attention to the individual; and, in fact, class instruction has profited much by their discoveries. At the present
time, however, home instruction has lost all significance. Even
when attempted, it must strain all energies to attain the high
standard of the modern school and must conform so closely to
the school curriculum as to render original experiments impossible   Yet the home is not only out of the question as a substitute for the school, it even lacks the time and the opportunity
to contribute something of its own individuality to the instruc-

---

[1] In another work, *Aus Horsaal und Schulstube* (Freiburg, 2nd ed , 1912,
p 387), Willmann approves heartily of the autonomy enjoyed by most American universities, which permits them to adapt themselves to changing conditions and to revive certain practices of medieval and Renaissance universities, and he adds, "This is academic freedom, genuine adacemic autonomy,
a great social boon for a nation and one that outweighs all the services, however great they be, that the government renders the state universities "

tion imparted in school. The modern school has often been charged with making such demands upon the time and energy of its pupils that the latter have hardly any breathing time left to enjoy the pleasures of home life, and even less opportunity to receive whatever the family might contribute to their mental life.

The modern system of education is in every regard well adapted to make intellectual attainments more uniform. But it is less well adapted to produce a strongly individual and characteristic personality. It is so rich in content as to satisfy all intellectual needs even before they can be felt by the individual. So much general knowledge is expected of the modern man that he cannot, till at a relatively late period in life, consult his own preferences in the selection of his studies; and in the case of most men individual taste can never assert its claim. The organization of modern education is responsible for the general activity witnessed in the field of learning and studies; but by reason of this very organization, the chief motives for studying are custom, the prospect of gain, and, at best, the sense of duty; and thus the spontaneous and individual inclinations are checked. The system of modern education is very comprehensive, but fails, nevertheless, to include all factors of intellectual growth and development, for it thwarts the work of some, while allowing undue influence to others.

ALPHABETICAL INDEX.

1

Lightning Source UK Ltd.
Milton Keynes UK
UKHW030633220321
380773UK00009B/776

9 781245 648172